Education and the State

In most countries in the world, school education is the business of the state. Even if forms and functions differ, the imparting of elementary knowledge is universally regarded as a public function. Yet this is neither self-evident nor self-explanatory. The degree of involvement of state agencies in the supervision, financing and organization of the school system sometimes varies so much that the usual assumption of a common understanding of 'the state' seems to be an illusion.

Making international comparisons and focusing strongly on the historical conditions of the current form of state education, this volume paints a nuanced picture of how the relationship between 'education' and 'state' has been and is conceptualized. Insights into this relationship are gained by considering and analysing both specific processes such as financing and bureaucracy; and conceptual ideas, for example community, authority and political utopias. The book presents comparative studies and analyses of regional and local conditions, arguing that the history of each country or region is critical to educational success, and the relationship between the education and the state must be reconsidered, both internationally and historically, in order to be of actual conceptual value.

Education and the State presents a broad variety of approaches and examples that provide a significant contribution to the understanding of the relationship between education and the state. It will be of key value to academics and researchers in the fields of the history of education, the politics of education, and educational administration.

Carla Aubry is Lecturer in Education, Psychology and Didactics at Pädagogische Maturitätsschule in Kreuzlingen, Switzerland.

Michael Geiss is Researcher and Senior Lecturer in the Department of Vocational Education at the Institute of Education, University of Zurich, Switzerland.

Veronika Magyar-Haas is Researcher and Assistant Lecturer in the Department of Social Pedagogy at the Institute of Education, University of Zurich, Switzerland.

Jürgen Oelkers is Emeritus Professor of General Pedagogy at the Institute of Education, University of Zurich, Switzerland.

Routledge Research in International and Comparative Education

This is a series that offers a global platform to engage scholars in continuous academic debate on key challenges and the latest thinking on issues in the fast-growing field of International and Comparative Education.

Books in the series include:

Teaching in Primary Schools in China and India
Contexts of learning
Nirmala Rao, Emma Pearson and Kai-ming Cheng with Margaret Taplin

A History of Higher Education Exchange
China and America
Teresa Brawner Bevis

National Identity and Educational Reform
Contested classrooms
Elizabeth Anderson Worden

Citizenship Education around the World
Local contexts and global possibilities
Edited by John E. Petrovic and Aaron M. Kuntz

Children's Voices
Studies of interethnic conflict and violence in European schools
Edited by Mateja Sedmak, Zorana Medari and Sarah Walker

Culture, Transnational Education and Thinking
Case studies in global schooling
Niranjan Casinader

The Changing Landscape of International Schooling
Implications for theory and practice
Tristan Bunnell

Leading and Managing Indigenous Education in the Postcolonial World
Zane Ma Rhea

Multi-campus University Systems
Africa and the Kenyan experience
Ishmael I. Munene

Education and the State
International perspectives on a changing relationship
Edited by Carla Aubry, Michael Geiss, Veronika Magyar-Haas and Jürgen Oelkers

Education and the State

International perspectives on a changing relationship

Edited by
Carla Aubry, Michael Geiss,
Veronika Magyar-Haas and
Jürgen Oelkers

LONDON AND NEW YORK

First published 2015
by Routledge
2 Park Square, Milton Park, Abingdon, Oxon OX14 4RN

and by Routledge
711 Third Avenue, New York, NY 10017

Routledge is an imprint of the Taylor & Francis Group, an informa business

© 2015 C. Aubry, M. Geiss, V. Magyar-Haas and J. Oelkers

The right of the editors to be identified as the authors of the editorial material, and of the authors for their individual chapters, has been asserted in accordance with sections 77 and 78 of the Copyright, Designs and Patents Act 1988.

All rights reserved. No part of this book may be reprinted or reproduced or utilized in any form or by any electronic, mechanical, or other means, now known or hereafter invented, including photocopying and recording, or in any information storage or retrieval system, without permission in writing from the publishers.

Trademark notice: Product or corporate names may be trademarks or registered trademarks, and are used only for identification and explanation without intent to infringe.

British Library Cataloguing in Publication Data
A catalogue record for this book is available from the British Library

Library of Congress Cataloging in Publication Data
Education and the state: international perspectives on a changing relationship/edited by Carla Aubry, Michael Geiss, Veronika Magyar-Haas and Jürgen Oelkers.
  pages cm – (Routledge research in international and comparative education)
  1. Education and state – Cross-cultural studies. 2. Education and state – History – Cross-cultural studies. 3. Education – Economic aspects – Cross-cultural studies. 4. Comparative education. I. Aubry, Carla, 1967–
  LC71.E2885 2014
  379 – dc23
  2014010288

ISBN: 978-1-138-77785-9 (hbk)
ISBN: 978-1-315-77238-7 (ebk)

Typeset in Bembo
by Florence Production Ltd, Stoodleigh, Devon, UK

Contents

List of contributors vii

PART 1
Introduction 1

1 Bringing education back in: international perspectives on the relationship between state, culture and society 3
   CARLA AUBRY, MICHAEL GEISS, VERONIKA MAGYAR-HAAS AND JÜRGEN OELKERS

PART 2
Comparing school systems 15

2 The national state, the local and the growth of mass schooling: history lessons from England, France and the United States 17
   MIRIAM COHEN

3 State intervention in backward countries: some case studies of state education systems in Hispanic America (c.1870–1920) 39
   GABRIELA OSSENBACH

PART 3
Financing education 59

4 The provision of education and the state: from equity to more equality 61
   CARLA AUBRY

5 State education, crisis and austerity: a historical analysis through the lens of the Kondratiev cycles 78
   VINCENT CARPENTIER

PART 4
Educational administration — 103

6 To write like a bureaucrat: educational administration as a cultural phenomenon — 105
   MICHAEL GEISS

7 Bureaucratizing from the bottom up: the centralization of school discipline policy in the United States — 121
   JUDITH KAFKA

8 The state of education in the States: the US Department of Education and the evolving federal role in American school policy — 138
   PATRICK MCGUINN

9 'Governing by numbers': social work in the age of the regulatory state — 159
   HOLGER ZIEGLER

PART 5
Power, myths of community and Utopia — 169

10 'Among School Children': the churches, politics and Irish schooling, 1830–1930 — 171
    DEIRDRE RAFTERY

11 Make the nation safe for mass society: debates about propaganda and education in the United States in the twentieth century — 178
    NORBERT GRUBE

12 Conceptualizations of dignity and exposure in critiques of community: implications for ethics and educational theory in the work of Plessner and Nancy — 196
    VERONIKA MAGYAR-HAAS

13 'Taking the path of least resistance': expulsions from Soviet schools in the Stalinist 1930s — 219
    E. THOMAS EWING

14 Utopia, state and democracy — 234
    JÜRGEN OELKERS

Index — 258

Contributors

Carla Aubry worked as Research Assistant at the Institute of Education at the University of Zurich, Switzerland from 2006 to 2012. She is currently Lecturer in Education, Psychology and Didactics at Pädagogische Maturitätsschule in Kreuzlingen, Switzerland.

Vincent Carpentier is Reader in History of Education at the Institute of Education, University of London, UK.

Miriam Cohen, Evalyn Clark Professor of History at Vassar College, USA, is completing a manuscript with Michael Hanagan on the comparative history of the welfare state in England, France and the United States, 1870–1950. She has published numerous articles dealing with various aspects of this work. She is also writing a biography of American social welfare activist Julia Lathrop for the 'Lives of American Women' biography series, edited by Carol Berkin, forthcoming from Westview Press.

E. Thomas Ewing is Professor of History and Associate Dean for Research and Graduate Studies in the College of Liberal Arts and Human Sciences at Virginia Tech, in Blacksburg, Virginia, USA.

Michael Geiss is currently Researcher and Senior Lecturer in the Department of Vocational Education and Economy at the Institute of Education, University of Zurich, Switzerland. From 2008 to 2012 he worked as a research assistant at the Institute of Education at the University of Zurich. In 2013 he was holder of a scholarship from the Forschungskredit of the University of Zurich.

Norbert Grube is Lecturer at the Centre for School History, Zurich University of Teacher Education, Switzerland.

Judith Kafka is an Associate Professor of Educational Policy and History of Education at Baruch College and the Graduate Center of the City University of New York (CUNY), USA. She is the author of *The History of 'Zero Tolerance' in American Public Schooling* (2011) and her work has appeared in a range of journals, including *History of Education Quarterly* and *Teachers College Record*.

Veronika Magyar-Haas has been Researcher and Assistant Lecturer at the Institute of Education, University of Zurich, Switzerland since 2008, initially in the Department of General Education, currently (since August 2012) in the Department of Social Pedagogy. She had a research scholarship from the German Research Foundation (DFG) from 2005 to 2008.

Patrick McGuinn is Associate Professor of Political Science and Education and Chair of the Political Science Department at Drew University, USA. His first book, *No Child Left Behind and the Transformation of Federal Education Policy, 1965–2005* (2006) was honoured as a *Choice* outstanding academic title. He is also the editor (with Paul Manna) of *Education Governance for the 21st Century: Overcoming the Structural Barriers to School Reform* (2013).

Jürgen Oelkers is Professor Emeritus at the Institute of Education, University of Zurich, Switzerland. He held the Chair of General Education from 1999 to 2012.

Gabriela Ossenbach is Full Professor of Contemporary History of Education at the National University of Distance Education (UNED), Madrid, Spain. Her main research areas are the history of educational systems and school textbooks in Latin America in the nineteenth and twentieth centuries. She is currently the Director of the MANES Research Centre, based in the UNED, dedicated to the study and preservation of textbooks of Spain, Portugal, and Latin America in the last two centuries.

Deirdre Raftery, based at University College Dublin, Ireland, is the author of, among others, *Gender Balance and Gender Bias in Education: International Perspectives* (2010); *History of Education: Themes and Perspectives* (2013); and *Educating Ireland: Schooling and Social Change, 1700–2000* (2014). She was also joint editor of *History of Education* (2008–2013), and has been Visiting Research Fellow, University of Oxford (2010) and Visiting Research Scholar, University of La Trobe, Australia (2014).

Holger Ziegler is currently Professor of Social Work at the Faculty of Education, Bielefeld University, Germany. He was Member of the Research Training Group Youth Welfare and Social Services in Transition of the German Research Foundation (2000–2003), Fellow at the Department of Criminology at Keele University, UK (2003) and Assistant Professor of Social Pedagogy at Westfälische Wilhelms University Münster, Germany.

Part 1

Introduction

Chapter 1

Bringing education back in

International perspectives on the relationship between state, culture and society

Carla Aubry, Michael Geiss, Veronika Magyar-Haas and Jürgen Oelkers

In the opinion of the OECD (Organisation for Economic Co-operation and Development) in Paris, the UNESCO Institute for Statistics in Montreal, and the World Bank in Washington, the nation state is the central organizational unit for modern education systems. State-organized education systems that display historically developed, regional characteristics can only be compared by abstracting their distinctive features in order to identify criteria that can serve as measurement variables. These parameters, used as the basis for reports about the performance of the corresponding systems, are established independently of national peculiarities (OECD/UNESCO, 2002). The assumption is that these international performance tests will provide information aimed at improving schools on a national level, as well as increasing the equality of opportunities, and encouraging more efficient utilization of available funds.

This, however, ignores what *state education* actually means. The concept of state organization of education provides an analytical backdrop, but the description of the relationship between education and the state still needs to be corroborated with both international and historical evidence in order to be of actual conceptual value. The goal must be to consider the distinctive features of the corresponding educational relationships both politically and theoretically. In other words, the diversities of education, rather than the state (Evans *et al.*, 1985), have to be brought back in.

In addition to the focus on the state education system, the major international comparative studies rely on numerous other assumptions, based on a supranational catalogue of criteria. Therefore, the idea of global 'governance' follows a specific model of state-organized educational systems. Behind this is Max Weber's bureaucracy theory, which has also attracted considerable attention in international debate (Holton and Turner, 1989; Lehmann and Roth, 1995; Swedberg, 1998; Turner, 2000). According to Weber (2005), 'bureaucracy' is tied to a hierarchy, functioning procedures, and the rational balancing of objectives (pp. 160, 721). The hierarchy stretches from the centre to the periphery, the procedures are respected, and the decrees have consequences. In other words, the system responds to the requirements of the top echelons of the hierarchy. National, regional or local specificities are not considered in this approach. Although forms of administration other than bureaucracy were also considered by Weber for classification, these seem to have been lost on his readers. Thus the state aspect seems to be present as soon as bureaucratic procedures are implemented.

International comparative studies further assume that school education represents an investment in the human capital of a society. The lack of consideration given to national specifics was shown by the OECD's many years of criticism of what it considered insufficient tertiary education in Switzerland. It was only because of rampant youth unemployment in Southern Europe that the specificities of the Swiss vocational education system were increasingly acknowledged and its dual education system appreciated (UNESCO, 2012). The hegemonic norming of the various definitions of education can also be seen in state attempts at standardization during the nineteenth century (see, for example, Crotti, 2008; Binder and Boser, 2011). The concept of education is deconstructed into various factors and skills that can be measured and tested.

Even though attempts at standardization have a long history, national education systems have maintained their cultural specificities to a far greater extent than they have allowed themselves to be globalized (Aubry and Westberg, 2012). The first things to be globalized are the discourses and language of experts, from which no direct assumptions can be made about the various education systems. Standards can be seen as normative instruments of power, strengthening the inter- and intra-national competition between education systems. Programmes for the reform of national education systems on the basis of competition results are thus nothing more than guidelines, and cannot be implemented directly. Instead, historically developed levels of implementation must be observed, varying by country, federal state, canton or municipality. It should be noted that this is rarely a smooth process, and that it inevitably involves adaptations to national education systems. The objectives established at the outset have only been achieved in a limited number of cases. The less the specificities of an educational system are taken into consideration, the less likely it is that the reforms will achieve their goals.

In the nineteenth and early twentieth centuries, many modern states developed an extensive educational monopoly in the form of *state schools*. While this occurred at varying speeds, and major local differences existed, certain similarities cannot be ignored. The basis of the metaphorical 'educational monopoly' was the *compulsory education* established by each state in the form of laws obliging all parents to send their children to school. A homogenizing view of various schools and school systems is helped by a public perception that the same service can be provided everywhere. This assumption is encouraged by international organizations. It is also aided by the concept of national curricula, which have thus far contained similar objectives and been comparable in their content and structure. The underlying premises here are that everyone should learn to read, and that understanding higher mathematical operations requires a basic comprehension of calculation.

Compulsory education and similar curricula do not mean, however, that education is a closed system. Schools do not escape the influence of globalization, but they are often the centres of a national or local community, underpinning local knowledge rather than simply following a general pedagogical or economic theory. They are culturally and historically specific, and are therefore far from being easily comparable units.

Now, however, the state organization of education is taken for granted not only in the current debate on educational policy, but also increasingly in pedagogical research. The genesis of a state education system between the French Revolution (Stübig, 1974; Julia, 1981; Harten, 1990; Herrmann and Oelkers, 1990), Prussian reforms (Heinemann, 1974) and the various European culture wars (Lamberti, 1986; Abels, 1996; Stadler, 1996; Maier, 2000), and in the period following the American Civil War (Van Overbeck, 2008), has always determined the classifications of educational history. Once a national education system had been established in the nineteenth century, there was virtually no further analysis of the form that the relationship between education and the state should take.

This is why, even though the development of a state education system is generally seen as the major caesura in the history of education, and educational policy debates treat the state organization of education systems as self-evident, paradoxically little can be said about the form and the development of the pedagogical aspects of this state monopoly. Even in more recent research, little is revealed about the development of the various state educational monopolies, their functionality and, in particular, their public acceptance.

National and local differences can only be explained historically. Future research must engage with the subject without prematurely attempting to find commonalities in cases where the differences are actually more significant. These differences can be seen in the research itself. German-speaking educational history, much like its French counterpart, overwhelmingly emphasizes the central role of the nation state, while American studies have a more regional focus.

The idea of the state, and of state organization of education, forms a common basis without actually explaining what it entails. What happens when education is publicly controlled? Which developments, issues and challenges can be traced, differentiated or even compared in the individual countries? It is difficult to form a general overview due to conceptual blind spots and the diverging interpretations of 'education', the 'state', and the relationship between them.

Historical structural analyses of the various educational systems also required conceptual considerations in order to be able to suitably describe and explain the long-term changes in the relationship between education, the state and society. The focus of this interest was the changing relationship between the educational system and the state, the object of much political dispute (Nique, 1990; Nique and Lelièvre, 1993), as well as the relationship between discipline and mobilization through the education system (Müller, 1977; Jeismann, 1989; Kuhlemann, 1992). The specificity of the national and local development of educational systems was explained using concepts of system formation (Müller and Zymek, 1987), and this German concept was presented for international discussion (Müller *et al.*, 1987). Later, pedagogical and educational policy discussions were also brought into the analysis in Germany (Apel *et al.*, 2001) and the state perspective was expanded to include inter- and/or intranational aspects (Fuchs, 2004; Zymek, 2009).

In contrast to the German-speaking history of education, the discussion of the relationship between the state and education has developed differently in the English-speaking world. This is partly the result of the relevant national characteristics. The American history of education has produced a number of detailed studies (Beadie, 2010; Goldin and Katz, 2008; Kaestle and Vinovskis, 1980; Lindert and Go, 2010; Margo, 1990; Shipps, 2006), but has also tried for several decades to follow new conceptual paths, in response to the poorly developed central state structures and excessive bureaucracy in the educational system. The social history of the administrators (Tyack, 1976), the historical relationship between competition and bureaucratization (Labaree, 1988), or the analysis of the failure of state-led education reforms (Tyack and Cuban, 1995), provide the analytical material needed to create a historical image of the relationship between education and the state, without assuming a strong central power.

Other attempts to elucidate the relationship between the state and education come from Great Britain. The history of education in that country has focused on the complex relationship between 'private and public education', whereby the generalized use of both terms requires caution due to their English specificity (Aldrich, 2004; Shrosbree, 1988; West, 1975). West (1994) demonstrates that, following the Foster Act of 1870, the state system of education in Great Britain was superimposed over successful private efforts, thereby suppressing an emerging and increasingly robust structure of private, voluntary and competitive education funded by families, churches and charities. In contrast, Green (1990) undertook an international comparison of state education, focusing on the development and implementation of national education systems in England, France, Prussia and the United States. Even in this case, however, national specificities, which for England meant a significantly delayed nationalization process in comparison to the rest of Europe, determined the interest and focus of the study.

The importance attributed to the state in different research projects cannot be established solely according to national differences. If the state is seen as a welfare state and as a mutually supportive group (Castel, 2003), it takes on a certain importance in terms of the handling of social issues and therefore the education system. Consequently, the social state acts more as a guarantor, as both a structural opportunity and a challenge, charged with reducing social and material uncertainties and educational inequalities. With the propagation of a neoliberal perspective, however, in which the (educational) market is to be freed from state influence, the state is seen as having an entirely different significance. As formulated by Sparke (2006), this approach is accompanied by the 'educational and cultural cultivation of a new kind of self-promoting and self-policing entrepreneurial individualism' (p. 154). In relation to these divergences, it seems essential to consider the political question of the 'us' as well as of the 'social' in a historically and internationally focused study of the relationship between education and the state. It is on the basis of this assessment of the 'us' – in the sense of the conceptualizations of community and society – that differences are established, allegiances are formulated, inclusion and exclusion are determined, and the legitimacy of access to education is negotiated or decided. It is therefore also necessary to ask who has been regarded as belonging or not belonging to the state.

The above critique of the tendency to homogenize nationally and locally differentiated school systems and their varied historical development is not intended as a call for traditional country comparison studies. Nor do we mean to give the impression that, by highlighting local specificities, we wish to disregard the local relevance of global tendencies. The above delineation of diverging national perspectives on the relationship between education and the state is more of a general means of orientation and/or a heuristic framework to be honed or deconstructed in the various contributions. The association of states with specific models would be a reduction that sets the state as an absolute, without considering any further criteria. It is precisely the various economic perspectives and theories of power, administration and community subsumed in this volume that help to encompass and reconstruct the terms 'education' and 'state', and their possible relationships, in all their variety and complexity.

This work is intended to juxtapose the various approaches to the relationship between education and the state found in current research. Only a multi-perspective historical approach can do justice to the heterogeneity, ambiguity and changing nature of this relationship. On the one hand, this uses theoretical concepts whose objectives can only be understood in the context of national, transnational and international political and scholarly debate on the form and function of a state education system. They cannot be considered independently of political and business interests, as they require the consideration of actors, structural necessities, mentalities and/or culture.

This cohesive collection of studies is intended as a *first step* towards a better understanding of the changing relationship between education and the state. Here the focus lies especially on (Western) Europe and America. Even if two contributions (Ossenbach and Raftery) make reference to colonialism in their historical reconstructions, the book cannot – however necessary this seems – systematically consider the post-colonial states in its reflection on the relationship between education and the state. Individual studies in the context of post-colonial and historical research do engage with the profound changes and discontinuities in the political structures and systems in the colonies, and reconstruct various forms of state (the 'minority settler regime', the 'bureaucratic-patrimonial state', and the 'proconsular autocracy', see Osterhammel, 1995, pp. 55–77; Mamdani, 1996, pp. 9–34) and modes of exercising power ('direct' and 'indirect rule'; see Mamdani, 1996, pp. 9–34; Eckert, 2006) during colonial rule. The aspect of education, however, seldom attracts attention in this context. Exceptions include Bouche (1991, pp. 243–273) and Osterhammel (1995, pp. 100–111), who shows the extent to which (the withholding of) schooling functioned as an instrument of power, deployed in varying ways in the different colonies. Important issues in these conflicts were the language of instruction and 'native tradition' (Osterhammel, 1995, pp. 107ff.): in most colonies the 'high-culture' language of the colonizers was used, and the 'indigenous cultures' were disregarded in the area of education (Osterhammel, 1995, p. 109; Kerner, 2013, p. 27). In summary, the research does consider education in post-colonial states to some extent, but there has so far been no systematic analysis of the *relationship* between education and the state in this context.

The present book does not provide a complete, new analytical framework in the form of a consistent theory. But it helps us to ask better questions, and shows certain key starting points for a more complex, comprehensive approach, one which takes into account the ambiguities of the matter presented here. We contend that, if an adequate account is to be given of education and the state, *the history of education* as well as *its specific characteristics* in comparison to other state-related issues have to be kept in mind.

Historically, the creation and modification of state educational institutions can be seen as a transformation of state activity. In particular, this will be demonstrated from an administrative and financial point of view. New state responsibilities required regulatory organization and the provision of the corresponding resources. These newly acquired responsibilities and areas of activity led in turn to new problems that had to be dealt with in everyday organization. As a result, state education had to prove itself not only as an ideal, but also in practice.

Comparative presentations of the creation of various national education systems are accompanied by case studies of individual territories, cities and communities, in which processes of nationalization, standardization and centralization/decentralization are retraced in detail. These different approaches complement each other. On the one hand, the degree of abstraction required by a comparative study design may be criticized or called into question. On the other hand, studies on the emergence of national education systems are able to go into much greater detail in terms of source selection and the differentiation of interpretations – but such studies forego the possibilities offered by comparison. The volume includes discussions of the changing relationship between education and the state from the perspective of the history of ideas, as well as depictions stretching over entire periods and specific individual analyses. The historical projects also raise questions applicable to contemporary analyses. One concern here was not to reduce the 'state' to the nation state, or education to schooling. In line with the assumption that theories of the state are barely conceivable without social theory, or that ideas of community, society, solidarity and cohesion are inherent in theories of the state, some contributions deal with concepts of the social, both in theoretical interpretations and in references to state utopias that were explicitly conceived as social utopias.

The contributions of Miriam Cohen and Gabriela Ossenbach take a comparative approach. Cohen (Chapter 2) addresses the relationship between the country, local traditions and mass education in a comparison between England, France and the United States. She identifies significant differences in relation to the centralization/decentralization of school organization and financial autonomy, observing that the ability of the majority to implement changes is always dependent on coalitions at various levels, and that local financing is not necessarily linked to greater inequality between communities. During periods of economic depression, the United States and France reacted by expanding the school system, which was not the case in England.

Ossenbach (Chapter 3) focuses on Latin America between 1870 and 1920, where governments assumed varying degrees of involvement in the creation and control of their national education systems as a result of their histories. Significant factors in this process of nationalization were their colonial past, their economic backwardness in comparison with Western countries, and the influence of the Catholic Church. The study identifies different developments in the individual countries, as well as similarities, such as a shortage of funding on the municipal level. This led to more state involvement and meant that mass schooling could expand as the state gradually took charge of the public school system.

The above contributions, comparative in structure, permit the examination of a few clear developments such as centralization/decentralization (Cohen) and nationalization (Ossenbach). The historical analysis can be even more precise when the focus is on a city or a municipality. Carla Aubry's contribution (Chapter 4) uses the example of the city of Winterthur in Switzerland to demonstrate how the financing of state schools changed during the nineteenth century. Initially still in the hands of the city's citizens, the schools were financed using the revenues from city assets. Not all citizens benefited equally under this system. Over time, the increasingly pronounced influence of the state and efforts to achieve democracy eventually led to equal access. The level of detail of the analysis allows the historical financial focus to be expanded to include the perspectives of political participation and citizenship, and shows how complex the process of centralization/decentralization is.

Vincent Carpentier (Chapter 5) addresses the impact of not only economic backwardness (see Ossenbach) but also economic crises on investments in the educational system. By applying Kondratiev's cyclical theory to comparative educational research, he succeeds in showing how, prior to 1945, crises led to increased state investment in education. It was hoped that this would overcome the said crises, as Cohen demonstrates for the United States and

France. After 1945, however, a change can be seen, especially with the rise of neo-liberalism in the 1970s. During this period, reduced tax revenues led to increasing tension between wealth and public welfare, and financial crises brought a desire for savings in the educational sector.

Michael Geiss (Chapter 6) describes how, in the Grand Duchy of Baden in the second half of the nineteenth century, the educational administration and teachers joined forces in a common ideological project. History does not bear out the dualism of education and administration. Educational bureaucrats acted as 'intellectual doers' who, in their official capacity, sought to implement their ideas on child-rearing, education and the state. Moreover, the teachers, beneficiaries of national standardization, supported the bureaucratization of schools.

Judith Kafka (Chapter 7) deals with local events, examining the bureaucratization of American schools in the twentieth century. Focusing on the creation of formal procedures for the application of school discipline in Los Angeles, she is able to use a wide body of references to demonstrate that the teachers themselves wanted to regulate part of their everyday school experience in a bureaucratic way. Different institutional solutions developed in various districts, and the state then sanctioned the existing concepts at a higher administrative level. This also has implications for the examination of other aspects of educational bureaucratization, which can no longer simply be described as a top-down arrangement.

Patrick McGuinn (Chapter 8) also examines the growth of administration during the twentieth century. The starting point of his analysis is George W. Bush's No Child Left Behind Act, which generated controversy even beyond the United States. McGuinn traces the history of the law and gives a nuanced presentation of the gradual shift towards national responsibilities in the educational system throughout the twentieth century. He demonstrates how surprising the new national responsibilities in the American educational system are, considering the long anti-centralist tradition in this country: for its first thirty years, the US Office of Education had no significant administrative responsibilities. The new educational policy situation created by the NCLB Act can only be accurately assessed in the light of this history.

The problem of evidence-based educational and social policies is addressed by Holger Ziegler (Chapter 9). Focusing on social work in the twentieth century, he reconstructs the changing significance of the state, leading to the birth of the 'regulatory state', which abandons all attempts to increase welfare and assumes purely regulatory functions. A comparison with the analysis of changes after 1970 (see Carpentier) is productive. In this process, as Ziegler points out, the managerial approach replaces trust in professionals with organizational forms of government, which can be subsumed in the term 'management by measurement'.

Deirdre Raftery (Chapter 10) examines the distinctive development of the Irish school system under the conditions of British foreign rule. The focus is on the shifts towards pluralistic schooling in a country whose history has always been strongly marked by religious conflicts. Central structural frameworks in the educational system were determined by denominational differences for longer than in other countries. In the early twentieth century, the Catholic Church had the support of the population, as in Latin America (see Ossenbach), and had access to relevant personnel. Only now is the tendency towards a secular system gaining ground.

Norbert Grube's contribution (Chapter 11) considers the relationship between political propaganda and education. Using the opinions and approaches of scholars in communication studies, intellectuals and politicians in the United States during the first half of the twentieth century, he casts light on the construction of national homogeneity. In the historical context of the perceived threats of mass society, the two world wars, economic and social crises and uncertainty, he sees government propaganda as important for the creation of national coherence. Using a wealth of material, Grube demonstrates the extent to which propaganda must be seen as a means of educating mass society, and shows how American experts both discuss public opinion from a pedagogical perspective and make use of statistical data.

The relationship between the state and education is expanded to include a utopian aspect in the contribution of Jürgen Oelkers (Chapter 14). From the perspective of the history of ideas, covering different eras and using a wide range of sources, he shows how the genre of utopian narrative can be overwhelmingly broad if the classic Morus–Campanella–Bacon construction is not used as a limiting criterion. By means of utopian ideas from the philosophy of Ancient Greece, the Middle Ages and the modern era, Oelkers reconstructs the way in which the various utopias were linked to ideas of improved education. Democracy is seen not as a utopia, but rather as an experienced reality capable of convincing even its harshest critics.

However, as argued by Veronika Magyar-Haas (Chapter 12), state utopias can also be linked with community utopias, which leave little room for differences and the establishment of (inter)personal boundaries. Beginning with the social theory and community critique of Helmuth Plessner in the 1920s, and considering the 'left-Heideggerian' deconstructivist community theories of Jean-Luc Nancy, she demonstrates the possibility of theoretically and analytically reconsidering the 'limits of the community' beyond the context of Plessner's and Nancy's time. She discusses critiques of community and their implications for educational theory, going beyond the scholastic aspect of the term 'education' to include the notion of dignity as an objective of educational theory – but one which does not necessarily have explicitly normative connotations.

The fact that utopias do not simply become reality is hardly surprising. Nonetheless, E. Thomas Ewing (Chapter 13) demonstrates that the grim realities – for example, those of the communist social vision in Stalinist education – are not so easy to assess either. Using the example of the debates about exclusions from school, he reconstructs how, under Stalinism, dictatorial power led to the disciplining of students and teachers. 'Inclusive' discipline, as he explains, proved a successful alternative to exclusions.

This book presents a variety of elements, approaches and theses that provide a significant contribution to the understanding of the relationship between education and the state. The various scholarly cultures, experiential backgrounds, disciplinary contexts and objects of research allow readers to examine their own academic perspectives and reflect on individual approaches in the light of research on related topics. There is ample potential here for further research on the changing relationship between education and the state: on the one hand, these perspectives can be compared, in order to identify the differences and similarities between them, and on the other hand, their areas of focus can be considered across different time periods, objects of examination and theoretical contexts. Financing, bureaucracy, community, authority and utopia can be shown to be related fields that may be used to further examine and research the relationship between the state and education.

References

Abels, K., 1996. Lesebuch und nationale Bildung im Badischen Kulturkampf. *Rottenburger Jahrbuch für Kirchengeschichte*, 15, pp. 43–64.
Aldrich, R. (ed.), 2004. *Public or Private Education? Lessons from History*. London, Portland, OR: Woburn Press.
Apel, H.J., Kemnitz, H. and Sandfuchs, U. (eds), 2001. *Das Öffentliche Bildungswesen. Historische Entwicklung, Gesellschaftliche Funktionen, Pädagogischer Streit*. Bad Heilbrunn: Klinkhardt.
Aubry, C. and Westberg, J. (eds), 2012. *History of Schooling. Politics and Local Practice*. Frankfurt: Peter Lang.
Beadie, N., 2010. *Education and the Creation of Capital in the Early American Republic*. Cambridge: Cambridge University Press.
Binder, U. and Boser, L., 2011. Die Metrisierung der Pädagogik und die Pädagogisierung des Meters. Wie Pädagogik modernisiert wird. *Zeitschrift für Pädagogik*, 57(1), pp. 19–36.
Bouche, D., 1991. *Histoire de la Colonisation Française*, Bd. 2. Paris: Fayard.
Castel, R., 2003. *From Manual Workers to Wage Laborers: Transformation of the Social Question*. New Brunswick, NJ: Transaction.
Crotti, C., 2008. Bildungspolitische Steuerungsversuche zwischen 1875 und 1931. Die pädagogischen Rekrutenprüfungen. In: L. Criblez (ed.) *Bildungsraum Schweiz. Historische Entwicklungen und aktuelle Herausforderungen*. Bern, Stuttgart: Haupt, pp. 131–154.
Eckert, A., 2006. *Kolonialismus*. Frankfurt: Fischer.
Evans, P.B., Rueschemeyer, D. and Skocpol, T. (eds), 1985. *Bringing the State Back In*. Cambridge: Cambridge University Press.
Fuchs, E., 2004. Internationalisierung als Gegenstand der Historischen Bildungs-Forschung: zu Institutionalisierungsprozessen der edukativen Kultur um 1900. In: M. Liedtke, E. Matthes and G. Miller-Kipp (eds) *Erfolg oder Misserfolg? Urteile und Bilanzen in der Historiographie der Erziehung*. Bad Heilbrunn: Klinkhardt, pp. 231–249.

Goldin, C. and Katz, L.F., 2008. *The Race Between Education and Technology*. Cambridge: The Belknap Press of Harvard University.
Green, A., 1990. *Education and State Formation. The Rise of Education Systems in England, France and the USA*. Houndmills: Macmillan.
Harten, H.-C., 1990. *Elementarschule und Pädagogik in der Französischen Revolution*. Munich: Oldenbourg.
Heinemann, M., 1974. *Schule im Vorfeld der Verwaltung: Die Entwicklung der Preussischen Unterrichtsverwaltung von 1771–1800*. Gottingen: Vandenhoeck & Ruprecht.
Herrmann, U. and Oelkers, J. (eds), 1990. *Französische Revolution und Pädagogik der Moderne. Aufklärung, Revolution und Menschenbildung im Übergang vom Ancien Régime zur Bürgerlichen Gesellschaft*. Weinheim: Beltz.
Holton, R.J. and Turner, B.S., 1989. *Max Weber on Economy and Society*. London: Routledge.
Jeismann, K.-E. (ed.), 1989. *Bildung, Staat, Gesellschaft im 19. Jahrhundert. Mobilisierung und Disziplinierung*. Stuttgart: Franz Steiner.
Julia, D., 1981. *Les Trois Couleurs du Tableau Noir: La Revolution*. Paris: Belin.
Kaestle, C.F. and Vinovskis, M.A., 1980. *Education and Social Change in Nineteenth-century Massachusetts*. Cambridge: Cambridge University Press.
Kerner, I., 2013. *Postkoloniale Theorien zur Einführung*. Hamburg: Junius.
Kuhlemann, F.-M., 1992. *Modernisierung und Disziplinierung. Sozialgeschichte des Preussischen Volksschulwesens, 1794–1872*. Gottingen: Vandenhoeck & Ruprecht.
Labaree, D.F., 1988. *The Making of an American High School. The Credentials Market and the Central High School of Philadelphia, 1838–1939*. New Haven, CT: Yale University Press.
Lamberti, M., 1986. State, church, and the politics of school reform during the Kulturkampf. *Central European History*, 19(1), pp. 63–81.
Lehmann, H. and Roth, G. (eds), 1995. *Weber's Protestant Ethic: Origins, Evidence, Contexts*. Cambridge: Cambridge University Press.
Lindert, P. and Go, S., 2010. The uneven rise of American public schools to 1850. *The Journal of Economic History*, 70, pp. 1–26.
Maier, J., 2000. Kirche und Schule. Auseinandersetzung um Schulform und geistliche Schulaufsicht in konfessionell gemischten Staaten. In: H. Ammerich and J. Gut (eds) *Zwischen 'Staatsanstalt' und Selbstbestimmung. Kirche und Staat in Südwestdeutschland vom Ausgang des Alten Reiches bis 1870*. Stuttgart: Thorbecke, pp. 269–293.
Mamdani, M., 1996. *Citizen and Subject. Contemporary Africa and the Legacy of Late Colonialism*. Princeton, NJ: Princeton University Press.
Margo, R.A., 1990. *Race and Schooling in the South, 1880–1950: An Economic History*. London, Chicago, IL: University of Chicago Press.
Müller, D.K., 1977. *Sozialstruktur und Schulsystem. Aspekte zum Strukturwandel des Schulwesens im 19. Jahrhundert*. Gottingen: Vandenhoeck & Ruprecht.
Müller, D.K. and Zymek, B., 1987. *Datenhandbuch zur Deutschen Bildungsgeschichte. 2. Höhere und Mittlere Schulen. 1. Sozialgeschichte und Statistik des Schulsystems in den Staaten des Deutschen Reiches 1800–1945*. Gottingen: Vandenhoeck & Ruprecht.
Müller, D.K., Ringer, F. and Brian, S. (eds), 1987. *The Rise of the Modern Educational System. Structural Change and Social Reproduction (1879–1920)*. Cambridge: Cambridge University Press.
Nique, C., 1990. *Comment l'École Devint une Affaire d'État (1815–1840)*. Paris: Nathan.

Nique, C. and Lelièvre, C., 1993. *La République n'éduquera plus. La fin du mythe Ferry*. Paris: Plon.
OECD/UNESCO, 2002. *Financing Education – Investments and Returns. Analysis of the World Education Indicators. Executive Summary*. Montreal: UNESCO Institute for Statistics.
Osterhammel, J., 1995. *Kolonialismus. Geschichte – Formen – Folgen*. Munich: Beck.
Shipps, D., 2006. *School Reform, Corporate Style. Chicago, 1880–2000*. Lawrence, KS: University Press of Kansas.
Shrosbree, C., 1988. *Public Schools and Private Education. The Clarendon Commission, 1861–64, and the Public School Act*. Manchester: Manchester University Press.
Sparke, M.B., 2006. A neoliberal nexus: economy, security, and the biopolitics of citizenship on the border. *Political Geography*, 2, pp. 151–180.
Stadler, P., 1996. Kulturkampf und Kulturkämpfe im mittleren Europa des 19 Jahrhunderts. Versuch einer vergleichenden Orientierung. *Rottenburger Jahrbuch für Kirchengeschichte*, 15, pp. 13–25.
Stübig, F., 1974. *Erziehung zur Gleichheit: Die konzepte der 'éducation commune' in der Französischen Revolution*. Ravensburg: Maier.
Swedberg, R., 1998. *Max Weber and the Idea of Economic Sociology*. Princeton, NJ: Princeton University Press.
Turner, S. (ed.), 2000. *The Cambridge Companion to Weber*. Cambridge: Cambridge University Press.
Tyack, D., 1976. Pilgrim's progress: toward a social history of the school superintendency, 1860–1960. *History of Education Quarterly*, 16(3), pp. 257–300.
Tyack, D. and Cuban, L., 1995. *Tinkering Toward Utopia*. Cambridge, MA: Harvard University Press.
UNESCO, 2012. *Youth and Skills: Putting Education to Work*. Paris: UNESCO.
Van Overbeck, M.A., 2008. *The Standardization of American Schooling*. New York: Palgrave Macmillan.
Weber, M., 2005. *Wirtschaft und Gesellschaft. Grundriss der Verstehenden Soziologie*. Frankfurt: Zweitausendeins.
West, E.G., 1975. Educational slowdown and public intervention in nineteenth century England: a study on the economics of bureaucracy. *Explorations in Economic History*, 12(1), pp. 61–87.
West, E.G., 1994. *Education and the State: A Study in Political Economy*. Indianapolis, IN: Liberty Fund.
Zymek, B., 2009. Prozesse der Internationalisierung und Hierarchisierung im Bildungssystem. Von der Beharrungskraft und Auflösung nationaler Strukturen und Mentalitäten. *Zeitschrift für Pädagogik*, 55(2), pp. 175–193.

Part 2

Comparing school systems

Chapter 2

The national state, the local and the growth of mass schooling

History lessons from England, France and the United States[1]

Miriam Cohen

More than twenty-five years ago, political scientists Ira Katznelson and Margaret Weir argued that, since public schools have been partially:

> the guardian and cultivator of a democratic and egalitarian political culture in the US . . . [their history] cannot be excised from the treatments of the American welfare-state and more generally, from social democratic attempts by government to protect ordinary people from the ravages of the unfettered markets.
>
> (Katznelson and Weir, 1988, p. 5)

As an American historian working on the comparative history of the welfare state in England, France, and the United States from the late nineteenth to the mid-twentieth century, I am struck that, while the United States had little tradition of state spending for a great number of social welfare initiatives, few countries share its history of public expenditures on education. Yet Katznelson and Weir's call to integrate the history of public education with the broader history of the welfare states largely remains unheeded. While new approaches to the history of American state-making have been accumulating over the last two decades, because it is usually seen as an alternative to traditional programs of entitlement, outside of the field of educational history, few have paid much attention to schooling. This is beginning to change. Works by Lindert (2004) and Garfinkel et al. (2010) comparing American and European welfare states have included public expenditures on schooling. Kantor and Lowe (1995) have also addressed changing American education policy and its relationship to social welfare. Moreover, Katz (2010a, 2010b) is now integrating an analysis of public education into a history of the American welfare state. In our comparative study of the history of the welfare state in the United States, England, and France, my co-author, Michael Hanagan, and I are studying some of the usual features of the welfare state, which include entitlement programs, such as social insurance and protective labor legislation, but we are also focusing on the development of mass schooling.[2] Based on some of this work, and focusing on the years 1870 through World War II, this chapter shows that placing schools into the context of a comparative history of social welfare enables us to better understand the history of social welfare and state-making in two respects.

First, the commitment to schooling can be an important aspect of enhancing state capacity, which has implications for other aspects of social welfare. This is particularly true for the United States, where, because public education expenditures are social transfers, the American consensus about public education has been critical. In a country with a weak sense of public responsibility, the American attitude surrounding the importance of public education has stood out as a long-standing exception. Since the role of government in providing education was already an established tradition by the end of the nineteenth century, US reformers intent on enhancing state capacity have effectively used education to redefine the boundaries between state and family.[3] By connecting the history of education and history of the welfare state, we can recognize that state-sponsored education has been an important aspect of state-making in the United States. Its growth has, at some critical moments, not acted as a substitute for such social welfare approaches, as others have argued, but has contributed to the extension of other social welfare benefits, such as income support programs and workplace regulations (Flora and Heidenheimer, 1981; Patterson, 1994).

Second, paying attention to the history of mass schooling forces us to think carefully about the issues of centralization and decentralization in the making of the welfare state. Scholars of the welfare state have generally assumed that the growing centralization of democratic governments – which proceeded much more rapidly in Europe in comparison to the United States – meant advances in social benefits. Concentrating on the town of Winterthur in the Canton of Zurich, Carla Aubry's work in this volume, on the growth of public schooling in nineteenth-century Switzerland, shows that the increase in centralization of schools at the canton level increased equitable access to public schooling. Yet, the decentralized structure of the American and German school system, as Peter Lindert argued, in comparison to England and France, enhanced the reach of public schooling in the United States (Lindert, 2004).

My focus on both the local and the national in comparing the history of schooling picks up on Katz's recent call for a historical approach to evaluating the role of government in social policy, which "stresses the importance of time, place, context, the particular policy objective, the different levels of government and the different metrics that often separated their evaluation" (Katz, 2011, p. 337). Throughout the era between 1870 and World War II, the United States, with its more decentralized system of public education, remained the leader among the three countries in spreading access to public education. While central control and central funding of schools in the United States remained very limited, during the Depression, important New Deal initiatives provided critical support for the expansion of public schooling. In the case of England, growing centralization actually meant the limitation of equitable access with respect to public schooling. French education was subject to central control throughout this period, but it was only during the Great Depression that central state initiatives expanded the reach of schooling.

In all three countries, between 1870 and World War II, the inability to build lasting national coalitions favoring egalitarian expansion limited the potential of public schooling in the period between 1870 and World War II. As the United States begins to move closer to its European counterparts in the twenty-first century, with greater national mandates regarding public schooling, we see another example of growing centralization unaccompanied by growing equity.

Public education and state capacity: the United States in comparative perspective

In my earlier work on education and the American welfare state, I stressed the extent to which political activists appealed to widespread collective norms about the importance of schooling in order to make the case for a number of other social benefits. One of the best examples comes from the early twentieth century, when mostly women reformers promoted mothers' pensions, also called widows' pensions – that is, state-wide programs of income support for poor widowed mothers, so that they could keep their children at home rather than placing them in orphanages. In the second decade of the twentieth century, mothers' pension leagues campaigning throughout the country were remarkably successful. By 1920, the vast majority of states had enacted some sort of mothers' pension program. These government-funded initiatives were the precursors to the Aid to Dependent Children Program, which became federal law during the New Deal as part of the Social Security Act. Many historians have emphasized the extent to which campaigners on behalf of mothers' pensions had effectively practiced maternalist politics; reformers focused on issues that appealed to women as wives and mothers, and promoted the idea that women were particularly good at addressing such concerns (Ladd-Taylor, 1994; Muncy, 1991). I argued that the appeal to American values regarding the importance of education was also critical. Thus, advocates for mothers' pensions contended that, with the income provided to poor widowed mothers, children who might otherwise have worked could be kept in school (Cohen, 2005).

Thanks to recent work by Steffes (2012) and Provasnik (2006), we can now appreciate that these American activists were doing more than appealing to collective norms. In the United States, unlike England or France, legislation on both the state and national levels is legitimated not only because it represents the majority will of legislatures; laws also have to pass constitutional muster as determined by American courts. At the turn of the twentieth century, American reformers pushing to build the welfare state looked to an emerging American jurisprudence on the enforcement of school attendance laws, in order to build the case for the constitutionality of a whole host of social legislation, such as income support programs and workplace regulations. Thus, in 1914, the state of New York, in defending the implementation of widows' pensions, argued that while adults did not have rights to income, "government was morally obligated to dependent children, because of its right to compel all children to be educated" (State of New York, 1974, p. 19). Moreover, because the income helped to keep poor children in schools, in many states, mothers' pensions were implemented as school pensions.

Turning to labor law, American scholars of the progressive era have by now written many volumes showing how activists used the politics of maternalism as a successful strategy in arguing for the constitutionality of workplace regulation (Hart, 1994). In a country with a strong celebration of individual and, indeed, the corporation's right to free contract – and with American courts able and willing to strike down any legislation that they believed intruded on this right – reformers used appeals to the special needs of women to redefine the relationship between public responsibilities of the state and the private rights of individuals. The most famous instance of this successful strategy came with the Supreme Court's 1908 decision in *Muller* v. *Oregon*, which enhanced the police powers of the American states to regulate working hours for women. Attending to the special health needs of women, the future mothers of the race, the Court concluded, was deemed a legitimate role for the government, even though the Court had just concluded three years earlier, in *Lochner* v. *New York*, that such laws regulating men were unconstitutional. Yet, even before cases such as *Muller* in the early twentieth century, which turned on gender and public health, the American judiciary's willingness to enforce government prerogatives with respect to school attendance marked a major moment in American state-making, increasing the police powers of the state (Provasnik, 2006; Steffes 2012).

References to schooling, largely ignored by American social policy historians, can be repeatedly found in the arguments of proponents seeking to legitimate the growth of the regulatory state. Child labor laws were legitimated at the end of the nineteenth century because, as a New York official noted, "Compulsory Education Law makes it everybody's business to see to it that the Penal Code protecting children from machine labor is enforced" (State of New York, 1888, p. 416). However, it was not only in order to legitimate child labor laws that progressives looked to school attendance laws; they also used school laws to justify other workplace legislation. In 1905, Justice Oliver Wendell Holmes dissented from the majority view of the US Supreme Court in *Lochner* v. *New York*: a decision that, in striking down New York's hours laws for men, expressed the extreme laissez faire, narrow vision of police powers of the state. In doing so, he noted, "the liberty of the citizen to do as he likes so long as he does not interfere with the liberty of others to do the same, is interfered with [first] by school laws" (Holmes, 1905, p. 198).

If the widespread commitment to compulsory school attendance, at least across the American north, played a critical role in expanding the power of the state, it was the school bureaucracy, more than any other institution of government, that Americans turned to in order to administer these new welfare functions. America, in contrast to Europe, did not have government bureaucracies to oversee social welfare, so officials made use of one government institution they did have – the schools. Thus, mothers' pensions were largely administered by school districts, something that most historians of social welfare have failed to recognize. Child labor laws were mostly administered by school districts, not factory inspectors.

Under the New Deal, while the federal government did not provide direct aid to school systems, it did act to keep youth from the job market through aid to education. The national government, often in partnership with the local one, built schools through its various work relief programs; indeed, almost one-half of the counties in the United States could boast a school project built by the Roosevelt administration (Smith, 2006). The federal government also administered funds through the National Youth Administration to keep teenagers in school. That such programs were primarily efforts to tighten the adult labor market is evidenced by the fact that they disappeared once the United States recovered from the Great Depression. England and France also experienced the collapse of the job market in the 1930s, but neither country sought to solve the problems of unemployment, or the social problems of idle youth, by putting huge numbers of youth into schools.

The local and the national in comparative perspective

During the Great Depression, most US states and some municipalities increased school spending and access to high school education. The steady uptick in the proportion of teenagers – through age 17 – staying in school was part of broader trends established in the 1920s and continuing through the 1940s, with the sharpest growth taking place in the Depression. In both Pittsburgh and New York – the two American cities that are part of the focus of our study – the increases in high school attendance, in comparison to that of only a decade earlier, were well out of proportion to the increase in the size of the teenage population (Cohen, 2005). Nevertheless, it is no news to note that the decentralized school system that characterized the American system, during the New Deal and beyond, certainly limited an equitable expansion of schooling, particularly by race and class.

But greater power on the local level does not always imply less equity in social welfare provisions, in comparison to national initiatives, nor has increasing centralization enhanced equity. Our comparative study of the welfare state in the three countries, which focuses on national-level histories as well as developments in two major cities for each of the three countries, allows us to reconsider the issues of centralization and decentralization. Whether greater social provision comes at the initiative of the local or more central government, depends on the issue and the power of progressive coalitions at the local and national levels at any given historical moment. On a number of occasions over the course of almost one century, local welfare initiatives in England and France proved more egalitarian than were those of the central government. The history of public schooling in England and France is one area where centralization did little to enhance equity; sometimes, an increase in the power of the central government actually hindered such progress.

First, England. From the 1870s to the 1890s, educational reform triumphed. New mechanisms created by successive legislative enactments encouraged local school boards in individual cities to lay the foundation for a great expansion of public secondary schools – that is, schooling for students of 11 years and older – modeled on private secondary schools, making access to them much more widely available to working-class and middle-class populations. Birmingham, England – one of the cities that Hanagan and I have studied – exemplifies this trend. The Birmingham Education Society (BES) and the National Education League (NEL) provide models of how middle-class social movement organizations used their strong local organization to lobby for national-level reform. Formed in 1867, under the leadership of Birmingham's mayor, George Dixon, the BES recruited volunteers who gathered information on the state of education and school facilities in Birmingham to challenge the then Prime Minister, Benjamin Disraeli, who denied that "the British nation generally is an uneducated one" (Disraeli, 1882, p. 486). Later that year, Joseph Chamberlain replaced Dixon as Birmingham's mayor and he and other Birmingham reformers played a leadership role in the formation of the NEL in 1869. The League was instrumental in the passage of the Education Act of 1870, which laid the basis for compulsory schooling in Britain (Armytage, 1970; Marcham, 1976).

Organized workers in Birmingham provided support for middle-class initiatives; but their role was strictly subordinate. On the League's behalf, trade unionists organized speaking tours, delegations, and debates to propagandize the ideals of compulsory, secular education (McCann, 1970). While several prominent trade unionists supported the BES's work, its annual subscription of a guinea precluded working-class participation (Marcham, 1976).

One reason for the widespread effectiveness of the reformers' appeals was that the need to educate the masses for citizenship had taken on a new urgency in the eyes of many middle-class voters. The 1867 suffrage reforms had expanded the electorate to include many skilled workers, and some social commentators turned to education to "civilize" the newly franchised voters. Still, other, more progressive, reformers saw the link between education and democracy as interrelated; democratization would bring more education and, in turn, education will lead to more democracy. F.A. Channing, the MP from Northampton, near Birmingham, the son of the American Unitarian reformer, W.E. Channing, was probably influenced by the course of American educational reform. He was to portray educational expansion as a democratic and progressive force that had no natural limits. According to Channing:

Working-men throughout the country should think what it means to control the schools themselves by direct election, and what it would mean for their children to leave the secondary and technical instruction, to which their children ought to have access, also under direct popular control, instead of being walled off from elementary education, and handed over to nominated "cabin-window" bodies, in the interest of privileged classes and sects.

(Channing, 1918, p. 264)

Armed with local authority, educational reformers used successful local experiments to urge further national legislation. The Education Act of 1870 provided for the creation of locally elected school boards, the levying of rates for education, and giving authorities the right to make schooling compulsory through age 14; in July 1871, the Birmingham school board passed by-laws fixing the period of compulsion at the maximum allowed by the Act – the years 5 to 14 (Coley, 1911; Smith, 1982). The Birmingham experience was used to justify the enactment of compulsory elementary education throughout England in 1880 (Shewell, 1951).

English middle-class reformers used the leeway given to them by the government to great advantage. The foundations of a public system of secondary education began to emerge as local school boards authorized elementary schools to provide further education for older pupils, forming higher-grade schools and elementary "tops" that began to adopt a curriculum similar to that of private secondary schools. While Birmingham had been among the leaders of the movement toward secondary education, London, the other city we studied, also followed the trend. By 1886, promoting higher-standard schools became the official policy of the London School Board and fees in these schools were abolished in 1891 (Landon, 1900).

In many respects, the course and character of social reform in England and the United States shared a common spirit in the 1880s and 1890s. The driving force behind educational expansion was the autonomous school board – an independent unit that, like many American school boards, was concerned exclusively with educational policy and was authorized to raise taxes.[4] In contrast to city councils, which often had to justify spending public money among a variety of social goods, the boards had only to concentrate on making an effective case for education. From 1870 onward, school board elections were open to all ratepayers, leading to a wider suffrage than for parliamentary elections. Women ratepayers, denied the vote in parliamentary elections, could vote for school board elections.

Still, even as more egalitarian approaches to English education were spreading at the local level, this approach was losing saliency among important middle-class reformers, as issues of national efficiency became increasingly important to a country that saw itself as losing its industrial supremacy to both Germany and America. Some English reformers focused on the American educational system, but the majority of activists, more narrowly concerned with industrial education, centered their attention on Germany (Searle, 1971). The American historian David Labaree has explored the contradictory American expectations that schools ought to promote democratic equality, social efficiency, and individual social mobility. Labaree argues that "ideological characteristics" of both the commitment to individual mobility and democratic equality share a widespread progressive common ground (Labaree, 1997, p. 37). Both goals generate support for expanding access to education because, to paraphrase Labaree, those concerned with promoting democracy believe that education is essential so that all can participate politically on equal terms, and those committed to social mobility believe that access to schooling is necessary for all to have an equal chance at success (Labaree, 1988, 1997). Thus, to the extent that social efficiency in England became the dominant goal with respect to education, the egalitarian impulses lost out.

If the major argument for extending secondary education was put in terms of industrial efficiency, it made sense to consult businessmen and industrialists about their needs. Between 1880 and 1902, businessmen and industrialists lobbied for a reform of secondary education that would be vocationally oriented and specialized to produce the special workforce they required. Small businessmen hoped for government-provided secondary education that would provide language and commercial training (Association of Chambers of Commerce, 1892). Industrialists who spoke of their needs usually found a sympathetic audience among Liberals, who, along with the Conservatives, made up the two major political parties at the time (Emy, 1973). The labor movement, on the other hand, was divided into those who supported technical education following primary school, those who wanted to democratize access to secondary schooling for the talented elite, and a small number who seemed at least sympathetic to the need for generalized secondary education (Griggs, 1983).

Increasingly, as they embraced industrial efficiency, reformers from Joseph Chamberlain to the majority of the Fabian society became indifferent or opposed to the leeway given to local school boards and the new broadening of education. Educational reformers dedicated to education for industrial requirements now joined forces with private educators and members of the Anglican and Catholic churches to uproot the foundations of mass secondary education.

With the 1895 split in the Liberal Party, and the power of the Conservative Party on the increase, the Conservative Prime Minister, Arthur Balfour, decided to take the educational bull by the horns. The Education Act of 1902 charted a centralized, elitist course for English education that lasted for decades. According to scholar G.K. Searle, writing in 1971, "If the British educational system of the present day has much in common with that of France or Germany, but has diverged from the American patterns, this is largely the consequence of the 1902 Education act" (p. 212). Essentially, the Act struck at the heart of the issue, by abolishing the school boards, whose local initiatives had been expanding quality secondary education, and transferring their authority to the County or County Borough authorities. In large urban areas, such as Birmingham, this meant that education was brought under the control of a committee of the Birmingham City Council and, in the case of London in 1903, the London County Council. From this point on, the costs and needs of education would be weighed and balanced against other urban needs that pressed on local authorities, not justified on their own merit.

Local initiatives now had to be submitted for approval before implementation by the newly empowered national Board of Education (Banks, 1955; Kazamias, 1966). In the years that followed, the Board did not abolish existing higher-grade schools that competed with secondary schools; it acknowledged their secondary status and limited their accessibility. The Board required fees for entry into state-supported secondary schools, declaring that "A fee of a substantial amount is desirable both in order to ensure the financial stability of the school and also to emphasize the fact that the education provided is of a superior kind" (Simon, 1960, p. 242).

Nor did a Liberal electoral victory undo the centralization of educational policy. Four years after the Education Act of 1902, the Liberal Party took power with a crushing majority and, despite its own explicit pledge to restore local initiatives, and limit church-subsidized education, it failed to repeal the 1902 law. Thus, just at the time that Liberal power ushered in social legislation in the form of national income support, so, too, did it preside over the increasing use of public schooling as a vehicle for promoting the needs of social efficiency. By preventing the growth of a mass secondary education system, the 1902 Educational Act may or may not have encouraged national efficiency as intended, but it certainly strengthened educational inequality. In this system, key educational decisions for children were made by the time they were 11 years of age.

In the interwar years, industrial worker families increasingly favored expanded secondary education. However, educational policy remained a national initiative, and with this, a recursive pattern evolved that repeated itself over and over again. First came periods of bold educational initiative, in which commitments were made to raise the school-leaving age and new educational goals espoused; next came the increasing realization that such reforms were costly, followed by increases in unemployment and budgetary deficits, leading to the decision that school expenditures must be cut and ending in a restoration of the status quo ante. The pattern of support by a key committee, by an important political leader or even by Acts of Parliament, for an increase in the school-leaving age followed by its repudiation, occurred in 1918, 1924, 1926, 1929–1930, and 1936.

For example, the Fisher Bill, named after the President of the national Board of Education, Herbert Fisher, which was passed in 1918, involved the extension of secondary education, abolishing almost all exemptions from school attendance for those under the age of 14 and authorizing school authorities to establish a school-leaving age of 15, if they so chose. One of the most important aspects of the Fisher Bill, and a surprise to political leaders, was its popularity. In August 1919, Fisher himself noted that "All over the country I find the cry goes up; More secondary schools, and, again more secondary schools! We cannot build them fast enough to hold the pupils who want to get into them" (Kazamias, 1966, pp. 250–251). The emergence of educational issues and the popularity of secondary school expansion led the growing Labour Party to formalize its position, calling on the enlargement of secondary education, though throughout the 1920s and 1930s Labour's biggest concern remained unemployment.

The Fisher Bill, however, could not survive the increasing unemployment in 1920–1921, and the increasing domination of Conservatives in the ruling coalitions sealed the law's fate. Chairing a select parliamentary committee in 1922, formed to make recommendations for cuts in the budget, Sir Eric Geddes famously pronounced that he would do it "with an axe" (Bernbaum, 1967, p. 28). A main target of the ax was the educational budget for which he recommended brutal cuts in expenditures for secondary schools and increases in fees.

In the interwar period, during the tenure of Minister of the Exchequer and then Prime Minister Neville Chamberlain, Birmingham lost the educational leadership that had developed under the mayoralty of Neville's father, Joseph Chamberlain. Part of the reason for this loss of leadership was the changing character of the British government. Chamberlain's Birmingham had been such a model because much could be accomplished by strong-minded wealthy elites at the local level. Nevertheless, the centralization of British government, a centralization in which Joseph's son Neville played such a crucial role, now limited what local government could do.

By contrast, during the 1920s, major American cities accelerated the expansion of high schools. Certainly even on the local level, as school bureaucracies were centralized and structured to reflect the goals of professionals; the ability for ordinary citizens to actually participate in decisions regarding the functioning of local schools diminished. Yet, to the extent that American schools remained dependent on local property taxes, community support remained crucial. As Tracy Steffes notes, "While experts might control the school, the success of education required the cooperation, support and active efforts of teachers, children, parents and communities" (2007, p. 117). Mobilizing support for public schooling through the press and such organizations as the PTA (parent–teacher association), proponents of school expansion were remarkably effective. American historian Dan Amsterdam shows that, in contrast to the federal government in the 1920s – an era thought of as one of limited government – public spending at the state and local government level exploded; along with improvement in infrastructure, the largest expenditures in urban government consisted of public education (Amsterdam, 2009; Goldin and Katz, 2008; Reese, 2005).

During the Great Depression, the British Conservative Party dominance at the national level meant little government sympathy for enhancing the reach of secondary school. The effects of the Depression hit youth equally hard in England and the United States. English employment trends also showed a decrease in the need for manual workers that paralleled the situation in the US job market. In contrast, clerical jobs, which required extended schooling, were in higher demand, yet England experienced no such comparable increase in schooling. In 1938, as many American states were raising the compulsory age of schooling to 16, British parliamentary reports on education recommended that the mandatory school age be increased from 14 to 16; however, the extension of compulsory schooling to age 15 did not occur until after World War II. Even after the war, when local school committees once again looked to make the reach of secondary school more egalitarian, the national level government, now dominated by Labour, while it gave lip service to the idea, considered this a low priority. Money for experimental, comprehensive secondary schools, comparable to the typical American high school, where children of varying social classes were housed in one school, was only slowly forthcoming from the national government, and even less available after 1950, when the Conservatives took power. Only in the mid-1950s did experimental comprehensive schools begin to take shape (Fenwick, 1976; Gosden, 1983; Parkinson, 1970; Pedley, 1956).

During this same time period, 1870–1950, the French state, famous for its highly centralized approach, carefully monitored and regulated secondary school education. The need to pass the *baccalauréat*, as well as entry exams for specialized schools, allowed the state to set the overall rhythm of secondary education. Age 11, when a child was eligible for admission to a *lycée*, was a first key turning point in a child's educational life. Although French children were required to attend school until age 13, after age 11 it was practically impossible for a child to enter the elite secondary system of *lycées* and *collèges*. Age 17 was the second turning point in French secondary education, when the student took an exam for graduation, the *baccalauréat*. Successful completion of the *baccalauréat* opened the student's way to the prestigious institutions of higher learning.

All French schools were subject to state inspection and the uniform curriculum imposed by the state severely limited local experiments. Before 1906, when the effects of a republican landslide took hold, private schools – typically Catholic – had somewhat greater freedom to experiment and sometimes edged out their secular competitors in the fiercely competitive exam taking. While *lycées* and *collèges* were usually located in large cities, the former generally ignored their urban environment and remained impervious to local politics. For example, Paris, one of the cities in our study, was the capital of the *lycée*; the most famous, such as the Lycée Louis-le-Grand, the Lycée Henri IV, or the Lycée Charlemagne, were Parisian. But Parisian secondary schools were not dominated by Parisians. In fact, students from Parisian primary schools were disproportionately excluded from entry to the *lycée*.

The tiny *lycées* in Saint-Etienne, the other French city that Hanagan and I have studied, were somewhat more rooted in the locality, but only because of their proximity to a local engineering school. A boys' public *lycée*, the Lycée Claude Fauriel, had only been established in 1890 and a girls' in 1895. Together, they served a little over one hundred students, a miniscule number in that city, situated in a metropolitan area of 264,000. Slightly larger numbers of secondary students were enrolled in a Catholic school, until 1906, in the Jesuit *collège* of Saint-Michel. Outside the religious and the few state-run secondary schools, there was little in the way of post-elementary instruction available in the Stéphanois, the region that included Saint-Etienne (Ronin, 1948).

Whatever their relationship to the local environment, decisions that affected secondary school education were made in Paris. In the French National Assembly, laws were enacted by a series of coalitions brokered between fiscally conservative republicans and radical republicans, who were more inclined toward social reform. After 1893, socialists played an ever-growing part in this coalition. While religion played a role in the formation of educational policy in all three countries, nowhere was it so polarizing as in France, where major religious division, Catholic/non-Catholic, was a significant cleavage in national politics. Unlike Ireland, where, as Raftery shows us in this volume, most nationalists and republicans supported religious education, in France the battle for secular education was a fight for the republic. In the early days of the Third Republic, during the 1870s, a broad spectrum of republicans, including conservatives, came to believe that the secure foundation of the republic required the elimination of the church's role in public education. The republican landslide of 1905 strengthened the cause of separation of church and state and the secularization of education. With educational policy a lightning rod for debates between the religious and the secular, relatively little attention was paid to the elitism of secondary education (Auspitz, 1982).

During the interwar years, France saw some serious efforts to expand secondary education. Right after World War I, a group of military intellectuals assigned to Marshall Petain's staff proposed a common school curriculum for youngsters in the primary grades and greater access to secondary schools with a common curriculum, sometimes referred to as the *école unique*. The Confédération Générale du Travail (CGT), the confederation of French trade unions, also endorsed a common curriculum, which was supported by the teachers' unions (CGT, 1931). Throughout the period, the biggest push for a more egalitarian education system, as in England, came not from the labor Left, but the Radical Socialists – a rather moderate, predominantly rural party at the time. Their leader, Édouard Herriot, the perennial mayor of Lyons, saw education as the principal vehicle of social progress. In 1925, the French expanded the more commercially oriented, tuition-free school, the *école primaire supérieure* (EPS), providing it free of charge if no *lycées* were available. The EPS expansion was similar to the short-lived experiments of the local school boards in England prior to 1902; the EPS offered two to four additional years of schooling to train for a number of white-collar occupations, including teaching. In 1930, France established free secondary education for children through the sixth class, for ages 11 to 12.

As in the United States, the Depression brought change in French education; yet, the biggest development, the spread of free secondary school education, occurred in the years 1930–1933, before the Popular Front years. Although the socialists supported efforts to expand free education, it was driven by Radical Socialists. During Edouard Herriot's brief tenure as Prime Minister (June 3–December 18, 1932), the Radical Socialists and the socialists partnered to form an educational coalition that resulted in the gradual extension of free *lycée* schooling. By 1933, all seven classes of the *lycée* became free – for those who qualified. The availability of space in existing educational institutions, due to the decline of the size of the age cohort (an effect of the population loss during World War I), removed one of the great financial obstacles to the expansion of schooling. In any case, the French state, in comparison to the English, had always contributed far more to secondary schooling and the financial cost was relatively cheap (Jaubert, 1938).

As the Depression deepened in France, secondary school enrollments increased. And if socialist militants were divided about the importance of moving masses of working-class children into education beyond traditional vocational training, like the British, the parents wanted to send their children not just to vocational training schools but also to the free secondary schools – either the elite *lycées* or, in the case of most, the EPS.

In some ways, the increase in secondary school attendance was similar to that which took place in the United States, where high school enrollments increased during the hard years of the 1930s. But if the trends pointed in the same direction as the United States, the overall size of the French increase was very small. In 1930, 3.5 percent of French children were in upper secondary school, which encompasses children aged 10–19. In 1935, 5 percent were in school; by 1940, their number rose to 7.4 percent (UNESCO, 1952).

In addition to the expansion of secondary schools, the Popular Front years also saw curricular changes in an effort to promote a more egalitarian system. While the left-wing parties are often seen as the architects of the major educational change during the Popular Front years, the major designer, and the builder, Jean Zay, was a politician of the more moderate Radical Socialist party. There is no question that, in terms of educational reform, the years between 1936 and 1937 were exciting. Both big plans and small were in the works. Although he ultimately failed in the years before World War II, Zay was able to make a serious assault on the French old-fashioned educational system because he was in power at the educational ministry throughout the rise of the Popular Front and after its collapse. The Leon Blum government came and went, but Zay remained in his ministry. Zay's major accomplishments in extending the school age to 14 and introducing a common curriculum in elementary schools occurred during the early days of the Popular Front, and even though his proposals met with growing opposition within his own party, as a Radical Socialist he could still draw on party loyalties to remain in office and count on a commitment to education that long characterized the Radical Socialists.

Zay realized from the start that an ambitious program of school expansion would depend on increased spending for school structures and the search for funding was his first priority. He sought to unify a bifurcated system that consigned groups to separate spheres early on. Zay was not afraid to use power and many of his most daring measures were implemented by ministerial decree. He began experimenting with a new system in which all students age 13–14 would take a common orientation class, where they would explore a variety of educational alternatives, all the while sharing the same school building and the same overall curriculum. Unfortunately, experiments tried out in select schools did not constitute a clear educational program. Opponents found much to attack but supporters were not always sure what to defend (Ory, 1994, pp. 709–710; Ruby, 1969). Although Zay raised the school-leaving age from 13 to 14, it took a long struggle to implement this reform. Moreover, his attempts to democratize French secondary education by offering more fellowships and better coordinating the transition from primary to secondary school, while retaining basic divisions within secondary education, met ferocious opposition, not only from the right, but from some teachers' unions. Unlike British unionists, who were relatively united in their demand for more egalitarian schools, French education was sharply divided between teachers in the elite *lycées* and those outside them.

As the Popular Front ebbed, all things connected with it became open targets. With so many of the Popular Front leaders outside of government by the end of 1937, Zay became a special target of right-wing attack. The price of moving the *école unique* – the common school – to the center of the political arena meant exposing it to political divisions. Imprisoned with fellow left-wing prisoners by the Pétain government, as one of the republicans who had contributed to France's collapse, Zay was assassinated by right-wing *miliciens* in 1944. While the number of students attending French secondary schools increased in the interwar period, particularly during the years of the Great Depression, the idea of a common school with a melange of students of all classes – so dear to Radical Socialists – seemed to be no nearer.

France in the mid-twentieth century, with its centralized education system, had emerged ahead of the centralized English system, in terms of access to secondary school. However, it still lagged behind the Americans, with their decentralized approach. In 1949, roughly three-quarters of all Americans aged 14–17 were full-time students, while only one-half of the French and one-third of the population of England and Wales were still in full-time education. At the same time, one out of every five Americans who graduated secondary school went on to college, compared to a little more than one in twenty of French graduates and one in fifty of their English counterparts (UNESCO, 1952).

National coalitions and public schools

By 1945, France was unable to build strong national coalitions to push for an egalitarian school system. The strongest push came from the Radical Socialists, whose influence was short-lived; the major players on the right were opposed and those on the left were divided, at best, in their concern. So too, as we have seen in England, the great faith in education came from Liberals, whose attitude about a common education changed, and who in any case played an increasingly limited role, as we move to the middle of the twentieth century. As for the major political parties – Labour was only nominally interested in massive access to college preparatory schools, and the Conservatives were openly hostile. Still, if England and France were unable to build such national coalitions, so too – despite the widespread consensus about the importance of public education – was the United States slow in building national coalitions that could push for egalitarian schooling.

While the spread of education in the United States was dependent on local- and state-level capacities, federal efforts were few and far between. In the early post-World War I years, many education reformers and national organizations coalesced around a federal education bill that called for the establishment of a federal department of education. It also provided for matching funds to those states requiring that children be in school for twenty-four weeks, and until age 14. The bill received support from the National Educational Association, the National Mothers' Congress, the Women's Joint Congress, the General Federation of Women's Clubs, the League of Women Voters, and the Women's Trade Union League. But the proposed legislation left most issues of standardization to the states; thus the issue of race as well as religion split the coalition. W.E.B Dubois of the National Association for the Advancement of Colored People (NAACP) blasted the bill for perpetuating states' rights to deny African Americans any sort of meaningful education. When it became clear to the great reformer Florence Kelley, head of the National Consumers League at the time, that the bill would not require states to fund black and white schools equally, she withdrew her support. The Catholic Church mounted sustained opposition to the bill. While, as Lynn Dumenil points out, many Catholics supported other aspects of social reform, they were unanimously opposed to a bill that funded public schools. At a time when many anti-Catholic organizations were mounting rather unsuccessful state-wide campaigns to mandate attendance at public schools, the church was concerned about any efforts to privilege the institution (Duminel, 1991; Mink, 1996). The bill never even came to a vote; most Congressmen and their constituents were content to keep federal funds out of public education, save for the little amount available for vocational training.

The next important federal initiatives came during the New Deal, which, as I have argued, along with Paula Fass, have been an underappreciated aspect of the Roosevelt years (Cohen, 2005, Fass, 1983). Yet FDR did not push for direct federal aid to school systems; he knew that powerful southern congressman were hostile toward any federal aid package that would reduce racial inequalities and open the door for greater federal regulation of the schools. Moreover, he did not want to alienate urban Catholics (Tyack et al., 1984).

After World War II, groups came together on a few important occasions, resulting in increased access to education. The GI Bill of Rights represented one successful effort to put together a coalition of those committed to military benefits, with liberals committed to a federal role in expanding access to education. The National Defense Educational Act of 1958, enacted in the wake of the Sputnik Crisis of 1958, provided many millions in federal aid dollars between 1959 and 1962 to enhance education at all levels, and exemplified the power of the Cold War coalition of liberals pushing federal aid to education with national security allies (Urban, 2010). The civil rights community's decision to put schooling front and center in the struggle to guarantee citizenship rights across race, that is, *Brown* v. *Board of Education*, was a key moment of increasing involvement by the federal government in American education (McGuinn, 2006).

The passage of the Elementary and Secondary School Act of 1965 as part of Lyndon Johnson's War on Poverty represented an important increase in federal involvement. And, more recently, as McGuinn shows in this volume, both the Bush and Obama administrations implemented an "ambitious and controversial expansion of federal power that has long been based on the principal of local control." The United States is now living with the largest federal intervention into schooling to date – No Child Left Behind (NCLB) (McGuinn, 2006; see also Chapter 8 in this volume). NCLB, implemented under George W. Bush, used federal funding to force state and local school systems to implement testing programs. These assessments are meant to hold education officials accountable for raising student proficiency in reading and mathematics. Schools that fail to make improvements in achievement could face a variety of punitive sanctions, including school closure. In some cases, parents of children in failing schools could exercise "choice," by using federal funds to transfer their children into successful schools. Participating in NCLB is a voluntary program; however, because schools need all the financial aid they can get, they have no choice but to cooperate.

The US approach to measuring education achievement nonetheless remains far more decentralized in comparison to Europe. Under NCLB, American states have been free to choose which tests to use and how rigorous the standards would be. Even so, state and local communities pushed back forcefully against the mandates and the punitive measures; by early 2014, some 85 percent of the states have received waivers, allowing them to accept NCLB funds if they have shown good faith efforts to improve achievement (McNeil, 2013).

The Obama administration has nevertheless continued federal efforts to institute reforms through financial incentives, offering badly needed funds, for which states must compete. In early 2014, nineteen states have obtained such funding, totaling four billion dollars, through the US Department of Education

(DEA) Race to the Top (RTT) program (White House, 2014). RTT "winners" are those states that show a continuing commitment to testing, the use of testing to reward and punish teachers, and a willingness to use tax dollars to expand the number of charter schools, institutions that operate outside of the rules and regulations of the district public schools. The DEA has also used RTT funds to encourage the adoption by states of Common Core standards of achievement, created by the National Governors' Association, in the area of mathematics and language arts. At this writing, forty-five states and the District of Columbia have adopted the Common Core standards for measuring achievement in elementary and secondary schools. Such uniformity might be closer to the national standards we associate with Europe, but unlike Europe, no uniform curriculum was enacted to achieve the goals. Moreover, the intense pushback from parents and teachers against even this much standardization, and the fact that some school districts have opted out of RTT funds rather than follow the requirements of the Common Core, suggests that the United States is a long way from standardizing its educational policies at the level of the individual school.

To the extent that centralization of schooling in the United States has proceeded at all, it has not, despite the stated goals of many involved in the school reform movement, resulted in greater parity in educational opportunities for children across class and race. Thus, a central approach regarding public schooling in the United States, as I have argued for an earlier time period in England and France, is no guarantee of more egalitarianism. Today, NCLB has not truly confronted the issues of class and race. Schools where the most severely disadvantaged are educated can only avoid NCLB's penalties for failure if they focus almost exclusively on reading and math, to the detriment of all other subjects. RTT similarly concentrates on reading and math (Bjork, forthcoming). Such a development, Kantor and Lowe have argued, actually widened the disparities between urban and suburban schools. Moreover, the emphasis on parental "choice" has not truly provided better options for the vast majority of poor children. NCLB's provisions do not offer incentives for better suburban schools to accept these students, nor are there enough good public and charter schools in the urban districts, which could enable poor families to truly exercise "choice" (Kantor and Lowe, 2013).

Michael Katz wrote recently that public schooling is still one of America's largest programs of economic redistribution. The dependence on local property taxes, which results in a public school system that so disadvantages poor and minority children in the United States, makes it hard to view American public schooling as redistributive. But not only has it always been redistributive, our public school system still is. Thus, "the average family with children receives benefits worth much more than they have contributed and wealthier families, childless and empty-nest households, and businesses subsidize families with children in school" (Katz, 2010a, p. 52). Rather than expanding on that commitment to education as a public good, however, the United States is now sponsoring a proliferation of privately subsidized initiatives as part of its national public school system. Often, these initiatives stress the adoption of business models that apply market models to school reform. They rely on managers, rather than professional educators, and place a heavy emphasis on rewards and sanctions, along with testing, to hold teachers accountable. Holger Ziegler, in this volume, charts a similar approach to the reform of social work in Germany, with its new emphasis on managerialism. As Diane Ravitch has noted, "with the collapse of Communism and the triumph of market reforms in most parts of the world, it did not seem to be much of a stretch to envision the application of the market model to [American] schooling" (2011, p. 10). The emphasis on school vouchers, to be used by families who become individual consumers in the market, lessens the sense of collective responsibility. In the United States, this is a particular worry, because losing the sense of public responsibility for the schools may leave Americans with almost no sense of public responsibility at all.

Ultimately, only a national approach can address the American problem, so well articulated by Roosevelt advisor and President of the University of North Carolina, Frank Graham, who in 1939 declared that:

> we do not have a democracy in America when we invest $220 in one child's education and less than $20 in another child's . . . if you say "Leave it to the States." You simply say we don't believe in equality of educational opportunities for the children in this country.
>
> (US Children's Bureau, 1939, p. 100)

Still, as I hope this historical analysis has suggested, we cannot assume that, even in modern democracies, central initiatives necessarily offer this important promise.

Notes

1 An earlier version of this chapter was delivered to the University of Zurich Conference on Education and the State: Historical Perspectives on a Changing Relationship, September 15, 2011. I thank the audience members at the Conference, as well as Christopher Bjork, Michael Hanagan, Harvey Kantor, and an anonymous reader for their comments and suggestions.
2 Cohen and Hanagan, "Democracy and Demography: Political Coalitions in the Making of the American Welfare State in England, France, and the United States, 1870–1950" (manuscript in progress). The study involves a comparison of national policies in England, France, and the United States and focuses on politics and policies in two cities for each country. In the United States, we study New York City and Pittsburgh, as well as London and Birmingham for England, and Paris and St Etienne for France.
3 To quote, social transfers "flow to the citizens as a matter of law or entitlement and they are paid for by other members of the community by law or requirement" (Garfinkel et al., 2010, p. 2). I am also grateful to Lisa Tiersten and Lars Tragardh,

"The Child and the Nation-State, France, Sweden and the United States," Conference on the Child and the State, New York, May 2006, for their introductory comments, which helped me to think about the role of schooling in drawing new boundaries between the state and the family.
4 For a discussion of how the establishment of separate school funding in Winterhur, imposed by the Canton of Zurich, enhanced the democratic reach of schools, see Aubry, in this volume.

References

Amsterdam, D., 2009. *The Roaring Metropolis: Business, Civic Welfare, and State Expansion in 1920s America*. PhD thesis, University of Pennsylvania.
Armytage, W.H.B., 1970. The 1870 Education Act. *British Journal of Educational Studies*, 18, pp. 121–133.
Association of Chambers of Commerce, 1892. *Thirty Second Annual Meeting . . . On March 8th, 9th & 10th, 1892*. London: Vacher & Sons, pp. 129–133.
Auspitz, K., 1982. *The Radical Bourgeois: The Ligue de L'enseignement and the Origins of the Third Republic, 1866–1885*. New York: Cambridge University Press.
Banks, O., 1955. *Parity and Prestige in English Secondary Education*. London: Routledge and Kegan Paul.
Bernbaum, G., 1967. *Social Change and the Schools 1919–1944*. London: Routledge and Kegan Paul.
Bjork, C., forthcoming. *Transforming Japanese Education: A Nation's Attempts to Reduce Academic Pressure*.
Channing, F.A., 1918. *Memories of Midland Politics*. London: Constable and Copy.
Cohen, M., 2005. Reconsidering schools and the American welfare state. *History of Education Quarterly*, 45(4), pp. 511–537.
Coley, A.H., 1911. The council schools. In: J.H. Muirhead (ed.) *Birmingham Institutions*. Birmingham: Cornish Brothers, pp. 365–400.
Confédération Générale du Travail (CGT), 1931. Rapports adopté par la commission confédérale de l'enseignment et de l'education ourvière. *La Voix du Peuple*, March, pp. 237–239.
Disraeli, B., 1882. *Selected Speeches of the Right Honourable Earl of Beaconsfield*. London: Longmans, Green.
Duminel, L., 1991. The insatiable maw of bureaucracy: antistatism and the educational reform in the 1920s. *Journal of American History*, 77(2), pp. 499–524.
Emy, H.V., 1973. *Liberals, Radicals, and Social Politics 1862–1914*. Cambridge: Cambridge University Press.
Fass, P., 1982. Without design education policy in the New Deal. *American Journal of Education*, 91(1), pp. 36–64.
Fenwick, I.G.K., 1976. *The Comprehensive School 1944–1970: The Politics of Secondary School Reorganization*. London: Methuen.
Flora, P. and Heidenheimer, A., (eds), 1981. *The Development of the Welfare State in Europe and America*. New Brunswick, NJ: Rutgers University Press.
Garfinkel, I., Rainwater, L., and Smeeding, T., 2010. *Wealth and Welfare State: Is America a Laggard or Leader?* New York: Oxford University Press.
Goldin, C. and Katz, L., 2008. *The Race Between Education and Technology*. Cambridge: Belknap Press of Harvard University Press.

Gosden, P., 1983. *The Education System since 1944*. Oxford: Martin Robinson.
Griggs, C., 1983. *The Trades Union Congress & the Struggle for Education*. London: Falmer Press.
Hart, V., 1994. *Bound By Our Constitution: Women, Workers, and the Minimum Wage*. Princeton, NJ: Princeton University Press.
Holmes, O.W., 1905. *Dissent, Lochner v. New York*. 198 US 45.
Jaubert, L., 1938. *La Gratuité de L'enseignement Secondaire*. Dissertation in law. Bordeaux: Imprimerie Delmas.
Kantor, H. and Lowe, R., 1995. Federal welfare policy: from the New Deal to the Great Society. *Educational Researcher*, 24(3), p. 24.
Kantor, H. and Lowe, R., 2013. Educationalizing the welfare state: the evolution of social policy since the New Deal. In: R. Lowe (ed.) *Educationalizing the Welfare State and Privatizing Education: The Evolution in Social Policy Since the New Deal* (e-book). Available at: http://epublications.marquette.edu/cgi/viewcontent.cgi?article=1252&context=edu_fac (accessed January 25, 2014).
Katz, M., 2010a. Public education as welfare. *Dissent*, 57, pp. 52–56.
Katz, M., 2010b. The American welfare state and the social contract in hard times. *Journal of Policy History*, 22, pp. 508–529.
Katz, M., 2011. Was government the solution or the problem? The role of the state in the history of American social policy. In: M. Hanagan and C. Tilly (eds) *Contention and Trust in Cities and States*. New York: Springer, pp. 323–338.
Katznelson, I. and Weir, M., 1988. *Schooling for All: Class, Race and the Decline of the Democratic Idea*. New York: Basic Books.
Kazamias, A.M., 1966. *Politics, Society, and Secondary Education in England*. Philadelphia, PA: University of Pennsylvania Press.
Labaree, D.F., 1988. *The Making of an American High School: The Credentials Market and the Central High School of Philadelphia, 1838–1939*. New Haven, CT: Yale University Press.
Labaree, D.F., 1997. *How to Succeed in School Without Really Learning: The Credentials Race in American Education*. New Haven, CT: Yale University Press.
Ladd-Taylor, M., 1994. *Mother Work: Women, Child Welfare and the State, 1890–1933*. Urbana, IL: University of Illinois Press.
Landon, F.G., 1900. Higher grade schools. In: T.A. Spalding (ed.) *The Work of the London School Board*. London: P.S. King, pp. 193–199.
Lindert, P., 2004. *Growing Public: Social Spending and Economic Growth Since the Nineteenth Century*. Cambridge: Cambridge University Press.
McCann, W.P., 1970. Trade unionists, artisans and the 1870 Education Act. *British Journal of Educational Studies*, 18(2), pp. 134–150.
McGuinn, P.J., 2006. *No Child Left Behind and the Transformation of Federal Education Policy, 1965–2005*. Lawrence, KS: University of Kansas Press.
McNeil, M., 2013. NCLB waivers: a state by state breakdown. *Education Week* (online) (last updated January 30, 2014). Available at: www.edweek.org/ew/section/infographics/nclbwaivers.html (accessed January 28, 2014).
Marcham, A.J., 1976. The Birmingham Education Society and the 1870 Education Act. *Journal of Educational Administration and History*, 8, pp. 11–16.
Mink, G., 1996. *The Wages of Motherhood, Inequality in the Welfare State*. Ithaca, NY: Cornell University Press.

Muncy, R., 1991. *Creating a Female Dominion in American Reform, 1890–1935*. Oxford: Oxford University Press.

Ory, P., 1994. *La Belle Illusion: Culture et Politique sous le Signe du Front Populaire, 1935–1938*. Paris: Plon.

Parkinson, M., 1970. *The Labour Party and the Organization of Secondary Education 1918–65*. London: Routledge and Kegan Paul.

Patterson, J., 1994. *America's Struggle Against Poverty 1900–1994*. Cambridge, MA: Harvard University Press.

Pedley, R., 1956. *Comprehensive Education*. London: Victor Gollancz.

Provasnik, S., 2006. Judicial activism and the origins of parental choice: the court's role in the institutionalization of compulsory education in the United States, 1891–1925. *History of Education Quarterly*, 46(3), pp. 311–347.

Ravitch, D., 2011. *The Death and Life of the Great American School System: How Testing and Choice Are Undermining Education*. New York: Basic Books.

Reese, W.J., 2005. *America's Public Schools: From the Common School to No Child Left Behind*. Baltimore, MA: Johns Hopkins Press.

Ronin, P., 1948. *Saint-Etienne: Cité Méconnue*. Saint-Etienne: Editions Espoir.

Ruby, M., 1969. *La Vie et l'Oeuvre de Jean Zay*. Paris: L'imprimerie Beresnick.

Searle, G.R., 1971. *The Quest for National Efficiency: A Study in British Politics and Political Thought, 1899–1914*. Berkeley, CA: University of California Press.

Shewell, M.E.J., 1951. *An Historical Investigation of the Development of a Local System of Education in the City of Birmingham from 1870–1924*. London: University of London.

Simon, B., 1960. *The Two Nations and the Educational Structure, 1780–1870*. London: Lawrence & Wishart.

Smith, D., 1982. *Conflict and Compromise: Class Formation in English Society, 1830–1914*. London: Routledge and Kegan Paul.

Smith, J.S., 2006. *Building New Deal Liberalism: The Political Economy of Public Works*. New York: Cambridge University Press.

State of New York, 1888. *Second Annual Report of the Factory Inspectors of the State of New York, for the Year Ending December 1, 1887*. In: G. Abbott (ed.), 1938. *The Child and the State, Vol. 1, Legal Status in the Family, Apprenticeship and Child Labor, Select Documents and Introductory Notes*. Chicago, IL: University of Chicago Press, p. 416.

State of New York, 1974. *Report of the New York State Commission on Relief for Widowed Mothers*. Transmitted to the legislature, March 27, 1914. New York: Arno Press.

Steffes, T.L., 2007. *A New Education for a Modern Age: National Reform, State-building, and the Transformation of American Schooling, 1890–1933*. PhD thesis, University of Chicago.

Steffes, T.L., 2012. *School, Society, and State: A New Education to Govern Modern America, 1890–1940*. Chicago, IL: University of Chicago Press.

Tiersten, L. and Tragardh, L., 2006. Introduction. Paper presented at The Child and the Nation-State: France, Sweden and the United States symposium, Columbia University, New York, May 2006, unpublished.

Tyack, D.B., Lowe, R. and Hansot, E., 1984. *Public Schools in Hard Times: The Great Depression and Recent Years*. Cambridge, MA: Harvard University Press.

UNESCO, 1952. *World Handbook of Educational Organizations and Statistics*. Paris: United Nations.

Urban, W., 2010. *More than Science and Sputnik: The National Defense Education Act of 1958*. Tuscaloosa, AL: University of Alabama Press.
US Children's Bureau, 1939. *Papers and Discussions at the Initial Session*, White House Conference on Children in a Democracy, April 26.
White House, 2014. *Race to the Top* (online). Available at: www.whitehouse.gov/issues/education/k-12/race-to-the-top (accessed January 27, 2014).

Chapter 3

State intervention in backward countries
Some case studies of state education systems in Hispanic America (c.1870–1920)

Gabriela Ossenbach

Although, in Latin America, new educational systems came into being immediately after the achievement of independence, when education was seen as crucial to the construction of political legitimacy, this chapter will primarily focus on the consolidation of these educational systems beginning in the last quarter of the nineteenth century.[1] The intervening years were too rife with political instability, armed conflict, regional tensions, the establishment of borders and of political institutions, and the articulation of an economic model that would guarantee institutional development and consensus among the different factions struggling for power. All of these factors contributed to a delay in the consolidation of national educational systems that were very much on the minds of the region's political leaders from the first moments of political independence.

The model of state that took shape at the end of the nineteenth century in Latin America was what has come to be known as an *oligarchy state*. Under this type of organization, political society consisted solely of members of the dominant class, with practically everyone else being excluded. Oligarchies were made possible by the interdependence of the rural world (landowners) and the urban bourgeoisie, which maintained contacts in the exterior and worked toward expanding the international commerce of primary products. The integration of this increasingly consolidated urban, illustrated, modernizing group with the rural elites created the conditions for putting into place an effective power system. As a social group, peasants were the least involved in the concept of a national identity, while the cities became the foundation and base for the building of national states (Carmagnani, 1984, pp. 141–143; Germani, 1962, pp. 147–150; Graciarena, 1984, pp. 49–51). The establishment of state educational systems from this period was also an essentially urban phenomenon.

Although, after their independence, all of the Latin American countries implemented educational systems that were based on the Western model associated with the ideological and political concept of the liberal state (a veritable "cultural model," according to Ramírez and Ventresca, 1992, p. 124), we shall refrain from considering the Brazilian model, which underwent a somewhat different evolution due to its own particular emancipation process. This took place under the monarchy, with the Portuguese royal family itself moving to Brazil in 1807, due to the Napoleonic invasion of the metropolis.

We will, however, examine the role played by the state in the educational systems of various countries of Spanish America, defining two broad categories. On the one hand, we shall refer to those countries that inherited a more traditional socio-political structure in which the influence of the colonial legacy and the Catholic Church was considerable (Colombia, Ecuador, and Chile). On the other hand, we will look at models of "early modernization," implemented in countries in which the influence of the Catholic Church was not so preponderant, economic development was more uniform, and where civilian society had become more consolidated, due at least in part to the influx of European immigrants (Argentina and Uruguay). The aim is to provide a general overview of these countries and make observations regarding common aspects as well as national particularities in order to identify both consistencies and peculiarities that may serve as analytical categories for a comparative study.

In using the term "backward countries" in the title of our chapter, we are referring to the concept put forth by the economic historian Alexander Gerschenkron (1904–1978), whose 1962 work *Economic Backwardness in Historical Perspective* is still relevant to this type of study. According to Gerschenkron, the further a country's economy lags behind the economies of the most industrialized countries (the author applied the Industrial Revolution in Great Britain model), the greater the role that government intervention plays in encouraging development and implementing reforms.[2] An economy that lags behind is also conducive, in Gerschenkron's view, to the emergence of ideologies that place great faith in progress.

The absolute "backwardness" of industrial development in Latin America during the nineteenth century led the national governments to assume an important role in economic development and in the consolidation of a new independent order. Indeed, the role of the state was more decisive there than in those countries where capitalism had originally developed. The reference to their being "behind" – and the need to do something about it – became a constant in the political discourse of much of Spanish America throughout the nineteenth century. This discourse also emphasized the importance of educating the new generations as an indispensable condition for the progress of these fledgling nations, and it tended to place the blame for their "backwardness" on the old metropolis, Spain (Ossenbach and del Pozo, 2011, pp. 586–587; Ossenbach, 2001b). The Argentinian Domingo Faustino Sarmiento, one of the most renowned and influential politicians to promote the expansion of public education in Chile and Argentina, expressed this idea, which is so central to the epoch we are studying, unequivocally in the following passage in 1849:

> There can be no doubt that our task is arduous, given that we must make up for the deficit of sufficiency that has placed Spain on the dubious line that separates civilized people from barbarians and from the increase of

barbarism that came with colonization and that was preserved by the natives. But there is a movement in all the Christian Nations toward a social organization with a base so broad and grand that it is difficult for us to imagine ... and this gives us no choice but to ... prepare us for this new existence which all Christian Societies will soon be a part of, this society being based on the greatest possible development of all of the individuals making up the nation and overcoming the obstacles that the current organization places in the way of the free development of man's active and intellectual faculties. The state, or the joined national forces, shall watch over and protect individual needs and make all citizens beneficiaries of the advantages of association, including all of those who until now were unable to care for themselves.

(Sarmiento, 1849, pp. 24–25)

This awareness of how behind they were would lead these newly independent countries to practice a compulsive importation of foreign models that were adopted with an unflappable faith in their usefulness for solving the theoretical and practical problems involved in organizing the new nations.[3] In the realm of education, there was a special propensity for the importation of foreign models, especially those originating from France, England, Germany, and the United States. The historian Gregorio Weinberg would affirm that this receptive attitude toward tendencies coming from more advanced countries, evident throughout the nineteenth century and the first decades of the twentieth century, was due to a growing awareness of the way in which Latin America was "out of synch," as it were, slipping further behind the progress of Europe and the United States.[4] A need was felt to find ideas and inspirations in the more advanced countries that would help these nations "catch up" and put them in the same time frame, "homogenizing the diversity of times" (Weinberg, 1993, pp. 19–55). The Uruguayan Arturo Ardao speaks of "setting the national clock – a clock running decades behind" (Ardao, 1964, p. xxv).[5]

Yet, we should be careful when deciding whether to attribute the active role of the state in the new Hispanic American nations solely to their need to catch up economically. We must not forget that these societies lacked the social force of a bourgeois class, that there was little sense of national unity, and that their economic articulation was weak. Unlike the more advanced countries, these emerging states were thus obliged to play a critical part in the search for national and territorial unity, in the struggle for political legitimacy and in the creation of a nationally defined economic space (state reform implied an effective transition to a system of capitalist production). In rejecting the old colonial order, these countries faced a series of institutional inadequacies, which they attempted to address by means of governmental initiatives, by the use of the state's administrative machinery, and by virtue of sheer political authority (essentially, by forcing numerous matters and policies – education included – into the political arena). In contrast to other countries, in Hispanic

America investments of private capital in public initiatives of the kind mentioned in the chapter by Vincent Carpentier (in this volume) were practically non-existent. The exiguous industrialization during this period did not produce capital that investors would be inclined to put toward the progress of urban labor forces. In rural areas the scant need for qualified workers did not encourage the establishment of schools on plantations or estates either, although some countries contemplated the creation of on-farm schools that would be the responsibility of the large landowners (Ossenbach, 1996b).

Alluding to the rather limited capacity of civil society to address certain matters that then had to be taken up by the state, the Uruguayan educational reformer José Pedro Varela wrote the following in 1874:

> We are all well aware of the miracles that have taken place in the realm of education in the United States. This has been made possible by the joint effort of the authorities and the population, by the enormous investment made by the state together with the enormous sums donated by the intelligent philanthropy of the wealthy. In our case the opposite is true; if the amount of money that the state dedicates to education is scant to begin with, the contributions made by civilians are more pitiful yet ... The only explanation would seem to be that our concept of philanthropy in Uruguay is misguided; whereas we're likely to respond generously to causes of all sorts – for the sick, for the poor, even for festivities, the contributions made to education are insignificant in comparison.
>
> (Varela, 1874, vol. 49, pp. 9–10)

Yet, the active involvement of the new national governments cannot be attributed exclusively to the organizational challenges that followed these countries' independence and their need to join the international capitalist system. There were other historical reasons, going back considerably, for the active role taken on by the state. First and foremost was the bureaucratic tradition inherent to the administration of the Spanish colonial empire, together with the existence of a pre-industrial urban culture, which included a vast tertiary sector that was intimately associated with those institutions and bureaucratic practices (Véliz, 1984, pp. 15–16). The administrative apparatus inherited from the colonial era was greater in those countries where the state had played a more significant role in the colonial economy (Mexico and Peru). In other regions that had been more marginal (Rio de la Plata), the minimal administrative system needed for an incipient economy based on livestock breeding had been much smaller; as a result, its influence in the post-colonial era was by comparison smaller (Oszlak, 1981, p. 30).

All of these circumstances would have another important consequence for the expansion of literacy in Latin America. One in particular can be singled out in comparative research on the subject, namely the way in which literacy in these countries only became widespread as a result of the establishment of primary schools by national governments. This was done at a considerable cost to governments and is in direct contrast to the process in the United States and Canada, where the spread of literacy started *before* the establishment of universal, obligatory education, with the family playing a vital role in the process (Núñez, 1993). This phenomenon, though, is not attributable solely to the different types and degrees of state intervention (which also existed in southern and northern Europe), but rather has a clearly religious origin that can be traced to the importance of family readings of the Bible, as this was practiced in Protestant countries. The importance of these contrasting "approaches" to literacy should not be underestimated when analyzing the significance of the state's role in Latin American education. Models of analysis put forth by Boli *et al.* (1985) are also relevant in this regard, particularly in the distinction they make between countries in which civil society is dominant and countries in which the predominant social force is the government. In the former, "nation-oriented" countries, education would be seen as an eminently individual process of mobilization, from the "bottom up," in which the combined efforts of different groups move in the direction of progress. In the latter, "state-oriented" countries, by contrast, it is the government that educates its citizens, establishing and regulating the expansion of education in a movement that goes "top down" (Boli *et al.*, 1985, pp. 158–161).

These authors contend that, in those countries, where the impulse for a modernizing process came primarily from the government – as was the case in Spanish America – the state incorporated "the individual through the institution of citizenship, which both granted participatory rights in political, economic, and cultural arenas and imposed strong obligations to participate in state-directed national development" (Boli *et al.*, 1985, p. 159). In this process of converting an individual into a citizen, education assumed a key role, as is attested by the fact that most countries required their citizens to be able to read and write in order to be allowed to vote; in other words, only literate individuals could be considered full citizens (Caruso, 2010). This represented in effect the founding of a new political community based on the written word. Even women's education was viewed from the perspectives of politics and citizenship, encouraged not so that women could become citizens themselves, but rather so that they could become educators of children and future citizens.

Another feature of the model in which the state's power is predominant was the suppression of corporative power in favor of the consolidation of government power. This shift would have important consequences for the formation of the elite classes, as it resulted in the reform or elimination of the universities established under colonial rule. These universities were placed under the direction of the state governments, which took over control of their administration, norms, examination processes, and the issuing of professional degrees (Serrano, 1994). We should remember that the Spanish colonial empire maintained a practice of establishing universities in its American territories, unlike the Portuguese empire, which throughout the entire colonial period failed to establish even a single university in Brazil. In fact, throughout much of the nineteenth century, the Brazilian elite class still journeyed back to the metropolis to study at the Portuguese university of Coimbra.

Although the expansion of general education was an important part of Hispanic American political discourse, it was the reforms in higher education that were treated as a priority, beginning almost immediately after independence was achieved. Between 1810 and 1830, notwithstanding the armed conflicts taking place, public universities were established in Argentina, Venezuela, Colombia, Ecuador, Peru, and Bolivia, setting a trend that would continue throughout the century in the entire continent. In other instances, profound reforms were carried out at existing colonial universities, as in the case of Venezuela's Universidad Central or at the Universidad de San Carlos in Guatemala. In some cases, the colonial universities were abolished; the Real y Pontificia Universidad de México was closed in 1833, while the Universidad de San Felipe in Chile ceased to operate in 1839 (the Universidad de Chile was then inaugurated in 1842 and in 1910 the Universidad Nacional de México was established). All of these changes pursued the same objective: to wrest the universities from the power of the traditional ruling classes and, in essence, to convert higher education into a matter of national interest. Indeed, the state maintained a virtual monopoly over university education in almost all of these countries until the second half of the twentieth century (whereas in the realm of primary and secondary education the Catholic Church and the religious orders would continue to enjoy the freedom to found and run private schools). In the nineteenth century, Hispanic universities and institutions of higher learning became important centers for the formation of professionals and civil servants, with the study of law predominating. One consequence of this initiative was that the ecclesiastically oriented formation that had traditionally been taught in these centers was phased out and relegated to other institutions. Hans Albert Steger has referred to this new type of nineteenth-century university as "the Lawyer's University," one whose role would be to provide the base for a new governing class (Steger, 1974). In light of this, it is not surprising that, in the study of philosophy and law, new ideas and trends of thought were rapidly introduced and propagated, generating important ideological debates that would then have an impact on the organization of new state institutions.

We have seen how the active role of the state in founding and consolidating educational systems in Hispanic America throughout the nineteenth century and the first decades of the twentieth century cannot be doubted seriously. Yet, there are at least three concrete issues relevant to the government's role in education that became sources of considerable tension during this period. First, we will take a look at the establishment of compulsory education, after which we will examine the relationship between the state and the Catholic Church, followed by a brief look at the dynamic between the centralizing tendencies of the national governments and the attributions corresponding to the municipal and regional authorities within these countries.

The debate over the compulsoriness of education

In those countries where the government took over the initiative of forming its citizens (members of the nation-state), educational policies had the adoption of institutional rules of compulsory education as their principal strategy. Starting in the last third of the nineteenth century, all Spanish American countries established the basic structures of their school systems – structures that would remain virtually unchanged at least until World War II – that took the form of General Education Laws (Ossenbach, 2001a, p. 22; Ossenbach, 2008, p. 433). In most cases, these laws served mainly to organize primary education, with secondary and higher education being addressed by separate legislation. Nonetheless, these laws did establish a central body or system of learning institutions – structured in primary, secondary, and higher education levels – while at the same time giving a formal guarantee to the equality of educational opportunities. They also introduced the principle of a common, universal, and free elementary education. Compulsory education was also generally introduced, with some exceptions that we will analyze here. It was the state that took over the function of organizing and directing the school system and of creating the administrative infrastructure necessary to do so, and in general these new educational attributions were assumed by a specific ministry, either exclusively or in collaboration with other sectors of the government administration.

The principle of primary education's being made compulsory was defended by virtually all liberal politicians throughout Latin America. We should note that liberalism, as it was understood in the region at the time, maintained a firm conviction about the importance of the state's role in education as well as in other areas of social life. The liberal ideology also ardently defended the separation of church and state, which put it in direct opposition to conservative thought. Regarding the establishment of compulsory education, myriad arguments were made in its favor, as we shall see below.

One of the arguments reiterated most often in favor of the compulsoriness of education was that man's freedom, especially the freedom of man in society, is not without limits. Often this idea was associated with the belief in the state's obligation to be a "guardian" of minors, and with the issue of the need to be literate in order to enjoy the right to vote:

> If the state makes certain requirements for the exercise of citizenship that may only be fulfilled through education, then the parent who deprives their child of that education is committing an abuse. The public authority is obliged to address that abuse, both in defence of the child, whose rights have been ignored, and in defence of the society, which is thus being attacked at its foundation through the conservation and propagation of ignorance.
>
> (Varela, 1874, vol. 49, p. 83)

This argument took on another dimension with the conviction that the state was responsible not only for material needs but also for moral matters. The pedagogical and political discourse of the time abounds with arguments about the advantages and the goals of education, in particular those referring to the search for happiness, the instilling of (non-religious) moral values, the avoidance of bad habits, etc.:

> It is an essentially materialistic doctrine ... the idea that the state need not care for more than the body and the material aspects of our society. No, sir! – the state is also there to take care of hearts and souls, and its greatest mission is not that of maintaining the current material order but rather helping in the development of the eternal or moral order.
> (Letelier, 1888, p. 43)

In countries such as Uruguay and Argentina, where the conformation of society was heavily influenced by the massive influx of immigrants in the last quarter of the nineteenth century, we can also find arguments that view compulsory education as a means of integrating immigrants into the national society:

> Given the role of education in relation to the prosperity of a people, both in its economic needs as well as in the realm of democratic practices; given the way in which schooling helps to prevent crime and helps to integrate the immigrant; ignorance therefore has no place and it is the state, by definition and in its very essence, that has the obligation to require attendance at school, having every right to actively enforce this requirement.[6]
> (Cucuzza, 1986, p. 47)

It is curious how defenders of compulsory education such as the Uruguayan José Pedro Varela – previously cited (1874) – resorted to examples from other countries of his time, which, although they may not have originally been supporters of the concept, had begun to implement it. This shows how, by the end of the nineteenth century, the compulsoriness of education had become widespread, even in those countries where civil society had played an important part in the expansion of public schools and the state had been much less involved:

> In practice, the results produced by compulsory education could not be more satisfactory, whereas the effort made in education in those places where it is not obligatory leave much to be desired. Schooling is only widespread in those countries where it is compulsory, Mr Cousin said, and the facts prove this to be true, with the sole exceptions of the United States and Holland. In Germany, Switzerland, Sweden, Norway, and Denmark, which

have had it for some time now, ignorance has been eradicated, whereas in France, England, Italy, Spain, and Russia, the number of ignorant people has reached alarming proportions. Yes, even in the first of these countries that for so long have marched ahead of the rest of the world wielding their power and influence. And yet the examples of Germany and Switzerland have given the results that we would have expected, and today, according to Mr Laveleye, compulsory education has been introduced into all of the countries in Europe, with the exception of Russia, Belgium, and Holland. In the United States, since the need has been felt, the states of Massachusetts and Connecticut have adopted it, while people everywhere are clamoring for it. In England, the latest education law from 1870 has authorized the school committees to establish it. London and numerous other important cities have already implemented it.

(Varela, 1874, vol. 49, p. 88)

Varela admired the "remarkable effort made by the North American people in favor of education" and felt that in this country it was the "harmonious union of public authorities and individual action" that made it possible to achieve the great goal of a country, whereby every last person received an education. He did recognize, however, the need for North Americans to establish obligatory schooling due to the significant number of children who received no education or who attended school only sporadically, as was especially true among the children of poor Irish immigrants (Varela, 1874, vol. 49, p. 89).

In Uruguay, education was made compulsory by the introduction of the 1877 Law of Common Education, while Argentina made primary school obligatory in 1884 with the famous Law no. 1420 of Common Education. In Chile, however, where the educational system had been implemented earlier than in other countries we have been considering (1860), schooling was only made compulsory in 1920. This delay was not due to any ideological debate about compulsory education, but rather to arguments regarding the state's incapacity to undertake such a task and cover its basic needs. That such an endeavor was the responsibility of the government was not questioned. The historian Loreto Egaña, in her study of the debates that took place in the National Pedagogical Congress of 1889 in Santiago, affirmed that:

a law of compulsoriness seemed to place more of a responsibility on the government than on parents. For the speakers at this Congress, the major problem was the available educational offer, not the means for obliging people to attend school.

(Egaña, 2000, p. 44)

This author also draws our attention to another important obstacle for the establishment of obligatory schooling – namely child labor, an issue very much present in the debate in Argentina and Uruguay as well (Cucuzza, 1986, pp. 47–50).[7] The Catholic press in Chile did declare its opposition to compulsory schooling, arguing that education was not the state's job, that there should be more space for private education, and that state intervention in such an area was no guarantee of progress or success, as evidenced by the poor state of Chilean primary education at the time. None of these arguments managed to sway the view of the liberals, who – in close association with the mercantile sectors of the country's economy – saw a direct relationship between generalized education and economic modernization. Compulsory education was finally established in Chile in 1920 (Egaña, 2000, pp. 45–60).

A very peculiar case is that of Ecuador, where a Catholic republic was established under the dictatorship of Gabriel García Moreno during the decades of 1860 and 1870. This regime gave a considerable impulse to education and, as a result, the entire school system was strongly centralized and compulsory education was introduced. In 1895, the triumph of the Ecuadorian liberal revolution, which provided access to political power to the economic sectors from the coastal areas involved in exportation, continued the strengthening of the central government's role and led to the establishment of compulsory education in primary school with the Public Instruction Law from 1897 (later rewritten in 1906). In Colombia, where the Catholic tradition was as firmly rooted as it was in Ecuador, as there was no developed, modernized economic sector to offset its influence, a more rigid societal structure prevailed and a conservatism that managed to put off the establishment of obligatory education until 1927. Between 1886 and 1930 (known as the period of *Regeneration*), the previous liberal reform, which had established compulsory education in 1870, was repealed. In its place, the church was given widespread attributions in education, frontally opposing any attempt by the Colombian state to become involved in governing education. Those opposing the 1870 Decree of Public Instruction had gone as far as to say that "an individual is free, free to the extent that he is free to remain ignorant, and no one can oblige him to receive an education" (Loy, 1982, p. 11). We will further explore the relations between church and state in the following section.

Relations between the state and the Catholic Church

A decisive factor in the consolidation of public school systems in Hispanic America was the issue of secularization and the relations between the Catholic Church and the state. The tensions that grew out of this relationship produced legislative and ideological skirmishes that in countries such as Ecuador and Colombia resulted in considerable delays in the establishment of stable educational systems, as we have seen.

During the process of nationalization of the Catholic Church following independence, and up until at least 1850, the Spanish American governments took possession of ecclesiastical assets and the right to name bishops. This led to conflicts of sovereignty between the new national states and the Vatican (Mecham, 1966). Yet, most of the first constitutions drawn up in these countries declared Catholicism the official state religion, with the judicial norms that were created during emancipation not only ratifying the continuity of the prevailing Catholic faith, but even restoring to the church many of its previous privileges. Thus, in a sense, the Catholic religion was able to play a unifying role in the nation-building process, while at the same time the conflicts that arose between it and the national governments exercised a divisive influence. Spanish America did not have to face conflicts between Catholics and Protestants as did some European countries (see the chapter by Raftery in this book), nor did it ever really experience religious dissidence; the anticlericalism of the nineteenth century was no exception. On the contrary, Hispanic American anticlericalism had from its origins a markedly legal and political nature; no serious religious movement ever took place.

Since the colonial period, the Catholic Church in Hispanic America had been closely allied with political power; it did not have an autonomous "grass-roots" support system gained through the people's sense of religious solidarity or *lay spirituality*, as was the case in the Puritan colonies of North America. The arrival of independence, however, put the church, with its lack of autonomy, in a position in which it had no choice but to be tied to the political power, against which it was forced to defend its attributions and privileges. In defending its interests, the church found itself allied with conservative groups that vowed to protect it as an institution, while at the same time confronting it with the tendencies by which government was consolidating its power. As a result, significant conflicts between liberals and conservatives arose. As previously noted, the liberals believed firmly that the separation of church and state was crucial in order for the state to consolidate its structure and implement its goals. Conservative thought, however, maintained that the state should not only rely on the church to carry out certain functions – thus providing, among other aspects, a guarantee of order – but that the government had a responsibility to provide it with support and protection, so that the church could better carry out these functions.

The fact that the constitutions of some countries conceded a preferential status to Catholicism does not necessarily imply that concessions were made to clerical demands. The new governments kept a close watch over the church and gradually took over functions that had traditionally been in the church's hands – among them, education, charity, the civil registry, etc., all of which would play a major role in the process of political institutionalization. Tensions between the conservative and liberal oligarchies diminished as the economic structures linking these countries to the international market began to take shape. Negotiation and consensus led to a relative stability and helped to neutralize conflicts with the ecclesiastical power. Although each country came up with its own solutions to the problems of secularization, the separation of church and state was not a generalized formula for overcoming discrepancies.

In Uruguay and Argentina, countries that enjoyed a relative political stability and whose economic growth had occurred relatively early on, the formal union of church and state lasted well into the twentieth century. It is true that, in these countries, the state gradually assumed full control of areas such as education and established a balance that included the authorization for the practice of other religions – a way of handling the massive European immigration to these countries at the time. The expansion of public education in Argentina and Uruguay was far ahead of other countries in Latin America.

The principle of freedom of education, understood primarily as the freedom to create and found schools, was another general feature of educational systems throughout Latin America. Although the policy applied to all private schooling, it affected mostly those schools run by the Catholic Church and by religious orders (numerous foreign orders arrived in the second half of the nineteenth century). With very few exceptions, the state reserved the rights of authorization, supervision, certification, issue of diplomas and degrees, and even the funding of these private institutions.

In the case of Chile, the historian Sol Serrano maintains that, when the educational system was first being established (1830–1860), the difficulties encountered by the state were, for the most part, not ideological, given that both the conservatism that was in power at the time as well as the incipient liberalism had their roots in a common, illustrated, republican formation – one that considered education to be of primordial importance on the path to civilization. They also shared the conviction that it was the state's responsibility to regulate the educational system. This was possible, at least in part, because a consensus existed at the time that affirmed the Catholic nature of the state. The Law of Primary Education, passed in 1860, included the teaching of religion in primary school under clerical supervision, a measure that liberals criticized for, among other reasons, not respecting the foreigners living in Chile (Egaña, 2000, pp. 53, 57). After 1873, and as a consequence of a debate about new regulations in secondary education, the forward push of liberal ideas in Chile clashed with a strengthened Catholic Church, with the ensuing debate reflecting a more clear-cut struggle of the church vs. the state. The collapse of a Catholic ideal shared by virtually the entire political class now brought under fresh scrutiny the role of the state as the provider of education. Where it was previously seen as part of a struggle in the fight against ignorance and against an oppressive legacy, education now became part of an ideological struggle in which two distinct world views were in fierce competition with each other. This struggle does not seem to have affected the stability of the Chilean educational system, in Serrano's opinion, since the system's foundations were already firmly in place by the time this religious conflict arose (Serrano, 1994, pp. 443, 448–450). After 1873, certain governmental controls were implemented in the secondary private schools, where religious education ceased to be obligatory. However, as a consequence of this debate private education began to play an important role in Chile at this time, leading liberal politicians such as Valentín Letelier to protest:

> These [private] schools open in large cities with greater culture and less of a need for them, and not in the backward towns, where the need is greater due to their limited culture. They are not like industry or business, which respond to the laws of supply and demand. They are moral institutions, subject to the needs of culture.
>
> (1892, p. 334)

In 1888, the founding of the Catholic University of Santiago marked the end of the monopoly that the state had thus far held over higher education in Chile. The Catholic University of Valparaíso was created in 1928.

Ecuador's case is peculiar; as we mentioned, its educational system was organized around 1870, with the state not only playing a major role but also collaborating closely with foreign religious orders that had come to the country (most notably the Frères des Écoles Chrétiennes). The Catholic dictator Gabriel García Moreno was a great believer in scientific progress and it was he who laid the foundation for an educational system that was intended to be a central part of the construction of a national Ecuadorian state in which Catholicism would be one of its most important distinguishing features.[8] Moreno undertook an important reform of the church and placed the school system under the strict supervision of Catholicism. With the Liberal Revolution of 1895, the pending issue of the secularization of school was made possible, as mentioned above, by the triumph of the liberal groups from the coast, where trade and export dominated the economy. Notwithstanding the powerful Catholic tradition in Ecuador at the time, a radical alternative took form in the stand-off between church and state; the Political Constitution of 1906 and the Law of Public Instruction passed the same year established lay education in all official and municipal institutions and prohibited public funding of any religious schools. This Constitution officially declared the separation of church and state and eliminated the existing declaration by which the state was officially Catholic (Ossenbach, 1996a). From the perspective of President Leonidas Plaza, one of the most renowned of the Ecuadorian liberal thinkers, the church's role needed to be consigned to the private realm, which was where it belonged. He also believed that religious congregations, which had traditionally made up a part of a "government organism," should not be given the consideration of legal persons, or benefit from the rights corresponding to public entities:

> The state needs to take over the functions – as well as the means to exercise them – that have been entrusted to them [the religious congregations]. The state must regain those means that were given to them for public objectives, such as education, social care, etc., for which the legislator is the judge and against which private individuals, even in dedicating their own means toward these objectives, may not act. Public welfare is the responsibility of public powers; private welfare, of private individuals.
>
> (Plaza, 1905, p. 156)

In 1906, the Ecuadorian minister of Public Instruction expressed alarm at the fact that the children "were ignorant of the fact that they were Ecuadorian republicans, but were well aware that they were Roman Catholics" (Monge, 1906, pp. 22–23).

As noted above, in 1870, Colombia underwent a radical liberal reform of its education that excluded obligatory religious instruction in its public schools. The reform was short-lived though, due to the opposition of the Catholic Church. This educational reform actually played an important part in the civil war that took place in 1876, which came to be known as the "Guerra de las Escuelas" (The Schools War). The only solution found for carrying out the task of organizing and stabilizing the public school system in Colombia was that of accepting Catholicism as an inseparable part of Colombian nationality. After 1886, a radical change took place in the country's public education, resulting in an overwhelming presence of the Catholic Church and religious congregations, to the detriment of the national government, whose role was significantly reduced. Only after the Education Law of 1903 was passed did the government slowly begin to take on more responsibilities in public education, gaining momentum in the 1920s and especially the 1930s, when the liberals regained power (Farrell, 1997).

The centralizing tendencies of the state

In order to conclude our contribution, we will discuss, albeit briefly, the subject of the centralizing of educational policy by the state, which was a fairly widespread phenomenon in Spanish America during the era this work focused on. In general, mass schooling could expand while the state gradually took charge of a primary education that had originally been the responsibility of municipalities (Newland, 1991). A shortage of funding on the municipal level had always been one of the important obstacles for the consolidation of a public school system. However, the centralizing process was not limited to providing financial support, as it also involved many other aspects of the organization and management of school systems. School inspection, for example, was one of the strategies for progressing in a centralizing process that was closely associated with the consolidation of the liberal state. For the most part, a certain consensus was reached, recognizing that only a central government was in a position to achieve the conditions necessary for the stability, progress, and institutional order that such public matters required.

Centralization was the result, on the one hand, of overcoming conflicts with provincial *caudillos* and, on the other, of the urban and rural worlds' finding their place at the service of an "outward" model of growth, that is, one based almost exclusively on the exportation of raw materials. This model, built upon a fundamentally urban base, resulted in a very weak expansion of educational systems in rural areas (especially in those countries with large indigenous populations). It also led to an "uneven modernization" in which the demand

and the budgets for secondary education in the cities – for the formation of workers in government bureaucracy, in commerce and in exportation – grew, even as the levels of primary education and literacy lagged far behind (Núñez, 1993, pp. 374–379). This is a historical example of how the centralization of educational systems does not necessarily lead to equity (growing centralization unaccompanied by growing equity), as can be observed in various cases that Cohen and Aubry examine in this book.

Another form of centralization took effect in countries with federal regimes, such as México, Argentina, Colombia, and Venezuela, where the central government held on to important attributions in the realm of public education and resorted to a variety of mechanisms in order to intervene and exercise its authority in the federated states. The pressure exerted by the central governments did lead to tensions, however, which have only recently been acknowledged due to the fact that the historiography of education and its evolution in Hispanic America has also tended to follow a centralist bias. Only in the last few decades has a regional history of education begun to emerge, helping to shed more light on the centralizing process as well as on the resistance that this tendency came up against in different regions and provinces (see, for example, Alarcón, 2011; Puiggrós and Ossana, 1993, 1997; Rockwell, 2007).

A final reflection

Despite considerable pressure to limit the central government's role in the imposition of educational policy in Latin America, the interventionist tradition of the continent was still very much in place until quite recently. The large-scale expansion of the region's educational systems after World War II, carried out in part thanks to international organisms such as UNESCO and CEPAL, relied quite heavily on state intervention (Ossenbach and Martínez Boom, 2011). However, only since the 1990s, with the promotion of the *Washington Consensus* and its push for a reduced government role in education (as well as in other realms of social and economic activity), can we see the evidence of the beginnings of a reversal in this trend. In some countries – most notably in Chile, during the Pinochet era – a variety of educational attributions were ceded to municipal authorities and even to individual schools (Martínez Boom, 2004). The disastrous results of this policy can be attributed both to insufficient funding and to the glaring lack of any kind of autonomous tradition in the organization of educational systems. In spite of the fact that Latin America has been seeking, in a more or less generalized tendency, to define an appropriate subsidiary role for the central government to play in the administration of educational systems, for the most part, the state still reserves the right to mandate and supervise a national curriculum.

Paradoxically, the tendency to limit the state's role and to decentralize educational systems in Hispanic America is accompanied by an opposite trend in such influential countries as the United States, where the last several decades have witnessed an increase of the federal role in school policy (see McGuinn's chapter in this book).

Notes

1. In alluding to educational systems we are referring to what Margaret Archer called state educational systems, "a nationwide and differentiated collection of institutions devoted to formal education, whose overall control and supervision is at least partly governmental, and whose component parts and processes are related to one another" (1979, p. 54).
2. An application of the typologies of A. Gerschenkron for the History of Education was made by Lundgreen (1973). In a chapter included in this book, Vincent Carpentier makes a comparable study of the way in which public and private investment as well as government backing of education increased in France, England, and the United States during the successive phases of depression from the nineteenth century all the way to 1945 (Carpentier studies the oscillations in state intervention using as a reference the upturns and downturns of the economy expressed by the *Kondratiev cycles*).
3. With regard to this theory, Gerschenkron also proposed the idea of "the advantage of being behind," based on the assumption that less advanced countries have a shorter route to cover in the development process as they can adopt the latest technologies.
4. K. Leroux points out in this regard, referring to Domingo F. Sarmiento's plan to transplant the North American educational model to Argentina, that:

    > Sarmiento's project to Americanize Argentine schools [. . .]challenges the paradigm of Americanization as a strategy of imposing U.S. values and practices on a less powerful society to foster relations of dependency. The driving force for this educational project came by invitation from within Argentina's leadership, not any official representative or agency of the U.S. government.
    > (Leroux, 2012, p. 66)

5. Similar reflections on the need to "catch up" can be found in the concept of "dischronic development" elaborated by Soriano (1987).
6. Speech by the Dean of the Colegio Nacional of Tucumán, Argentina, in the First Pedagogical Congress (*Primer Congreso Pedagógico Argentino*), 1882.
7. Cucuzza also recorded declarations of Uruguayan participants in the Buenos Aires Congress of 1882.
8. The construction of a national state with a Catholic identity in Ecuador under Garcia Moreno shares many similarities with the Irish state after its independence in 1922: education in the hands of priests, brothers, and nuns; obligatory religious content in school textbooks; symbiosis between patriotism and Catholicism, etc. (see the chapter by Raftery in this book).

References

Alarcón, L., 2011. Educación, nación y ciudadanía en el Caribe colombiano durante el periodo federal (1857–1886). Unpublished doctoral thesis, Universidad Nacional de Educación a Distancia, Madrid.

Archer, M., 1979. *Social Origins of Educational Systems*. London and Beverly Hills, CA: Sage.

Ardao, A., 1964. Prólogo. In: J.P. Varela 1874. *La Educación del Pueblo*. Montevideo: Ministerio de Instrucción Pública y Previsión Social (Biblioteca Artigas. Colección de Clásicos Uruguayos, vol. 49).

Boli, J., Meyer, J., and Ramírez, F., 1985. Explaining the origins and expansion of mass education. *Comparative Education Review*, 29(2), pp. 145–170.

Carmagnani, M., 1984. *Estado y Sociedad en América Latina, 1850–1930*. Barcelona: Crítica.

Caruso, M., 2010. Literacy and suffrage: the politicisation of schooling in postcolonial Hispanic America (1810–1850). *Paedagogica Historica*, 46(4), pp. 463–478.

Cucuzza, H.R., 1986. *De Congreso a Congreso. Crónica del Primer Congreso Pedagógico Argentino*. Buenos Aires: Besana.

Egaña, L., 2000. *La Educación Primaria Popular en el Siglo XIX en Chile: Una Práctica de Política Estatal*. Santiago: Dirección de bibliotecas, archivos y museos/LOM ediciones.

Farrell, R.V., 1997. Una época de polémicas: críticos y defensores de la educación católica durante la regeneración. *Revista Colombiana de Educación*, 35, pp. 5–39.

Germani, G., 1962. *Política y Sociedad en una Epoca de Transición. De la Sociedad Tradicional a la Sociedad de Masas*. Buenos Aires: Paidós.

Gerschenkron, A., 1962. *Economic Backwardness in Historical Perspective. A Book of Essays*. Cambridge, MA: Belknap Press of Harvard University Press.

Graciarena, J., 1984. El estado latinoamericano en perspectiva. Figuras, crisis, prospectiva. *Pensamiento Iberoamericano. Revista de Economía Política*, 5a, pp. 39–74.

Leroux, K., 2012. Sarmiento's self-strengthening experiment. Americanizing schools for Argentine nation-building. In: R. Garlitz and L. Jarvinen (eds) *Teaching America to the World and the World to America. Education and Foreign Relations since 1870*. New York: Palgrave Macmillan, pp. 51–71.

Letelier, V., 1888. El estado y la educación nacional. Discurso pronunciado en la sesión solemne celebrada por la universidad el 16 de Septiembre de 1888. In: V. Letelier *La Lucha por la Cultura. Miscelánea de Artículos Políticos i Estudios Pedagójicos*. Santiago: Imprenta i Encuadernación Barcelona, pp. 43–53.

Letelier, V., 1892. *Filosofía de la Educación*. Buenos Aires: Cabaut y Cia., 1927.

Loy, J.M., 1982. Los ignorantistas y las escuelas. La oposición a la reforma educativa durante la Federación Colombiana. *Revista Colombiana de Educación*, 9, pp. 9–24.

Lundgreen, P., 1973. *Bildung und Wirtschaftswachstum im Industrialisierungsprozess des 19. Jahrhunderts*. Berlin: Colloquium Verlag.

Martínez Boom, A., 2004. *De la Escuela Expansiva a la Escuela Competitiva. Dos Modos de Modernización en América Latina*. Barcelona: Ed. Anthropos/Convenio Andrés Bello.

Mecham, J.L., 1966. *Church and State in Latin America. A History of Politic-Ecclesiastical Relations*. Chapel Hill, NC: University of North Carolina Press.

Monge, A., 1906. Informe del Ministro de Instrucción Pública del año 1906. In: T. Baquero 1948. *Apuntes Para la Historia de la Educación Laica en Ecuador*. Quito: Imprenta del Ministerio del Tesoro (Publicaciones del Colegio Normal "Juan Montalvo"), pp. 22–23.

Newland, C., 1991. La educación elemental en Hispanoamérica: desde la independencia hasta la centralización de los sistemas educativos nacionales. *Hispanic American Historical Review*, 71(2), pp. 345–353.

Núñez, C.E., 1993. Educación y desarrollo económico en el continente americano. In: C.E. Núñez and G. Tortella (eds) *La Maldición Divina. Ignorancia y Atraso Económico en Perspectiva Histórica*. Madrid: Alianza Editorial, pp. 359–380.

Ossenbach, G., 1996a. La secularización del sistema educativo y de la práctica pedagógica: laicismo y nacionalismo. *Procesos. Revista Ecuatoriana de Historia* (Special issue *El Laicismo en la Historia del Ecuador*), 8, pp. 33–54.

Ossenbach, G., 1996b. La educación y la integración nacional del indígena en la revolución liberal ecuatoriana, 1895–1912. In: P. Gonzalbo and G. Ossenbach (coord.) *Educación Rural e Indígena en Iberoamérica*. México/Madrid: El Colegio de México/UNED.

Ossenbach, G., 2001a. Génesis histórica de los sistemas educativos. In: J.L. García Garrido, G. Ossenbach, and J. Valle (eds) *Génesis, Estructuras y Tendencias de los Sistemas Educativos Iberoamericanos*. Madrid: OEI (Serie "Cuadernos de la OEI: educación comparada", no. 3), pp. 13–60.

Ossenbach, G., 2001b. El concepto de "emancipación espiritual" en el debate sobre la educación en Hispanoamérica en la primera mitad del siglo XIX. *Revista Brasileira de História da Educação*, 1, pp. 143–159.

Ossenbach, G., 2008. La Educación. In: E. Ayala Mora and E. Posada Carbó (eds) *Historia General de América Latina, vol. VII: Los Proyectos Nacionales Latinoamericanos: Sus Instrumentos y Articulación (1870–1930)*. Paris/Madrid: UNESCO, pp. 429–452.

Ossenbach, G. and del Pozo, M.M., 2011. Postcolonial models, cultural transfers and transnational perspectives in Latin America: A research agenda. *Paedagogica Historica*, 47(5), pp. 579–600.

Ossenbach, G. and Martínez Boom, A., 2011. Itineraries of the discourses on development and education in Spain and Latin America (ca. 1950–1970). *Paedagogica Historica*, 47(5), pp. 679–700.

Oszlak, O., 1981. The historical formation of the state in Latin America. Some theoretical and methodological guidelines for its study. *Latin American Research Review*, 16(2), pp. 3–32.

Plaza, L., 1905. Mensaje del Presidente de la República al Congreso Nacional, de 10 de Agosto de 1905. In: A. Noboa 1908. *Recopilación de Mensajes Dirigidos por los Presidentes y Vicepresidentes de la República, Jefes Supremos y Gobiernos Provisorios a las Convenciones y Congresos Nacionales Desde el Año de 1819 Hasta Nuestros Días, 5*. Guayaquil: Imprenta de El Tiempo.

Puiggrós, A. and Ossana, E. (eds), 1993. *La Educación en las Provincias y Territorios Nacionales, 1885–1945*. Buenos Aires: Ed. Galerna.

Puiggrós, A. and Ossana, E. (eds), 1997. *La Educación en las Provincias, 1945–1983*. Buenos Aires: Ed. Galerna.

Ramírez, F.O. and Ventresca, M., 1992. Institucionalización de la escolarización masiva: isomorfismo ideológico y organizativo en el mundo moderno. *Revista de Educación* (Madrid), 298, pp. 121–139.

Rockwell, E., 2007. *Hacer Escuela, Hacer Estado. La Educación Posrevolucionaria Vista desde Tlaxcala*. México: Colegio de Michoacán, Centro de Investigaciones y Estudios Superiores en Antropología Social (CIESAS) y Centro de Investigación y de Estudios Avanzados (Cinvestav).

Sarmiento, D.F., 1849. *De la Educación Popular*. Santiago: Imprenta de Julio Belín.

Serrano, S., 1994. La ciudadanía examinada: el control estatal de la educación en Chile, 1810–1870. In: A. Annino, L. Castro Leiva, and F.X. Guerra (eds) *De los Imperios a las Naciones: Iberoamérica*. Zaragoza: IberCaja, pp. 439–450.

Soriano, G., 1987. *Hispanoamérica: Historia, Desarrollo Discrónico e Historia Política*. Caracas: Universidad Central de Venezuela, Facultad de Ciencias Jurídicas y Políticas.

Steger, H.-A., 1974. *Las Universidades en el Desarrollo Social de la América Latina*. México: FCE.

Varela, J.P., 1874. *La Educación del Pueblo*. New edition: Montevideo: Ministerio de Instrucción Pública y Previsión Social (Biblioteca Artigas, Colección de Clásicos Uruguayos, vol. 49), 1964.

Véliz, C., 1984. *La Tradición Centralista de América Latina*. Barcelona: Ariel.

Weinberg, G., 1993. *Tiempo, Destiempo y Contratiempo*. Buenos Aires: Leviatán.

Weinberg, G., 1995. *Modelos Educativos en la Historia de América Latina*. Buenos Aires: UNESCO/CEPAL/PNUD/AZ Editora.

Part 3

Financing education

Chapter 4

The provision of education and the state

From equity to more equality

Carla Aubry

'Education and the state' is the title of an anonymous article published in the *Pall Mall Gazette* in 1865 (Lover of Light, 1865). The London evening paper had been the place of a dispute on whether schools for 'the people of the land' came under the jurisdiction of the state, or should rather be dealt with by private initiatives at a local level.[1] The author argued vehemently for schools subsidized by the state: 'to establish elementary schools [. . .] is the State's duty – [. . .] it has no right to hand over this duty to the "noblemen and gentry of the diocese"'. If financed privately, he argued, 'it can be applied exactly as the donors please' (Lover of Light, 1865) and this arbitrariness was undesirable. The article was signed 'a Lover of Light', as the author clearly saw himself as the representative of a 'better liberalism' (Lover of Light, 1865). The man behind the pseudonym was Matthew Arnold, the British poet and cultural critic, who – in his function as inspector of schools – received orders in 1865 to study the secondary education system on the continent and provide a detailed report by commission of Her Majesty (Lang, 2006).[2] His travels led him to Switzerland in the same year, and he seems to have been impressed by the local educational system. 'In Switzerland, more than in any other country [. . .] all classes use the same primary school' (Arnold, 1964, p. 15). Since it was the holiday season, the schools in Zurich were closed. Thus, he travelled to the nearby small town of Winterthur, on which he noted, 'Winterthur is, I think, for its school establishments the most remarkable place in Europe. The schools of this small place [. . .] are the objects of first importance in the town, and would be admirable anywhere' (Arnold, 1964, p. 281).

However, such praise seems suspect. Would Arnold have noticed difficulties of the local education system on such a short visit? Or would he have simply ignored them, given the amount of convincing he was planning to do back home? What he witnessed in Winterthur was the result of a long process in education policy. There had been drawn-out battles about the jurisdiction and orientation of schools, which had not immediately been made accessible for everyone; the state had only slowly started to play an active role, and the ways of financing the system had changed. The story of this process will be told here; and I suspect that it is a story that Arnold would have liked to hear.

I will examine the period between the abolition of school fees in the town of Winterthur in 1789 and the general abolition of school fees in the entire Canton Zurich in 1869, as ruled by the state. The following aspects, which change and interact in the course of this period, will be relevant to the analysis: changing property situations, the role of the state[3] in relation to local decision-makers, and the potential for political participation in local educational and political decision-making processes – as Cohen points out in her chapter, a wider suffrage has an effect on local school politics. A central issue is the fact of public involvement in the financing and organization of schools (see, e.g., Engermann *et al.*, 2009; Lindert and Go, 2010; Mitch, 1986, 2004; Westberg, 2013), especially when it comes to equal opportunities in education (Cohen, 2005; Margo, 1990). To depict the process in its changing political and economic dimensions, I will focus on the question '*Who is entitled to what?*', or, somewhat more off-hand: Whose money was supposed to fund the schooling of whose children, and whose decisions were such school issues at the time? I will chronologically pick out three historical periods. The first part (1789–1810) will depict the introduction of free schools in Winterthur and the social differentiation of schooling within the town, caused by the foundation of an 'Ansässen school'. In this context, I will also discuss the relevance of the local citizenship and its economic significance. In the second part (1830–1839), the 1830s will be outlined as years of increased citizens' participation rights and increased influence of the state, with ramifications for the organization of schools. The foundation of new local school authorities in the period discussed in the third part (1859–1869) led to considerable changes regarding participation rights and ownership structures that also influenced the funding of schools. It was towards the end of this period that Arnold visited Winterthur.

1789–1810: the logic of the common and equity

In the year 1789/1790, a revised school plan led to changes for the schools in the town of Winterthur.[4] The previously obligatory three-monthly and New Year's payments for schooling were abolished, resulting in 'free teaching' that was somewhat revolutionary (Winkler, 1947). The introduction of free schools reduced the income teachers earned, as they were no longer paid by school fees. However, they were compensated for their losses by an increase in the town's contributions. The fiscal authority of the town was given the task of carefully examining the town's economic situation, with the goal to discreetly find out 'if the budget was capable of bearing the increased expenses without danger' (Troll, 1842, p. 152). This seemed to be the case, inasmuch as the two privately run charter schools in town were also declared free schools (Troll, 1842). The municipal authorities had been repeatedly trying to make life difficult for these privately run schools. Nevertheless, despite the sanctions, the charter schools did not cease to exist, not least because the lower classes of the municipal school were often overcrowded. The school fees paid by the students were the main source of teachers' income at private schools (Troll, 1842). According to the revised school plan, all the youngest pupils were now to attend the first two years at these charter schools, and the teachers were to be paid from the municipal budget. This way, the schoolmasters of the charter schools finally exchanged 'their private status for protection and payment by the town' (Troll, 1842, p. 134).

The competition of the free education market was terminated by its inclusion into the municipal school organization. The financial inclusion of previously privately run schools is an indication of the attempts to create a uniform school system in Winterthur and to make it subject to control by municipal authorities. However, any attempt at exerting control, organizing and enforcing topical guidelines, such as age of enrolment, teaching objectives and curriculum, cannot be achieved without a financial commitment. Schools were funded by the revenue from municipal estates. Originally, the municipal lands and the commons (*Allmenden*) served as reserve property, mainly securing the grounds for livestock and pasture farming. Purchases, exchanges and loans, and not least the improvement of land use and the resulting conversion of less valuable ground to valuable meadows and fields, led to common land increasingly becoming a municipal property protected by the municipal authority (Weber, 1971). The woods, whose timber could be sold or used for the town's own building activities, were particularly significant for the town's treasury. Interest-bearing capitals, transaction levies and customs revenue, as well as a variety of taxes, provided further funds for the town's treasury (Ganz, 1979). However, the municipal property had no connection to the state and was considered the town's private property (Weber, 1971). Revenue generated by this property paid for the many municipal tasks, of which schools were just a part, and by introducing free schools, those responsible proved generous. In retrospect, the retired headmaster Troll called the school year of 1789 a 'blessed school year' because 'our schools started, as much as possible, being everything to everybody' (Troll, 1842, p. 137). The question of what 'everybody' meant in this context and how this 'everybody' was being differentiated shall be pursued in the following.

Until the end of the eighteenth century, students were mainly the children of burghers.[5] Until 1764, those inhabitants of the town who had not been granted local citizenship – the so called '*Ansässen*'[6] – were not allowed to 'have their own hearth' ('*einen eigenen Rauch zu führen*') (Winkler, 1947, p. 60). Ansässen were mainly servants and maids, without families of their own. Both the right of settlement and any political rights were an inherited privilege reserved for the offspring of established citizens in the sense of the '*ius sanguini*' (Guzzi-Heeb, 2009; Studer et al., 2008). In the seventeenth and eighteenth centuries, access to this local citizenship right was increasingly restricted, leading to the establishment of two different classes of inhabitants: the burghers and the Ansässen without citizenship rights.[7] In 1764, the ban on 'having an own hearth' was lifted, to the advantage of the rich burghers, who were now able to have their country estates run by foreign workers and their families

(Winkler, 1947, p. 60). As a result, and because teaching was free in Winterthur, the number of students of Ansässen background increased successively. In 1793, their share was about 13 per cent (Winkler, 1947, p. 60).

In the same year, the school inspector referred to the growing number of foreign children attending the local schools, competing with the children of the burghers (Winkler, 1947). For the children of the Ansässen, school was not compulsory and their attendance depended on the decision of their parents. Still, as it was free, more and more Ansässen children attended the town schools, making the classes overcrowded (Troll, 1842). In the eyes of Winterthur's burghers, this was increasingly causing problems:

> For our offspring, this meant overcrowding and introduced a heterogeneous element. Soon the effects of this intermingling became obvious. For the children of burghers, the schools of the town had become gradually worse, for the village children they were much too good and [even] beyond their needs.
>
> (Troll, 1842, p. 193ff.)

Thus, the Ansässen were not only a legally different group of the population, but from the point of view of the burghers, the schooling needs of the foreign children were not comparable to the significantly higher demands of their own children.

To ease this heterogeneous intermingling, a separate school for the Ansässen was established in 1810.[8] The separation of schools was permeable in both directions. Occasionally, gifted Ansässen children could be granted access to burgher schools, just like burgher children with weak school performance could be sent to the Ansässen school, by order of the school council (Winkler, 1947). Consequently, the Ansässen school quickly gained a reputation of being a low-level school for the poor. The separation of Ansässen children and burgher children at school also had a financial effect. The Ansässen school was provided with a location and fuel for heating only. The foreign parents had to pay the teachers, through school fees, just as they had to pay for their children if they attended the burgher school. For the burgher children, attending school was still free. Thus, the basic principle of free schools for all children was abandoned. This seemed to be appropriate, for the unequal financial treatment resulted from the 'logic' of funding schools from the town's estates, which were the property of the Winterthur burghers. This property produced revenue that could be used for funding the schooling of their own children. The Ansässen were not entitled to this kind of support, as – not being owners of the town's estates – they were not entitled to benefits their revenue provided.

How essential the economic dimension of the citizenship right was can be illustrated by the decisions on granting citizenship right by the burgher assembly. Ansässen could apply for citizenship rights and, if granted, they had to buy themselves in (Suter, 1992). These buying-in fees seemed to be justified, as the increase in the number of those having bought themselves in meant a rise in the number of those benefiting from the town's revenue. These fees were high, roughly equivalent to the annual expenses of a family with three children.[9] To gain citizenship rights, a person had to be living in the town for several years and needed to be in possession of an orderly baptism certificate as well as a good reputation. To rule out that the newly accepted burghers would in the foreseeable future become so poor that they became dependent on public welfare, they needed to prove that they had sufficient wealth or landed property. Citizenship rights were countered by certain municipal obligations, such as providing help in any distress that was not self-inflicted.[10] If all the conditions were met, the application was usually successful. Those who were denied are of special interest, as their cases provide important insight into the decision-making process. A certain Moritz Blickli, for instance, met all the conditions and was nevertheless only granted provisional citizenship rights. As a Catholic, it was argued, he was not eligible to have any share in the church property reserved for the Protestant culture. Furthermore, it was deemed that his buying into this property could later lead to claims that would prove 'unfavourable to the local parish'.[11] There were also worries that the admission of Catholics into the affairs of the Protestant Church would sooner or later lead to friction and disagreement, 'in the beginning likely only in economic matters, but later in denominational ones, and bring discord into the parish'.[12]

This example illustrates several important points. The citizenship right granted participation and was part of a social economy following the logics of 'proportional equality'. This does not mean an arithmetical, formal equality in the sense of 'equal shares', but rather an 'equity in correspondence to proportionate equality which calls for distribution according to relevant differences'. In this sense, a distribution of goods is just if it is done in an appropriate or adequate way (Aristoteles, 1964, esp. book V), such as, for example, the granting of suffrage or the distribution of revenues from goods according to class, honour, wealth, need or status. The restrictive handling of granting citizenship rights was meant to protect the burghers' property from excessive exploitation and thus, in the long term, maintain the revenue covering the town's expenses. In her economic studies about the use of commons, Elinor Ostrom refers to certain factors that contributed significantly to the preservation of joint resources (Ostrom, 1990, 2005). Those include local decision-makers with similar interests and occasional actors with leadership potential. The most significant factor, though, was the strict limitation of the number of authorized users and lack of clear rules of usage. Cooperative estates were managed economically, and as far as possible, the capital stock was not used (Schläppi, 2011). According to this 'logic', the use of resources in Winterthur was subject to strict regulations, aimed at preventing overexploitation. Furthermore, in the context of granting citizenship rights, those responsible strived to ensure that the community of burghers would stay as religiously and morally homogeneous as possible.

1830–1839: the 'democratic paradox' and reforms

When it came to competences in decision-making and political power, the burghers of Winterthur formed a less homogeneous group than expected. The fate of the town was mostly in the hands of the town council, which has often been called a 'paternalistic regiment' (Ganz, 1979, p. 17). The town council, as the town's highest authority, decided on almost all important issues.[13] This changed in the 1830s when state control was getting more important. At the annual municipal assembly of 29 June 1830, a burgher demanded the right of free speech, to the irritation of the town's authority. The inflexible and meaningless way in which the assembly of burghers was held, the impossibility of free speech and the sweeping way in which the magistrates reported were publically criticized (Ganz, 1980). The right to have a say in financial decisions was one of the main demands raised at the assembly. It was argued that 'if the town's property [is] the property of all burghers, it is in the nature of free concepts that then indeed all citizens [. . .] [may] themselves decide about expenses, sales, purchases [and] this will not only be done by a small selection of burghers'.[14] However, participation rights require transparency and insight into the administration of estates and the accountancy. Thus, it was also demanded that:

> to make any burgher capable of reasonably judging on cases of this kind, the situation of our budget must not be hidden behind dark and complicated ways of accountancy but any citizen must be allowed to have an understanding of its importance. Why should he who entrusts not be allowed to know what he entrusts.[15]

The call for the right to more say in financial matters must be seen against a background of a political and economic liberalization. Under the impression of the July Revolution in France, of mass petitioning and people's assembly, the old elites in several cantons of Switzerland were deprived of their powers, and liberal state constitutions were introduced. Among others, the latter enforced direct elections and a system of checks and balances, and they extended suffrage and passive franchise to broader parts of the male population (Koller, 2010).

In the Canton Zurich, the new state constitution of 1831 stipulated that the state's sovereignty was based on the entirety of the people and was to be executed by elected authorities and public officials.[16] Paupers and people under tutelage, as well as those who were made bankrupt, were still excluded from suffrage and passive electoral rights.[17] As a consequence of the political upheavals, the assembly of burghers in Winterthur became the town's superior authority, and the demands for transparency and participation led to a reform of the administration as well as a standardization of procedures. Budget matters were centralized in an annual general account, which was meant to guarantee transparency for the citizens. This general account was displayed for all burghers in the town's office.[18]

The extended participation rights for the town's burghers were balanced by an increased subjection to state regulations. Under the new state constitution of 1831, Winterthur lost a variety of special municipal rights (Ganz, 1979, p. 34ff.). The organization of schooling and church matters, as well as the municipal budget, became increasingly subject to framework conditions and directives by the state (Ganz, 1979, p. 37). Despite improved participation rights for broader parts of the population, the town was increasingly made subject to regulations and control by the state. This 'democratic paradox' resulted in confrontations (Aubry, 2012a). One of the most controversial subjects was school reform and the different ways of funding local schools.

In the course of a number of committee meetings and community assemblies, a new school plan for Winterthur's schools was worked out. Right from the beginning, one of the essential goals was not to give up on the right to decide on 'local school institutions'[19] and to be able to decide as independently from state interference as possible in the future. The assembly was ready to adjust the system of obligatory elementary schools to the 'general laws on school', but intended to reserve the right to 'establish the higher departments [. . .] according to *our own decisions*'[20] for itself. In the eyes of most of the burghers, this demand for autonomy could be justified, as, until then, they had always provided the funding of their municipal schools themselves. In their opinion, the fact that this was a high sum provided sufficient evidence that the improvement of schools was an obvious concern for the majority of the burghers.[21] In the 'long assembly' held on 22 and 23 June 1833, the new school plan was passed after lengthy discussions.[22] Considering the time-consuming debates, it is not surprising that only half of the burghers attended. The minutes record 270 attendants, and it is not clear if every one of them was in agreement with retired headmaster Troll, who noted later: 'In the long and hot days [. . .] the burghers of Winterthur celebrated their first educational assembly' (1842, p. 244).

The school plan was sent to the state's educational council, which, as feared, demanded adjustments and changes, in particular, requesting that access to burgher schools for girls and boys should be also open to the Ansässen. The burghers still wanted these schools to be accessible only by their special permission. The town council expressed its displeasure with the state's interference, particularly regarding the financial decision-making competence: 'How disturbing and deep the changes of the municipality's decisions as stipulated by the State Council of Education [are] and how they [will have] a negative effect particularly regarding the economy'.[23] In its 'General Basic Regulations', the revised constitution of Winterthur of 1831 stated that, for the benefit of future generations, the municipal property had to be maintained and, if possible, extended as the burghers' continuous property, for 'funding their common matters'.[24] In the eyes of the burghers, the indivisibility of the municipal property had the highest priority, as it still formed the basis of financing the town's needs and was supposed to remain as such in the future. The '*nervus rerum*' was supposed to be used both by 'the current generation and by our offspring'.[25]

The school regulations for Winterthur, which were finally agreed on after heated debates, distinguished three types of school, just as they had existed previously – the boys' and girls' schools for the burghers, as well as the former Ansässen school.[26] However, as a result of political and financial considerations, each school type was now divided into two main departments. The lower department, for which the state stipulated compulsory education, was distinguished from the higher department of senior schools, which were considered the town's 'own schools' that were maintained voluntarily.[27] According to a majority of the burghers, this separation was advantageous, in that '[a] clear and true relation of our parish towards the state [. . .] will be drawn'.[28] The burghers would not tolerate any interference by the state in matters of municipal senior schools because they considered them their *private* affair.[29] The state was not entitled to interfere, even more so as it did not contribute to the funding of the municipal senior schools. Financial regulations going beyond the obligatory part of the school system, as formulated by the state law on schools, were exclusively a matter for the burghers.

This differentiation also had an impact on financing. An analysis of the distribution of school expenses shows how unequally the schools were provided for by the town. By far the most was spent on the voluntarily established senior boys' school (147 francs per head and per year), more than double than for the senior girls' school (63 francs per head and per year), which received about as much as the senior Ansässen school.[30] The lower department of the obligatory system shows the same difference. The girls' school and the Ansässen school received about the same amount of money (19 and 16 francs per head and per year respectively), whereas the burghers invested 30 francs in the boys' school.[31] Meanwhile, Ansässen still had to pay school fees, for the rule was: 'For the children of local burghers education is free in all departments of the municipal school [. . .]. Non-burgher students pay a fee'.[32] Although the state demanded the reduction of the fees as early as in 1835, it was rejected by the burghers. Eventually, the state's educational council prevailed, and the school fees for Ansässen had at least to be reduced.

Progressive reforms meant that school costs were rising under the new liberal government in Zurich. As Cohen points out in this volume, it was the liberals who believed passionately in education, as in England and France. Ossenbach, also in this volume, refers to the liberals in Hispanic America, and their firm convictions about the importance of the state's role in education. The same trend was present in Switzerland, with economic consequences. Between 1832 and 1851, school costs in Winterthur rose from 6 to 29 per cent of total expenditure,[33] while on the state level they increased sevenfold in the same period (Kägi, 1954, p. 68). The state had made primary schooling compulsory, but its grants to the municipalities did not cover the attendant costs. Its meagre funds were used for covering significant deficits in local school-building projects, while taking into consideration the budgetary and tax situation of the communities in question. This way, poorer municipalities particularly benefited from state support. However, this system was prone to misuse, and trust in figures announced by municipalities was low. To prevent possible misuse, in 1832, the municipalities were made to establish separate school funds, whereby the interest payments were used for running school expenses, thus avoiding the introduction of additional tax payments.[34]

The idea of establishing a proper school fund was first introduced in Winterthur as early as 1819. It was to be endowed from the municipal estate, so that a central school authority would be able to meet all school expenses from this fund (Troll, 1842, p. 240). However, this idea did not prevail. Over the years, the school fees paid by the Ansässen had generated a steady surplus. After 1811, the Ansässen paid more in school fees than was needed to cover the expenses. In 1825, this surplus was used to establish a local school fund (Ganz, 1979, p. 115), the aim of which was to, at least partially, relieve the municipal budget.[35] In 1833, following efforts by the state government, Winterthur began the separation of the estates for schools, the poor and the church from the general burgher estates.[36] The entirety of income and expenses was split between the four titles of estates – those designated for the poor, church estates, school estates and municipal estates. Thus, the town achieved what was later explicitly put down in its constitution of 1839: all collective estates were considered the burghers' estates, now simply split into four categories for administrative reasons.[37] The first three estates were to be endowed in a way that allowed each one to meet the annual expenses that arose from the interest generated by the endowed capital funds. The school estates also liquidated the school fund established in 1825, which had increased steadily over time.[38] The expected annual interest was to cover at least the costs for the obligatory school types.[39]

In a financial and administrative context, the separation of the school department was complete. The higher and voluntarily run schools were still funded directly by the town's budget, with the obligatory types being the responsibility of the school estates. With this separation into an obligatory branch under the school laws of the state and a voluntarily run higher town school, for which Winterthur did not demand any financial support, the town managed to obtain a certain independence from demands of the state concerning school matters. As far as the local burghers regarded the matter, the state had no participation rights until it was able to financially support all the required reforms. However, the burghers of Winterthur did not completely disregard the state's regulations, because ultimately they were convinced that good local schools were crucial for the economic development of their town (Aubry, 2012b). With the administrative separation of the school estates from the collective common estates, the funding of schools was furthermore secured, since by way of item-related funding, the expenses for schooling were protected from rival municipal projects that might also need funding. The separation did not, however, affect the local ownership situation. The sustainability of the use of the property still had priority, and from the burghers' point of view, this could still only be guaranteed by way of strict regulations.

The 1830s were characterized by reforms in educational politics, which, as shown, can be seen as part of a political liberalization. Nonetheless, the claim formulated in the state constitution of 1831, according to which the sovereignty of the state was supposed to be based on the entirety of the people, must be seen against the background of the census suffrage. 'People' could not be equated with the population, and participation rights were still restricted. Consequently, the liberalization of certain circumstances in society could not yet be equated with a democracy of the people. This was to come years later.

1859–1869: new institutions and changing property situations

In the early 1860s, criticism of the representative democracy in the Canton Zurich grew stronger, and calls for a direct democracy could no longer be ignored (Craig, 1988). A newly formed democratic movement opposing the 'liberal regime' made claims for a constitutional revision (Kölz, 2000). There were calls for a restriction of parliamentary powers and the abolition of indirect elections, as well as a free press and unrestricted association law, the expansion of popular education and more autonomy for local authorities (Kölz, 2000). The aspiring industrial town of Winterthur became the centre of the middle-class opposition (Dünki, 1990; Suter, 1991). Before voting took place on a comprehensive state constitutional revision, a first step towards democratization had been taken in educational matters. The new cantonal school law of 1859 stipulated the creation of independent school communities, with separate competences and financial decision-making powers.[40] This meant the creation of a local institution that was more or less independent of other political committees and responsible solely for local educational issues.

In Winterthur, the creation of the new institution that was the school community led, above all, to wider participation rights. Inhabitants without burghers' rights were entitled to vote on matters of education, even – and this was particularly significant – on questions of financial nature. The number of Ansässen voters in the school community roughly equalled that of the burghers, so that an impasse situation in votes was theoretically possible and was feared by some of the burghers. The new school law thus led to a change in property rights, something that understandably gave rise to disputes. Once more, debate took place in Winterthur about the state 'illegally' issuing decrees to which, from the point of view of some burghers, it was not entitled: separating the school estates as 'lawful school estates belonging to the school community' was said to be a 'gross violation of [. . .] the property rights of the community of burghers'.[41]

The majority of burghers did not feel obliged to make this substantial split. Nevertheless, there were understandable reasons for doing so, for otherwise, in order to cover the rising school costs, taxes would need to be raised, which in the end would have been a burden most of all for themselves. The separation between the community of burghers and the school community was made by way of a treaty. In this treaty, the burghers obliged themselves to erect a new school building 'which shall meet all needs of the obligatory elementary school', as well as to provide an additional sum of 50,000 francs for the new school fund. Furthermore, all revenue from marriage fees was to be transferred to this fund over the following ten years. The school community accepted the obligation to pay the full costs for the local school as soon as the fund had grown appropriately and to give up any further claims on the burghers' property.[42]

By the newly created institutions of the school community and the municipal schools board, the economic separation from the common estate was completed:

> From May 1st, 1860, the School Community of Winterthur will take over control and administration of the previously citizen-administered obligatory school institutions and will pay for them [. . .] which in all respects will be made subject to the regulations of the Canton's law on schools.[43]

Indeed, if compared to previous 'separations', which were rather administrative simplifications, the separation of 1859 was a substantial one, due to the change of property situation, as the school community was not restricted to the exclusive circle of the burghers. This meant that even those parts of the population not holding Winterthur citizenship rights were provided with decision-making authority and rights of use of municipal property, at least as far as the separate new school fund was concerned.

The revenue from the school fund was not enough to cover the costs for the local primary schools. In contrast to Ossenbach's findings for Hispanic America (in this volume), the shortage of funding on the municipal level did not lead to more state involvement. The local school community was authorized to raise taxes, and in Winterthur taxes were collected to cover the deficit from 1861 on.[44] In addition, all children had to pay an annual school fee of 3 francs. With the introduction of school communities, the distinction between the children of citizens and those of Ansässen came to an end.

Another step towards democratization was made by the partial revision of the state s constitution in 1865. With the implementation of the 'community of inhabitants', the traditional assembly of burghers lost its significance and power (Ganz, 1979). From now on, all adult male inhabitants were eligible to vote and be elected, provided they were Swiss citizens.[45] With this act, the remaining burgher property became municipal property, meant to satisfy the public needs of the municipalities.[46] Thus, only six years after the implementation of school communities, the common estate was again an issue of heavy debates. The

Winterthur burgher law had allowed a user share, which could not only be accessed indirectly via institutions, such as school or welfare for the poor, but also directly, on an individual level. This individual burgher's share in the form of wood, wine or grazing rights seemed to be endangered by the introduction of the community of inhabitants. In a 150-page voluminous expert report, State Archivist Hotz commented that the revenue from the burghers' estates had always been shared between public needs and individual use by burghers. However, it was further explained, the regulations for the use of the revenue had tried to protect it from the desires of individuals and maintained the output of the estates in the interest of the public (Hotz, 1868, p. 131). Regarding the argument of a traditional practice, Hotz referred to the non-existence of any difference between inhabitants and burghers in the past; in other words, 'the institution of burgher right was a comparably young development' (Hotz, 1868, p. 4). Thus, the often stated argument of a tradition of private use by citizens had become obsolete. In the community assembly held on 28 February 1869, the matter was finally resolved, whereby those in support of a separation of usage for private purposes were defeated, with a share of only 30 per cent of the votes.[47]

The abandonment of the differentiation between burghers and Ansässen was not only sought by the introduction of school communities and those of inhabitants. On 18 April 1869, the Canton Zurich citizens voted in favour of a new State Constitution that defined a further democratization in several areas (Dünki, 1990). Article 62 abolished school fees for obligatory schooling, with explicit demands for an increased financial commitment for schooling from the state.[48] By the introduction of 'free teaching', the financial inequality in Winterthur had come to an end, at least in respect of obligatory schooling. Now, there was one school for everybody. Typically for Switzerland, the press talked about a people's school (*Volksschule*) rather than a 'state school' in their debates about 'free teaching', for 'the state is nothing else than the entirety of its citizens who make themselves subject to this compulsion'.[49] Matthew Arnold, the 'Lover of Light', had a similar view of this on his travels through the Canton Zurich: 'but what is important to be observed is that it is still a school for the people, or Volksschule, and also a school which the public provides for them' (Arnold, 1964, p. 276). In Switzerland, the school laws were built upon a bold idea 'about the citizen's claim, in this matter, upon the State, and the State's duty towards the citizen' (Arnold, 2001, p. 70).

Conclusion: financing schools and the social order

School was – and is, of course – an institution within society. The way of funding was co-determined by political and economic rules. My tour through the history of school funding in the town of Winterthur has shown a process I call 'from equity to more equality'. For a long time the situation in Winterthur was determined by the local citizenship right as a powerful tool of social exclusion; at a purely formal level, it was understood as a membership organization with significant, sociologically interesting, effects. The citizenship right was the basic condition for participation in local political decision-making processes as well as for having certain usage and property rights. Consequently, not everybody was able to fetch from the pool of the municipal *oikos*. The citizenship right granted participation and was part of a social economy, following the logic of 'proportional equality'. The principle of equity as treating 'the equal equally and the unequal unequally' had effects on school funding and came to bear when, after 1800, there was an increasing 'foreign inundation' at schools. According to this principle, the social order within the town was differentiated; unequal school opportunities became equivalent to unequal economic treatment.

In the course of democratization attempts in the 1830s, the right to participate in political decisions was extended, although mostly pertaining to extended possibilities within the circle of burghers. The social and economic differentiation between burghers and Ansässen regarding school funding remained. The state increasingly acted as a corrective, but the majority of Winterthur burghers were in support of attempts at autonomy, as well as of the lowest possible degree of state interference in school matters in their town. As municipalities and local school authorities saw their administrative business as part of the town's budget, there were attempts at dissociation from the state. Those were justified by financial independence in the sense of 'who pays is the one to order'. Thus, the state was not deemed entitled to interfere in the 'private' affairs of the town.

Independence was only possible for those being financially independent to a certain degree. By the further differentiation of the school community in 1860, Winterthur did not only see a change of decision-making and administrative competence regarding schools but also – and I believe this to be crucial – of property matters. In the final separation, the burghers' estates lost their direct significance for school funding. In the school community, the Ansässen were now entitled to decide not only about educational issues but also about financial matters regarding schools. In the context of the democratic movement opposing the liberal regime in the 1860s, the introduction of the community of inhabitants led to a suspension of the difference between burghers and Ansässen. As a result, all male Swiss citizens were now entitled to vote and be elected. Thus, the participation rights were extended once more, to a bigger share of inhabitants of Winterthur. In the field of obligatory schooling, increased social democratization was achieved when the state stipulated the abolition of school fees, thus providing more equal opportunities in education.

As a conclusion, we may state that, within the analysed period (1789–1869), it is possible to sketch a multi-faceted process of change regarding the funding of schools, and the process of centralization/decentralization is far more complex than assumed. The answer to the question of 'who is entitled to what?'

was debated and subject to change. Significant in this context were the following aspects: the increased influence of the state *as well as* the introduction of local and independent school communities, the change in administering the municipal estates, the extension of potential for political participation, as well as changing ideas of how resources should be used and by whom. The techniques of transforming material resources into the immaterial good of education were, and are, significant when we analyse the funding of schools. It enables and restricts educational opportunities and is a result of political decision-making processes.

Notes

1. This debate can be seen against the backdrop of a revised educational code, which, in 1862, predicated paying grants on the performance of the pupils. As a result of these changes, many feared an underfunding of schools. In many places, private donations were used to cover expenses. For assessments of the consequences of this policy, see, for example, Marcham (1979).
2. Arnold had already travelled to Europe, including French-speaking Switzerland, in 1859, in order to research popular education.
3. Due to a strong tradition of federalism in Switzerland, the cantons were (and still are) responsible for much government activity. In line with this tradition, the term 'state' here refers to the political entity of the Canton Zurich.
4. A revised school plan for the boys' school was introduced in 1789, and in 1790 for the girls' school.
5. The term 'burgher' refers to an established citizen of the town of Winterthur, who held local citizenship rights.
6. The term 'Ansässen' refers to the parts of the population living in the town but having originally come from outside, where 'outside' could also mean the nearby villages.
7. On the historic relevance of different forms of citizenship, see also Brubaker (1994) or Fahrmeir (2000).
8. StAW B 2 106. Minutes of the town council, 10 September 1810. See also Ganz (1979, p. 114).
9. StAW B 2d 4. Minutes of the municipal assembly, 29 May 1837, and StAW II B 30 k6. Report Scherr, 1842.
10. StAW B 2d 4. Minutes of the municipal assembly, 29 May 1837.
11. StAW B 2d 4. Minutes of the municipal assembly, 29 May 1837.
12. StAW B 2d 4. Minutes of the municipal assembly, 29 May 1837.
13. StAW II B 34b 1. 21 June 1816, as well as 5 August 1816. Its members were appointed from the ranks of a committee of thirty-nine persons, who had been elected by the assembly of burghers.
14. StAW II B 34b 1. 23 January 1831.
15. StAW II B 34b 1. 23 January 1831.
16. FBP ZH HA I 14. Constitution of the Canton Zurich, 1831 Art 1.
17. FBP ZH HA I 14. Constitution of the Canton Zurich, 1831 Art. 24.
18. They refrained from publishing the report because, by doing that, the complete estate of the town would have been known in the whole canton, and 'no housefather would ever disclose his wealth to the public'. StAW II B 34b 1. Introductory report of the commission on the revision of the town constitution, 1831.

19 StAW B 2d 2. Municipal and guild minutes, 31 January 1831.
20 StAW B 2d 2. Municipal and guild minutes, 31 January 1831.
21 StAW II B 34b 1. Report and application to the burghers, 16 April 1831.
22 StAW B 2d 3. Minutes of the municipal assembly, 22 and 23 July 1833.
23 StAW B 2d 3. Minutes of the municipal assembly, 22 and 23 July 1833.
24 StAW II B 34b 1. Municipal constitution of the town of Winterthur, 1831.
25 StAW II B 34b 1. Hints and allusions. The notion '*nervus rerum*' refers to 'money, because it allows for getting or doing almost everything' (Flörke, 1802).
26 StAW B 2d 3. Minutes of the municipal assembly, 22 and 23 July1833. On this, ref. Ganz (1979, p. 116) or Troll (1842, p. 247).
27 StAW B 2d 3. Minutes of the municipal assembly, 22 and 23 July 1833.
28 StAW B 2d 4. Minutes of the municipal assembly, 24 August 1840.
29 StAW II B 30k 6. Minutes of the meeting of the commission on revision of the school plan, 10 September 1838.
30 StAW Kc1.
31 StAW Kc1.
32 StAW II B 30k 6. Minutes of the meeting of the commission on revision of the school plan, 10 September 1838.
33 StAW II B 10k 1.
34 StAW II B 10k 1. Circular district council 'Call for formation of a schools estate', 10 December 1832.
35 StAW II B 30k 6. Reverend Hanhart to mayor, 21 March 1827.
36 FBP ZH HA I 3,4. Law concerning the administration of the municipal estates, 1838.
37 StAW II B 34b 1. Constitution of the town of Winterthur, s. 62, 11 December 1839.
38 StAW II B 34b 1. Constitution of the town of Winterthur, s. 62, 11 December 1839.
39 StAW II B 10k 1. Report to the burghers on the state of the municipal estate and applications, 1842.
40 FBP ZH HA I 14. Law on schooling in the Canton Zurich, 1859, s. 32 and 264.
41 StAW II B 30k 6. Report to commission regarding changes to town constitution, 23 July 1859.
42 StAW II B 30d 3. Draft for agreement between burghers and the school community of the town of Winterthur, regarding rejections of the latter, 2 August 1859.
43 StAW LBc 2. See also Winkler (1947, p. 113).
44 StAW LB/26.
45 Constitution of the confederate government Zurich, 18 April 1869, Art. 17.
46 Constitution of the confederate government Zurich, 18 April 1869, Art. 55.
47 Votes: 544 to 270. The turnout seems to have been rather low. It is interesting that the proportion of supporters of a private share of the commons was about the same as the number of those handing in the first petition.
48 State constitution of the canton Zurich, 1869, Art. 62, and Law regarding the replacement of school fees, January 1869. On this see also Bloch (1999).
49 *Neue Zürcher Zeitung*, 25 November 1868.

Archives

StAW: Stadtarchiv Winterthur
FBP: Forschungsbibliothek Pestalozzianum

References

Aristoteles, 1964. *Nikomachische Ethik*. Berlin: Akademie-Verlag.
Arnold, M., 1964. *Schools and Universities on the Continent*. Ed. R.H. Super. Ann Arbor, MI: The University of Michigan Press.
Arnold, M., 2001. *Culture and Anarchy*. Ed. J.D. Wilson. Cambridge: Cambridge University Press.
Aubry, C., 2012a. Die Bedeutung ökonomischer Ressourcen. 'Öffentliche Schulaufsicht zwischen kantonaler Einflussnahme und Widerständigkeit vor Ort. *Jahrbuch für historische Bildungsforschung*. Band 17. Bad Heilbrunn: Julius Klinkhardt, pp. 126–143.
Aubry, C., 2012b. The 'value of schooling': rising expenditures on education in Winterthur, 1830–1850. In: C. Aubry and J. Westberg (eds) *History of Schooling. Politics and Local Practice*. Frankfurt: Peter Lang, pp. 90–106.
Bloch, A., 1999. Schulpflicht, Unentgeltlichkeit und Laizität des Unterrichts im Kanton Zürich zwischen 1770 und 1900. In: L. Criblez, R. Hofstetter and C. Magnin (eds) *Eine Schule für die Demokratie. Zur Entwicklung der Volksschule in der Schweiz im 19. Jahrhundert*. Frankfurt: Peter Lang, pp. 123–153.
Brubaker, R., 1994. *Staats-Bürger. Deutschland und Frankreich im Historischen Vergleich*. Hamburg: Junius.
Cohen, M., 2005. Reconsidering schools and the American welfare state. *History of Education Quarterly*, 45(4), pp. 511–537.
Craig, G.A., 1988. *Geld und Geist. Zürich im Zeitalter des Liberalismus 1830–1869*. Munich: C.H. Beck.
Dünki, R., 1990. *Verfassungsgeschichte und Politische Entwicklung Zürichs 1814–1893*. Zurich: Stadtarchiv.
Engermann, S., Mariscal, E.V. and Sokoloff, K.L., 2009. The evolution of schooling in America, 1800–1925. In: D. Eltis, F.D. Lewis and K.L. Sokoloff (eds) *Human Capital and Institutions. A Long Run View*. Cambridge: Cambridge University Press, pp. 93–142.
Fahrmeir, A., 2000. *Citizens and Aliens. Foreigners and the Law in Britain and the German States, 1798–1870*. New York, Oxford: Berghahn Books.
Flörke, H.G., 1802. *Oekonomische Encyklopaedie, oder Allgemeines System der Staats-, Stadt-, Haus- und Landwirthschaft in Alphabetischer Ordnung*. Band 102 (e-book). Available at: www.kruenitz1.uni-trier.de/xxx/n/kn02132.htm (accessed 14 July 2011).
Ganz, W., 1979. *Geschichte der Stadt Winterthur. Vom Durchbruch der Helvetik 1798 bis zur Stadtvereinigung*. Winterthur: Verlag W. Vogel.
Ganz, W., 1980. Winterthur und der Ustertag von 1830. *Winterthurer Jahrbuch*. Winterthur: Druckerei Winterthur AG, pp. 65–82.
Guzzi-Heeb, S., 2009. Niederlassungsfreiheit. In: *Historisches Lexikon der Schweiz* (online). Available at: www.hls-dhs-dss.ch/textes/d/D10369.php (accessed 27 July 2011).
Hotz, I.H., 1868. *Historisch-juristische Beiträge zur Geschichte der Stadt Winterthur des Gemeindgutes und der Nutzungen nach Urkundlichen Quellen*. Winterthur: Bleuler-Hausheer.
Kägi, E., 1954. *Der Finanzhaushalt des Kantons Zürich in der Regenerationszeit. Wirtschaft, Gesellschaft, Staat. Zürcher Studien zur Allgemeinen Geschichte*. Band 11. Zurich: Europa Verlag.
Koller, C., 2010. Regeneration. In: *Historisches Lexikon der Schweiz* (online). Available at: www.hls-dhs-dss.ch/textes/d/D9800.php (accessed 28 July 2011).

Kölz, A., 2000. *Der demokratische Aufbruch des Zürchervolkes. Eine Quellenstudie zur Entstehung der Zürcher Kantonsverfassung von 1869.* Zurich: Schulthess.

Lang, C.Y., 2006. *The Letters of Matthew Arnold* (e-book). Available at: http://rotunda.upress.virginia.edu/arnold (accessed 23 August 2012).

Lindert, P. and Go, S., 2010. The uneven rise of American public schools to 1850. *The Journal of Economic History*, 70(1), pp. 1–26.

Lover of Light, 1865. Education and the state, *The Pall Mall Gazette*, 11 December 1865 (online). Available at: British Newspapers 1800–1900, http://newspapers11.bl.uk/blcs/ (accessed 8 August 2012).

Marcham, A.J., 1979. Recent interpretations of the Revised Code of Education, 1862. *History of Education*, 8(2), pp. 121–133.

Margo, R.A., 1990. *Race and Schooling in the South, 1880–1950. An Economic History.* Chicago, IL: University of Chicago Press.

Mitch, D.F., 1986. The impact of subsidies to elementary schools on enrolment rates in nineteenth-century England. *The Economic History Review, New Series*, 39(3), pp. 371–391.

Mitch, D.F., 2004. School finance. In: G. Johnes and J. Johnes (eds) *International Handbook on the Economics of Education.* Cheltenham: Edward Elgar, pp. 260–297.

Ostrom, E., 1990. *Governing the Commons. The Evolution of Institutions for Collective Actions.* Cambridge: Cambridge University Press.

Ostrom, E., 2005. *Understanding Institutional Change.* Princeton, NJ: Princeton University Press.

Schläppi, D. 2011. Verwalten statt regieren. Management kollektiver Ressourcen als Kerngeschäft von Verwaltung in der alten Eidgenossenschaft. *Traverse: Zeitschrift für Geschichte*, 18(2), pp. 42–56.

Studer, B., Arlettaz, G. and Argast, R., 2008. *Das Schweizer Bürgerrecht.* Zurich: Neue Zürcher Zeitung-Buchverlag.

Suter, M., 1991. Winterthur und der Schweizer Staatsgedanke im 18. und 19. Jahrhundert. *Winterthurer Jahrbuch.* Winterthur: Druckerei Winterthur AG, pp. 81–99.

Suter, M., 1992. *Winterthur 1798–1831. Von der Revolution zur Regeneration.* Winterthur: Stadtbibliothek.

Troll, J.C., 1842. *Geschichte der Stadt Winterthur nach Urkunden bearbeitet. Zweiter Theil Enthaltend die Schulgeschichte der Stadt Winterthur.* Winterthur: Hegner's Buchdruckerei.

Weber, H., 1971. *Die Zürcherischen Landgemeinden in der Helvetik 1798–1803.* Frauenfeld: Huber.

Westberg, J., 2013. Stimulus or impediment? The impact of matching grants on the funding of elementary schools in Sweden during the nineteenth century. *History of Education*, 42(1), pp. 1–22.

Winkler, H., 1947. *Schulgeschichte der Stadt Winterthur bis zum Jahre 1922.* Winterthur: Buchdruckerei Geschwister Ziegler.

Chapter 5

State education, crisis and austerity

A historical analysis through the lens of the Kondratiev cycles

Vincent Carpentier

Introduction

Socioeconomic crises represent crucial opportunities to explore the connections and tensions between wealth and welfare and their implications for the public sphere and educational policy. The global economic downturn that unfolded in 2008 is no different, and has generated alternative diagnoses and policy responses that directly question the relationship between education, the state, social justice and economic performance. A first type of interpretation of the economic downturn focuses on the fiscal crisis and considers the implementation of austerity policies as a key condition for restoring economic growth and, in the longer term, reducing inequalities through a trickledown effect. A second approach considers those same inequalities as a cause rather than a consequence of the crisis and sees their reduction through the implementation of a countercyclical increase of public funding as the way forward to reactivate economic growth by an increase of demand and an investment in the quality of the labour force.

State education (considered in this paper as the public funding and provision of education) is at the interface of these debates connecting taxation and the production and distribution of growth. This is an important issue because, especially during economic crises, the particular virulence of such debates question and sometimes threaten the connections amongst the cultural (creation and transmission of knowledge), social (contribution to social cohesion, mobility and citizenship), productive (impact on employability and productivity through innovation and training) and financial (public or private funding) dimensions of public educational systems. Moreover, because of its potential to either reinforce or address socioeconomic inequalities (Apple, 1982; Unterhalter and Carpentier, 2010), education has been increasingly considered either as a driver of the crisis or a solution to it.

Thus, during hard times, the public educational system is often blamed for not reinforcing social cohesion, for not supporting productivity, and for being a financial burden for growth. However, the analysis at the interface of political economy and history of education developed in this paper suggests that, from a historical point of view, the relationship between austerity and crisis is not as straightforward as it might seem today. The lens of the long economic cycles shows that, before the Second World War, the growth of state education used to take place during economic crises as a key part of a broader historical expansion of a social infrastructure of human development (Carpentier and Michel, 2010), which played a key role in reducing the tensions between inequality and economic performance. Thus, the successive phases of historical expansion of public educational systems were responses (and indeed solutions) to socioeconomic crises, rather than their cause. Such mechanisms contrast with the austerity policies which have been implemented to address the various economic crises which have unfolded since the mid 1970s. Therefore, there could be a historical case we can refer to when attempting to develop countercyclical public policy today.

Section 1 presents the empirical findings and their theoretical interpretation. The quantitative historical data reveal a correlation between public funding in education and Kondratiev cycles. These trends are interpreted by applying the theory of systemic regulation, which considers that the historical connections and tensions between the public funding of social activities driving human development (including education) and the economic structure lead to the upturns and downturns of the economy expressed by the Kondratiev cycle. Thus, the fluctuations in funding in education can be understood as part of a wider trend linking the State and the transformations of the socioeconomic system. The lens of economic cycles designates crises as turning points in the recurrent build up of tensions between economic growth and inequalities. Section 2 shows that prior to 1945, economic crises were contemporary of countercyclical expansion of public educational systems that acted as a response to blockage of the growth regime. Section 3 examines a reversal from countercyclical to procyclical expenditure on education after 1945, whereby education shifted from a corrector of crisis to a driver of the postwar growth until the 1970s crisis led, unlike its predecessors, to a slowdown of public funding in education. Section 4 reflects on how this historical lens can help us to interpret the post 2008 crisis and discusses some potential scenarii.

Kondratiev cycles, crises and state education

Reactions to what was commonly called the 'credit crunch', which engulfed the world economy in 2008, are worth careful examination. At first, analysts believed that this crisis would be short-lived and that some adjustments would correct the external turbulences. Then, as the crisis deepened, the idea emerged that these exogenous factors were, in fact, revealing internal dysfunctions at the heart of the economic system. In other words, this crisis was systemic and the mechanisms that drove the growth could be the same as those that had provoked the crisis. The recurrence of such crises makes it worth exploring existing historical interpretations of the long economic cycles. The approach developed here considers that education, as a key interface of economic and human developments, is crucial in explaining the cyclical fluctuations of the economy and the recurrence of economic crises and their overcoming. Similarly, economic cycles can help us to (at least partially) understand the mechanisms behind the historical phases of expansions and setbacks of education.

Crisis and economic cycles: debates and interpretation

Galbraith concludes his book on the depression of the 1930s by saying that:

> the wonder, indeed, is that since 1929 we have been spared so long. One reason, without doubt, is that the experience of 1929 burned itself so deeply into the national consciousness. It is worth hoping that a history such as this will keep bright that immunizing memory for a little longer.
> (1954, p. 29)

The world economy has faced major structural crises since Galbraith's warning and the most recent one has sparked revived interest in his analysis of the tensions between the financial and economic spheres. Although the depression of the interwar years perfectly illustrates these tensions and has become the point of reference for making historical parallels with the current crisis, it is worth noting that the recurrence of phases of crisis since the Industrial Revolution of the late eighteenth century has also been observed and interpreted in major works on economic cycles.

Although other cycles of shorter periodicity have been identified, this chapter focuses on the Kondratiev cycle (or long wave), named after the Russian economist Nikolai Kondratiev (1892–1938). In the 1920s, he analysed historical economic and financial statistics in major industrialized countries and identified a succession of twenty- to twenty-five-year phases of prosperity and depression. Four long waves of approximately fifty years have since been identified, each showing expansion and depression phases: 1790–1820/1820–1848; 1848–1870/ 1870–1897; 1897–1913/1913–1945; 1945–1973/1973–?.

Kondratiev cycles remain highly contentious and there are ongoing debates among economists and historians about their existence, as well as reservations about the deterministic view of history they tend to represent (Louçã and Reijnders, 1999). These are valid and important criticisms. However, a cautious interpretation of Kondratiev cycles may contribute to productive debate, not least in responding to Hobsbawm's (1997) call for collaboration between historians and economists to understand socioeconomic transformations (Milonakis and Fine, 2009). Kondratiev cycles have also been politically contentious. Their depiction of alternations of phases of growth and crisis has been criticized by some on the left for inferring that the capitalist system can always regenerate itself and others on the right for implying that crises are inevitable features of the capitalist development.

The theory of systemic regulation and the Kondratiev cycle: education and the historical connections and tensions between human and economic developments

The theory of the systemic regulation interprets the Kondratiev cycle as the expression of the dialectical relationship between economic and human developments (Boccara, 1988; Fontvieille, 1976; Marx, 1894). The cyclical economic upturns and downturns are seen as the results of the long-term interactions and tensions between the development of social activities contributing to human development (and indirectly to economic performance) and the economic structure.

Therefore, Kondratiev cycles can be considered as the product of internal systemic connections and tensions between wealth and welfare. Within that approach, crises are caused by the cyclical re-emergence of socioeconomic inequalities, which eventually contribute to the disruption of economic efficiency and profitability. Reversibly, economic recovery depends on periodic transformations of the socioeconomic structure contributing to the reduction of inequalities and the revival of productivity. In other words, economic crises represent critical turning points when the social justice and economic agendas are 'forced' to meet in order to revive the system. The following will suggest that social spending on human development (including education) is a key driving force behind this cyclical process of transformations.

The chapter will look at the long-term relationship between education, the state and economic cycles using empirical data produced by a research programme on the historical development of social spending. They have highlighted important specificities but have also revealed a common correlation between the fluctuations of public funding towards human development and Kondratiev cycles. Thus, it is important to note that, although this chapter focuses on education, similar trends have been observed in relation to other social spending, such as health and pensions (Domin, 2000; Michel and Vallade, 2007; Reimat, 2000).

Methodologies, key empirical observations and potential interpretation: the fluctuations in public expenditure on education and economic cycles and the 1945 reversal

The findings discussed below are based on a construction of historical statistics on education using the method of quantitative history. This method follows the principles of national accounting and provides a stable frame to integrate financial and other data, and allows comparisons across time and space (Marczewski, 1961). A research programme of quantitative histories of funding in education in the UK (Carpentier, 2001, 2003), France (Carry, 1999; Fontvieille, 1990), Germany (Diebolt, 1997) and the United States (Carpentier, 2006a) reveals three key trends and patterns discussed here from the British and French perspectives:

- The first finding reveals a huge historical expansion of public expenditure on education (Figure 5.1).
- The second finding shows substantial fluctuations in public expenditure on education connected to long economic cycles (Figure 5.2).
- The third key finding signals that these fluctuations in public expenditure on education were countercyclical before 1945 and became procyclical afterwards (Figure 5.2).

These empirical findings led to considering the possibility of a reversal of the historical relationship between economic growth and public expenditure on education around the Second World War. Based on the theory of systemic regulation, the idea of a 1945 reversal led us to formulate two key assumptions about the links between education and economic crisis:

- Until 1945, public educational systems played a key role in responding to economic crises by contributing to the political, social and technical changes necessary for economic recovery. The expansion of public expenditure on education is contemporaneous of the socioeconomic crises and contributes to their overcoming by using underused capital to reduce inequalities and revive the perspectives of growth and profitability.
- The post-1945 procyclical expansion of funding in education shows that public investment in education became a driver of growth rather than a corrector of crisis. The slowdown of public funding in education following the post-1970s' downturn contrasts with what happened during previous economic downturns. This questions the effectiveness of the current austerity policies that are supposed to respond to the crisis since 2008.

Before examining in more detail the links between public funding of education and economic fluctuations, it is important to acknowledge some of the limitations of an analysis of education based on the sole economic and financial dimensions. First, it is important to note that this interpretation of the phases of expansion and setback of education in relation to economic cycles should be considered alongside other political, social and cultural analyses (Apple, 1982; Ball, 2007; Dale, 1989). Second, inequalities in education are not only related to income or social class, but also intersect with gender and ethnicity and other potentially underrepresented groups (Carpentier and Unterhalter, 2011; Gillborn, 2008). Third, funding in education is a necessary but not sufficient way to evaluate educational development. Changes in funding were contemporary of key other qualitative developments in policy and practices explored by historians of education (Aldrich, 2006; McCulloch, 2011; Simon, 1960). Goodson has also highlighted some connections between the Kondratiev cycles and non-financial areas, such as curriculum reforms (2005). Fourth, an increase in funding should, but does not necessarily, lead to improvements in equity and quality.

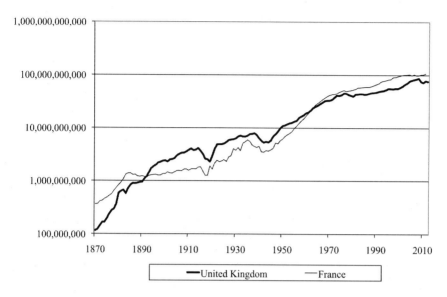

Figure 5.1 Public expenditure on education (1990 Geary-Khamis USD) 1870–2012.[1]

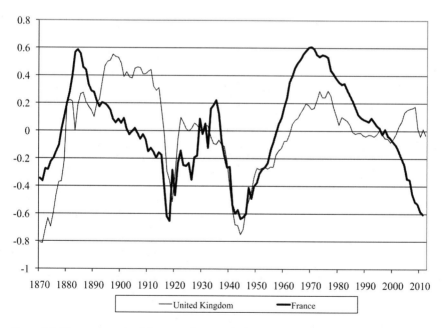

Figure 5.2 Fluctuation of public expenditure on education (1990 Geary-Khamis USD) (second-order deviation from the regression curve) 1870–2012. $R^2 = 0.97$ (UK) and 0.967 (France).[2]

The next two sections will explore the ways in which the post-1945 reversal can help us to reflect on the relationship between public education, prosperity and austerity.

Crises as opportunities for socioeconomic transformations: the countercyclical growth of public education before 1945

The idea that, before the Second World War, fluctuations in public funding in education were reversed to economic cycles is rather counterintuitive. In today's world, it seems rather paradoxical that educational funding could expand at a faster rate during hard times and at a slower pace during phases of prosperity. One possible way to interpret this trend is to consider the role of education in the growth regime inherited from the Industrial Revolution that prevailed until the Second World War.

Growth model, social systems and public funding in education before 1945

The typical pre-1945 growth model born out of the first wave of industrialization was based on a productivity regime mainly driven by the reduction of the cost of productive forces rather than their qualitative progression. A key problem with this model – which privileges physical over human capital – is the inherent development of inequalities that constitutes both its short-term success and its long-term unsustainability. The cost reduction on wages and social spending increased immediate profitability but, in the long term, led to a recurrent structural underinvestment in the development of the workforce (and the population), which harmed productivity. This decline in efficiency, coupled with the widening of the gap between production and consumption, produced a situation of overaccumulation of capital (an abundant capital that cannot be invested efficiently and turned into profit), leading to a socioeconomic crisis.

It is in this context that the approach of the systemic regulation (Fontvieille, 1976) considers the countercyclical acceleration of public funding in social activities as a key driver of economic recovery. During the crisis, the transfer of the overaccumulated capital towards productive social spending (in education but also health, pensions, housing, sanitation and wage policies) rebalanced the productive forces and produced a qualitative shift in production. Social spending helped redynamize the historical construction (and funding) of a social infrastructure of human development (Carpentier and Michel, 2010), reducing inequalities and reviving the perspectives of growth and profitability. Thus, crises offered opportunities to realign the economic structure, social change and technological innovation. This can be connected to neo-Schumpeterian analysis of the crisis as a period of reassessment of the connections between technological and social systems contributing to the development of a new sociotechnological paradigm driving the recovery (Freeman and Louçã, 2001; Perez, 2002).

The combination of the systemic regulation and neo-Schumpeterian frameworks help to explain (at least partially) why the successive crises that took place from the Industrial Revolution to the Second World War were decisive moments for the expansion of education as part of wider transformations to reduce inequalities and revive growth. Crucially, this economic interpretation of educational development must be considered alongside other political and social analyses of the historical expansion of education. The state of the economy affects (negatively or positively) the social justice rationale by creating the conditions permitting allocation of more (or less) funding to the social sphere. In other words, pre-1945 economic crises were key moments when the economic urgency to develop education in order to revive growth and profitability met the political and social rationales for social change and the reduction of social inequalities.

Importantly, the examination of the process of mediation by which the overaccumulated capital is invested in social activities offers an interpretation of the cyclical advances and setbacks in state intervention alongside other funders or providers of education, such as industrialists, philanthropists, workers' associations or voluntary enterprises. What is important is that those countercyclical education developments contribute to the resolution of the crisis because they took place outside the rules of the market and do not claim a share of profit. This may include private and public funding. For example, during the first crises of the nineteenth century, countercyclical funding in education was initially carried out by industrialists themselves (for example, through donations to voluntary schools or hospitals), who used philanthropic educational activities as opportunities to channel overaccumulated capital towards social activities that would benefit their workers and, in the longer term, their productivity and future profits (Fontvieille, 1990).

However, these private contributions gradually reached their limits. The transformations necessary to overcome each new phase of depression required further investment in order to sustain more sophisticated innovations and the qualitative development of a larger proportion of the labour force. This was beyond the financial capacity or the will of industrialists or other private contributors. This prompted the state to play a role of mediation and redirect, through taxation, the overaccumulated capital towards education, thus contributing to the development of technology and skills in order to find a new path of productivity.

It is important to note that such transformations, which were clearly driven by economic necessity, also combined with social and political unrests and demands that transcended the sole needs from the productive system. This led to a generalization of some of the rights initially given to workers to the whole population. Crises were therefore also key moments when the state synchronized its economic role and legitimation (Hartley, 2010). This gradual shift towards more state intervention and social rights after each of the successive crises explains partly the reversal of the relationship between education and economic growth that took place after 1945 and the emergence of the welfare state. This also explains the ongoing tensions between educational and economic systems that have built up since the 1970s. This explains why it is important to explore in further detail the historical process prior to 1945.

The countercyclical expansion of educational systems: the cases of France and the UK, 1833–1945

The following traces the origins of the countercyclical development of educational systems in France and the UK until the Second World War.

The first Kondratiev cycle (1790s–1840s): first setback of the Industrial Revolution and early development of state involvement in elementary education

The upturn and downturn of the first Kondratiev cycle corresponded respectively to the emergence of the first Industrial Revolution (1790s–1820s) and its first setback (1820s–1850s). The rapid industrialization led to previously unimaginable increases in productivity levels, but also put some strain on social systems and contributed to the expansion of unsustainable social inequalities that slowly led to economic slowdown and political instability across Europe (Hobsbawm, 1962). Responses to overaccumulation of capital and demands for political and social change included the expansion of a mix of voluntary and state initiatives in education (but also in housing, health, etc.), which helped to address some of the existing inequalities and eventually contributed to overcoming the productivity crisis.

In Britain, child labour and the lack of funding put pressure on the existing charity schools (Carpentier, 2003; Sanderson, 1999) with a significant long-term social and economic cost, and it is noticeable that the economic downturn coincided with the vote of the first annual central grant to elementary schools in 1833. The grant provided regular public funding to existing voluntary schools, which were, until then, funded by donations and fees. That same year, Parliament voted in the Factory Act, which banned child labour. Private attempts to recycle abundant capital for future profit included donations to schools, as well as traditional universities, and contributions to the vocationally orientated mechanics' institutes (Sanderson, 1972).

Similar countercyclical developments took place in France. The 1833 Loi Guizot made it compulsory for communes of more than 500 people to fund a primary school for boys. Partial gratuity and an obligation for districts to run a teacher training college were also introduced by this law. In 1841, work was banned for children younger than 8. A new legislation in 1851 ensured that children younger than 14 and those between 14 and 16 worked no more than 10 and 12 hours a day, respectively (Heywood, 1998).

These legal and financial educational responses to economic problems and social and political unrest have laid the basis for the development of a public education system (financed by overaccumulated capital), preparing for a longer-term qualitative transformation of the productive system. Bringing the children out of the factory and into the classroom would be crucial in developing the next phase of growth in both countries.

The second Kondratiev cycle (1850s–1890s): the Long Depression and the drive to free and compulsory elementary education

The upturn of the second Kondratiev cycle (1850–1873) was a prosperous phase for both countries, even representing the apogee of British capitalism. However, once profitability was restored, the growth model soon returned to its tendency to favour physical capital over human investment. In Britain, this is symbolized by the introduction of the 1862 revised code, a system of payment by results seeking to increase efficiency through inspection (Aldrich, 2006, p. 60). However, it has been questioned whether this new system led to a slowdown in funding rather than an increase in quality (Carpentier, 2003; Marcham, 1981; Morris, 1977). In France, the return of economic growth also led to a slowdown in public funding despite mixed signals sent by legislative reforms. In 1850, the Loi Falloux proclaimed the freedom of teaching and sought to drive an expansion of religious schools (which could obtain grants from the state). It suppressed the obligation to fund higher elementary schools. However, it obliged every commune of more than 800 people to run a school for girls.

The potential long-term social and economic costs of this limited funding effort – during this era of prosperity – were foreseen by some contemporaries. For example, Forster introduced into Parliament his ambitious 1870 Elementary Education Act as a way of countering the catching up by German and US competitors and the potential loss of British industrial supremacy. However, the economic conditions leading to such change had yet to be met.

It was during the depressive phase of the second Kondratiev cycle (1873–1895), known as the Long Depression, that the conditions to properly resource the implementation of the Forster Act gradually emerged. Figure 5.3 shows that the major economic and political turbulences following the financial crash of 1873 were contemporaneous with a countercyclical increase of public funding to voluntary schools and new schools established by local authorities in order to fill the gap. Once again, the need to address an overaccumulation of capital combined with a stagnating productivity required social transformations, including in education. The rise in public funding drove compulsory (1880) and free (1891) elementary education and ensured that children effectively moved from the factory to the school. Countercyclical developments also include the 1889 Technical Instruction Act, funded by whisky money and local

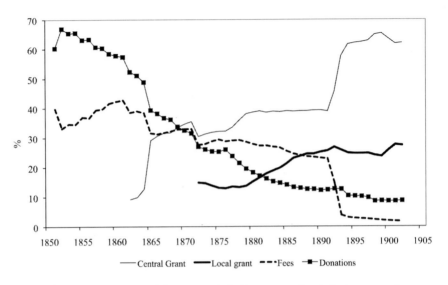

Figure 5.3 Income structure of the state-aided elementary schools (voluntary and state schools), England and Wales, 1851–1902.

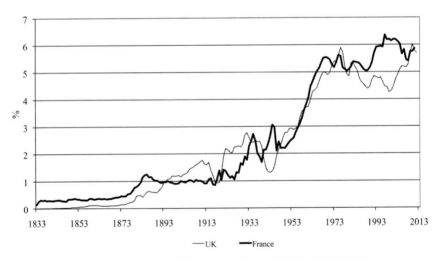

Figure 5.4 Public expenditure on education as a share of GDP, 1833–2012.

taxation. The Long Depression was also a turning point for philanthropy in higher education with the creation of the civic universities. Moreover, many higher education institutions in difficult financial situations benefited from the first annual treasury grant to university colleges, voted for in 1889 (Shinn, 1980). Importantly, these trends suggest that countercyclical public funding operated as an addition to, rather than a substitute for, private resources (Carpentier, 2010; 2012).

The Long Depression was also a key era for the development of French education (Fontvieille, 1990). In 1874, free schools were instituted and legislation that bans work for children younger than 12 was introduced. In 1881–1882, the Lois Ferry were a landmark in defining the three principles of the republican school, namely free, compulsory and secular primary education (Prost, 1970). French higher education benefited from an increase in state funding from 1875 to 1890, coinciding with the creation of several new universities (Verger, 1984, p. 329). These countercyclical educational developments contributed to the dynamics of the second phase of industrialization that was about to unfold in the next cycle.

The third Kondratiev cycle (1890s–1940s): the Great Depression and the shift beyond elementary education

The strength of the economic upturn of the third Kondratiev cycle (1895–1914) has been much debated (Solomou, 1987). These debates focused on the ways in which the UK emerged from the Great Depression and the impact on its relatively unsuccessful transition towards the second Industrial Revolution compared to competitors such as the United States and Germany. Some authors have blamed the lack of investment in education (Carpentier, 2003; Sanderson, 1999), while others have argued that the intrusion of the state destabilized an efficient private market of education and harmed growth (West, 1975). The variations in the degree of countercyclical response to the economic crisis might contribute to an explanation of the differences in the pace of expansion of public educational systems between countries. On the one hand, Figures 5.1 and 5.4 show that the countercyclical increase of public funding over the Long Depression led the UK to catch up with the level of financial effort of France and other competing countries. On the other hand, one could argue that the delay in constructing a formal educational system might have been detrimental to the capacity of the UK to adapt to the more sophisticated second Industrial Revolution at the end of the nineteenth century (Carpentier, 2006a). This economic interpretation – in conjunction with others, such as the idea that the construction of the nation state and social cohesion were more urgent in Germany, the United States and France than in the UK (Green, 1990) – can explain the differentials in development between public educational systems and their impact on the processes of catching up between countries (Carpentier, 2006a). These interpretations challenge the view that the intrusion of the state after the 1870 Education Act harmed the economic position of Britain (West, 1975). On the contrary, they suggest that public education might be considered as a response to the British relative decline rather than its cause (Carpentier, 2003).

Despite differences in rates of growth in the upturn of 1895–1914, the early years of the twentieth century did witness some economic recovery with the indicators of accumulation, price and interest rates back on track. However, the growth regime of the second Industrial Revolution slowly reverted to the usual preference for physical capital over human capital. The period can be characterized by major structural changes in education in both countries, albeit with a rather timid increase of funding. Figure 5.4 shows that education expenditure in reference to GDP rose only from 1.2 per cent in 1897 to 1.6 per cent in 1913 in the UK and remained stable in France.

On the contrary, Figure 5.1 shows that the economic downturn of the third Kondratiev cycle, which lasted from the powerful 1920–1921 crisis to the well-documented Great Depression that followed the 1929 crash, did lead to an overall increase of public funding in education (its share of GDP rising from 0.94 per cent to 2.46 per cent in the UK and from 1.38 per cent to 1.88 per cent in France). This was despite the prevalence of an anti-public spending discourse and tough fiscal lines expressed in the Geddes Committee in 1921 and the 1931 May Report in the UK. Indeed, a closer look at the figures suggests that the impact on funding was not as strong and sustained as suggested by the policy rhetoric. Although cuts were implemented in education, they only briefly affected the trends of expenditure. Over the whole period, spending remained high with a particularly important expansion of secondary education in both countries (Carpentier, 2006a). In France, the 1919 Loi Astier defined the organization of technical education. Public involvement in higher education also grew with the creation of the University Grants Committee in the UK. Financial means remain modest, but the share of GDP devoted to higher education increased from 0.0611 per cent in 1919 to 0.12 per cent in 1938 in both countries. Still, beyond financial support, the interwar era was clearly a crucial time for the construction of the public administration of higher education and a new structure of funding that would prepare for future expansion.

Thus, overall, the interwar years were contemporaneous with an increase in the level of educational funding combined with a change in its structure. Countercyclical public funding contributed to the consolidation of the elementary school system and significant increases in spending at secondary and higher education levels. With the powerful social, cultural and political changes provoked by the Great Depression and the Second World War, the stage was set for the substantial transformations revealed by the transition to procyclical growth of public educational systems after 1945. The next section aims to interpret the origins and consequences of this synchronization between the fluctuations of the economy and those of public expenditure on education.

The fourth Kondratiev cycle (1950s–?): the reversal of the link between education and the economy and the transformed relationship between crisis and austerity

Figure 5.2 reveals that, unlike its predecessors, the fourth Kondratiev cycle recorded high rates of growth of public funding in education during the economic upturn (1945–1973) and slower rates of growth during the economic downturn (1973–?). This shift from a countercyclical to procyclical trends in public funding in education is interpreted as part of a broader transformation of the relationship between economic and human developments after the Second World War. A new productivity regime – depending on the expansion rather than the control of the public social sphere – was established. This regime entered a crisis stage after the economic downturn of the mid-1970s, which revived the tensions between educational and economic systems that are ongoing.

The procyclical expansion of educational systems as a driver of the postwar growth regime (1945–1973)

The procyclical expansion of public funding in education (and other social activities) during the economic upturn of the fourth Kondratiev cycle (1945–1973) led to the assumption that education became a driver of growth rather than a corrector of crisis. This represented a dramatic departure from the productivity model born out of the first Industrial Revolution in the sense that growth became driven by the qualitative development of productive forces rather than the reduction of their cost. At the heart of this historical shift is the idea that the cumulative quantitative changes that operated during the preceding crises have produced a qualitative transformation of the system (Michel, 1999). This major change was facilitated by the intense shocks of the Great Depression, which showed the limit of the market economy (Keynes, 1936) and the market society (Polanyi, 1944) and the necessity for state intervention to correct them. The impact of the Great Depression combined with the changes in attitudes regarding solidarity (Lowe, 1993), and a higher acceptance of taxation (Peacock and Wiseman, 1994) provoked by the Second World War created a socioeconomic context favourable to the development of a new regime of production based on a fairer redistribution of wealth. This postwar fordist regime ensured a virtuous circle between mass production and consumption (Boyer and Saillard, 2002; Jessop and Sum, 2006). In this model, productivity gains were translated into redistributive wage policies and publicly funded investment in productive social spending that, in return, increased productivity levels. For once, overaccumulation of capital seemed to be under control and productivity and consumption in fine tune.

The fordist regime has been contemporaneous with a significant expansion of educational systems after the war. Education played a key part in this new regime by contributing to the joint interests of the Keynesian consensus on public spending and the agenda of the knowledge economy. The consensus drove the increase of public expenditure on education and sustained the gradual implementation of reforms conceived during the Second World War, such as the 1944 British Education Act and the French plan Langevin-Wallon, which form the basis of the generalization of secondary education (Lowe, 1992). The procyclical expenditure drove the development of comprehensive education in England and the creation of the *collège unique* in France in the 1960s. The major expansion of higher education systems that started in the mid-1960s was also driven by increasing state funding to institutions and student financial support in both countries (Carpentier, 2006b, 2012). Increased funding, rising participation rates and improved student/staff ratios characterized this period. However, the idea of a golden age should be treated cautiously. While the opportunities to study in higher education improved overall, some barriers remained, contributing to unequal access according to social class, ethnicity and gender (Bourdieu and Passeron, 1964; Reay et al., 2005).

Overall, the procyclical growth of the public investment in productive social spending, such as education, was part of a conscious strategy of growth rather than a corrective mechanism aimed at overcoming crises, as was the case during previous cycles. However, the belief that wealth and welfare had been reconciled and that an inclusive economic growth coincided or, indeed, was driven by a relative reduction of inequalities was going to be heavily challenged by the economic storm of 1973 and the neoliberal policies that followed (Unterhalter and Carpentier, 2010).

The post-1970s downturn and the pressure on the public sphere and education (1973–?)

The virtuous circle between growth and public funding in education was broken by the downturn of the 1970s, characterized by the apparition of stagflation. This unusual combination of economic stagnation and inflation was interpreted by the opponents of Keynesian policies as the result of unsustainable wages and public spending policies. In complete opposition to the mechanisms adopted to overcome the crises of previous cycles, the neoliberal response to the 1970s' downturn was based on the idea that limitation of taxation and public spending would revive growth and employment. This time, the attempts to divert the overaccumulated capital and restore profitability did not drive the expansion of the social sphere, but rather found other channels – the financial system and new markets created by the deregulation of public services.

It is important to note that these new trends have not been created but accelerated by the contemporary form of globalization and its influence on deregulation. Although the international mobility of capital also contributed to reduce overaccumulation during previous crises, such as those of the 1870s and 1930s, the transnational financialization of the economy has been much stronger under the latest phase of globalization, which started in the 1980s. This has favoured the export of underused capital rather than its use for the development of the social sphere at the national level. A second key change is that domestic and international pressure for lower taxation combined with the adoption of new national and global common practices, such as the GATT, which has driven a commodification of the social sphere (Robertson, 2003). This led to a reduction in public funding towards these services that became new markets and new sources of profits for underused capital. As a result, most social activities recorded a slowdown of their public funding and witnessed the re-emergence of private resources and providers.

These transformations produced two main patterns in education, which are well advanced in the UK and emerging in France. The first development is the introduction of competition and choice and a growing space given to private funding or (and) providers within the compulsory education sector (Ball, 2007; Van Zanten, 2005). The second aspect is the emergence in the UK of cost-sharing policy in higher education (Johnstone, 2004), which introduced loans and an increase in tuition fees and combined with the emergence of new private and global providers (BIS, 2011; Carpentier, 2012).

These policies have strongly impacted on the trends in public funding since the mid-1970s. Figure 5.4 shows that, despite a renewed public effort to fund education from New Labour, UK investment, as a share of GDP, remains below the pre-1970s' levels. Thus, the revival of public funding that took place after 1997 can be seen only as a countermovement to the previous slowdown that seems to be jeopardized by the re-emergence of austerity policies since the 2008 crisis. In France, the effort to fund education in the early 1990s has been weakened by strict budgets from governments in place since 2001 and, as a result, public expenditure, as a share of GDP, remains similar to its 1970s' levels. These policies raised questions about the impact of private funding and provision on equity and efficiency and whether they can be considered as substitutive or additional resources capable of raising the overall investment in education necessary to stimulate both the economy and social cohesion (Carpentier, 2012).

These questions and concerns are not futile in the sense that these trends designate the economic downturn that started in the mid-1970s as unique in the sense that, for the first time, an economic crisis led to a slower growth of public funding in education. This raises questions in relation to the origins of the post-2008 crisis and the potential solutions to it.

The post-2008 crisis: the beginning or the end of a downturn? Education, inequalities and growth

These historical changes in the public–private dimension of educational funding are important to consider when looking at the aftermath of the 2008 global economic downturn. The crisis re-uncovered key tensions between the economy and society and inspired radically different ways of seeing the relationship between public funding, wealth and welfare. Associated solutions range from imperative cuts to necessary countercyclical spending. These scenarios have, of course, different implications for education policy. Should we pause and reflect on the impact of the retreat of state funding on education? Should we move faster towards marketization of education by increasing both private funding and provision?

Is public funding part of the problem or the solution?

Scenario 1 sees public expenditure as the problem behind the crisis. This corresponds to current policy that seems to have shifted most of the responsibility for the 2008 crisis on to the state rather than initial market failure. This neoliberal approach has led to previously unimaginable developments, such as the threat of countries defaulting and the current mechanisms systematically conditioning lower states' cost of borrowing on the reduction of deficit. Within this framework, the 2008 crisis stressed the need to complete the unfinished market reforms started in the 1980s, including in education.

Scenario 2 considers that the 2008 crisis brought back to the fore the contested relationship between inequality and the economy (Atkinson and Piketty, 2007; Stiglitz, 2012; Wilkinson and Pickett, 2009; Piketty, 2014). It sees the difference between production and distribution of wealth as a contributing factor in hindering growth, leading Krugman to argue that 'distribution deserves to be treated as an issue as important as growth' (2008, p. 33). Using that lens, the credit crunch can be seen as the consequence of unsustainable levels of private debt (rather than public debt) associated with new financial products that have (alongside cheap imported products) masked increasing levels of inequalities. The following restraint of credit from the banks exposed these inequalities and hampered growth. This interpretation contests the priority given to the sole reduction of deficit (to the exclusion of any other indicators) and the idea that policies aimed at reducing the deficit focus on the control (rather than efficiency) of public spending, rather than fairer taxation. Within this approach, the global economic downturn that started in 2008 might be an opportunity to address the disconnection between wealth production and redistribution and to revive public investment towards human development in order to address social issues and political unrest and to raise productivity levels.

2008: the beginning or the end of a downturn?

The lens of the Kondratiev cycle opens the possibility to consider the 2008 crisis either as the start of a new downturn or the continuation of the one started in the 1970s. For some, the return of growth in the 1990s – which coincided with the expansion of globalization, the development of new information technologies and the take-off of new emerging countries, such as India, China and more recently Brazil – represented the end of the 1970s' downturn and the beginning of the upturn of a fifth Kondratiev cycle. The 2008 crisis would therefore signify the beginning of the downturn of this fifth Kondratiev cycle.

Others have questioned the viability of the recovery from the 1980s' crisis and argued that indicators, such as productivity levels and profitability, suggest that the economic downturn of the fourth Kondratiev cycle is still unfolding (for a comprehensive discussion, see Bosserelle, 2010). The 2008 crisis would not represent the end of the boom of the 1990s but the deepening of (or possibly a conclusion to) the structural economic downturn of the 1970s. The contemporary crisis suggests that the neoliberal response to the 1970s' downturn was not efficient and that the increasing levels of private debts and the reliance on cheap imports from emergent countries could not sustain an increasingly unequal dynamic of growth indefinitely. The slowdown of the funding of the social sphere identified above can be linked to historical trends and patterns that reveal growing tensions between wealth and welfare over the last three decades. The resurgence of inequalities from the 1980s is marked by the degradation of the Gini index and increasingly diverging trends between economic and social indicators (Carpentier and Michel, 2010; Gadrey and Jany-Catrice, 2007; Michel and Vallade, 2007). Graphs represented in Figures 5.5 and 5.6 show that another key element to consider is the correlation between lower public spending and the increase of the GDP owned by top income earners since the early 1980s, especially in the UK (Atkinson and Piketty, 2007), suggesting that the growing inequalities in income were not mitigated by taxation policies.

The long-term view offers a different perspective on the contemporary discourses, practices and policies of austerity associated with scenario 1 and questions whether they could have been responsible for the absence of a resolution of the structural crisis since the 1970s. Looking at the past might lead to consideration of a shift to countercyclical policies associated with scenario 2.

It has been shown above that, during previous crises, the dynamics of the economy were revived by the development of a social infrastructure whose logic was not characterized by profit but by the use of an excess of capital in order to develop new sources of productivity. Since the 1970s, in the context of stagflation, neoliberal policies represented new strategies aimed at overcoming this kind of crisis by reducing taxation and switching back the regulation of the social infrastructure of human development to a capitalist form. The tensions between these two forms of regulation have yet to be resolved. Within such interpretation, the 2008 crisis might be seen as an opportunity to pause and reflect on the tensions between economic growth and inequalities since the 1980s and to think about the possibility of bringing back some collective

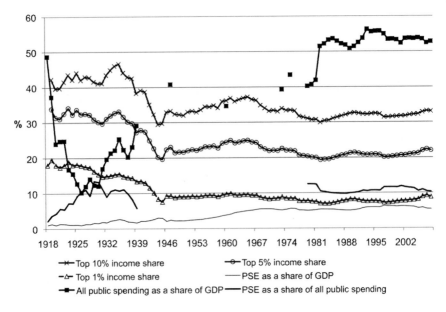

Figure 5.5 Public spending (PS), education and socioeconomic indicators in France, 1918–2008.

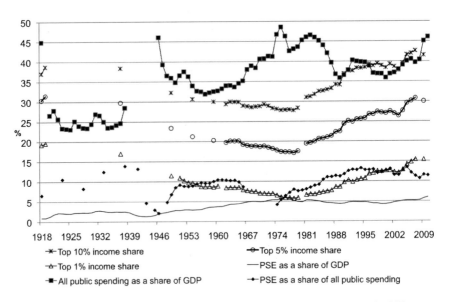

Figure 5.6 Public spending (PS), education and socioeconomic indicators in the UK, 1918–2008.[3]

(not necessarily state) forms of social spending in order to address the tensions between wealth and welfare. This shift is prompted by concerns about whether the marketization of the social sphere can resolve the overaccumulation of capital and continue to drive productivity while taking on board the wider aims of education.

A return to countercyclical education?

Educational systems have recently experienced increasing tensions between public funding and enrolment. The risk is that the austerity policies in the post-2008 era, which are aimed at increasing competition with reduced public funding, could lead to a heavily polarized system of compulsory education and reinforce existing inequalities. Currently, choice is constrained and, especially in time of austerity, only the best informed people will be able to navigate such a system (Ball, 2013; Whitty *et al.*, 1998). As far as higher education is concerned, there is a danger that cost sharing could be turned into a public/private substitution, which would lead to a transfer rather than an increase of resources with strong implications for equity (Carpentier, 2010, 2012).

Thus, there is a risk that the intensification of austerity policies in education following the 2008 crisis could further increase existing social inequalities and compromise the chance of economic recovery. Such tensions have been explored by Goldin and Katz in their historical analysis of the links between education, technology, inequality and growth in the United States (Goldin and Katz, 2008). The authors found that the historical steady and relatively egalitarian supply of education has allowed the United States to generate growth. However, they show that the setback in educational attainment since the 1980s explains the re-emergence of inequalities, prompting growing concerns about the long-term capacity of the US economy to grow and compete internationally. These trends on declining attainment and the increasing privatization and its impact on the erosion of a public good (Cohen, 2011) seem to correlate with the Kondratiev fluctuations of public expenditure on education observed in the United States (Carpentier, 2006a), which mirror those of the UK and France explored in this chapter.

These developments point at the shortcomings of the austerity policies that have been implemented since the 1970s. The analysis of the mechanisms that led to overcoming previous crises offers alternatives to current policy by making a historical case for a countercyclical policy that would reconcile political, social and economic rationales of education. This requires tackling the question of the public deficit differently, by considering not only the question of the efficiency of public spending, but also the development of fairer taxation systems. A countercyclical policy founded on these principles would ensure that the agenda of austerity does not compromise those of economic growth and equity (Carpentier, 2009, 2012).

Conclusion

The historical perspective indicates that the relationship between education and economic crisis is not as straightforward as we might think today. It shows that the successive phases of development of state education were responses rather than causes of the economic downturns that punctuated the development of the capitalist economy. Past crises have been provoked by tensions between wealth and welfare, which eventually led to an increase in social inequalities, political unrests and a decline of levels of productivity. The recoveries from economic crises prior to the Second World War were the results of transformations of the socioeconomic system, which included the transfer through taxation of unused capital to develop the activities of human development to revive growth. This included a renewed effort to fund public educational systems in order to respond to socioeconomic and technological innovations. The policy response to the crisis of the 1970s was very different in the sense that it channelled the unused capital to the financial sector rather than the public sphere and pursued an agenda of lower taxation combined with a marketization of social sectors, including education systems. The crisis that unfolded in 2008 might be the reminder that those remedies have backfired. They increased the tensions between wealth and welfare and, as a result, failed to address the productivity challenge and exacerbated the political and social issues. The post-2008 crisis, therefore, could be considered as a potential end of the 1970s' downturn, whereby the necessary structural transformations to rebalance wealth and welfare are about to take place, as they did during the previous downturns in the 1830s, 1870s and 1930s. In that sense, countercyclical public spending on education and other areas related to human development might contribute to jointly addressing social inequalities and revive economic performance.

Notes

1. Financial series are expressed in purchasing power parity in 1990 Geary-Khamis USD (PPP). PPP can be defined as a conversion rate that quantifies the amount of a country's currency necessary to buy in the market of that country the same quantity of goods and services as a dollar would in the United States. Such a tool is necessary in order to give a comparative estimate of the value of educational expenditure, eliminating differences in price levels between countries. The PPP indices series are derived from Maddison's calculation of GDP at PPP USD (Maddison, 1995, 2000) and updated (www.ggdc.net/maddison). The GDP at PPP USD was then divided by the GDP expressed in current USD to obtain the PPP index and applied to the expenditure series. After 2008, data are updated, using the OECD as a source (http://stats.oecd.org/Index.aspx?DataSetCode=PPPGDP).
2. A regression curve is the best-fitting curve drawn through a scatter-plot of two variables. It is chosen to come as close to the points as possible and thus represents the shape of the relationship between the variables (here the expenditure and the time) and the long-term trend if the series were regularly distributed. The deviations from the regression curve represent the cyclical fluctuations around the trend. Nine-year moving averages are sliding averages that smooth the data in order to ease the examination of the trend and changes.

3   Sources: On income: Alvaredo, F., Atkinson, T., Piketty, T and Saez, E. *The World Top Incomes Database*. http://g-mond.parisschoolofeconomics.eu/topincomes/. Other indicators: Carpentier (2007) updated.

References

Aldrich, R., 2006. *Lessons from History of Education. The Selected Works of Richard Aldrich*. Abingdon: Routledge.
Apple, M., 1982. *Cultural and Economic Reproduction in Education*. London: Routledge and Kegan Paul.
Atkinson, A.B. and Piketty, T., 2007. *Top Incomes over the Twentieth Century. A Contrast between European and English-Speaking Countries*. Oxford: Oxford University Press.
Ball, S.J., 2007. *Education plc: Private Sector Participation in Public Sector Education*. London: Routledge.
Ball, S.J., 2013. *The Education Debate*. Bristol: Policy Press.
BIS, 2011. *Students at the Heart of the System. The Higher Education White Paper*. Department of Business, Innovation and Skills.
Boccara, P., 1988. *Etudes sur le Capitalisme Monopoliste d'État, sa Crise et son Issue*. Paris: Editions Sociales.
Bosserelle, E., 2010. *La Crise Actuelle Apporte t-elle un Démenti aux Approches Menées en Termes de Kondratiev?* Conference: La Crise: Trois ans après, quels enseignements? Université Blaise Pascal IUFM Auvergne, Février.
Bourdieu, P. and Passeron J.C., 1964. *Les Héritiers, les Étudiants et la Culture*. Paris: Editions de Minuit.
Boyer, R. and Saillard, Y., 2002. *Regulation Theory. The State of the Art*. London: Routledge.
Carpentier, V., 2001. *Système Éducatif et Performances Économiques au Royaume-Uni: 19ème et 20ème Siècles*. Paris: L'Harmattan.
Carpentier, V., 2003. Public expenditure on education and economic growth in the UK, 1833–2000. *History of Education*, 32(1), pp. 1–15.
Carpentier, V., 2006a. Public expenditure on education and economic growth in the USA in the nineteenth and twentieth centuries in comparative perspective. *Paedagogica Historica*, 42(6), pp. 683–706.
Carpentier, V., 2006b. Funding in higher education and economic growth in France and the United Kingdom, 1921–2003. *Higher Education Management and Policy*, 18(3), pp. 1–26.
Carpentier, V., 2007. Educational policymaking: economic and historical perspectives. In: D. Crook and G. McCulloch (eds) *History, Politics and Policy Making in Education*. London: Bedford Ways Papers, pp. 30-48.
Carpentier, V., 2009. Viewpoint: the credit crunch and education: an historical perspective from the Kondratiev cycle. *London Review of Education*, 7(2), pp. 193–196.
Carpentier, V., 2010. Public-private substitution in higher education funding and Kondratiev cycles: the impacts on home and international students. In: E. Unterhalter and V. Carpentier (eds) *Global Inequalities and Higher Education*. Houndmills: Palgrave MacMillan, pp. 142–171.
Carpentier, V., 2012. Public-private substitution in higher education: has cost-sharing gone too far? *Higher Education Quarterly*, 66(4), pp. 363–390.
Carpentier, V. and Michel, S., 2010. Towards an Index of Social Infrastructure of Human Development (ISIHD). In: *Twenty Years of Human Development: The Past and The*

Future of the Human Development Index. Von Hügel Institute/UNDP/HDRO, University of Cambridge, 28–29 January.

Carpentier, V. and Unterhalter, E., 2011. Globalization, higher education, inequalities: Problems and prospects. In: R. King, S. Marginson and R. Naidoo (eds) *A Handbook on Globalization and Higher Education.* Cheltenham: Edward Elgar, pp. 148–168.

Carry, A., 1999. Le compte satellite rétrospectif de l'éducation en France: 1820–1996. *Economies et Sociétés,* Série AF(25), pp. 1–281.

Cohen, M., 2011. The national state, the local, and the growth of mass schooling: history lessons from England, France, and the United States. Paper presented at the University of Zurich Conference on Education and the State, Zurich, 17 September, unpublished (see Cohen's chapter in the present volume).

Dale, R., 1989. *The State and Education Policy.* Milton Keynes: Open University Press.

Diebolt, C., 1997. L'évolution de longue période du système éducatif Allemand XIXème et XXème siècles. *Economies et Sociétés,* Série AF(23), pp. 1–370.

Domin, J.P., 2000. Evolution et croissance de longue période du système hospitalier français: 1803–1993. *Economies et Sociétés,* Série AF(26), pp. 71–133.

Fontvieille, L., 1976. Evolution et croissance de l'état français 1815–1969. *Economies et Sociétés,* Série AF(13), pp. 1657–2149.

Fontvieille, L., 1990. Education, growth and long cycles: the case of France in the 19th and 20th centuries. In: G. Tortella (ed.) *Education and Economic Development since the Industrial Revolution.* Valencia: Generalitat Valenciana, pp. 317–335.

Freeman, C. and Louçã, F., 2001. *As Time Goes By. From the Industrial Revolutions to the Information Revolution.* Oxford: Oxford University Press.

Gadrey, J. and Jany-Catrice, F., 2007. *Les Nouveaux Indicateurs de Richesse.* Paris: La Découverte.

Galbraith, J.K., 1954. *The Great Crash, 1929.* Boston, MA: Houghton Mifflin.

Gillborn, D., 2008. *Racism and Education. Coincidence or Conspiracy?* London: Routledge.

Goldin, C. and Katz, L.F., 2008. *The Race Between Education and Technology.* Cambridge, MA: Harvard University Press.

Goodson, I., 2005. Long waves of educational reform. In: I. Goodson (ed.) *Learning, Curriculum and Life Politics. The Selected Works of Ivor F. Goodson.* Abingdon: Routledge, pp. 105–129.

Green, A., 1990. *Education and State Formation. The Rise of Education Systems in England, France and the USA.* London: Macmillan.

Hartley, D., 2010. Rhetorics of regulation in education after the global economic crisis. *Journal of Education Policy,* 25(6), pp. 785–791.

Heywood, C., 1998. *Childhood in Nineteenth-Century France. Work, Health and Education among the Classes Populaires.* Cambridge: Cambridge University Press.

Hobsbawm, E.J., 1962. *The Age of Revolution.* London: Abacus.

Hobsbawm, E.J., 1997. *On History.* London: Abacus.

Jessop, B. and Sum, N.L., 2006. *Beyond the Regulation Approach.* Cheltenham: Edward Elgar.

Johnstone, B., 2004. The economics and politics of cost sharing in higher education: comparative perspectives. *Economics of Education Review,* 23(4), pp. 403–410.

Keynes, J.M., 1936. *The General Theory of Interest, Employment and Money.* London: Macmillan.

Krugman, P., 2008. Inequality and redistribution. In: N. Serra and J.E. Stiglitz (eds) *The Washington Consensus Reconsidered*. New York: Oxford University Press, pp. 31–41.
Loucã, F. and Reijnders, J., 1999. *The Foundations of Long Wave Theory*. Cheltenham: Edward Elgar.
Lowe, R., 1992. *Education and the Second World War*. London: Falmer.
Lowe, R., 1993. *The Welfare State in Britain since 1945*. Houndmills: Macmillan.
McCulloch, G., 2011. *The Struggle for the History of Education*. Abingdon: Routledge.
Maddison, A., 1995. *Monitoring the World Economy 1820–1992*. Paris: OECD.
Maddison, A., 2000. *The World Economy: A Millennial Perspective*. Paris: OECD.
Marcham, A.J., 1981. The Revised Code of Education, 1862: reinterpretations and misinterpretations. *History of Education*, 10(2), pp. 81–89.
Marczewski, J., 1961. Histoire quantitative, buts et méthodes. *Cahiers de l'Institut de Sciences Économiques Appliquées*, Série AF(15), pp. 3–54.
Marx, K., 1894. *Capital, vol. 1*. London: Laurence and Wishart, 1970.
Michel, S., 1999. *Education et Croissance Économique en Longue Période*. Paris: L'Harmattan.
Michel, S. and Vallade, D., 2007. Une Analyse de long terme des dépenses sociales. *Revue de la Régulation*, 1, pp. 1–32.
Milonakis, D. and Fine, B., 2009. *From Political Economy to Economics: Method, the Social and the Historical in the Evolution of Economic Theory*. London: Routledge.
Morris, N., 1977. Public expenditure on education in the 1860s. *Oxford Review of Education*, 3(1), pp. 3–19.
Peacock, A.T. and Wiseman, J., 1994. *The Growth of Public Expenditure in the United Kingdom*. London: Oxford University Press.
Perez, C., 2002. *Technological Revolutions and Financial Capital: The Dynamics of Bubbles and Golden Ages*. Cheltenham: Edward Elgar.
Piketty, T., 2014. *Capital in the 21st Century*. Cambridge, MA: Harvard University Press.
Polanyi, K. 1944. *The Great Transformation: The Political and Economic Origins of Our Time*. Boston, MA: Beacon Press.
Prost, A., 1970. *L'Enseignement en France, 1800–1967*. Paris: Armand Colin.
Reay, D., David, M. and Ball, S., 2005. *Degrees of Choice: Class, Race, Gender and Higher Education*. Stoke-on-Trent: Trentham Books.
Reimat, A., 2000. Histoire quantitative de la prise en charge de la vieillesse en France, XIXème–XXème siècles: assistance et prévoyance. *Economies et Sociétés*, Série AF(27), pp. 7–114.
Robertson, S., 2003. WTO/GATS and the global education services industry. *Globalisation, Societies and Education*, 1(3), pp. 259–266.
Sanderson, M., 1972. *The Universities and British Industry 1850–1970*. London: Routledge and Kegan Paul.
Sanderson, M., 1999. *Education and Economic Decline in Britain, 1870 to the 1990s*. Cambridge: Cambridge University Press.
Shinn, C.H., 1980. The beginnings of the University Grants Committee. *History of Education*, 9(3), pp. 233–243.
Simon, B., 1960. *Studies in the History of Education (1780–1870)*. London: Lawrence and Wishart.
Solomou, S., 1987. *Phases of Economic Growth, 1850–1973, Kondratieff Waves and Kuznets Swings*. Cambridge: Cambridge University Press.

Stiglitz, J., 2012. *The Price of Inequality: How Today's Divided Society Endangers Our Future*. New York: WW Norton.

Unterhalter, E. and Carpentier, V., 2010. *Global Inequalities and Higher Education. Whose Interests Are We Serving?* Houndmills: Palgrave Macmillan.

Van Zanten, A., 2005. New modes of reproducing social inequality in education: the changing roles of parents, teachers, schools and educational policies. *European Education Research Journal*, 4(3), pp. 155–169.

Verger, J., 1984. *Histoires des Universités en France*. Toulouse: Bibliothèque Historique Privat.

West, E.G., 1975. Educational slowdown and public intervention in nineteenth century England: a study on the economics of bureaucracy. *Explorations in Economic History*, 12(1), pp. 61–87.

Whitty, G., Power, S. and Halpin, D., 1998. *Devolution and Choice in Education: The School, the State and the Market*. Buckingham: Open University Press.

Wilkinson, R. and Pickett, K., 2009. *The Spirit Level*. London: Allen Lane.

Part 4

Educational administration

Chapter 6

To write like a bureaucrat
Educational administration as a cultural phenomenon

Michael Geiss

Talking about bureaucrats usually includes a mention of narrow-mindedness, inefficiency or formalism. There are few groups of people in cultural history more readily associated with a certain fixed set of characteristics and procedures. The bureaucrat is thought to be part of a hierarchy with certain competences, methods and chains of command. His medium is the written word. He uses texts to communicate with the world outside his office.[1]

To the educationalist, bureaucracy often appears as a serious threat. Laments about an all-powerful administrative apparatus are an intrinsic part of his rhetorical inventory.[2] They are found in teachers' colleges, educational programmes or the pedagogical press. Administrators and their directives are regarded as threatening to smother the realities of teaching. The freedom of the teacher, according to this well-established litany, is diametrically opposed to the educational bureaucracy's desire for standardization.[3]

However, discussions on the polarity of bureaucratic and pedagogical actions have made their way into the academic realm. There are many examples of socio-academic literature distinguishing analytically between two forms of action that govern the educational sphere.[4] The dualism can also be found in the historiography of education. Here, the national standardization of education is regarded as a hostile embrace, unduly limiting the teacher's initial freedoms.[5] This criticism, still applicable today, has thus been back-projected on to history, which, in turn, serves to validate it.

Bureaucracy, based on writing and therefore always distanced, is the polar opposite of the comforting rhetoric that aims at direct educational interaction.[6] However, scepticism and opposition to a school system determined by bureaucracy are to be found in progressive, as well as in Catholic, radical democratic, neoliberal and conservative writings. Administration always seems to be a foreign object, threatening intrinsic coherences.[7]

State officials write. Their principal means of communication is the ministerial letter, their memories are composed of minutes and notes, and their main references are laws and decrees (Luhmann, 1983). The highly standardized letter is the symbol of bureaucratic logic. It is a prime example to symbolize a perceived idiosyncratic order of everyday administration, and to explore its distance from educational realities.

It cannot be denied that this point of view captures parts of the administrative reality. Anybody who has worked in a state school or a university will be familiar with absurd demands of the administration that can only be explained by taking into account its *specific code*. Applied to the history of education, however, the dualism of education and administration suffers from the sharp lines it draws. It captures too much of reality and, given that it enables definite classifications, it removes important ambivalences and inaccuracies.[8]

I would like to illustrate this problem by using an example of the bureaucrat as a writer. My case study examines the Grand Duchy of Baden, one of the smaller southern states of the German Reich in the nineteenth century. Baden was a monarchy that adopted a constitution early on (Hug, 1998). From 1860 onwards, a string of reforms moved the competences within the education system away from the churches towards newly installed national authorities.

In order to understand the relationship of administration and education in the second half of the nineteenth century, it is important to recall the manifold writing activities undertaken by the school functionaries of Baden. Composing a ministerial letter was only one form of bureaucratic writing, even though it constituted an important part of administrative reality. Higher-level functionaries, however, also practised other forms of text production. They wrote scientific papers, edited the pedagogical classics and published on questions of teaching or psychology in the prospering pedagogical press. They reflected on the theoretical relationship of education and state and attacked the continuing demands of the church. Some school functionaries excelled in composing textbooks or editing and commenting on collections of school laws. School inspectors gave practical lectures, which were then published in the organized teachers' magazines. One even propagated his own model for his town's organization of schools.

Writing bureaucrats: legitimizing a state-controlled education system

In order to understand the manifold activities of the administrators of Baden, it is important to consider the specific communicational situation in the second half of the nineteenth century, that is, the potential circle of recipients. *Teachers* were the real winners of the national standardization of the education system and, as such, often the recipients of the writings of members of the educational bureaucracy.

The profession's eventual assumption under the regulations of the civil service law in 1892 had been preceded by many small steps towards an improvement of the professional and financial situation of teachers (Kimmelmann, 1926; Wunder, 1993, 2000). By the beginning of the 1860s, teachers had every reason to pin their hopes for improvements of their legal and financial situation on the new, by now liberal, government and its administration (Gall, 1968).

The new educational administration could therefore rely on the support of the organized teachers.[9] They propagated and supported changes in the supervision and administration of elementary schools, enthusiastically embraced the offer of cooperation that had been extended early on during the reforms, discussed the respective steps of those reforms in an exhaustive and mostly benevolent manner and widened the discursive resonant space through meetings and publications. The state aimed to include teachers in their processes, albeit without giving them a permanent right to collaborate on a higher level of administration.[10]

The teachers thus ensured the local presence of the state's objectives. Without them, those objectives had little chance of being implemented, as the state's power did not reach that far. After the reforms, the clergy no longer acted as local representatives of the supervisory structure. A fierce *Kulturkampf* in the 1860s and 1870s had curtailed the educational authorities of the church in Baden.[11] In the Catholic municipalities, priests initially refused to enter the new local school boards. Occasionally it was not even possible to organize valid elections (Becker, 1973; Maier, 2000). The inclusion of teachers by the state authorities was thus a part of a strategy to stabilize the new supervisory structures.

However, it wouldn't be possible to fully understand the emergence of Baden's state-controlled education systems under a central administration, partly bureaucratically organized inspectorates and a wide-reaching enforcement of pedagogical standards in the course of the nineteenth century without including a new type of *intellectual doer* as bearer and designer of these transformational processes into the analysis. These 'doers' – the term coined by Peter Becker and Jeroen Dekker (2002) – who were not just intellectuals but interested and involved in the actual implementation of programmes, could be found both within and outside national institutions, and in universities as well as authorities (see also Tenorth, 2003). Supported by a more or less institutionalized transnational technical discourse (see Fuchs, 2004; Leonards and Randeraad 2010) and equipped with detailed knowledge of the local conditions, they were often school functionaries themselves and, as such, cared about the practical implementations of their pedagogical concepts.

The first important position to be filled in the newly organized educational administration in Baden was that of head of the highest school authority. The choice fell upon Karl Knies, who was indeed an intellectual *doer*, but had neither qualified for the role of a functionary by means of a legal education nor proven himself to be an expert on education in his publications. Up to the point of his coming into office, Knies's dealings with educational matters had merely included the draft for a polytechnic school in Kassel (1849) and a few years of practical experience as a teacher in a cantonal school in Schaffhausen, which he had only taken because he had been denied an academic career after 1849.[12] In 1853, he still regarded the *railway* as a 'new, great elementary school' (Knies, 1853, p. 119), which would blur all class distinctions, unite the nation and secure peace and progress forever.

Only a year after the establishment of the State Board of Education, Knies did, however, publish forty-four theses concerning the reform of the educational system in Baden, which would remain one of the central documents of the discussions in educational policies over the following fifteen years. In addition to his proposals of a reduction in religious instruction and the establishment of interdenominational schools, it was his view on school supervision that caused controversial discussions. Knies postulated local school boards, separated by religious denomination, whose number of elected members was to exceed that of the appointed ones. He also proposed full-time district school inspectors.

With his calls for a local school board elected by the local public, Knies fell into line with positions criticizing bureaucracy, which had been widely discussed during the eve of the 1848 revolution and had found its way into national administration in 1863 (Krosigk, 2010). At the same time, the theses also included a strictly bureaucratic element in the shape of the full-time district school inspector, which diametrically opposed the pre-revolutionary ideas of self-government.

The forty-four theses were referred for discussion to a committee of teachers. They were published in the professional organ of the organized teachers, which also documented the discussions of the advisory council in the following issues.[13] Following their publication, the theses were initially not received in view of their bureaucratic (district school inspectors) or their democratic elements (local school boards), but rather as an anticlerical pamphlet that radically curtailed the churches' right to participate in matters of education. In 1864, most of the aspects of Knies's theses were implemented by law.

When Ernst von Sallwürk, at only 38 years of age, was elected into the State Board of Education in 1877, he held credentials of a different kind. It is hard to imagine a person in the second half of the nineteenth century with a wider pedagogical expertise than Sallwürk's. He had practical experience as a high school teacher as well as in the fields of teacher training and school administration, was well read in international didactical literature and published about the history of education. During his time as a school functionary, Sallwürk translated, edited and commented on Rousseau's *Emile* (1876–1878) and published a German edition of John Locke's *Some Thoughts Concerning Education* (1883), along with a string of didactical and pedagogical essays in academic papers. Between 1893 and 1907, Sallwürk worked as a lecturer at the technical university in Karlsruhe, where he read history of education and supervised tutorials for academically trained teachers (Dauer, 1919). A recent bibliography lists 138 published titles that can be attributed to Ernst von Sallwürk.[14]

Academic reasoning about education was never an end in itself for Sallwürk, but rather fulfilled a specific function for the newly organized and, by now, state-controlled education system. In an essay published in 1893, he explained the current situation of educational discourse to an English-speaking audience as being 'in a very peculiar position'. It had spent the first half of the nineteenth century developing theories on how to establish a strong education system, and now, when it was essential to actually build one, nobody wanted to consider those theories: 'no one cares to hear what it has to say' (Sallwürk, 1893a, p. 313). Political and religious interests, as well as pressing practical problems, were dominating all educational matters.

While Karl Knies's arguments were conceptual ones and, for him, a state-regulated organization was only one of many possible forms of supervising the education system, Sallwürk had no doubts that a state-controlled education system was a necessity that could not only be justified historically, but also permeated theoretically. According to him, the state could only do justice to its role as a cultural force by monopolizing all questions of education. Even religious education could not, at the highest level of authority, be left to the church. The supervision of the entire education system by the state was, according to Sallwürk, a sort of 'pedagogical custody' (1893b, p. 48).

In the second half of the nineteenth century, it was by no means clear if and how a state-controlled education system could deliver on the promise of providing education for a steadily and incalculably growing population.[15] Apart from this clearly described goal, the state's pedagogical orientation had another, somewhat hidden, function. It provided a normative foundation for the newly created educational administration and thus guaranteed its survival. Unlike the national interest, which could be applied to all parts of government, the pedagogical orientation of the educational administration provided legitimation, sustainability and autonomy for this very administration. Sallwürk's demands for the separation of the 'general governmental mechanism', that is, the state administration, from the actual administration of education was the foundation for steady growth, increasing differentiation and the separation of education and its controlling instances from the administration of other aspects of society.

Educational administrators: talking to an expert audience

Theoretical deliberations on the relationship between education and the state, as openly discussed by some high-level school functionaries, only constituted a small part of their publications. Even Sallwürk published much more on questions of psychology, didactics or the pedagogical classics than on the theories of nationalized education. Other, often high-ranking, members of the State Board of Education did not address a wider audience but remained close to the everyday business of the administration in their writings: August Joos, who headed the department from 1881 to 1895, initiated and published a collection of Baden's school laws and decrees that is still being used by historians of education.

Some administrators were more ambitious, yet they still remained unknown outside Baden. Georg Peter Weygoldt, a farmer's son who had initially completed teacher training and afterwards studied widely and received a doctorate, had worked his way up from being a district school inspector to becoming a member of the State Board of Education. He published works on Platonic philosophy and the relationship between Darwinism and religion, as well as subjects such as musical instruction and the problem of teacher shortages. Weygoldt was well liked among teachers and became a distinguished member of the teachers' association of Baden.[16]

However, even those who did not belong to the highest school authority, and instead worked as district school inspectors over long periods of time, distinguished themselves through theoretical and didactical publications. Ferdinand Leutz, who had initially studied theology and philology, worked as director of a grammar school before taking on the role of head of the district school inspectorate in Heidelberg. He published on the psychology of learning and children's psychology, developed guides for teachers and researched on the history of education. His publications appeared in the annual reports of the teachers' training college in Karlsruhe, to whose directorate he belonged.

The publications of Anton Sickinger, who worked as a city school inspector in Mannheim from 1895 onwards, were aimed directly at changing the organization of the elementary schools. Sickinger developed a model that responded to the different aptitudes of pupils with a corresponding differentiation of the school structure. Mannheim was one of the few industrially prosperous cities in a predominantly rural state. In a memorandum, Sickinger demonstrated, aided by statistical information, that, although capable, many pupils would not successfully complete elementary school. In 1901, his model for a differentiation into standard and remedial classes was adopted with slight modifications by the city council and was later applied in other cities and countries. Sickinger himself was an expert propagator of his ideas. He strove to get the support of well-known personalities, and his programmatic writings attracted attention in professional journals as well as the daily press (Niess, 1997). He introduced his own system, known as the 'Mannheim School System', in a pedagogical encyclopedia, talking about himself in the third person and paraphrasing his own publications on the subject. Finally, he listed 230 essays as relevant publications at the end of the entry.[17]

Just as certain administrators had their say about didactical, psychological or philosophical matters, teachers showed a profound understanding of administrative ideas and advocated their own concepts. Even before Knies published his forty-four theses, there had been several proposals from teachers on how to restructure the educational administration. Those had come very close to the government's ideas. In this regard, teachers were able to draw upon concepts that had been discussed earlier.[18] A special memorandum painted a bleak picture of the existing conditions in the education system and confirmed the need for a reform of the supervisory structures from the teachers' point of view. It argued that a perfidious pervasion of both the professional and the private sphere in the shape of a 'double observation' served to constantly confront teachers with their poor standing. They could neither teach freely, according to their beliefs and based on their skills, nor could they develop freely in their personal lives or choose their private company. They had to give account of their alcohol consumption and even their intellectual activities outside the school.[19]

Questions of supervision retreated into the background after the implementation of the supervisory law in 1864 and a comprehensive Education Act in 1868. It was the call for higher wages and the inclusion into the civil service that now became the main focus of the liberal teachers. Meanwhile, the teachers' right to increased participation in school matters was still widely discussed in the German-speaking surroundings. The second half of the nineteenth century saw an extensive journalistic output on questions of school administration and teachers' selfgovernance that, early in the twentieth century, led the *Allgemeine Deutsche Lehrerzeitung* to publish a compilation of fifty characteristic texts that had made significant contributions to the conceptual debate about these issues.[20] The self-administration of teachers was thought to be partly organized according to the democratic concept of self-government, although it did not mean a democratic control by the general public, but rather a professionalization of the supervisory personnel. During the last decades of the nineteenth century, the demands for a truly free school under a consistent peer control, without any interference from pedagogically unqualified staff, found an increasingly receptive audience, once again in Baden.[21]

Everyday practices: communication in hierarchies

But what about the actual administrative work? First, we need to distinguish the different levels on which written communication was carried out. Administrative communication in Baden rarely took place between equal players. For the most part, the correspondence mirrors the hierarchical characteristics defined by public authorities or officials. Thus, the highest authority wrote to the appropriate ministry, and the district school inspector wrote to his superior central school authority or the local school boards in his department. The different positions in the administrative structure found their expression in differing writing styles. To a higher administrative level, issues had to be justified, whereas downwards, they were directed. This became the norm for administrative communication, a fact that can also be demonstrated empirically.

This hierarchical structure was, however, only one avenue for written encounters. When it came to organizationally demanding changes, authorities were often forced to canvass for the support of their subordinates. The construction or extension of school buildings, for instance, had to be paid for by the municipalities.[22] Those were adept at ignoring, reinterpreting or delaying urgent requests.[23] In such cases, the superior authorities would, apart from threatening with sanctions, try to convince the councils by using arguments of hygiene or pedagogy, or even quoting statistics that documented the projected number of pupils in the district. They would use protocols of district visits or expert opinions to illustrate their demands. They also had the option of offering long-term government loans to help councils with the financing of projects.[24]

When Baden attempted an organizational democratization of the education system in the twelve years from 1864 onwards, it was essential to ensure the cooperation of the members of the local school boards. As some of the board members were elected, they had to keep protocols of their meetings, and democratic majority decisions had to be accepted by the defeated minority. This was not always the case, and the superior authorities often had to remind the local school boards to adhere to the democratic process. It is this transitory introduction of democratically legitimized authorities that helps us to appreciate the complexity of administrative communication: if the functioning of procedures was achieved by means of persuasion and cooperation, valid elections were then almost forced after big parts of the Catholic population had abstained (Geiss, 2011).

The higher the level of administration, the more sophisticated the style of communication became. In 1862, the State Board of Education was set up as a central entity, which inevitably marked the end of the old denominational structures of the education system. However, since it was subordinate to the ministry of the interior, decisions had to be made there, although the school board was still in charge of determining the daily organization of the education system.

Over time, the competences and abilities of the members of the central authority grew. Its distinctly pedagogical orientation took shape not only in the amount of decrees that seemed almost impossible to address by the turn of the century. Teachers were increasingly pressing for an administration that took into account the actual requirements of the schools – a demand that seemed to be fulfilled in 1911, when the authority became a ministry in its own right.

The teachers demanded an administrative communication less focused on bureaucratic principles and better equipped to cope with the educational realities. These demands were met with the appointment of pedagogically skilled personnel. In particular, Sallwürk's rise through the ranks was applauded in this context. At the beginning of the twentieth century, the teachers' demands began to focus on the establishment of an independent Ministry of Education. This was seen as the way to consistently and finally transform the entire education system in the sense of a pedagogical supervisory control. Discussions in the Second Chamber on the question of homogenization of the educational administration under a specialized management began in 1902[25] and were taken up again over the following years. In 1911, Baden provided a specialized ministry to take into account the state's diverse educational landscape with its many decrees and the resulting communication effort.

Administrative overacting: the case of school inspector Bopp

District school boards were bureaucratic institutions, albeit staffed with pedagogically trained personnel. For the elementary school teachers, those boards signified the first step towards a genuine peer control. District school inspectors, however, took great care to distance themselves from teachers. They emphasized the distinctiveness of their office, which demanded a particular double qualification of pedagogical knowledge and administrative skills.

In the teachers' press, criticism of bureaucracy was seldom voiced, or was voiced indirectly through repeated publication of articles that dealt with examples of educational administration outside Baden. Still, even such cautious criticism shows that teachers did not have a universally positive regard for the work of the district school inspectors. In order not to jeopardize the continuing improvement of their financial situation and the possible inclusion into the civil service, teachers' organizations remained cautious in their publications and mostly loyal towards their employers.

Meanwhile, accusations of bureaucratism were raised in the Second Chamber of the state parliament of Baden, which sparked a debate questioning the entire organization of the educational administration. In late April of 1902, the State Board of Education was publicly attacked and accused of bureaucracy. Minister of Justice Dusch, who was in direct command of the authority, repudiated the allegations.[26]

The subject remained virulent in parliamentary debate. A few days later the main focus of the criticism was not the State Board of Education, but rather Pius Bopp, one of the eighteen district school inspectors, who was directly attacked and openly criticized for his bureaucratic behaviour. In the presence of the Minister of Justice and the director of the State Board of Education, one member of the parliament claimed that Bopp had caned pupils and verbally abused teachers during a school inspection. Yet another member of parliament believed Bopp to have shown a 'pathological moment'.[27]

The subject of such debates, however, was not only the misconduct of a single civil servant. It was the entire administrative system that was up for discussion. Karl Heimburger, an educationalist and progressive member of the Second Chamber, took the criticism to another level: for him, the improper behaviour of district school inspectors towards teachers was by no means an exception and deserved a stern reprimand, as indicated by this statement: 'Teachers should not be burdened with bureaucratic matters. If there is one institution that cannot tolerate bureaucratism, it is the schools.'[28]

The teachers, however, did not voice their complaints publicly, instead choosing to write letters to the director of the highest school authority and the responsible minister. They depicted the district school inspectors as inconsiderate bureaucrats browbeating teachers with absurd demands. The openly discredited inspector Bopp was ridiculed in those letters, and depicted as an incompetent inspector and ill-mannered man who smoked during school prayers and exams. This was presented as a well-known fact and by no means an isolated case.[29]

The Bopp case serves to illustrate the fact that such instances of bureaucratic self-authorization among district school inspectors were based on real events, rather than just allegations for political purposes. In the files of the State Board of Education is a circular sent by district school inspector Bopp to the local school boards within his jurisdiction in early 1902. It contains detailed demands regarding the 'Advancement and safeguarding of the correspondence between teachers, local school boards and the district school board.' Bopp commented on the filing of documents and the drawing up of letters and lists, and defined appeal stages and chains of command.[30]

Ever since the implementation of inspectorates, district school inspectors had wanted to be able to issue their own decrees. In April 1865, the State Board of Education reacted to a suggestion by one of the district school inspectors proposing to publish their proclamations to local school boards and elementary school teachers in the official bulletins of the district authorities. However, this would have meant coercing the publishers of those papers to distribute free copies to all local school authorities, as purchasing copies for every teacher and every local school board was considered too expensive. But directives by the district school boards seemed to happen 'very seldom and irregularly' and were thought to be distributed by one-off prints or circulars.[31] Nonetheless, the possibility to publish their directives was still considered a necessity by the district school inspectors.

The State Board of Education, sensing danger for the good relations between the authorities and elementary school teachers, reacted sympathetically to the 'degree of resentment' that the many, often useless new demands in Bopp's circular had caused. Thus, Bopp was reminded that his business conduct was meant to show a 'finer tact and understanding for schools, pupils and teachers'. Subsequently, the separate points of the circular were subjected to a detailed examination by the State Board of Education, which then voiced its criticism in detail and reminded him to stay sympathetic in his dealings with teachers and pupils.[32]

Even though the teachers were restrained in their communiqués, the letters to the State Board of Education and the Ministry of Justice show that district school boards were, indeed, seen as bureaucratic. They also serve to illustrate how fragile the construction of the state-controlled educational administration as a genuinely pedagogical inspectorate was. Within a short period of time, the case of an administratively overambitious district school inspector managed to mobilize the ministry, the State Board of Education, the district school boards, the political public and the teachers alike.

Facing educational bureaucracy

In conclusion, it is evident that a bureaucratic administration did exist and was based on formal methods, strictly following the letter of the law that was applied to the field of education. This fact needs to be considered in any historical reconstruction of the relationship between education and the state in the nineteenth century.

An analysis that focuses only on the powerful top-down communication along the administrative hierarchy, however, would not be sufficient, as it neglects the negotiation process that secured the cooperation of the subordinate authorities. Without their help, even a fully developed bureaucracy could not function. In the nineteenth century, in particular, when big parts of the state administration were still being established, differentiated and stabilized, an administration could not work if it was based on constant threats of sanctions. It could hardly have imposed those without blocking its own progress.

A historical analysis of the educational administration that focuses on power relations alone loses sight of the specifics of such an administration, in which many school functionaries doubled as educationalists. They were well versed in the contemporary expert discussions on good tuition, teaching psychology, the pedagogical classics, and the history of education or the theories of state education, with some even contributing publications to the discourse. The high-level functionary of the nineteenth century was indeed a 'doer'. He was working as both an academic writer and an administrator, who not only wanted to lecture on his ideas, but also apply them.

Educational administration was subject to particular public scrutiny and occasionally became a matter for parliamentary debate in Baden. The authorities communicated in writing with the representatives of teachers and medical associations, church authorities, the ministries within their jurisdiction or individual delegates. As a public institution, they relied on the legitimation of their activities. Only if they were met with trust, at least for a certain period of time, could their organizational processes be stabilized (Meyer and Rowan, 1977).

This means, however, abandoning the historiographical dualism of education and administration. We cannot truly understand the expansion of the educational administration without historically reconstructing its pedagogical legitimization. In this case, the pedagogical code enabled the educational administration to employ semantics that were unspecific enough to fill them with any necessary meaning, yet at the same time clearly distinguishable from an economical, nationalistic, etatistic or confessional orientation. Additionally, teachers served as a strong representation of the administration in the schools and in public. They felt that they were working on the same pedagogical project as the supervisory authorities.

This alliance also stabilized a school that was continually losing its functions for the local communities and was turning into an institution that was meant purely for teaching. Correct reading, writing and arithmetic were becoming the central elements of a school education, rather than religious education or civic instruction, although those remained part of the curriculum in both a discursive and practical sense.

Conversely, this abandonment of the dualism has consequences for the general history of administration. Modern bureaucracy could not prevail simply by the spread of an abstract 'state spirit', which was shared by all members of the administration. The educational administrators did, in fact, share an etatistic attitude that absolutized the state as an all-redeeming institution. Sallwürk's theoretical pieces contain such elements. A mere etatistic orientation, however, would not have been enough for an outward legitimization of the new structures or an inward normative saturation, as a specific semantics was needed – one that served to distinguish the educational administration from other administrative bodies. This would then help to justify and promote its development.

The school functionaries of nineteenth-century Baden tried to establish an elementary school founded on pedagogical aspects. In doing so, they ensured the loyalty of the teachers and stabilized their own position as the public administration of schools and teaching. Paradoxically speaking, it was this liberation that made it possible to protect the educational freedom from state intervention, even though it was, and still is, dependent on it.

Notes

1. For the history of the German term '*Bürokratie*', see mainly Wunder (1987, 1992). For the cultural history of administration, see Becker (2011) and Becker and Krosigk (2008). For the analytical possibilities and boundaries of the concept of bureaucracy, see Blau (1956).
2. This concept was canonized for the German-speaking area in an article by the co-founder and first director of the Max Planck Institute for Human Development in Berlin, Hellmut Becker (see Becker, 1954). The principal point of reference for the pedagogical criticism of administration in this context is Theodor W. Adorno's topos of the 'administered world'. See also the attempts to confront the perspectives of the Frankfurt School with Max Weber's organizational sociology (Greisman and Ritzer, 1981).
3. In this context, the teacher and pedagogical author Horst Rumpf (1966) used the term 'administrational distress of the school'.
4. For the United States see, for example, Wise (1979). For a historization of this dualism see Labaree (2011). In this volume, Holger Ziegler traces the shift of a bureaucratical orientation towards a new managerialism.
5. Particularly marked for Germany in Berg (1975). This historiographical perspective is strongly relativized by Scholz (2012).
6. For the German version of progressive education ('*Reformpädagogik*') as a rhetorical strategy, see Oelkers (2005). For the significance of a romanticized language for teacher training in the United States, see Labaree (2005).
7. Social technocratic designs of the nineteenth and early twentieth centuries (Auguste Comte, Friedrich Engels, Lenin), on the other hand, have a positive view of the 'administration of things', which is always strictly distinguished from an administration of people. See Geiss (2012, pp. 154–158).
8. Rita Casale (2011) has recently argued that educational theory should try to capture also the ambivalences of historical developments.
9. For a 'bureaucratizing from the bottom up', see also Judith Kafka's chapter in this volume.

10 Über die Verhandlung der Beiräthe. *Badische Schulzeitung*, 1863, pp. 31–38; Friedberg, E.A., 1871. *Der Staat und die katholische Kirche im Großherzogtum Baden*. Leipzig: Duncker & Humblot, pp. 78–89.
11 For the transnational dimension of the *Kulturkampf*, see Müller (2013).
12 The biographical information was taken from 'Badische Biographien' (Heidelberg 1875–1935) and Löwe (1998).
13 Über die Verhandlungen der Beiräthe. *Badische Schulzeitung*, 1863, pp. 31–38.
14 www.uni-jena.de/Herbartianismus_Forschungsstelle.html (accessed 14 January 2014).
15 There were alternatives in both a discursive and practical sense. The priest and author, Friedrich Wilhelm Dörpfeld, propagated a cooperative family model; another alternative was the democratic model of 'self-governance' that was practised in the United States or Switzerland, and for a short period of time also in Baden, albeit in a reduced form. For the competition between organizational models, see the more recent studies Brockliss and Sheldon (2012), Glenn (2011) and Loss (2012).
16 The biographical information was taken from 'Badische Biographien' (Heidelberg, 1875–1935).
17 Sickinger, A., 1908. Schulsystem, Mannheimer. In: W. Rhein (ed.) *Encyklopädisches Handbuch der Pädagogik VIII*. Beyer: Langensalza, pp. 324–336.
18 Ortsschulpflege. *Badische Schulzeitung*, 36 (September), p. 2.
19 *Die Neugestaltung des Volksschulwesens in Baden. Eine Denkschrift. Zweite, durch einen Anhang vermehrte Auflage* (Heidelberg, 1861).
20 Literatur zur Frage der Schulleitung und Schulaufsicht. *Allgemeine Deutsche Lehrerzeitung*, 1909, 61/16, pp. 197–199.
21 For example, Zum neuen Jahre. *Neue Badische Schulzeitung*, 1880, 1(Januar); Die fachmännische Schulaufsicht, ein Lehrerideal. *Badische Schulzeitung*, 1900, 43.
22 For the shift in meaning of the school building in the administrative process, see Geiss (2010).
23 For the resistance of the local supervisory authorities, see De Vincenti *et al.* (2011).
24 For the history of educational financing, see Carla Aubry in this volume.
25 The 72nd public session of the Second Chamber on 29 April 1902.
26 The 73rd public session of the Second Chamber on Wednesday, 30 April 1902. Extract from the verbatim minutes (GLA 235/7152).
27 The 76th session of the Second Chamber on 5 May 1902. Extract from the verbatim minutes (GLA 235/29170).
28 The 76th session of the Second Chamber on 5 May 1902. Extract from the verbatim minutes (GLA 235/29170).
29 An elementary teacher, to Arnsberger, 8 May 1902 (GLA 235/29170); Weiland, teacher, to von Dusch, 8 May 1902 (GLA 235/29170).
30 Circular of the District School Inspectorate Offenburg, 1 January 1902 (GLA 235/29170).
31 State Board of Education to District School Inspectorate Baden, 4 April 1865 (STAF B 648/1, no.6).
32 State Board of Education to district school inspector Bopp, 17 June 1902 (GLA 235/29170).

Archives

GLA: Generallandesarchiv Karlsruhe, Germany
STAF: Staatsarchiv Freiburg im Breisgau, Germany

References

Becker, H., 1954. Die verwaltete Schule. *Merkur*, 8(12), pp. 1155–1177.
Becker, J., 1973. *Liberaler Staat und Kirche in der Ära von Reichsgründung und Kulturkampf. Geschichte und Strukturen ihres Verhältnisses in Baden, 1860–1876*. Mainz: Matthias-Grünewald-Verlag.
Becker, P., 2011. Sprachvollzug: Kommunikation und Verwaltung. In: P. Becker (ed.) *Sprachvollzug im Amt. Kommunikation und Verwaltung im Europa des 19. und 20. Jahrhunderts*. Bielefeld: Transcript, pp. 9–42.
Becker, P. and Dekker, J.J.H., 2002. Doers: the emergence of an acting elite. *Paedagogica Historica*, 38(2–3), pp. 427–432.
Becker, P. and Krosigk, R.V. (eds), 2008. *Figures of Authority. Contributions Towards a Cultural History of Governance from the Seventeenth to the Twentieth Century*. Frankfurt: Peter Lang.
Berg, C., 1975. Schulpolitik ist Verwaltungspolitik: die Schule als Herrschaftsinstrument staatlicher Verwaltung. *Vierteljahrsschrift für Wissenschaftliche Pädagogik*, 51(3), pp. 211–236.
Blau, P.M., 1956. *Bureaucracy in Modern Society*. New York: Random House.
Brockliss, L. and Sheldon, N. (eds), 2012. *Mass Education and the Limits of State Building, c.1870–1930*. Basingstoke: Palgrave Macmillan.
Casale, R., 2011. Zur Abstraktheit der Empirie – Zur Konkretheit der Theorie. Anmerkungen über die versäumte Auseinandersetzung mit den Folgen des Positivismusstreits. In: I. Breinbauer and G. Weiss (eds) *Orte des Empirischen in der Bildungstheorie. Einsätze Theoretischer Erziehungswissenschaft*. Wurzburg: Königshausen und Neumann, pp. 45–60.
Dauer, A., 1919. *Ernst von Sallwürk zum 80. Geburtstag*. Langensalza: Beyer.
De Vincenti, A., Grube, N. and Rosenmund, M., 2011. Öffentliche Schulaufsicht zwischen pastoraler Verantwortung, Laienmitwirkung und rationalisierter Expertise. *Jahrbuch für Historische Bildungsforschung*, 17, pp. 110–125.
Fuchs, E., 2004. Internationalisierung als Gegenstand der Historischen Bildungsforschung: zu Institutionalisierungsprozessen der edukativen Kultur um 1900. In: M. Liedtke, E. Matthes and G. Miller-Kipp (eds) *Erfolg oder Misserfolg? Urteile und Bilanzen in der Historiographie der Erziehung*. Bad Heilbrunn: Klinkhardt, pp. 231–249.
Gall, L., 1968. *Der Liberalismus als Regierende Partei. Das Großherzogtum Baden Zwischen Restauration und Reichsgründung*. Wiesbaden: Steiner.
Geiss, M., 2010. Die Leiche im Schulhaus: amtlicher Schriftverkehr als Quelle für eine Kulturgeschichte der Bildungsverwaltung. *Zeitschrift für Pädagogische Historiographie*, 16(1), pp. 59–66.
Geiss, M., 2011. Verordnete Öffentlichkeit. Der Versuch einer demokratisch legitimierten Ortsschulbehörde im Großherzogtum Baden, 1864–1876. Unpublished paper. Zurich.
Geiss, M., 2012. Die Verwaltung der Dinge: einige Überlegungen zur pädagogischen Geschichtsschreibung. In: K. Priem, G.M. König and R. Casale (eds) *Die Materialität der Erziehung. Zur Kultur- und Sozialgeschichte Pädagogischer Objekte (Beiheft der Zeitschrift für Pädagogik)*. Weinheim: Beltz, pp. 151–167.
Glenn, C.L., 2011. *Contrasting Models of State and School: A Comparative Historical Study of Parental Choice and State Control*. New York: Continuum.

Greisman, H.C. and Ritzer, G., 1981. Max Weber, critical theory, and the administered world. *Qualitative Sociology*, 4(1), pp. 34–55.
Hug, W., 1998. *Geschichte Badens*, 2nd edn. Darmstadt: Wissenschaftliche Buchgesellschaft.
Kimmelmann, A., 1926. *Zur Geschichte der Lehrer-Bewegung in Baden, 1876–1926*. Bühl-Baden: Konkordia.
Knies, K., 1853. *Die Eisenbahnen und ihre Wirkungen*. Braunschweig: C. M. Schwetschke.
Krosigk, R.V., 2010. *Bürger in die Verwaltung! Bürokratiekritik und Bürgerbeteiligung in Baden. Zur Geschichte Moderner Staatlichkeit im Deutschland des 19. Jahrhunderts*. Bielefeld: Transcript.
Labaree, D.F., 2005. Progressivism, schools and schools of education: an American romance. *Paedagogica Historica*, 41(1&2), pp. 275–288.
Labaree, D.F., 2011. How Dewey lost: the victory of David Snedden and social efficiency in the reform of American education. In: D. Tröhler, T. Schlag and Fritz Osterwalder (eds) *Pragmatism and Modernities*. Rotterdam: Sense.
Leonards, C. and Randeraad, N., 2010. Transnational experts in social reform, 1840–1880. *International Review for Social History*, 55, pp. 215–239.
Loss, C.P., 2012. *Between Citizens and the State: The Politics of American Higher Education in the 20th Century*. Princeton, NJ: Princeton University Press.
Löwe, J., 1998. *Kontextuale Theorie der Volkswirtschaft. Der Ansatz von Karl Knies als Grundlage zukünftiger Wirtschaftspolitik*. Amsterdam: Fakultas.
Luhmann, N., 1983. *Legitimation durch Verfahren*. Frankfurt: Suhrkamp.
Maier, J., 2000. Kirche und Schule. Auseinandersetzung um Schulform und geistliche Schulaufsicht in konfessionell gemischten Staaten. In: H. Ammerich and J. Gut (eds) *Zwischen 'Staatsanstalt' und Selbstbestimmung. Kirche und Staat in Südwestdeutschland vom Ausgang des Alten Reiches bis 1870*. Stuttgart: Thorbecke, pp. 269–293.
Meyer, J.W. and Rowan, B., 1977. Institutionalized organizations: formal structure as myth and ceremony. *American Journal of Sociology*, 83(2), pp. 340–363.
Müller, C., 2013. 'It has been a wordy war'. Die Frühphase des Schulstreits in Belgien, Frankreich und den Niederlanden im Vergleich und die transnationalen Grundlagen der 'Culture Wars', 1857–1870. In: T. Schulze and S. Ehrenpreis (eds) *Grenzüberschreitende Religion: Vergleichs- und Kulturtransferstudien zur Neuzeitlichen Geschichte*. Gottingen: Vandenhoeck & Ruprecht, pp. 116–139.
Niess, U., 1997. Mannheims Schul- und Bildungsgeschichte im Kaiserreich. Das Beispiel der Elementarschulen und der höheren Lehranstalten. In: B. Kirchgässner and H.-P. Becht (eds) *Stadt und Bildung*. Sigmaringen: Jan Thorbecke Verlag, pp. 136–156.
Oelkers, J., 2005. *Reformpädagogik. Eine Kritische Dogmengeschichte*, 4th edn. Weinheim, Munich: Juventa Verlag.
Rumpf, H., 1966. *Die Administrative Verstörung der Schule*. Essen: Neue Deutsche Schule Verlagsgesellschaft.
Sallwürk, E. v., 1893a. Contemporary educational thought in Germany. *Educational Review*, 5(April), pp. 313–324.
Sallwürk, E. v., 1893b. *Art und Bedeutung einer Kulturgemäßen Schulaufsicht*. Gotha: Verlag von Emil Behrendt.
Scholz, J., 2012. Verwaltung und Reform der Elementarschulen Brandenburgs in der Zeit der Preußischen reformen. In: M. Geiss and A. De Vincenti (eds) *Verwaltete Schule: Geschichte und Gegenwart*. Wiesbaden: Springer VS, pp. 39–52.

Tenorth, H.-E., 2003. Schulmänner, Volkslehrer und Unterrichtsbeamte: Friedrich Adolph Wilhelm Diesterweg, Friedrich Wilhelm Dörpfeld, Friedrich Dittes. In: H.-E. Tenorth (ed.) *Klassiker der Pädagogik. Bd.1: Von Erasmus bis Helene Lange*. Munich: C.H. Beck.

Wise, A.E., 1979. *Legislated Learning. The Bureaucratization of the American Classroom*. Berkeley, CA: University of California Press.

Wunder, B., 1987. Bürokratie, Geschichte eines politischen Schlagworts. In: A. Windhoff-Héretier (ed.) *Verwaltung und Ihre Umwelt*. Opladen: Westdeutscher Verlag, pp. 277–301.

Wunder, B., 1992. 'Verwaltung', 'Bürokratie', 'Selbstverwaltung', 'Amt' and 'Beamter'. In: O. Brunner, W. Conze and R. Koselleck (eds) *Geschichtliche Grundbegriffe*. Stuttgart: Klett-Cotta, pp. 69–96.

Wunder, B., 1993. *Vom Dorfschulmeister zum Staatsbeamten. Die Verbeamtung der Badischen Lehrerschaft im 19. Jahrhundert*. Buhl (Baden): Konkordia.

Wunder, B., 2000. Die Verstaatlichung der Volksschule im 19. Jahrhundert. In: U. Andermann and K. Andermann (eds) *Regionale Aspekte des Frühen Schulwesens*. Tübingen: Bibliotheca Academica, pp. 221–229.

Chapter 7

Bureaucratizing from the bottom up

The centralization of school discipline policy in the United States

Judith Kafka

The bureaucratization of American education is usually told as a top-down tale, with external, often elite, actors developing and enacting policies and structures that over time have given increasing educational authority to centralized officials at the district, state, and federal levels (Murphy, 1990; Tyack, 1974). Yet the case of school discipline veers sharply from this narrative. In the decades following World War Two, local actors – teachers, principals, and community members – promoted the bureaucratization of school discipline, albeit often for different purposes. This chapter offers a brief explanation of how and why they did so, through an examination of the Los Angeles City School District, which was one of the first school systems in the nation to adopt a centralized discipline policy. In the case of Los Angeles, and nationally, authority over school discipline shifted from local educators to centralized officials in response to multiple pressures, which at times conflicted, but which converged around the notion that bureaucratic solutions could solve local educational problems. The centralization of school discipline policy in the United States thus raises larger questions about the bureaucratization of American schooling, and suggests that, at least since the second half of the twentieth century, this phenomenon has not been exclusively imposed from above. Indeed, while many groups and actors in the United States today articulate opposition to the centralization of educational authority more broadly, their efforts to reverse the process have thus far been quite weak, perhaps indicating the absence of viable alternatives.

The centralization of school discipline

For most of American history, school discipline was largely a local matter. Classroom teachers made individual decisions about how students should behave, and they used whatever methods they deemed appropriate for making sure this happened. Educators, school leaders, philosophers, parents, and social critics often disagreed about what the term discipline actually meant, what it should look like, and even what its purpose was, but there was very little debate about the fact that the teacher was ultimately in charge of school discipline.

American educators derived their disciplinary authority from the longstanding doctrine of *in loco parentis* – the notion that teachers act in place of the parent while children are under their charge (Bybee and Gee, 1982). Teachers maintained this parental prerogative even in the face of opposition from students' *actual* parents. Teachers were thus not expected to act as a child's parent *would* act but rather how he or she *should* act to ensure appropriate social and moral development. This distinction was crucial because public education was understood to be a socializing institution for the new nation; children of all backgrounds would learn to embrace American values and ideals of democracy through a common schooling experience. For children whose parents were deemed morally suspect – either because they were poor, immigrant, non-Protestant, or non-white – schooling offered the chance for self-betterment. In this context, discipline was often considered *the* most important purpose of public education. Academic skills and content mattered, but not as much as teaching the nation's youth how to behave (Kaestle, 1983; Kafka, 2011).

Yet while common schooling was intended to both unify and socialize American children around a broad set of Protestant-based beliefs about God, family, and country, the government provided no regulations or guidance about what those beliefs were or how teachers should go about ensuring that they were learned. On a national level, this is not terribly surprising: As McGuinn details in his chapter in this volume, the federal government had very little to do with public schooling in the United States until the middle of the twentieth century. Yet even at the state level, which is where most aspects of American public education have traditionally been governed, there were almost no rules or regulations regarding school discipline. This remained true even as states began playing an increasingly important role in education – from implementing and enforcing mandatory attendance laws, to regulating teacher qualifications, to issuing basic standards about school content and curriculum. Discipline was considered a central purpose of education, but teachers and other school-based educators enjoyed considerable disciplinary autonomy as "acting parents."

In truth this autonomy did not lead to a great deal of variation. Teachers and principals relied on social norms to guide their disciplinary decisions, and while those norms changed with time and were always being contested in some way, for the most part behavioral expectations and the way schools and teachers worked to ensure that students internalized those expectations were markedly similar from school to school, district to district, and state to state (Meyer *et al.*, 1983). Yet while their disciplinary practices may not have significantly differed, school-site educators nonetheless enacted them based on their own discretion.

Today, school discipline in the United States is a far more regulated affair. School systems issue phonebook-sized handbooks with codes of conduct and the rules and procedures school personnel must follow when responding to errant behavior. Most districts and states also have so-called "zero-tolerance" discipline policies, which mandate student suspension and expulsion for acts of misbehavior ranging from drug and weapon possession to tardiness, smoking, and disrespect (Johnson et al., 2000; Skiba and Raush, 2006). The federal government even began regulating school discipline with its passage of the Gun Free Schools Act of 1994, which requires all schools that receive federal funding to expel any student in possession of a weapon on school grounds and inform local law enforcement of the incident. Today American educators are not expected to act as parents, but as agents of rules and regulations established by district, state, and federal officials. Indeed, zero-tolerance policies are explicitly intended to *limit* teachers' and principals' individual discretion: The policies are supposed to prohibit educators from "tolerating" certain kinds of misconduct, and they grant increasing disciplinary control to district supervisors, centralized boards of education, and state legislatures (Kafka, 2011).

The most common explanation for the centralization of disciplinary authority in the United States is that government intervention in school discipline began in the 1960s with judicial decisions recognizing students' constitutional rights in school.[1] This explanation essentially asserts that granting youth the same kind of rights that adults enjoyed weakened teachers' ability to act *in loco parentis*. From this perspective, once children possessed constitutional rights, teachers could no longer make disciplinary decisions based on what they believed was in the best interest of the child and his or her classmates; instead, educators were required to consider the legal ramifications of their disciplinary actions. More importantly, according to many critics of students' rights decisions, teachers' *moral* authority was irrevocably undermined by the very notion that students *could* challenge disciplinary decisions in court. The result, from this perspective, was that school systems and eventually government authorities were forced to implement bureaucratic rules and regulations to replace *in loco parentis* (Arum, 2003; Thernstrom, 1999; Weinig, 2000).

Another common explanation for the centralization of disciplinary authority in American public schooling is that rising rates of school violence in the late 1960s and 1970s, along with a general disregard for adult and institutional authority on the part of youth, and especially minority youth, led to increased police intervention in schools and the eventual development of bureaucratic disciplinary systems (Crews and Counts, 1997; Devine, 1996; Noguera, 1995).

These two explanations of the centralization of disciplinary authority in the United States are significantly different, but they share two common characteristics. First, they both locate the impetus for change in the late 1960s and 1970s. Second, they both portray students and their advocates as instigating these changes by successfully challenging – either directly or indirectly – the doctrine of *in loco parentis*. While there is some truth in both of these explanations, they are incomplete, even when taken together. First, both narratives begin too late. In reality, some school districts began developing centralized discipline policies in the 1950s – a full decade before the court decisions, unrest, and violence of the 1960s and 1970s. Second, neither explanation adequately recognizes the role that *educators* played in shifting control over school discipline away from schools and classrooms and toward district and state officials. Indeed, both explanations portray educators as responding to cultural and institutional changes far beyond their control – essentially forced by others (either the courts or confrontational youth and their families) to give up *in loco parentis*. Yet in truth teachers often led the way, demanding the creation of district-wide policies that shifted control over discipline to centralized authorities. School administrators later followed suit, appealing to government authorities at all levels – city, county, state, federal – for help maintaining order in their schools. Other actors and factors also played a part in shifting control over discipline away from classroom teachers. At different times, students, parents, civil rights activists, and politicians all promoted policies that weakened or rejected the doctrine of *in loco parentis*. Court decisions recognizing students' constitutional rights in school ultimately played a supporting role in this process, as did student unrest and concerns about school violence in the 1960s and 1970s. By that time, however, the bureaucratization of school discipline had already begun.

1950s Los Angeles: teachers push for a centralized policy

One of the first districts in the nation to adopt a centralized discipline policy and begin formally shifting disciplinary authority away from school-site educators was that of the city of Los Angeles. It implemented a district-wide discipline policy to great fanfare and some national attention in 1959, and continued to lead the country in the bureaucratization of school discipline in the decades that followed. The policy's creation was the direct result of actions taken by Los Angeles teacher organizations and professional groups, which had begun complaining about the district's apparent discipline problem several years earlier. Los Angeles teachers and their representatives officially lodged their concerns both with the Board of Education, which had governance power over the school system, and with the office of the superintendent, which was the central administrative authority of the district, and they urged these centralized officials to enact district-level reforms to address the issue.

The idea that school discipline was, in fact, a problem was one that no one refuted. At the time, the nation was in the midst of a widespread juvenile delinquency scare – a product of both Cold War paranoia and significant cultural, social, and demographic changes that many Americans found destabilizing and frightening (Gilbert, 1986). Parents, politicians, law enforcement officials, and social commentators were concerned about the nation's youth and convinced that juvenile crime and anti-social behavior were on the rise. FBI director J. Edgar Hoover went so far as to term the apparent delinquency epidemic a "menacing cloud, mushrooming across the nation" (1958, p. 8). A popular book and then film called *Blackboard Jungle*, which portrayed a rough urban high school where teachers were terrorized and attacked by their students, brought considerable attention to the supposed problems of crime and violence in urban schools across the country, and national leaders began asking what could be done to restore order to the American classroom.

In truth, there were few data to corroborate this near consensus that discipline was a universal problem in American schools. School districts did not collect any information about student discipline, and, while anecdotal reports included some disconcerting stories about both student behavior and teachers' methods of punishment, these were rare and not considered typical. National surveys revealed that the vast majority of teachers found their students to be well behaved (Lambert, 1956). In Los Angeles, the student behaviors elementary school teachers identified as most troubling seemed relatively mild, such as "speaking out of turn" and "restless (inattentive)"; one behavior they identified, "emotionally disturbed," seemed to describe a *cause* of student indiscipline rather than a specific behavior.[2] Nonetheless, with the exception of the district superintendent, who claimed that discipline was no more or less a problem than it had ever been, no one in Los Angeles seemed to doubt that discipline was deteriorating in the city's schools and that something needed to be done about it.[3]

For teachers, the answer to the district's discipline problem was twofold: create more specialized settings for problem youth outside of the regular classroom, and implement a district-wide discipline policy to be followed by all students, teachers, and staff. Taken together, these solutions would serve to both centralize and specialize disciplinary authority, and reduce classroom teachers' disciplinary discretion in the process. Los Angeles' teacher representatives offered many arguments in support of their requests, all of which were premised on the notion that *in loco parentis* was no longer an operable principle in the Los Angeles school district.

One central justification for shifting disciplinary authority away from classroom teachers was that too many students required disciplinary interventions beyond a regular classroom teacher's expertise. These students, teachers argued, required the help of specially-trained professionals, such as psychiatrists and social workers, rather than the ministrations of "acting parents." The Los Angeles Elementary Teachers Club, for example, informed the Board that its members were encountering "an increasing number of discipline problems due to emotional disturbances," and asserted that these children required "immediate" professional attention outside of the regular classroom. "We are told that one out of every three children in our classroom will suffer from some mental disorder during his lifetime," its representatives noted. Club members acknowledged that elementary school teachers had a professional responsibility "to guide children into desirable patterns of behavior using imposed discipline, when necessary," but they argued that students with "mental and emotional defects" and "psychopathic tendencies" required specialized help beyond the skills and expertise of a regular classroom teacher.[4]

Charles McClure, a high school teacher and representative of the local chapter of the American Federation of Teachers, articulated a similar position in a speech before the Board in November of 1956:

We are qualified to do a good job of teaching but we are not qualified as psychiatrists ... We cannot take time out day after day to reprimand a small group, or to restore order, without cheating most of the students out of valuable instructional time.[5]

In addition to maintaining that discipline for many students required more specialized skills than classroom teachers possessed, Los Angeles teachers argued that formalizing discipline with a written policy would help restore social order in a district that was suddenly booming with a growing and increasingly diverse student population.[6] As families in search of new jobs and better opportunities poured into greater Los Angeles in the postwar years, teacher representatives pointed out that the student body was "growing and moving constantly" and that "incoming families represent[ed] every section of the nation." A centralized discipline policy, they reasoned, would help schools and teachers with the "problem of assimilating newcomers" unfamiliar with local norms and behavioral expectations.[7] Teachers also pointed out that many *teachers* were new to the district, and that they, too, would benefit from a policy that clearly stated disciplinary rules and regulations.[8] Los Angeles teachers thus sought the implementation of a formal centralized policy to replace the informal norms that had governed school discipline for so long, even though the development of such a policy would inherently limit their individual discretion.

An obvious question in the context of twentieth-century American schooling is, what role did race play in teachers' desire to shift some of their disciplinary authority to centralized officials and specialists? This is an especially relevant question in Los Angeles, where a once-small black population was suddenly growing quite rapidly and Mexican American students comprised close to 20 percent of the student body, while the teaching force remained predominantly white (Kafka, 2011; Los Angeles City School District, 1966).[9] In this case, however, in 1950s' Los Angeles, the answer seems to be that race did not play a significant role in teachers' efforts to create a centralized discipline policy and expand specialized settings for problem youth – for a number of reasons. First, at the time, those concerned about juvenile delinquency focused on the idea that any child, from any type of family or home, no matter how wealthy, was at risk of becoming a delinquent. Indeed, despite the fact that juvenile arrest rates were highest among minority youth in urban centers in the 1950s, experts spent considerable time warning of "split-level delinquency," borne out of the social isolation and corrupted family values of the growing suburbs (Hoover, 1958; Salisbury, 1958). Moreover, in Los Angeles, concerns about student misbehavior during this period were often directed at new *white* migrants, who were considered less sophisticated and less "adjusted" than their locally-raised classmates (Randall, 1957). In fact, Los Angeles teachers highlighted the San Fernando Valley, a newly-developing suburb that at the time was almost exclusively white, as a neighborhood in need of additional disciplinary resources.[10] Meanwhile, concerns about minority youth were rarely mentioned.

This was no doubt in part due to the effects of so-called de facto segregation and the fact that most Los Angeles teachers did not interact with non-white students.

Instead of focusing on race or ethnicity, Los Angeles teachers identified a bureaucratic cause of the apparent school discipline problem. Specifically, they argued that their disciplinary role as educators was poorly defined – both in the context of the classroom and within the structure of the district – and that greater articulation of disciplinary expectations would help to maintain order in the schools. Teachers wanted clear rules and regulations that they could show to parents and students who might question their authority, but they also wanted clear rules and regulations that they could present to principals and district officials. In short, they wanted their disciplinary responsibilities – and accountability for those responsibilities – codified within the formal district bureaucracy. Moreover, Los Angeles teachers wanted a role in determining the district policy. Indeed, their representatives complained that teachers felt they were in a "disciplinary no man's land," in which they possessed neither a "voice in determining school disciplinary problems" nor "the authority to follow through" when problems arose.[11] Through the development of centralized rules and regulations about how students were expected to behave and who was responsible for taking action when those expectations were not met, Los Angeles teachers hoped to both more clearly delineate their disciplinary responsibilities and gain a voice in the policy process.

Both of the teachers' discipline-related proposals – to expand specialized settings for problem youth and create a district-wide discipline policy – were well received by centralized officials and quickly implemented. In an era of bureaucratic expansion, and a time in which technical responses to social problems seemed to rule the day, the notion that problematic student behavior could be improved through centralized rulemaking and bureaucratic expansion was compelling to school authorities.[12] Moreover, a centralized policy would cost little more than the paper it was printed on, and while expanding specialized resources for problem youth would require additional expenditures, in April of 1957, local voters approved a school bond measure that funded, among other things, new specialized settings and services for misbehaving youth.[13] The new discipline policy took somewhat longer to develop, but it was drafted (with some teacher input), adopted, and implemented before the decade was over. One board member termed it "possibly the most important reform in public school administration that has occurred in the United States in the last twenty years."[14]

The 1960s: minority youth and activists join in

In the 1960s, local educators were joined in their efforts to further bureaucratize discipline by minority youth, parents, and activists, who – while often operating in direct opposition to teachers – nonetheless viewed the centralization of disciplinary authority as preferable to allowing for local disciplinary discretion. If racial conflict did not play much of a role in efforts to bureaucratize school discipline in Los Angeles in the 1950s, by the 1960s, issues of race, ethnicity, and language were central to the process. Like many urban school systems across the United States in the 1960s, the Los Angeles city school district was a site of great social and racial unrest – particularly after the violence of Watts in 1965. Minority youth and their advocates protested both structural inequities in the school system at large and specific incidents at their local schools, at times directly challenging the authority of their school-site educators and appealing for district-level intervention (Kafka, 2011).

The most famous school protests in Los Angeles in the 1960s were the so-called East L.A. school blowouts, or walkouts, in the spring of 1968. The blowouts lasted several days and eventually involved 10,000 students, most of whom were Mexican American; they have been credited with catapulting the Brown Power, or Chicano, movement on to the national stage and sparking a sense of self-empowerment and political activism within the Mexican American community (Muñoz, 1989; NLCC Educational Media, 1996).[15] Student leaders framed the protests as an effort to achieve greater racial and ethnic equity within the school system; they sought better facilities and improved instruction in their schools, as well as recognition of their language and culture, and more Spanish-speaking teachers. At the same time, however, many of the student demands were related to more narrow issues of disciplinary discretion. For example, students wanted to change their schools' dress and grooming codes, which were established on a school-by-school basis, and they sought to eliminate the use of corporal punishment, which at the time could be conducted by teachers and principals at their own discretion.[16] Other protests demanded the replacement of white administrators in predominantly black schools with black principals, and greater community voice in school-based disciplinary decisions (Kafka, 2011; Mauller, 1976).

Although the blowouts and other student protests in Los Angeles achieved very little in terms of acquiring increased resources for minority youth, they did play a role in limiting teachers' and principals' disciplinary discretion. First, and most importantly to many at the time, the Board of Education granted amnesty to all student protesters involved in the blowouts. This decision effectively overruled school-site educators who had sought to suspend and even expel participants. The amnesty was a practical move on the part of the Board, but it nonetheless infuriated many teachers and principals, who rightly noted that their disciplinary authority had been usurped by the Board's decision. Second, the Board directed a subcommittee to investigate students' requests regarding dress and grooming codes and the use of corporal punishment – issues that had long been matters of local jurisdiction. In the short term, the Board's decision to direct these concerns to subcommittees for further investigation had no immediate results, although it did signal to students and educators alike that these matters were no longer strictly the purview of teachers and principals.

In the long term, dress and grooming codes were eventually eliminated district-wide as a direct result of the subcommittee's deliberations.[17] The student walkouts and protests, then, clearly played a role in shifting disciplinary decision-making to the centralized authority of the district.

Many Los Angeles teachers and principals opposed these Board decisions on the grounds that they were too lenient toward disobedient youth and thus weakened school-site educators' authority.[18] Teacher and principal representatives argued that the Board had essentially condoned unlawful behavior by granting protesters amnesty from punishment and that, in doing so, the Board had also effectively diminished school-site educators' ability to maintain discipline. As the president of a faculty club in East Los Angeles complained to the Board, a student could now walk into class and say, "I was absent and you can't do anything about it," and the student would be right.[19] Even teachers working in white, more affluent neighborhoods that were not directly affected by the protests registered their displeasure. As a faculty representative from one such school complained, "Our classroom authority and achievement weakens . . . as your guidelines fall slack."[20]

Yet teachers' and principals' response to the Board's centralized decision-making was not a request for increased autonomy. Instead, they asked the Board to enact more punitive centralized disciplinary measures that they believed would help restore order and their disciplinary authority. As the Los Angeles Association of Secondary School Administrators told the Board, its members did not want to view every incident of student misbehavior as a matter of individual discretion; they preferred a district-wide policy to which they could adhere.[21] Of course, the district *did* have a system-wide discipline policy in place, but with students and community members openly rejecting school-site educators' authority, and with the Board making decisions that seemed to legitimate protesters' actions, Los Angeles teachers and principals wanted the Board to develop a new policy that was both more specific and, crucially, more punitive.

In time, the Board began to develop a firmer stance toward student protests and walkouts. When a large-scale school boycott erupted across South Central Los Angeles in the spring of 1969, for example, the Board took a hard line. After disrupting sixteen predominantly-black schools in the area, forcing the closure of two, and inspiring other walkouts and boycotts across the district, protesting students in South Central Los Angeles returned to classes five days later without obtaining any concessions from the Board.[22] Instead, the Board issued a statement asserting that "disorder and disruption" would "not be countenanced" and that the Board would "seek the prosecution of those who violate the law."[23] It followed up this announcement with a formal reminder that site administrators had the right to ban or suspend any organization that had violated school regulations, which soon led to the removal of a chapter of the United Mexican American Students from Roosevelt High School in East Los Angeles.[24]

The centralization of school discipline in Los Angeles in the late 1960s was thus primarily the result of, and a response to, the actions of local actors – student protesters on the one side and teachers and principals on the other. Yet it was also largely the outcome of a broader political struggle over the city's public schools. Student protesters and their advocates, who pushed the Los Angeles Board of Education to develop policies that limited teachers' and principals' control over school discipline, did so in pursuit of greater equity and dignity for the district's poor minority youth. They targeted the organization of school discipline only to the degree that they viewed local school rules and disciplinary procedures as serving to perpetuate injustice and preserve inequities. At the same time, the teachers and principals who urged the Board to expand the district's role in regulating school discipline did so in an effort to protect their authority at a time in which it was widely contested. Los Angeles educators viewed their ability to enforce school discipline as central to their capacity to maintain and promote social order – in their schools and classrooms, and in society at large. The result, however, was more centralized decision-making in the realm of discipline and a decrease in local control.

1970s: school and district leaders

The trend toward greater centralization of disciplinary authority in Los Angeles continued in the 1970s, as Los Angeles principals increasingly turned to district officials and other government agencies for help in maintaining order in their schools, and in the process promoted rules and policies that would limit their disciplinary discretion. By this time, as a headline in *U.S. News & World Report* blared in 1970, there seemed to be "a crime invasion" in American "big-city schools," and urban districts in particular were trying to clamp down on school violence and unrest.[25] Yet, as the same national magazine pointed out six years later, despite "filling their buildings with alarms and guards, and getting tough with expulsions and arrests," nothing school officials did seemed to work. Crime, violence, and terror had taken over the nation's urban schools.[26] Report after report and headline after headline made the same case: American schools – and urban schools in particular – were under siege.

Concerns about school violence were particularly prevalent in Los Angeles, where, in the 1971–1972 school year, the district documented 167 incidents involving the use of weapons on school grounds.[27] Two years later, the district reported 210 assaults against school personnel, 745 assaults against students, and a total of 10,041 school crimes (or "criminal incidents") during the course of one school year – a 20 percent increase in crime despite the district's declining enrollment.[28] It is difficult to know to what extent these figures represented true increases in school crime and violence and to what extent they reflected the growing presence of security personnel who were expected to monitor and report criminal incidents. Yet even if exaggerated, the numbers represented what many in Los Angeles already felt they knew – that the city's schools, and specifically its black and Mexican American schools, had become sites of violence and mayhem.

Indeed, Los Angeles became something of national media darling for showcasing the dangers associated with urban education in the 1970s. Nearly every government study, national news story, and academic report published on the topic of school crime and violence featured or mentioned Los Angeles, and many focused in particular on the city's growing gang problem – often to great dramatic effect.[29] Authorities reported that at least 150 gangs operated within the city, and they credited the gangs' presence for turning Los Angeles schools into "armed camps" where neither students nor faculty felt safe.[30] Many of the most horrific acts of violence that occurred in and around Los Angeles schools during the early 1970s were linked to gang conflict, including a shooting at a Jefferson High School homecoming game in the fall of 1972 that injured five students and brought a great deal of attention to youth gangs and school violence.[31]

For their part, Los Angeles inner-city school administrators tended to agree that violence was a problem on their campuses, and they sought support from district and local government officials to combat it – usually in the form of stricter rules, increased security measures, and the ability to remove dangerous students from school for longer periods of time. The principal of Crenshaw High School in South Central Los Angeles, for example, spoke before the Los Angeles County Board of Supervisors to ask for assistance in ridding his school of gang violence by keeping convicted youth offenders behind bars. He claimed that gangs had turned Crenshaw High School into a "garrison camp," where teachers and students were focused on survival rather than learning. His colleague from Washington High School had a similar view: "Security on our campuses is the problem in our schools today. Not curriculum or new approaches to teaching. You can't teach anything unless you have an atmosphere without violence."[32]

District officials largely agreed with these assessments. Although at times they took issue with proposed solutions – such as "combat pay" for teachers working in inner-city schools – they largely applauded any effort to fight crime in school and took active steps to signal that they were serious about cracking down on school crime and violence, primarily by implementing two strategies. First, the Los Angeles Board of Education enacted "get tough" centralized discipline policies that mandated strict penalties for certain kinds of criminal behavior in school; and, second, the Board delegated increasing disciplinary responsibilities to non-educators, such as school security and local police officers. The result of the Board's actions was a reduction in both disciplinary responsibilities and disciplinary discretion for teachers and principals – reductions that few at the time seemed to oppose – and an increase in suspension and expulsion rates across the Los Angeles school district, especially in predominantly-black schools.

Of course, centralized discipline policies had been in place in Los Angeles since the late 1950s, and in 1968 the Board had already demonstrated its willingness to overrule school-site educators' disciplinary decisions. In the 1970s, however, district officials focused on the *content* of the centralized policies by making them more specific and attached to greater, inflexible consequences – essentially creating "zero-tolerance" discipline policies in all but name. In 1971, for example, the Los Angeles City Board of Education implemented a rule basically mandating the suspension and eventual expulsion of any student found in possession of a deadly weapon at school; in 1974, district officials moved to suspend and expel all students arrested for drug sales as part of an undercover police operation.[33]

Prior to these new rules, principals had been able respond to weapon and drug possession on their campuses on a case-by-case basis, and reportedly often recommended counseling or another course of action that did not lead to student expulsion. Associate Superintendent Jerry Halverson explained in 1972 that this level of discretion had "fit the needs of individual schools and students" at the time, but was no longer appropriate. The district's "thinking changed," Halverson explained, "because of the tremendous increase in possession of guns at schools." In essence, the Board had ruled that principals' judgments about what would be in the best interest of a student and school were no longer relevant.[34] Yet, despite the fact that the new rules usurped their authority, principals did not oppose them; indeed, many expressed relief that these firmer policies had been put into place.[35]

Thus by the end of 1970s, the Los Angeles school district had shifted disciplinary authority away from school-site educators and toward centralized officials. These policies mandated strict and highly punitive penalties for certain behaviors, and guaranteed that students accused of crimes such as weapon or drug possession would be excluded from school. The results of the school district's disciplinary policies and procedures in the 1970s were similar to what is seen today: Student suspension and expulsion rates were high, and black youth were excluded from school at a much higher rate than their non-black classmates. In 1977, for example, although only 24.5 percent of students attending Los Angeles schools were black, black youth constituted 43.9 percent of all students suspended. Meanwhile white students comprised 33.7 percent of the student body and 32.1 percent of student suspensions, while Latinos comprised 34.9 percent of the student population but only 27.9 percent of its suspensions.[36]

In the next several decades, this centralization of disciplinary authority would move even further up the bureaucratic chain – to the state of California and, eventually, to the federal government. Yet the basic structures and processes of centralized discipline were already in place. This institutional transformation occurred slowly and had been promoted by multiple actors for multiple reasons: by teachers, who viewed the creation of centralized discipline policies as a way to formalize their broader authority within the structure of the district;

by minority students, parents, and activists, who sought the centralization of disciplinary authority as a means of both limiting racial discrimination and asserting their right to participate in educational governance; and by school and district leaders, who promoted district-wide, inflexible discipline policies in response to public concerns about school violence and safety. Other factors played a role as well, including judicial decisions granting students greater civil rights in school, and concerns about school desegregation and property values. Yet when viewed in its entirety, it is clear that the centralization of disciplinary authority in Los Angeles was borne out of local action.

Whether or not those who promoted the bureaucratization of school discipline in Los Angeles and elsewhere were happy with the results is an open question. Only a year after the Los Angeles City School District enacted its first district-wide discipline policy, more than half of surveyed high school teachers felt that the policy had "had no effect on the discipline problem at all," and many believed "that by putting the rules down in black-and-white," their disciplinary authority had been weakened.[37] Yet despite their disappointment with the policy, Los Angeles teachers did not seek to increase their disciplinary discretion or restore *in loco parentis*. Instead, they spent years seeking to adjust the *content* of the policy, hoping to somehow find the formula that would increase their disciplinary authority while limiting their disciplinary responsibility.

In 1972, when the Los Angeles Board of Education was considering its zero-tolerance policy on weapon possession, which it would ultimately pass, a student representative from the district's Black Education Commission questioned the motives behind a policy that was clearly intended to punish rather than educate wayward youth, and hinted at the rule's likely racial ramifications.[38] Yet while the student criticized the centralized regulation, neither he nor anyone else came forward in defense of local disciplinary discretion. Indeed, it does not appear that there were any attempts to reinstate the notion that educators could and should act in the place of the parent when conducting school discipline.

Today, there seems to be recognition in the United States that existing zero-tolerance policies are harmful to youth and communities and disproportionately affect black and Latino boys. Yet whether this recognition will lead to the decentralization of disciplinary authority and a return to local discretion remains to be seen. The larger trend toward greater centralization of educational authority in the United States – from No Child Left Behind to the Common Core – and internationally, as documented, for example, by Ziegler's chapter in this book, suggests otherwise.

Notes

1 The most prominent of these court decisions were two rulings by the United States Supreme Court: *Tinker* v. *Des Moines Independent Community School District*. 393 U.S. 503 (1969), and *Goss* v. *Lopez* 419 U.S. 565 (1975).

2. *Elementary Needs Report of the Los Angeles Elementary Teachers Club. Presented to Los Angeles City Board of Education, Superintendent Jarvis, Dr. Ralph Lanz*, May 1957, binder 543, locker 33, *Los Angeles Board of Education Subject Files: Discipline* (from here forward referenced as *DSF*).
3. Jarvis, E. quoted in *Minutes, Regular Meeting, Elementary, High School, and Junior College* (8 November 1956), DSF.
4. *A Report on Discipline Presented to the Los Angeles Board of Education by the Los Angeles Elementary Teachers Club* (8 November 1956), DSF, pp. 2, 3.
5. Teachers ask code on misbehavior. *Los Angeles Times*, 9 November 1956, Section III, pp. 1–2.
6. By the middle of the decade, district enrollment was increasing at the startling rate of 20 percent a year, and fast approaching 500,000. Classroom and faculty shortages were acute, and tens of thousands of students were forced to attend school in split-sessions. Los Angeles City School District, *Los Angeles City School District Annual Report, 1958–59*; Jarvis, E.A., 1959. *Progress and Achievement: A Report Submitted to the Honorable Members of the Board of Education of the Los Angeles City School District by Ellis A. Jarvis, Superintendent of Schools*. Los Angeles: Los Angeles City School District, p. x; Teachers pinpoint pupil problems. *Los Angeles Times*, 17 May 1957, p. 2.
7. *The Nature of Discipline Affecting Los Angeles City Secondary Schools* (8 November 1956), DSF.
8. *Discipline in the Elementary School: A Report Presented by the Committee on Discipline in the Elementary School, by the Los Angeles City School Districts Division of Elementary Education* (December 1956), DSF.
9. 763 Negro teachers in L.A. School District. *California Eagle*, 24 January 1957, p. 3.
10. Los Angeles City Schools Office of Public Information. *Board of Education Hears Proposals to Strengthen School's Discipline* (1957), DSF.
11. *Elementary Needs Report*.
12. Willett, H.C., 1956. *School Board Minutes* (8 November).
13. Get-tough discipline policy urged for problem pupils. *Los Angeles Times*, 12 April 1957, p. 1.
14. Burke, P., *Law and Rules Committee Reports No. 1 and 2* (27 April 1959), DSF.
15. Torgenson, D., "Brown Power" unity seen behind school disorders. *Los Angeles Times*, 17 March 1968, Section C, p. 1; West, R. and Larsen, D., Education Board halts meeting in climax to school disorders. *Los Angeles Times*, 8 March 1968, pp. 1, 3.
16. Information regarding student and community demands during the blowouts was drawn from the following sources: McCurdy, J., Demands made by East Side high school students listed. *Los Angeles Times*, 17 March 1968, Section A, p. 1; Section C, pp. 4, 5; *Memo to Members of the Board of Education from Jack Crowther*, 26 March 1968, *Los Angeles Board of Education Subject Files: Student Unrest*, binder 683, locker 4 (from here forward referenced as *SUSF*); *School Board Minutes*: 4 April 1968; 8 April 1968; 24 June 1968; 8 July 1968; 25 November 1968.
17. Corporal punishment was eventually abolished in the Los Angeles Unified School District as well, but not in response to these student protests.
18. Although some teachers were supportive of student protesters' efforts, their view tended to be in the minority. See letters sent to the Los Angeles Board of Education from teachers at Roosevelt High School, dated 13 March 1968 and 15 March 1968, *SUSF*, 682. Letter from teachers at Lincoln High School sent to the Board of Education, 17 March 1968, printed in *Inside Eastside*, 1(12) (26 April–9 May 1968), p. 2.

19 Quoted in Malnic, E., Angry teachers accuse Board of laxity on boycott. *Los Angeles Times*, 29 March 1968, pp. 1, 30.
20 Letter to Reverend James Edward Jones [president of the Board of Education] from the Hubert Howe Bancroft Junior High School Faculty Association, 3 May 1968, SUSF, *683.*
21 Presentation to the Board of Education by Dr. Frank B. Snyder, Executive Secretary, Los Angeles Association of Secondary School Administrators, 25 September 1968, SUSF, 683.
22 Torgenson, D., Negro militant strike closes 2 L.A. schools, disrupts 16. *Los Angeles Times*, 11 March 1968, pp. 1, 16. Most of the discussion of this event is drawn from: All schools in Black community open as Carver classes resume. *Los Angeles Times*, 14 March 1968, pp. 1, 25; Kumbula, J. and Powers, C., Attendance climbs as school tensions ease. *Los Angeles Times*, 15 March 1969, Part II, pp. 1, 10; Kistler, R., Black alliance and school aide differ on boycott support. *Los Angeles Times*, 1969, pp. 3, 26; Confrontation: Black parents – Black militants. *Herald-Dispatch*, 29 March 1969, pp. 1, 9; Torgenson, D., Disorder spreads: schools strife. *Los Angeles Times*, 12 March 1969, pp. 1, 3; Disruptions fail to close schools. *Los Angeles Times*, 13 March 1969, pp. 1, 3, 33; Thomas Bradley victim of planned school riot. *Herald-Dispatch*, 22 March 1969, pp. 1, 7. See also Mauller, R., 1976. *An Analysis of the Conflicts and the Community Relationships in Eight Secondary Schools of the Los Angeles Unified School District, 1967–1969*. PhD diss., University of California, Los Angeles, pp. 109–145.
23 Memorandum from the Los Angeles City School District's Public Information Office, to all schools and offices, 11 March 1969, SUSF, p. 684.
24 Los Angeles City Schools, Public Information Office, *City Schools Adopt 'Get Tough' Policy against Disruptions.* 19 March 1969, SUSF, p. 684. The organizations that were mentioned as being subject to such action, although they were not named specifically in the final motion, were: Students for Democratic Society, Black Students Union, UMAS, and Third World Liberation Front. *School Board Minutes*, 13 March 1969; *Statement by J.C. Chambers, Board of Education Member*, 13 March 1969, SUSF, p. 684; Mexican-American students unit banned at Roosevelt High. *Los Angeles Times*, 18 March 1969, p. 3; Memo to Roosevelt High School Teachers, from Dr. Dyer (school principal) and the administrative staff, reproduced in *Inside Eastside* (24 March–6 April 1969), p. 6.
25 Public schools, a crime invasion. *U.S. News & World Report*, 1970, 68(4), p. 9.
26 Terror in schools. *U.S. News & World Report*, 1976, 80(3), pp. 52–55.
27 US Congress, Senate Judiciary Committee, Subcommittee to Investigate Juvenile Delinquency, 1975. *Our Nation's Schools – A Report Card: "A" in School Violence and Vandalism*, Washington DC: US Government Printing Office, pp. 31–32.
28 Total enrollment in the district's elementary and secondary schools peaked at 650,324 in 1969 and then gradually declined; by the 1975–1976 school year the district's enrollment was 598,441 – a decrease of about 8 percent. Los Angeles Unified School District, 1975. *Racial and Ethnic Survey*, Fall.
29 For instance, Los Angeles figured prominently in six out of eight stories discussing school violence and the nation's response to it. *U.S. News and World Report* between 1969 and 1976.
30 Quoted in US Congress, *Our Nation's Schools*, p. 32.
31 Shooting spree interrupts Jefferson Hi homecoming. *Herald-Dispatch*, 1972, 16, pp. 1, 2.
32 Rosenzweg, D., Black principal describes school as 'Ft. Crenshaw', *Los Angeles Times*, 19 December 1972, pp. 1, 24.

33 Rule proposed by Board member Donald Newman, 9 October 1972. Adopted unanimously (with 3 absent but in support) on 12 October 1972. *School Board Minutes*, 9 October 1972; 12 October 1972, DSF; Sweeney, J. and Newton, T., 128 students seized as drug pushers in LA. *Los Angeles Times*, 4 December 1974, pp. 1, 34; Sweeney, J., Drug crackdown raises questions. *Los Angeles Times*, 7 December 1974 (Section II), p. 1.
34 School Board expected to OK tough new gun control rules. *Los Angeles Times*, 11 October 1972, Part II, pp. 1, 8. See also, Harris, L., Trend of high school violence in L.A. keeps students fearful. *Los Angeles Times*, 27 November 1972, pp. 3, 26.
35 West, R., 100 school drug-pusher suspects back on campus. *Los Angeles Times*, 5 December 1974, Part II, pp. 1–2.
36 US Commission on Civil Rights, 1979. *Desegregation of the Nation's Public Schools: A Status Report*. Washington, DC: US Department of Health, Education and Welfare, National Institute of Education, pp. 50–51.
37 Harold Holstein, Chairman, Professional Problems Committee, High School Teachers Association, in a presentation to the Los Angeles City Board of Education, 22 September 1960, DSF.
38 Statement submitted to the Board of Education by Darrell Jones, Chairman of the Student Support System of the Black Education Commission and Student Body President of Crenshaw High School, 12 October 1972, DSF.

References

Arum, R., 2003. *Judging School Discipline: The Crisis of Moral Authority*. Cambridge, MA: Harvard University Press.
Bybee, R. and Gee, E., 1982. *Violence, Values and Justice in the Schools*. Boston, MA: Allyn and Bacon.
Crews, G. and Counts, M.R., 1997. *The Evolution of School Disturbance in America: Colonial Times to Modern Day*. Westport, CT: Praeger.
Devine, J., 1996. *Maximum Security: The Culture of Violence in Inner-city Schools*. Chicago, IL: University of Chicago Press.
Gilbert, J., 1986. *A Cycle of Outrage: America's Reaction to the Juvenile Delinquent in the 1950s*. New York: Oxford University Press.
Hoover, J.E., 1958. Counterattack on juvenile delinquency. *Los Angeles Times, This Week Magazine*, October 26, p. 8.
Johnson, T., Boyden, J.E., and Pittz, W., 2000. *Racial Profiling and Punishment in US Public Schools*. Oakland, CA: Applied Research Center.
Kaestle, C., 1983. *Pillars of the Republic: Common Schools and American Society, 1780–1860*. New York: Hill and Wang.
Kafka, J., 2011. *The History of "Zero Tolerance" in American Public Schooling*. New York: Palgrave Macmillan.
Lambert, S., 1956. What a national survey of teachers reveals about pupil behavior. *NEA Journal*, pp. 339–342.
Los Angeles City School District, 1966. *Racial and Ethnic Survey, Fall 1966*. Los Angeles, CA: Los Angeles County (Calif.) Office of Superintendent of Schools.
Mauller, R., 1976. *An Analysis of the Conflicts and the Community Relationships in Eight Secondary Schools of the Los Angeles Unified School District, 1967–1969*. PhD dissertation, University of California, Los Angeles.

Meyer, J., Scott, W.R. and Deal, T., 1983. Institutional and technical sources of organizational structure: explaining the structure of educational organizations. In: J. Meyer and W.R. Scott (eds) *Organizational Environments: Ritual and Rationality*. Newbury Park, CA: Sage, pp. 45–67.

Muñoz, C., 1989. *Youth, Identity, Power: The Chicano Movement*. New York: Verso.

Murphy, M., 1990. *Blackboard Unions: The AFT and the NEA, 1900–1980*. Ithaca, NY: Cornell University Press.

NLCC Educational Media (1996) *Chicano!: The History of the Mexican American Civil Rights Movement, Taking Back the Schools* (video). Los Angeles, CA: NLCC Educational Media.

Noguera, P., 1995. Preventing and producing violence: a critical analysis of responses to school violence. *Harvard Educational Review*, 65(2), pp. 189–213.

Randall, H., 1957. The multiple roles of women. *Los Angeles School Journal*, February 19, pp. 9–11.

Salisbury, H., 1958. *The Shook-up Generation*. New York: Harper & Row.

Skiba, R. and Rausch, M.K., 2006. Zero tolerance, suspension, and expulsion: questions of equity and effectiveness. In: C. Everston and C. Weinstein (eds) *Handbook of Classroom Management: Research, Practice, and Contemporary Issues*. Mahwah, NJ: Lawrence Erlbaum Associates, pp. 1063–1089.

Thernstrom, A., 1999. Where did all the order go? School discipline and the law. In D. Ravitch (ed.) *Brookings Papers on Education Policy*. Washington, DC: The Brookings Institution Press, pp. 299–327.

Tyack, D., 1974. *The One Best System: A History of American Urban Education*. Cambridge, MA: Harvard University Press.

Weinig, K., 2000. The 10 worst educational disasters of the 20th century: a traditionalist's list. *Education Week*, 19(40), p. 31.

Chapter 8

The state of education in the States
The US Department of Education and the evolving federal role in American school policy

Patrick McGuinn

Introduction

The most striking feature of American governance is federalism – the allocation of constitutional authority across federal and state governments – and nowhere is its impact more profound than in education. Most other countries have unitary governments that centrally establish and administer policy for schools, including the creation of a single national curriculum and testing system. In the United States, the multi-level and fragmented education governance structure and strong tradition of local control have made the creation of national policy in education – national standards and assessments in particular – much more complex, both politically and administratively.[1] Yet, persistent racial and socio-economic achievement gaps, global economic competition, and the weak performance of US students on international tests have amplified the call for some common goals and yardsticks to measure our children's academic performance, as well as more ambitious efforts to turn around chronically underperforming schools.

Education in the United States has historically been characterized by local control and the federal government has no constitutional authority to dictate education policy to the states. Beginning with the National Defense Education Act of 1958 and the Elementary and Secondary Education Act of 1965, however, national policymakers have used the grant-in-aid system to pursue federal goals in public education. In order to claim their share of a growing pot of federal education funds, states have had to agree to comply with a wide array of federal policy mandates. These mandates initially focused on ensuring more equitable school funding and access rather than the academic performance of students and schools. A new federal focus on accountability for student achievement and school reform was outlined in the Improving America's Schools Act of 1994 and was given more "teeth" in the No Child Left Behind Act in 2001. These developments have involved the federal government for the first time in core matters of school governance – such as academic standards, student assessment, teacher quality, school choice, and school restructuring – and fundamentally altered the relationship between the federal government and the states in education policy. They have also severely strained the federal grant-in-aid system and the administrative capacity of the US Department of Education (USED). For the USED to be effective in gaining state compliance with federal education policies, it needs sufficient statutory authority, administrative capacity, and political support. Still, throughout most of the thirty-year history of the department these resources have not been present.

This chapter will provide an overview of the evolution of national administrative capacity and the implementation of federal education policy in the United States between 1965 and 2012. As most recent research on education policy implementation has focused on states' activity and compliance efforts, this chapter will examine the process by which federal power over schools has become institutionalized over time. The relationship between Washington and the states in the area of education has historically been predicated on cooperation rather than conflict, both due to the fact that state education agencies have long depended on the US Department of Education for a considerable portion of their budgets (about 40 percent on average) and because state and federal educational policy goals have generally been well aligned. The challenge in the current NCLB era is that the feds have demanded that states develop new systems for tracking and disseminating student achievement data and intervening in struggling schools. However, states resent this new level of federal involvement and have struggled to meet all of the federal mandates. Consequently, as federal goals and methods have diverged from those of the states, the intergovernmental relationship has undergone a significant transformation. A central contribution of the chapter will thus be to offer a detailed analysis of the new educational federalism in the post-NCLB era. It will assess how the policy mandates of the law have affected the institutional capacities and incentives for reform in state and federal departments of education in order to illuminate the administrative mechanisms through which this new federalism operates.

Origins: the US Office of Education and the early federal role in education

Education policymaking in the United States has traditionally been dominated by local and state governments. The Constitution's silence on a federal role in education, supplemented by tradition and the reserved powers clause of the Tenth Amendment, meant that schooling was a very decentralized and locally run affair, from colonial times through the early days of the Republic. It was not until the common school movement of the nineteenth century that the states began to develop organized systems of public schools, with Massachusetts opening the first public high school in 1821 and passing the nation's first compulsory school attendance law in 1852. It was not until 1918, however, that such laws were in force in the other forty-nine states (Newman, 1994). Even then, state supervision and control over the education policies of locally financed and run public schools remained weak, as evidenced by the fact that, in 1890, on average, state departments of education employed only two staffers (including the superintendent) (Tyack and Cuban, 1997). The origin of federal involvement in education can be traced to the Land Ordinance Act of 1785 and the Northwest Ordinances of 1787, which linked the drawing of property lines with the creation of schools. Beginning with the admission of Ohio as a state, Congress required that all subsequent states guarantee public education in their state constitutions as a condition of statehood. The federal government became more directly involved in education – and set a precedent for grant-in-aid programs – with the passage of the Morrill Act in 1862. The Act authorized the creation of a network of what became known as land-grant colleges and committed the federal government to support them financially through the sale of federally owned lands.

While the federal government played a crucial early role in the development of K-12 education, it stayed virtually absent from the management of public schools until the second half of the twentieth century. The size and scope of national administrative power in education has, until the past decade or so, been quite small – a fact that is both a cause and a consequence of limited federal educational goals. A US Office of Education (USOE) was created in 1867, but it was given little staff or resources and a very proscribed mandate to gather statistical data on schools.[2] Its founding legislation declared that the Office was:

> for the purpose of collecting such statistics and facts as shall show the condition and progress of education in the several states and territories, and of diffusing such information respecting the organization and management of schools and school systems, and methods of teaching, as shall aid the people of the United States in the establishment and maintenance of efficient schools systems, and otherwise promote the cause of education throughout the country.
> (Kursh, 1965, pp. 11–12)

Even this limited role encountered a great deal of opposition from states' rights advocates, who saw any federal role in education as inappropriate and threatening to their sovereignty. As Harry Kursh has noted, there was "a lingering fear that almost any Federal activity – even an ingenuous attempt to gather statistics on the per capita expenditures of the states for education – would sharpen the entering wedge for complete government control of education" (Kursh, 1965, p. 13). Opposition to the original Office resulted in it receiving a tiny initial budget and a staff of only six, and these were expanded only slowly and amid much political infighting. The federal role in education increased in 1917 with the passage of the Smith-Hughes Act, which provided the first annual federal appropriation for K-12 schooling for vocational education programs. Even as late as the first half of the twentieth century, however, the nation's school system remained extremely decentralized. The day-to-day management of schools – including such matters as personnel, curriculum, and pedagogy –

remained in the hands of local authorities, with state and federal governments having little influence.

Expansion: the ESEA, equity, and categorical compliance

In the 1950s, growing elite concerns around educational equity and economic and military competitiveness led to a more expanded federal role in education. The National Defense Education Act (NDEA) of 1958 and the Elementary and Secondary Education Act (ESEA) of 1965 fundamentally expanded and transformed the federal role in schools by providing sustained, large-scale education aid to the states for the first time. The aim of the combination of the NDEA and the ESEA was to dramatically increase federal funding for education, both in absolute terms and as a proportion of total education spending. Between 1958 and 1968, for example, federal spending on education increased more than tenfold, from $375 million to $4.2 billion, and the federal share expanded from less than 3 percent to about 10 percent of the total school funding. Even as federal spending and programs in education grew over time, however, the ends and means of federal policy were clearly circumscribed – the national government would limit its efforts to improving educational equity by providing targeted categorical programs and supplemental funding for poor schools and children.

The creation of federal categorical programs in the NDEA and ESEA required that federal educational institutions shift from what had been largely an information-gathering and disseminating role to a more supervisory responsibility in the administration of the new federal funds and programs. This shift necessitated the creation of new federal and state administrative capacities to oversee the administration of the programs and ensure state compliance. State eligibility for federal education funds was often contingent on the provision of state matching funds, the creation of central implementing offices, and the collection of a variety of statistical data, which necessitated that state education agencies expand their size and activities and become more institutionalized. This was a clear objective of the ESEA, as Title V of the original legislation provided $25 million over five years for the agencies to build up their administrative capacity so that they would be better equipped to handle their new, federally imposed, responsibilities. The result, as Paul Hill has noted, was that state education agencies often became so dependent on federal funding and pliable to federal direction that they were effectively "colonized" (Hill, 2000, pp. 25–26).[3]

State education agencies (SEAs) – which had generally been poorly funded and staffed prior to the ESEA – became a crucial partner of the USOE and the key implementing agency for federal education policy. For most of the next thirty years, this was a cooperative and symbiotic relationship, as the federal government depended on SEAs to funnel national grant monies to local school districts. Moreover, the states were thrilled to accept such funds, particularly when not accompanied by federal mandates. However, the federal reliance on SEAs created the potential for a serious principal-agent challenge for USOE and the department would later struggle to get SEAs to align state priorities and resources with federal educational goals.

As noted by Bailey and Mosher in *ESEA: The Office of Education Administers a Law* (1968), from the start the USOE faced tremendous challenges in implementing the ESEA. First, the legislation incorporated multiple goals and methods, some of which were incompatible with one another. Second, the original ESEA gave federal administrators few tools to force compliance with federal directives in the use of ESEA funds. (Given the political opposition to federal "control" in education, it had been impossible to include even the kind of basic requirements that were normally attached to categorical grants in other policy areas such as Aid to Families with Dependent Children (AFDC).) Third, even if such tools had been available, for several years after the law's passage, the USOE was disinclined or unable to make use of such compliance tools. Fourth, lingering opposition to federal control of education ensured that attempts to rigorously administer the ESEA would generate a strong political backlash. Finally, the politics and implementation of the ESEA were greatly complicated by the addition of new purposes and programs and an increasingly contentious racial politics around school integration in the years following 1965.

Though the goal of the ESEA – to improve educational opportunity for the poor – was clear, the legislation was vague on how this goal was to be achieved. The ESEA distributed funds to school districts according to the number of poor children enrolled, but did not specify which services districts should provide to 'educationally deprived' children (Jennings, 2000, p. 4). The consequence of the ESEA's initial flexibility was that federal funds were used in a wide variety of ways and for a wide variety of purposes and local districts often diverted funds away from redistributive programs.[4] As Graham observed, "the upshot of all this is that when Title I was implemented, it produced not *a* Title I program, but something more like 30 thousand separate and different Title I programs" (1984, p. 204). The original ESEA legislation gave the USOE little power to coerce states to comply with federal regulations or goals or to punish states and school districts that failed to do so. The great level of discretion accorded to states and school districts in spending the new federal money ensured that compliance with federal goals was spotty at best. In his examination of the implementation of the ESEA, Berke noted that:

> federal aid is channeled into an existing state political system and pattern of policy, and a blend distilled of federal priorities and the frequently different state priorities emerges ... Federal money is a stream that must pass through a state capitol; at the state level, the federal government is rarely able – through its guidelines and regulations – radically to divert the stream or reverse the current.
>
> (Berke, 1974, p. 143)

Initially the USOE relied on the assurances of state education officials that they were in compliance with federal guidelines.[5] However, one of the fundamental premises behind the idea of compensatory education, and of the ESEA more generally, was that state and local education authorities had failed to ensure equal educational opportunities for their students and that they could not be trusted to do so in the future without federal intervention. The distrust of local education authorities – and mounting evidence that states and localities were diverting federal funds to purposes for which they were not intended – ultimately led Congress and federal bureaucrats to increase the regulation and supervision of federal aid. By the 1970s, the additional resources available to the US Office of Education and the agency's gradual adjustment to its new administrative role led the USOE to more aggressively enforce federal education mandates (Hughes and Hughes, 1972, p. 57). The ongoing consolidation of school districts across the country facilitated this effort as administrative centralization at the state level ultimately made schools more susceptible to federal regulation.[6]

In the 1980s, John Chubb would note that "in federal programs that are not explicitly regulatory, as well as those that are, policy has come to be carried out by increasingly detailed, prescriptive, legalistic, and authoritative means" (Chubb, 1985, p. 287). Between 1964 and 1976, for example, the number of pages of federal legislation affecting education increased from 80 to 360, while the number of federal regulations increased from 92 in 1965 to nearly 1,000 in 1977 (Ravitch, 1983, p. 312). Continuing opposition to federal micromanagement in education and the lack of consensus on how to measure the effectiveness of school reform efforts, however, led federal administrators to focus on school districts' spending patterns and administrative compliance. The result of this shift was that large numbers of bureaucratic regulations were created during the 1970s without any kind of concomitant focus on student or school results – everything was judged by procedure and process. Federal spending on elementary and secondary education, meanwhile, continued to increase, doubling from 1965 to 1975 (with a 210 percent increase in inflation-adjusted dollars) (National Center for Education Statistics, 2000, p. 395). Equally important was that federal spending increased relative to other levels; between 1960 and 1985, the percentage of total education spending provided by the national government increased from 8 to 16 percent, while the share attributed to local governments declined from 51 to 31 percent, as the state share increased from 41 to 55 percent (Wright, 1988, p. 195).

Strong institutional and ideological obstacles to an expansion of federal influence in education persisted long after the passage of the ESEA in 1965 and a bi-partisan consensus of sorts developed around these limits imposed on the federal role. National administrative authority in education was severely fragmented, with operational authority for federal categorical programs dispersed across a number of different federal agencies (including the Departments of Defense, Labor, and Health, Education and Welfare). Liberals, meanwhile, fought to keep the federal role redistributive in nature and focused on disadvantaged students. In addition, because of their alliance with teachers' unions and the belief that inadequate school resources were the primary problem facing schools, Democrats also sought to keep the federal role centered on school inputs rather than on outputs or curricular or governance issues. Conservatives, however, were willing to tolerate a small federal role in education, as long as it was unobtrusive and did not threaten local control over schools. These structural and political constraints produced a strange dynamic in which the increase in federal education spending and programs was not accompanied by a comparable strengthening of national administrative power over core school governance issues, or by expanded influence over state school improvement efforts.

Institutionalization: the creation of the US Department of Education

As the quantity and size of federal education programs grew in the wake of the ESEA, there were calls from some quarters to consolidate national administrative capacity in a form of a single-cabinet level agency. Although legislation to create a new federal department for education had been introduced 130 times between 1908 and 1975, the idea had always generated a great deal of political opposition from a variety of interests that had a stake in preserving the status quo (Stallings, 2002, p. 677). Small government conservatives opposed the new department because it would expand the size of the federal bureaucracy and the power of the federal government, which they were committed to rolling back. Moreover, state rights advocates believed that education was a state and local responsibility and that any federal role would be intrusive and counter-productive (Stephens, 1983, p. 651).

It is important to note that the primary goal of the advocates who fought to create the USED was to protect and expand federal education spending and programs, rather than to build an organization that could pressure states to reform their school systems. President Carter led the successful effort to create the USED in 1979, fulfilling an earlier campaign promise he had made to win the first presidential endorsement of the National Education Association. That Congress viewed the USED largely as a clientele agency was manifest in the legislation that created the department and the way in which the department was structured, staffed, and empowered. Congress limited the managerial flexibility of the department's leadership by embedding a detailed organizational structure in the authorizing legislation. This was somewhat unusual and was to have important consequences; as one observer noted, "unlike many reorganization efforts, most decisions concerning the ED reorganization structure were made in the adoption stage of the policy process by Congress" (Radin and Hawley, 1988, p. 176).

In *The Politics of Federal Reorganization: Creating the Department of Education*, Radin and Hawley (1988) observed that the political compromises in the drafting of the authorizing legislation limited the flexibility and resources accorded to the department's leadership and diluted the effectiveness of the new department in the short term. The practical task of merging a large number of different programs with their disparate organizational structures, cultures, and procedures would take time and meant that "true" reorganization of the executive department would take many years. From the very beginning, the administrative functions of the department were under-funded and under-staffed and these issues persisted as the number and size of federal education programs grew over time. This reflected the vision of the USED as a mere grant-making and information-gathering organization, rather than one charged with pushing states to embrace school reform (Radin and Hawley, 1988, p. 188). The new department also had to adapt to the demands of extensive Congressional oversight. Members of Congress were very protective of certain education department programs and staff and were rather willing to intervene to protect them, further limiting the managerial flexibility of the Secretary.[7]

When Carter was defeated in the 1980 presidential election (only a year after the department was created), the Department of Education lost its most powerful proponent. President Carter's successor, Republican Ronald Reagan, announced his desire to abolish the department entirely and secured the passage of the 1981 Education Consolidation and Improvement Act (ECIA), which dramatically reduced its size and power.[8] Though Reagan's efforts to disband the ED were ultimately unsuccessful, the attacks succeeded in substantially reducing the department's staffing and budget and its regulatory authority, thereby further limiting its ability to promote educational coordination or improvement. Some scholars have estimated that the number of regulatory mandates imposed on states through federal education programs was reduced by 85 percent during the Reagan Administration (Glendening and Reeves, 1984, p. 243). The budget for the Department of Education was cut by 11 percent between FY1981 and FY1988 (in real dollars), while the National Institute of Education (the federal educational research and development body) lost 70 percent of its funding during the period (Verstegen and Clark, 1988, p. 137). As Maris Vinovskis has noted, these reductions significantly reduced the number and quality of program evaluations within the department and thus made it more difficult for the agency to gauge the effectiveness of its educational improvement efforts (Vinovskis, 1999). Moreover, the assault on the department's legitimacy occupied the time and energies of both policymakers within the department and its supporters in Congress. Consequently, the new department and its allies were preoccupied with its survival rather than the difficult task of adapting the organization to its new responsibilities.

The 1980s thus witnessed two contradictory trends in national administrative power in education. On one hand, the opening of a cabinet-level national Department of Education in 1980 was representative of the expansion and institutionalization of federal authority over public schools. On the other hand, however, this expansion was not accompanied by an increase in the administrative capacity or political will that would have enabled the USED to hold states accountable for the outputs of their school systems or to force them to adopt major reforms. By 1980, federal spending and influence on schooling had expanded dramatically and the new Department of Education administered approximately 500 different federal education programs.[9] Still, the federal focus remained on access and equity issues rather than on improving schools' or students' academic performance and there was little effort to measure the educational progress of students who received federal funds or protection. This became increasingly problematic as a number of prominent studies were released that found that ESEA funds and programs had largely failed to improve educational opportunity for disadvantaged students.[10] Berke and Kirst (1972), for example, analyzed data from over 500 school districts and concluded that ESEA aid had done little to redress the large inequality in per-pupil expenditures between rich and poor districts.[11] In addition, because the ESEA was premised on the provision of additional resources, rather than the promotion of school reform, federal education aid generally went to support existing state and local programs. Over time, this approach came under fire, as the additional resources failed to generate either new reform approaches or improvement in student achievement.

The creation of a national department of education, and the release of the widely discussed *A Nation at Risk* report (which the department commissioned) in 1983, created the potential for a reconfiguration and expansion of the federal role in school reform. Nonetheless, the new administrative capacity that the creation of the USED was intended to provide did not develop during the 1980s because of the control of the Executive branch (and for part of the time Congress) by a Republican party that was extremely hostile to increasing federal power over schools. The same political dynamics redirected the national momentum generated by *A Nation at Risk* to advancing state school reform efforts, despite the report's call for a more robust federal role.

Redirection: the IASA and the new focus on standards and accountability

The election of a Democratic President and a Democratic Congress in 1994 created a political environment more favorable to an expansion of federal education policy. In the 1994 ESEA reauthorization (the Improving America's Schools Act (IASA)), President Clinton – a former "education governor" and "New Democrat" – secured changes that would push states to increase performance reporting and embrace educational accountability. Under this new ESEA and a companion piece of legislation, Goals 2000, states were required to establish academic standards in each grade and create tests to assess whether students had mastered the standards. The tests were to be administered to all poor children at least once in grades 3 through 5, 6 through 9, and 10 through 12. Enforcement by the US Department of Education was lax, however, as Democrats were opposed to withholding funds from state education systems and Republicans resisted federal micromanagement of states. In the end, most states failed to comply: as late as 2002, two years after the target date for full compliance, just sixteen states had fully complied with the central components of the 1994 law (McGuinn, 2006). Meanwhile, on the heels of the passage of the 1994 ESEA reauthorization, Republicans won control of both the House and Senate for the first time in decades – partly on the strength of their "Contract with America" and its call to roll back the expanse and power of the federal government. Republicans used their control of Congress – and of the appropriations for the USED – to undermine the USED's ability to pressure states on school reform. During the next ESEA reauthorization debate in 1999, conservative Republicans in Congress introduced the Academic Achievement for All Act ("Straight A's"), which sought to reduce federal influence by combining most federal education programs into block grants.

Enforcement: NCLB and the new mission of the US Department of Education

The previous discussion has demonstrated that the USED has historically been unable or unwilling to use federal education dollars as leverage to force systemic change in state education systems. (The notable exception here was in ending segregation but this effort was pushed more by the courts than USED.) The USED lacked the combination of three resources essential to undertaking such an effort – statutory authority, administrative capacity, and political will. The passage of the No Child Left Behind Act in 2001 fundamentally expanded and redirected federal education policy. Furthermore, it placed the USED at the center of a bi-partisan effort to use federal education spending in order to pressure states to embrace test-based accountability and introduce a host of reforms to reduce racial and socio-economic achievement gaps. While the 1994 Goals 2000 and IASA reforms put in place much of the statutory scaffolding for a shift in federal policy, as noted above, the USED lacked the administrative capacity and political will to enforce the law's mandates vigorously.

NCLB requires states to create accountability systems, annually test children in reading and math in grades 3 through 8 (and once in high school), identify proficient students as well as schools where an insufficient number of students were proficient, ensure that specified measures were taken with regard to schools that failed to make "adequate yearly progress," and set targets that would ensure that 100 percent of children were proficient in reading and math by 2014. One of the most important mandates in the law is that school report cards must disaggregate student test score data for subgroups based on race or ethnicity, economically disadvantaged status, limited proficiency in English, and classification as in need of special education. Crucially and controversially, a school that does not meet the proficiency target for *any one of these groups* is placed in "in need of improvement status" and states are required to take an escalating series of steps and interventions (including the offering of public school choice, tutoring, technical assistance, and restructuring) aimed at schools and districts that persistently fail to meet AYP targets.

The scope, specificity, and ambition of the law's mandates signaled something akin to a revolution in federal education policy. As written, however, the NCLB legislation was a complex mix of federal mandates and state discretion – although states are required to put standards and tests in place and create a system for dealing with failing schools, they are also entrusted with setting the rigor of these. Given these cross-cutting currents, much would depend on the way in which the law was implemented by the Bush Department of Education, and how the department handled states' requests for flexibility, extensions, and waivers. On this count, states hoped that the administration would be as amenable as the Clinton administration had proved to be in implementing the 1994 legislation. Deeming it the most promising path to deliver the cultural shift in schooling it sought, the Bush administration took a hard line and pushed states to comply with the letter of the law. While this forced states to take the law's mandates more seriously than they otherwise would have, it unsurprisingly sparked vocal complaints among educators, who argued that the law's goals and timetables were unrealistic and that the resources and guidance provided were insufficient.

One awkward question was how the Bush administration would respond to states that pushed back against the law's requirements in the name of federalism. The administration faced a thorny choice: acquiescing and accepting the efforts to undercut the reach of NCLB or aggressively challenging states that threatened to forfeit federal dollars in order to opt out of the NCLB regime. In a decision that caused consternation among conservatives concerned about federal overreach and the integrity of federalism, the administration opted to use every tool at its disposal to keep states in line. Given the noble promise of NCLB's pledge that every child would be proficient in reading and math by 2014, along with its belief that allowing states to backslide would launch the nation on a slippery slope and undercut its effort to transform the culture of schooling, the administration successfully brought substantial pressure to bear when Utah and Connecticut publicly challenged NCLB.

The aggressive implementation approach of the Bush administration USED succeeded in getting states to comply with federal mandates and intervene to a greater extent than ever before in districts with failing schools. As Phyllis McClure, a longtime member of the Title I Independent Review Panel, has observed:

> NCLB has grabbed the education community's attention like no previous ESEA reauthorization. It has really upset the status quo in state and local offices . . . For the first time, district and school officials are actually being required to take serious and urgent action in return for federal dollars.
>
> (McClure, 2004)

NCLB's requirement that states conduct annual testing and report student scores has forced states to build new data-gathering and dissemination systems and has resulted in a greater degree of transparency in public education than ever before. Scholars Tiffany Berry and Rebecca Eddy have written that the law has "transformed the landscape of educational evaluation" and is "redefining what evaluation is within the education evaluation community" (Berry and Eddy, 2008, p. 2). By holding states clearly accountable for the performance of their public schools, NCLB has also prompted state departments of education to expand their capacity to monitor local districts, provide technical assistance, and intervene where necessary (Hess and Finn, 2007).

The major policy shifts imbedded in NCLB necessitated a corresponding shift in the structure, staffing, and operations of the USED, which is charged with implementing the new law. In particular, NCLB's new focus on raising student achievement necessitated that the department develop new research capacities that could permit the effective monitoring of state compliance, the implementation of new longitudinal student data systems, and the identification of effective classroom interventions (McGuinn et al., 2012, pp. 125–154). The Institute of Education Sciences (IES) was created by the Education Sciences Reform Act of 2002, replacing the Office of Educational Research and Improvement (OERI) (and its predecessor the National Institute of Education, NIE), which had been the primary federal education research institutions since 1972. The methodology and quality of the research studies funded by the OERI and NIE were widely criticized and they were generally seen as exerting little if any influence on state education policies or classroom practice. In response, the IES has adopted a new strategy of conducting and funding research, which is primarily based on randomized trials that can more precisely measure the effects and effectiveness of state and federal policies (Whitehurst, 2003).

Another important arm of the new ED was the Office of Innovation and Improvement, which was created early in President George W. Bush's first term. According to its website, the OII is:

> the nimble, entrepreneurial arm of the U.S. Department of Education. It makes strategic investments in innovative educational practices through two dozen discretionary grant programs and coordinates the public school choice and supplemental educational services provisions of the Elementary and Secondary Education Act as amended by No Child Left Behind.[12]

These institutional changes at USED serve a dual purpose. In the short term, they enable the department to more effectively carry out its new mission of monitoring state compliance with NCLB mandates. In the longer term, however, it was hoped that the reorientation and reorganization of the USED would institutionalize the new, more aggressive federal approach to school reform into the bureaucracy and make it harder for the approach to be undone by subsequent presidential administrations or congressional pressure.

Implementation: state education agencies

As Vergari has noted, states have rebelled against federal mandates in education and sought to reshape them on the ground (2012, pp. 15–34). However, NCLB mandates – combined with the rigorous enforcement by the USED – have pushed states to rapidly and fundamentally transform their student testing, data collection, and district monitoring systems. A 2008 Rand study, for example, concluded that "states, districts, and schools have adapted their policies and practices to support the implementation of NCLB" (Stecher et al., 2007, p. 64). The USED has closely monitored state compliance efforts on both the front end – through the use of detailed accountability plans that each state must submit for review – and on the back end, through regular state reporting and federal audits.[13] The USED's Office of Inspector General has conducted audits of state policies and their compliance with NCLB mandates and demanded that states make changes where necessary.

In New Jersey, for example, a federal audit in 2005 criticized the NJ Department of Education for not disseminating state assessment results effectively and for not exerting sufficient oversight of district compliance with either the choice or supplemental educational services (SES) provisions of NCLB (US Department of Education, 2005). The highly critical federal audit was sufficient to generate significant changes in state policies and has led to the creation of a more robust role for the NJ Department of Education in implementing NCLB and providing technical assistance to schools and districts. This vision became the basis for Collaborative Assessment and Planning for Achievement (CAPA) teams, which conduct week-long school reviews in low-performing Abbott and Title I schools.[14] In 2005, the Department of Education's monitoring and evaluation system was completely transformed with the creation of the New Jersey Quality Single Accountability Continuum (NJQSAC) and the development of a statewide student-level database.

This New Jersey example demonstrates the historically unprecedented level of federal monitoring and enforcement activities in state education systems in the wake of NCLB. In implementing NCLB, the Bush administration fundamentally altered the role of the federal Department of Education – shifting it from its historical role as a grant-maker and compliance monitor to a more active (if still relatively toothless) role as a compliance-enforcer and agitator. The administration has emphasized the importance of bottom-line results in student achievement, shifting the traditional focus from regulation and process. Despite all of the political controversy surrounding NCLB, one of the enduring legacies of the Bush administration will likely be the institutionalization of assessment and accountability in education. In this sense, NCLB's influence may ultimately be compared to the original ESEA in 1965 – which, for all its flaws and shortcomings, cemented in place a new and substantial federal role in education. While it is impossible to predict the outcome of the pending congressional reauthorization of NCLB, signs indicate that the law's central principles of standards, testing, and accountability are likely to continue – even if the name "No Child Left Behind" may be replaced and several of the law's original provisions substantially reworked.

President Obama and Race to the Top

The election of Barack Obama as president in 2008 – combined with Democratic control of Congress – gave the Democratic Party an opportunity to assert a new vision of education reform. Many observers initially assumed that this would lead to a move away from federal school accountability and a reassertion of a traditional liberal focus on school resources, integration, and social welfare programs. While his administration did in fact offer states waivers from some of NCLB's ambitious accountability requirements, it did so only on the condition that individual states were willing to support key elements of the Obama reform agenda (Cavanaugh, 2012). And President Obama has also increased the federal role in important ways, as he called for the growth of annual testing in the ESEA, expanded federal efforts to restructure the worst-performing schools, and created a new focus on innovation, charter schools, and teacher accountability. The centerpiece of the Obama education agenda was the $4.35 billion Race to the Top (RTT), $3.5 billion School Improvement Grant (SIG), and $650 million Investing in Innovation (i3) programs (McGuinn, 2012a, pp. 136–159).

Historically, almost all federal education funds have been distributed through categorical grant programs that allocated money to districts on the basis of need-based formulas. According to this traditional model, states and districts received funding automatically, regardless of the performance of their schools or the promise of their particular school reform policies. While there has always been variation across states and districts in the amount of federal funds received, this variance was due to differences in state educational needs (the number of poor, ESL, or special education students, for example), rather than differences in school policies. The RTT, SIG, and i3 funds, by contrast, were distributed through a competitive grant process in which states and districts were only rewarded for developing school reforms that were in line with federal goals and guidelines. In particular, state applications were graded according to the rigor of the reforms proposed and their compatibility with five administration priorities: the development of common standards and assessments; improving teacher training, evaluation, and retention policies; developing better data systems; the adoption of preferred school turnaround strategies; and building stakeholder support for reform.

The department also established a number of criteria that states had to meet to even be eligible to apply for the RTT funds. These requirements have had a major effect on state school reform efforts, independent of the specific grant proposals the states have submitted. Among the fourteen criteria for RTT eligibility was that a state did not have a cap on the number of charter schools that are permitted to operate and that it did not have a firewall preventing the linking of student achievement data with individual teacher information. This served to stir the pot politically over school reform as never before, by forcing different interest groups to publicly stake out their positions on the various reform components of RTT in the debate over whether to apply them and under what conditions (McGuinn, 2012b, pp. 25–31). The competition also attracted a tremendous amount of media attention to the issue of school reform, shone a bright light on dysfunctional state policies, and helped create new political coalitions at the local and state levels to drive reform. There is evidence, for example, that RTT's emphasis on expanding charter schools and revamping teacher evaluations helped change the political climate around these controversial issues, paving the way for the passage of reform legislation in many states. The Obama administration has initiated a second Race to the Top competition and announced its desire to distribute more federal education funding though competitive grant programs in the future.

In the area of teacher evaluation and compensation, Obama and Duncan have supported their tough talk with some important steps to tie federal funds to significant reform. They have expanded the federal Teacher Incentive Fund, which has distributed resources to experiment with alternative evaluation systems and performance pay systems. So far thirty-four states, districts, and non-profit groups have received money to develop approaches that use "objective measures" of student performance to compensate the most effective teachers. Most significantly, the Obama administration is leveraging the RTT funds to spur improvements in state teacher data collection and evaluation systems, as well as to link such information to student achievement information. As Stephen Sawchuk has noted, "the stimulus application for the first time, sets a federal definition of teacher effectiveness" and states receiving RTT funds "must commit to using their teacher effectiveness data for everything from evaluating teachers to determining the type of professional development they get, to making decisions about granting tenure and pursuing dismissals" (Sawchuck, 2009). These changes are pushing states to embrace the types of teacher evaluation, compensation, and tenure reforms that they have long resisted. The use of competitive grants – and more recently conditional waivers from NCLB's accountability provisions – to drive states' reform efforts thus represents a new and potentially transformative role for the USED in American education.

The Common Core effort

Another important recent development has been the effort by the National Governors Association (NGA) and the Council of Chief State School Officers (CCSSO) to develop a "Common Core" of national academic standards and parallel assessments. Earlier efforts to develop national standards and assessments in the United States – such as those by President George H.W. Bush and President Bill Clinton in the 1990s – were met with impassioned opposition from across the political spectrum by those who feared federal power in education and/or the idea of a national curriculum that would overwhelm traditional state prerogatives.[15] The implementation of NCLB, however, increased the pressure to develop national standards and assessments, as states used their discretion in this area to manipulate the accountability system by lowering their standards, making their tests easier, and/or decreasing their proficiency cut scores. Such actions were widely criticized for dumbing down the curriculum and undermining the law's school accountability system. The result was that school reformers from across the political spectrum came to see the creation of common standards and assessments – and the increased accuracy and transparency they would bring to school performance – as an essential part of the effort to improve schools going forward (Bush and Klein, 2011).

In the wake of the many centralizing and coercive NCLB mandates, however, concerns regarding federal authority had only increased and this led to the mantra that common standards and assessments should be "national, not federal" (Heise, 2006). In July 2009, the NGA and CCSSO created a task force comprising representatives from higher education, K-12 education, and the research community and released standards in English and mathematics in June 2010. Given the voluntary nature of this approach, each state must make its own decision about whether to adopt the Common Core, and thereby substitute the national standards and assessments for the state's own. By encouraging states to sign on as part of their RTT applications, the Obama administration was able to get forty-eight states to pledge to sign on to the Common Core Standards Initiative (with only Alaska and Texas declining to participate). Moreover, as of July 2012, forty-five states had gone further and formally adopted the common standards as a replacement for their own state standards. In addition, three different consortia competed for the $350 million in RTT funding set aside for the development of next-generation assessments. Conlan and Posner see RTT and the Common Core approach as part of the Obama administration's "hybrid model of federal policy innovation and leadership, which mixes money, mandates, and flexibility in new and distinctive ways ... The model represents a blend of, but is different from, both cooperative and coercive federalism" (Conlan and Posner, 2011).

Conclusion

The past thirty years have witnessed a dramatic shift in politics and policymaking in American K-12 education. That the problems identified by *A Nation at Risk* – large socio-economic and racial achievement gaps and concerns that even the country's "good schools" are not good enough – continue to persist almost thirty years later is not the subject of much dispute. The particular source of the country's educational maladies and the best prescription to remedy them, however, continue to engender substantial disagreement among educators, researchers, citizens, and politicians. The new federal focus on academic performance and the extension of federal policy to cover every student and every school in the country mark a major shift in the governance of elementary and secondary education in the United States. As states have struggled to meet NCLB's ambitious goals and chafed at the reforms rewarded by RTT, some of the initial philosophical reservations within the Democratic and Republican parties regarding the new federal emphasis on accountability have come storming back to the surface. Many Republicans resent the coerciveness of the new federal role, while many Democrats are concerned about the impact of standardized testing on instruction and the focus on schools over broader economic and social change (McGuinn, 2012c).

As Miriam Cohen argues in her chapter in this volume, education in America has long resisted centralization, in stark contrast to European systems such as those of France and England. Federalism, and the lack of national constitutional authority to directly impose school reform on the states, have greatly complicated American politics and policymaking in education as it has forced the federal government to pursue its goals for school reform indirectly – through the grant-in-aid system and state education agencies. Recent developments – particularly NCLB, RTT, and the development of national standards and assessments – are moving America closer to a single "system" of education such as that found in much of the rest of the world. At the same time, however, the troubled implementation of these new policies – and the political controversy surrounding them – highlights the continuing distinctiveness of the education state in the United States.

The intergovernmental relationship in education in the United States in the contemporary era is both cooperative and coercive – a duality that makes it complex and contingent on broader political forces. The relationship has a cooperative element because the USED must rely on state education agencies as a conduit for federal education spending and as the implementer of federal policies on the ground in school districts. It is also coercive, however, as federal spending and policies have increasingly been used to push states to undertake politically unpopular changes they would not have undertaken in the absence of federal pressure. Coercion relies upon incentives and sanctions and, in education, the promise or withholding of federal funding can serve both purposes. Federal efforts to use the grant-in-aid system to force changes in state education policies are ultimately dependent on the willingness and ability of the USED to withhold funds from non-compliant states. In the absence of such action – or the credible threat of such action – it is unrealistic to expect states to comply with federal directives.

For the USED to be effective in gaining state compliance with federal education policies, it needs sufficient statutory authority, administrative capacity, and political support. However, throughout most of the thirty-year history of the department, these resources have not been present. The 2001 No Child Left Behind Act represents a major shift in the ESEA and an ambitious and controversial expansion of federal power over an educational system that has long been based on the principle of local control. With its prescriptive mandates, timetables, and aggressive enforcement, NCLB represents nothing less than a transformative shift in educational governance in the United States. However, the ultimate impact of the law – as well as recent Obama initiatives, such as Race to the Top and the Common Core – on schools is contingent upon ongoing efforts to restructure state and federal departments of education to expand their administrative capacity and reconfigure inter-governmental relationships to adapt to the new demands placed upon them. The Bush and Obama administrations have initiated an unprecedented effort to empower and reorient the US Department of Education to pressure states to embrace federal school assessment and accountability mandates. Clearly, the ultimate outcome of these efforts will have significant ramifications for the future of educational equity and federalism in America.

Notes

1 For more on the history of educational politics and policy-making in the United States, see McGuinn (2006) and Manna (2006).
2 For more on the establishment and activities of the US Office of Education, see Kursh (1965).
3 By 1993, state education agencies nationwide relied on federal funds for on average 41 percent of their operating budgets, with the federal share as high as 77 percent in some states.
4 See Peterson and Rabe (1986, pp. 136–140) for a more detailed discussion of the local tendency to shift federal funds from redistributive programs to other purposes.
5 The USOE was ill-suited to a compliance role – it had long been a small, passive organization that focused on collecting and disseminating statistical data on education and did little else. The result, as John and Anne Hughes noted, was that:

> if USOE had limitations on its policymaking authority and capability – and these have been legion – its ability to enforce its policies has been even more limited. The state agencies and the local districts, by and large, were used to going their own ways, which often meant disregarding federal requirements.
> (Hughes and Hughes, 1972, p. 50)

6 The number of districts declined from approximately 150,000 in 1900 to 15,000 in 1993 (Newman, 1994, p. 166).
7 Hufstedler noted that:

> with respect to one man on the Hill, if I didn't call him up on Wednesday and wish him a happy Thursday, he would be petulant and would give me trouble on some aspects of departmental work. In terms of turf, there are projects that are protected either by staff or by a congressman or by a senator. They believe they own those programs and if you try to do something that you think is important to change the priorities of the department, they are all over you like a nest of bees.
> (Hufstedler, 1990, pp. 66–67)

8 The 1980 Republican platform called for "deregulation by the federal government of public education and . . . the elimination of the federal Department of Education." The platform fretted that "parents are losing control of their children's schooling"

and that Democratic education policy had produced "huge new bureaucracies to misspend our taxes" (Historic Documents of 1980, pp. 583–584).
9 For an extended discussion of the expansion of federal compensatory education programs and the accompanying increase in federal education regulations, see Peterson (1983).
10 See, for example, those by Bailey and Mosher (1968), Berke and Kirst (1972), and Berke (1974).
11 It found that while Title I – which was explicitly focused on disadvantaged students – had a somewhat redistributive effect, this was erased by the effects of the other titles of the ESEA and vocational aid, which went disproportionately to wealthier districts. By dispersing ESEA funds widely across school districts, not only was federal assistance poorly targeted to its intended beneficiaries, but the additional resources that came to any particular school were limited (Berke and Kirst, 1972, p. 45).
12 www.ed.gov/about/offices/list/oii/index.html.
13 For more information on the USED review process for state accountability plans, see *No Child Left Behind Act: Enhancements in the Department of Education's Review Process Could Improve State Academic Assessments*. Government Accountability Office, September 2009.
14 For additional information on the CAPA process, see State of New Jersey Department of Education, *Collaborative Assessment for Planning and Achievement*. Available at: www.state.nj.us/njded/capa]] (accessed May 23, 2007).
15 For more of the standards-setting effort during this period, see Ravitch (1995).

References

Bailey, S. and Mosher, E., 1968. *ESEA: the Office of Education Administers a Law*. New York: Syracuse University Press.

Berke, J., 1974. *Answers to Inequity: An Analysis of the New School Finance*. Berkeley, CA: McCutchan.

Berke, J. and Kirst, M., 1972. *Federal Aid to Education*. Lexington, MA: Heath.

Berry, T. and Eddy, R., 2008. Consequences of No Child Left Behind on educational evaluation. *New Directions for Evaluation* (Special issue), 117.

Bush, J. and Klein, J., 2011. The case for common educational standards. *Wall Street Journal*, June 23.

Cavanaugh, S., 2012. Some states skeptical of NCLB waivers: big strings attached to bid for flexibility. *Education Week*, January 18.

Chubb, J., 1985. Excessive regulation: the case of federal aid to education. *Political Science Quarterly*, 100(2), pp. 287–311.

Conlan, T. and Posner, P., 2011. Inflection point? Federalism and the Obama administration. *Publius: The Journal of Federalism*, 41(3), pp. 421–446.

Glendening, P. and Reeves, M., 1984. *Pragmatic Federalism*. Pacific Palisades, CA: Palisades Publishers.

Government Accountability Office, 2009. *No Child Left Behind Act: Enhancements in the Department of Education's Review Process Could Improve State Academic Assessments*. GAO-09-911, September 24 (pdf). Available at: www.gao.gov/products/GAO-09-911 (accessed February 14, 2013).

Graham, H., 1984. *The Uncertain Triumph: Federal Education Policy in the Kennedy and Johnson Years*. Chapel Hill, NC: University of North Carolina Press.

Heise, M., 2006. The political economy of education federalism. *Emory Law Journal*, 56, pp. 125–158.

Hess, F. and Finn, C., 2007. *No Remedy Left Behind: Lesson from a Half-Decade of NCLB*. Washington, DC: AEI Press.

Hill, P., 2000. The federal role in education. In: D. Ravitch (ed.) *Brookings Papers on Education Policy*. Washington, DC: Brookings Institution Press, pp. 11–58.

Historic Documents of 1980, 1981. Washington, DC: Congressional Quarterly.

Hufstedler, S., 1990. Organizing the Department of Education. In: K. Thompson (ed.) *The Presidency and Education*. Lanham, MD: University Press of America.

Hughes, J. and Hughes, A., 1972. *Equal Education: A New National Strategy*. Bloomington, IN: Indiana University Press.

Jennings, J., 2000. Title I: its legislative history and its promise. *Phi Delta Kappan*, March, pp. 516–522.

Kursh, H., 1965. *The United States Office of Education: A Century of Service*. New York: Chilton Books.

McClure, P., 2004. Grassroots resistance to NCLB. *The Education Gadfly*, 4(11) (online). Available at: www.edexcellence.net/gadfly/index.cfm?issue=140#a1723 (accessed July 10, 2005).

McGuinn, P., 2006. *No Child Left Behind and the Transformation of Federal Education Policy, 1965–2005*. Lawrence, KS: University Press of Kansas.

McGuinn, P., 2012a. Stimulating reform: Race to the Top, competitive grants and the Obama education agenda. *Educational Policy*, 26(1), pp. 136–159.

McGuinn, P., 2012b. Fight club: how new school reform advocacy groups are changing the politics of education. *Education Next*, May, pp. 25–31.

McGuinn, P., 2012c. The federal role in educational equity: the two narratives of school reform and the debate over accountability. In: D. Allen and R. Reich (eds) *Education, Democracy, and Justice*. Chicago, IL: University of Chicago Press.

McGuinn, P., Berger, L., and Anderson, D., 2012. Incentives, information, and infrastructure: the federal role in educational innovation. In: R. Hess (ed.) *Carrots, Sticks, and the Bully Pulpit: Sobering Lessons from a Half-Century of Federal Efforts to Improve America's Schools*. Cambridge, MA: Harvard Education Press, pp. 125–154.

Manna, P., 2006. *School's In: Federalism and the National Education Agenda*. Washington, DC: Georgetown University Press.

National Center for Education Statistics, 2000. *The Condition of Education 2000*. Washington, DC: NCES.

Newman, M., 1994. *America's Teachers*. New York: Longman.

Peterson, P., 1983. Background paper. In: *Making the Grade: Report of the Twentieth Century Fund Task Force on Federal Elementary and Secondary Education Policy*. New York: Twentieth Century Fund.

Peterson, W.K. and Rabe, B., 1986. *When Federalism Works*. Washington, DC: Brookings Institution Press.

Radin, B. and Hawley, W., 1988. *The Politics of Federal Reorganization: Creating the US Department of Education*. New York: Pergammon Press.

Ravitch, D., 1983. *The Troubled Crusade: American Education from 1945–1980*. New York: Basic Books.

Ravitch, D., 1995. *National Standards in American Education*. Washington, DC: Brookings Institution Press.

Sawchuck, S., 2009. Teachers and the Race to the Top fund. *Education Week Teacher Beat Blog*. Available at: http://blogs.edweek.org/edweek/teacherbeat/2009/07/teacher_provisions_in_the_race.html (accessed July 25, 2009).

Stallings, D.T., 2002. A brief history of the US Department of Education, 1979–2002. *Phi Delta Kappan*, 83(9), pp. 677–683.

State of New Jersey Department of Education, 2007. *Collaborative Assessment for Planning and Achievement*. Available at: www.state.nj.us/njded/capa (accessed May 23, 2007).

Stecher, B.M., Epstein, S., Hamilton, L.S., Marsh, J.A., Robyn, A., McCombs, J.S., Russell, J., and Naftel, S., 2007. *Pain and Gain: Implementing No Child Left Behind in three states, 2004–2006*. Santa Monica, CA: RAND Corp.

Stephens, D., 1983. President Carter, the Congress, and NEA: creating the Department of Education. *Political Science Quarterly*, 98(4), pp. 641–663.

Tyack, D. and Cuban, L., 1997. *Tinkering Towards Utopia: A Century of Public School Reform*. Cambridge, MA: Harvard University Press.

US Department of Education, Office of Inspector General, 2005. *Audit of NJDOE's Compliance with Public School Choice and SES Provisions. Final Report ED-OIG/A02-F0006*. Available at: www.ed.gov/about/offices/list/oig/auditreports/a02f0006.doc (accessed April 2, 2007).

Vergari, S., 2012. The limits of federal activism in education policy. *Educational Policy*, 26(1), pp. 15–34.

Verstegen, D. and Clark, D., 1988. The diminution in federal expenditures for education during the Reagan administration. *Phi Delta Kappan*, 70(2), pp. 134–138.

Vinovskis, M., 1999. *Missing In Practice? Systematic Development and Rigorous Program Evaluation at the US Department of Education*. Paper presented at the Conference on Evaluation of Educational Policies, American Academy of Arts and Sciences, Cambridge, MA, May 13–14.

Whitehurst, G., 2003. *The Institute of Education Sciences: New Wine, New Bottles*. Presentation to the American Education Research Association Annual Meeting, April 23, 2003.

Wright, D., 1988. *Understanding Intergovernmental Relations*. Pacific Grove, CA: Brooks/Cole.

Chapter 9

'Governing by numbers'
Social work in the age of the regulatory state

Holger Ziegler

'The more strictly we are watched, the better we behave'
(Jeremy Bentham, 1791)

'I can only steer what I can measure'
(CEO of the German Federal Employment Agency)

Social work and the state – the case of Germany

A number of academic commentators are currently suggesting that the assumption that the state is responsible for organizing education can no longer be taken for granted. While this observation seems both valid and analytically relevant, it is not actually new for some fields of education, such as social work in Germany. At least in some of its traditions, social work is an educational discipline. The relative complexity of capturing the ambivalent stake of the state in social work partially originates from the so-called principle of subsidiarity, which is a part of the German constitution (Art. 23 of the Grundgesetz) and is thus particularly relevant for welfare law. First, subsidiarity is a central dimension of Catholic social teaching, as it is based on a premise that there is a hierarchical line from the individual to the family, to the community or municipality, and to the state. Subsidiarity thus implies that the higher levels and, in particular, central state agencies *must* not provide services that can be supplied by subsidiary levels. Subsidiarity also implies that welfare and youth welfare agencies of the state *must* not intervene in cases where non-state agencies – the so-called *freie Wohlfahrtsverbände* – are able to do the job. Given this background, it is no coincidence that social work is largely provided by non-state third sector social welfare organizations. In Germany, approximately 75 per cent of all welfare services are provided by the *freie Wohlfahrtsverbände*, which are among the biggest organizations in the country, employing nearly one million staff. In addition, a large majority of the social workers in Germany are employed by such non-state organizations. Yet, ironically, non-state third sector social welfare organizations in Germany are hardly entities beyond the reach of the state. Not only are more than 90 per cent of the welfare activities of these *Wohlfahrtsverbände* directly financed by the state (most typically at the municipality level), but these organizations are also – as a matter of fact (rather than as a matter of self description) – more or less corporatively embedded within the state. Consequently, many choose to classify the social cooperation between these social welfare organizations and the state as 'corporatist trust' (*korporatistisches Kartell*). Against the background of the corporatist make-up of the German welfare system, it is plausible to argue that the *freie Wohlfahrtsverbände* are a part of the enlarged state rather than a part of a civil society understood as a sphere separate from the state. What makes this arrangement even more complex is the fact that the nature of *freie Wohlfahrtsverbände* has transformed over the last twenty years – from friendly societies into for-profit enterprises. Thus, interestingly, these organizations (which are allegedly a part of the civil society) act as market players within an arrangement within which they are actually a part of the corporatively enlarged state. Thus, the question arises at present, is social work a state agency and to what extent?

Generally, social work practices are a bundle of public interventions into the private life conduct of persons. In Germany, social work is more or less fully financed by the state. Analytically, social work might be described in terms of what Terrence Johnson (1972) used to call a 'mediated profession', which points to professions in which an agency – in the case of social work, a state agency – acts as mediator between the profession and its clientele. Its primary responsibility is deciding, in broad terms, who the clientele will be and what should be provided for them through a legal framework and through the overall allocation of resources and powers. Against this background, the social control functions of social work (which are functional for state tasks) are well known and have been sociologically more or less accurately described since the 1960s. As the aim of this chapter is not to provide a detailed discussion on whether social workers are the 'soft cops' of the capitalist state machine, or catalysts for social change, or even whether the reality is more contradictory and complicated, such issues will not be covered. Nonetheless, there is no doubt that state legislation embodies particular perspectives on the way individuals with 'problems' and 'needs' are defined and subsequently outlines the methods and modes in which welfare services may, or are obliged to, respond to them. What is of interest here, however, is that currently some observers posit a recent return of a supervisory authoritarian state within social work. Not only is there an increase in the overall interventions of social work and the overall social work expenditures, but also the more coercive, disciplinary and even punitive interventions have been amplified. For instance, in the last five years, the number of children taken into care in an immediate manner (*Inobhutname*) in Germany has risen by 42 per cent. In addition, the loss of parental custody has increased by 40 per cent in the last four years. The number of attempts to withdraw parental custody by public youth authorities has increased by an alarming 57 per cent in the same period. Moreover, custodial measures for deviant children are back on the agenda. At the same time, there is a quest to implement comprehensive early warning systems, based on screening procedures, in order to identify children and families at risk and to provide so-called early preventive measures. It is important to note that the discourse about the modes of the preventive measures does not only stress the responsibility of the state, but places an emphasis on the responsibility of the parents, which is to be monitored and supervised by the state. In these circumstances, the scope of legal enforcement rights of social work has evidently been increased. There is also some evidence that the willingness to enact these enforcements in a so-called 'confrontative' manner has increased.

Moreover, within the context of current social policy conceptions, such as the so-called 'activating welfare state' or the 'social investment state', social work plays an important role as service-based or in-kind transfers have increased relative to in-cash transfers. In particular, with respect to interventions aimed at addressing problems of inequality and social exclusion, 'pedagogical interventions' (Kaufmann, 2002) – that is, social competency-conveying measures – are portrayed as more efficient and appropriate than distributive measures. Some social policy commentators even argue that the social investment state is largely a social-pedagogization of social welfare, which is based on an activation and pedagogical transformation of the welfare state. Be this as it may, there is hardly any doubt that, in terms of social work, the state is very active in Germany.

The regulatory state

However, it is evident that, in Germany, the age of what conservatives and libertarians have called 'Big Government' is over. The notion of 'Big Government' – together with the notion of *ungovernability* – was mostly a denigration of an allegedly omnipresent, yet impotent, welfare state. In particular, since the late 1980s, the state was considered to be both omnipresent and impotent, that is, excessively large and costly and at the same time inefficient in performing its designated role. What was thus referred to as neo-liberalism within education and welfare was both a response to disenchantment with bureaucratic governance and a policy promising to reduce the alleged overload of the welfare state. This policy also delegitimated a pretend 'new class' of social workers, bureaucrats and intellectual consultants, who are said to have a large influence on public policy and a personal commitment to expanding the role of government. Consequently, it may be a contradiction to argue at the same time that the welfare state is increasingly interventive and to claim that policies that tried to force back the role of the expansive role of government have been successful. Yet, this might not be as contradictory as it seems.

Meanwhile, the well-established notion of the rise of a 'regulatory state' (see Majone, 1996; Rhodes, 1997; Scott, 2000) might be helpful when attempting to analyse this issue. The notion of the regulatory state indicates an overall shift towards the use of regulation over other governmental tools. In particular, a change in the welfare state is observed, whereby the conventional redistributory (or 'producing') welfare state – which provides money and social services through state bureaucracies or agencies close to the state – has been partly replaced by measures that mandate welfare tasks to non-state providers and agencies. Nevertheless, the state is still in charge of regulating the activities of the non-state providers and agencies. Thus, processes of 'deregulation' go alongside new regulatory measures ensuring that privatized spheres operate safely, namely rankings, ratings, inspection, '*Aufsicht*', audit and licensing. The notion of a regulatory state thus indicates that reduced state (in particular less redistribution) intervention may go alongside increased state power, in terms of more regulation and monitoring of the spheres beyond the state.

The regulatory state, with all its appeals to privatization and the civil society, is therefore not a retreat of the state. Rather, the state functions are shifted: instead of providing common goods in terms services, the new task is to supervise and monitor sectors responsible for providing these services. In the 'regulatory state', state functions are shifted from 'rowing to steering' (Osborne and Gabler, 1992), implying that patterns of direct service delivery (that is, rowing) are to be transformed into modes of governance based on setting policy direction and providing requirements and incentives for others to provide services. In this context, the 'others' may include third sector institutions or the so-called civil society. Governmental strategies of the regulatory state are twofold. The first part – accompanied by pseudo-democratic rhetoric – is about empowering communities to solve their own problems. The slogans 'it takes a community to prevent a crime' or 'it takes a community to raise a child' signify a shift in the 'rowing' responsibility, but not a reduction in the extent of the governmental steering power. The other and related part is about fostering competition among service providers, sometimes referred to as devolution or privatization. Yet there is not much private about this privatization. Rather, it allows the state to perform an alternative way of governing – 'Governing at a distance' (Rose and Miller, 1992, p. 181). This mode of governance provides governments with relatively more resources and, most importantly, with a maximum flexibility to respond to changing needs and tasks. Governments replace their propensity to reach their aims with governance by directing. Moreover, in the regulatory state, governance is tantamount to making more policy decisions, putting more social institutions into motion, and performing more regulating while shifting the operative task responsibility away from the central state. As the state regulates, rather than produces, welfare traditional boundaries between state and society, and those between the public and the private sector, seem to blur accordingly.

Ironically, in effect, this may come close to a reassertion of the central state or, more specifically, the idea of a core executive control over policy-making. I argue that the idea of the regulatory state marks a significant shift in state functioning. I will attempt to outline this with respect to the governmental logic of welfare provision. In a broad sense, it seems to be fair to argue that the service provision of the post-war welfare state was founded on two pillars. The first pillar was a legalistic – conditionally, rather than target programmed – hierarchically structured bureaucratic administration. The second pillar was a kind of deontologically oriented, largely self-regulated professionalism. Based on state-regulated training, the professionalism of service providers was considered sufficient for a rational and effective steering of services. Other tools of governance were understood as non-essential. Thus, hierarchical bureaucracy and professionalism were a foundation of the German welfare state, which was considered capable of performing its functional tasks more or less successfully and adequately. This constellation may be described as a bureau-professional regime, which combines two key aspects of the organization of state welfare: (1) the rational administration of bureaucratic systems, and (2) professional expertise in control over the content of services (see Otto and Ziegler, 2011; Rüb, 2003). Ironically, the traditional bureaucratic hierarchy was compatible with considerable discretion in the operative social work. While it is certainly true that bureaucratic hierarchies were the basis for the exercise of power *over* social workers, these hierarchies were as much a basis for the power exercised *by* social workers. In essence, social workers had the power to define who their clients were, what they needed and the type of measures that should be taken in order to meet specific aims (see Harris, 1998).

'Governing by numbers' – towards a managerialist governmentality

The bureau-professional arrangement is fundamentally challenged by a new kind of organizational governance that might be described with the term *managerialism*. First, I argue that managerialism – by introducing organizational forms of regulation such as hierarchy, target-setting, performance management, audits and accountability, but also market forms of customer relations – replaces trust in professionals as well as the trust relationships between practitioners and clients. In this context, Pat O'Malley's analysis of what he calls 'advanced liberalism' is particularly instructive. In social liberalism, O'Malley (2009) argues that governmental welfare programmes were closely linked to:

> the esoteric knowledges of the positive sciences of human conduct. Advanced liberalism transferred these powers to an array of calculative and more abstract technologies, including budget disciplines, audit and accountancy. These require professionals and experts to translate their esoteric knowledges into a language of costs and benefits that can be given an accounting value, and made 'transparent' to scrutiny. In the form of marketisation, the authority of experts is determined not by their own professional criteria, but by the play of the market.
>
> (O'Malley, 2009, p. 8)

Whereas in classical liberalism markets were understood as 'natural' phenomena, these natural markets are displaced by the conception of markets as purposively created as techniques of policy, in order to maximize efficiency, accountability and competition. O'Malley's thoughts about advanced liberalism dovetail well with the basic ideologies of managerialism. In other words, managerialism seems to be the central policy programme of advanced liberal or neo-liberal policies.

There is no doubt that social work is conducted in organizations and that management coordinates and facilitates professional practice, but also controls social work professionals by supervisory mechanisms that ensure workforce compliance and task accomplishment. Clearly, social work needs an efficient and enabling management. However, the aim of managerialism is rather different, for it legitimizes a particular version of 'how to manage', for what purposes, in whose interests, and with what knowledge.

As Christopher Pollit points out, it is a 'set of expectations norms, beliefs and practices at the core of which burns the seldom-tested assumption that better management will provide an effective solvent for a wide range of economic ills' (1990, p. 1).

Managerialism is, therefore, a kind of general ideology that legitimizes and seeks to extend the 'right to manage' and comprises overlapping, and sometimes competing, discourses that present distinctive versions of 'how to manage'. Most importantly, managerialism is a normative system primarily concerned with defining what counts as valuable knowledge and who is empowered to act on this knowledge base.

On this basis, the ideology that the 'the professional knows best' is replaced by the belief that managers 'do the right thing', which will provide the most effective and efficient solution for the kind of problems social work is engaged with.

Therefore, managers should have the power, agency and responsibility to provide solutions and the kind of value for money deemed to be lacking in professionally dominated welfare bureaucracies. In order to reach this goal, however, managerial judgement has to take precedence over professional judgement. In other words, managerialism works at the expense of professional control and discretion. Instead of acting as the passive custodians of services controlled by front-line staff, managers should determine policy goals and actively seek to implement them. The basic idea behind this assertion is that it is through the agency of managers, rather than professionals, that services need to be delivered.

This kind of managerialism is embedded within a shift towards a regulatory state, that is, a mode of public policy that denotes the importance of regulation relative to macroeconomic stabilization and income redistribution. Based on an implemented division between the purchaser and provider of services, the idea is that the state should focus on controlling and steering welfare provisions – provided not only by the market, local communities and volunteers, but also by local welfare agencies – rather than directly provide services. 'Steering instead of Rowing' is the central slogan of the catalytic government of a regulatory state.

Basic regulatory instruments are budgetary management, audits, standards and the setting performance indicators through which the central state tries to enhance its capacity to shape, monitor and steer local institutional practice. On the behalf of service providers, this is accompanied by the rise of a number of accountancy-derived concepts and technologies. In order to guarantee the accountability of the service providers – which is regarded as the core problem – evaluation, monitoring and performance management, or more general auditable management control systems, are the key tools that are replacing trust in professional decision-making.

The reason behind this shift is simple: the regulatory philosophy is devoted to the lure of the objectivity of numbers and calls for control and measurement in defining objectives and the quality of services, whereas public service delivery by professional social workers – who may insist on their professional autonomy – has many uncontrollable features. However, the ungovernability of professionals who may be resistant to control from politics is likely to lead to an exponential increase in costs of services and to diminish the quality and effectiveness of service provisions.

My basic argument is that the governing of social work within the regularity state is most of all a mode of 'management by measurement' (Noordegraaf and Abma, 2003, p. 854) or of 'governing by numbers'.

The corresponding audit culture (Power, 1997) in service organizations clearly represents a new mode for governing professionals. We should keep in mind that a central feature of all projects of professionalization is to gain a monopoly of credibility with the public, which restricts the control by outside agencies over the actual ethicality of the transaction of professional services (Freidson, 2001). With the rise of managerialism in social work, this project is over. The audit approach as a central element of managerialism profoundly alters professionals' relationships with their organizations. There is a shift from trust and relative autonomy to measurement, standardization and control, which favours a 'what works' approach to policy that operates through adopting a seemingly 'neutral' or rather 'technical' stance towards professional practice (see Otto et al., 2009).

As managerialism is based on the unproven and empirically doubtful belief that more managerial autonomy and managerial accountability for results will improve performance and efficiency, decision-making should be the right of the management, and it is the management that should be accountable for the practices and outcomes of service deliverance. As Bottery points out, managerialism is based on the 'measurement of professional work by external quantitative measures . . . emphasises a form of administrative control where professionals are "on tap" to managerial strategic decisions rather than "on top" autonomously deciding how their practice is best used' (2006, p. 7).

In that sense, managerialism is tantamount to anti-professionalism, or at least to an opposition to two central pillars of the professional idea. These pillars are the axiomatic assumptions that (1) welfare judgements are embodied in the person of the professional, and (2) the regulation of professionals is enshrined in the ethos of the profession and its bodies. The background for the shift to managerialism might not be economic in the strict sense of the word. Rather, it is a cultural background. The cultural and discursive views of professionals have changed over the last fifty years, from ones of high trust, peer-based accountability and autonomous practice, to a view that is predominantly low-trust, involves extensive external quantitative accountability, and grants only limited professional discretion. How could this happen?

Instructive is a short view on Elliot Freidson's analyses of professionalism. Freidson (2001) argues that professionalism *inter alia* contains a cognitive or competence-based as well as a cultural dimension. The cognitive dimension includes 'a body of knowledge and skill that is officially recognized as one based on abstract concepts and theories and requiring the exercise of considerable discretion' (Freidson, 2001, p. 180). The cultural dimension is an 'ideology serving some transcendent value and asserting greater devotion to doing good work than to economic reward' (p. 180). The central question is whether the public and policy, as well as the professionals themselves, believe that professionals have these virtues. There is reason to doubt that they do. Professional power over clients was demeaning, patronizing, creating dependence, and in the interests of service providers rather than the clients or the welfare of the population. Professional autonomy did not, in fact, guarantee clients the highest standards of service provision, but rather led to unacceptable variability in the nature and quality of interventions. A basic element is the augmentation of statistical diagnosis by judgements embodied in intelligent devices, such as tests, norms, tables, charts and risk levels. This comes close to a standardization of classification and diagnosis required for documentation, regulation and reimbursement.

In his seminal work 'From dangerousness to risk', Robert Castel argued in the early 1980s that:

> [new] strategies of social administration are currently being developed, which seem to me to depart in a profoundly innovatory way from the traditions of mental medicine and social work. The innovation is this. The new strategies dissolve the notion of the *subject* or a concrete individual, and put in its place a combinatory of factors, *the factors of risk*. Such a transformation carries important practical implications. The essential component of intervention no longer takes the form of the direct face-to-face relationship between the carer and the cared, the helper and the helped, the professional and the client. It comes instead to reside in the establishing of *flows of populations* based on the collation of a range of abstract factors deemed liable to produce risk.
>
> (Castel, 1991, p. 281)

As a result, specialist professionals who have regular face-to-face contact with clients are cast in a subordinate role, while managerial policy formations take over. What Castel describes seems to be exactly the modification of the relationship between front-line professionals and welfare administrators. The managerial technologies reduce the autonomy of frontline practitioners, de-skill and subordinate professionals and consequently diminish the possibility for direct face-to-face work. The professional seems to be 'reduced to a mere executant' (Castel, 1991, p. 281) whose primary task is generating low-level data inputs for managerial decision-making.

Nearly a century ago, in Siegfried Bernfeld's *Sisyphos oder die Grenzen der Erziehung*, a fictitious state secretary of education, called 'Citizen Machiavelli' gives the following speech:

> You have to understand that the organization of the educational system is the crucial problem. This organization we have to dominate forcefully, adamantly, and completely, while we do not have to worry to leave issues of curricula, instruction and even education to pedagogues, ideologists and even to social democrats.[1]
>
> (Bernfeld, 1925, p. 99)

The insights of 'Citizen Machiavelli' seem to guide the new governance of education. Yet, against the background of managerialism, organizational forms of regulation have been refined in terms of strategies of standardization and rationalization, which reflect a pursuit of 'measurable' results and come close to what Harrison (2002) describe as a 'scientific bureaucratic model':

> [which] is 'scientific' in the sense that it promises a secure knowledge base that can provide rational foundations for clinical decisions. It is bureaucratic in the sense that this knowledge is codified and manualized through the use of protocols, guidelines and targets such as time-scales for assessments which are monitored by managers, sometimes using computer systems or through internal and external audit.
>
> (Lawler and Bilson, 2010, p. 83)

This outlines a new relationship between the state and social work whereby 'governing by numbers' seems to be a core dimension of a new governmentality of education.

Note

1 'Sie müssen nämlich verstehen, daß die Organisation des Erziehungswesens das entscheidende Problem ist, das wir konsequent und unerbittlich unserem Einfluss restlos vorbehalten müssen, während wir die Lehrplan-, Unterrichts-, selbst Erziehungsfragen beruhigt den Pädagogen, Ideologen, ja selbst den Sozialdemokraten überlassen können' (Bernfeld, 1925, p. 99).

References

Bernfeld, S., 1925. *Sisyphos oder die Grenzen der Erziehung*. Reprinted in 1967. Frankfurt: Suhrkamp.

Bottery, M., 2006. Education and globalization: redefining the role of the educational professional. *Educational Review*, 58(1), pp. 95–113.

Castel, R., 1991. From dangerousness to risk. In G. Burchell, C. Gordon and C.P. Miller (eds) *The Foucault Effect: Studies in Governmentality*. Hemel Hempstead: Harvester Wheatsheaf, pp. 281–298.

Freidson, E., 2001. *Professionalism. The Third Logic*. Cambridge: Blackwell.

Harris, J., 1998. Scientific management, bureau professionalism, new managerialism: the labour process of state social work. *British Journal of Social Work*, 28, pp. 839–862.

Harrison, S., 2002. New Labour, modernisation and the medical labour process model. *Journal of Social Policy*, 31(3), pp. 465–485.

Johnson, T., 1972. *Professions and Power*. Basingstoke: Macmillan.

Kaufmann, F.-X., 2002. *Sozialpolitik und Sozialstaat*. Opladen: Leske und Budrich.

Lawler, J. and Bilson, A., 2010. *Social Work Management and Leadership: Managing Complexity with Creativity*. Abingdon: Routledge.

Majone, G., 1996. *Regulating Europe*. London: Routledge.

Noordegraaf, M. and Abma, T., 2003. Management by measurement? Public management practices amidst ambiguity. *Public Administration*, 4, pp. 853–871.

O'Malley, P., 2009. Genealogy, systematisation and resistance in 'advanced liberalism'. *Legal Studies Research Paper 09/121*. Sydney: Law School, University of Sydney.

Osborne, D. and Gabler, T., 1992. *Reinventing Government: How the Entrepreneurial Spirit is Transforming the Public Sector*. Reading: Addison-Wesley.

Otto, H.-U. and Ziegler, H., 2011. Managerialismus. In: H.-U. Otto and H. Thiersch (eds) *Handbuch Soziale Arbeit*. Munich: Reinhardt, pp. 901–911.

Otto, H.-U., Polutta, A. and Ziegler, H. (eds), 2009. *Evidence-based Practice. Modernising the Knowledge Base of Social Work?* Opladen: Barbara Budrich.

Pollit, C., 1990. *Managerialism and the Public Services: The Anglo-American Experience*. Oxford: Basil Blackwell.

Power, M., 1997. *The Audit Society: Rituals of Verification*. Oxford: Oxford University Press.

Rhodes, R., 1997. *Understanding Governance*. Buckingham: Open University Press.

Rose, N. and Miller, P., 1992. Political power beyond the state: problematics of government. *British Journal of Sociology*, 43, pp. 173–205.

Rüb, F., 2003. Vom wohlfahrtsstaat zum, 'manageriellen Staat'? Zum wandel des verhältnisses von markt und Staat in der Deutschen sozialpolitik. In: R. Czada and Zintl, R. (eds) *Politik und Markt. PVS – Politische Vierteljahresschrift. Sonderheft 34*.Wiesbaden: VS Verlag für Sozialwissenschaften, pp. 256–299.

Scott, C., 2000. Accountability in the regulatory state. *Journal of Law and Society*, 27, pp. 38–60.

Part 5

Power, myths of community and Utopia

Chapter 10

'Among School Children'

The churches, politics and Irish schooling, 1830–1930[1]

Deirdre Raftery

Within this chapter, 'education' largely refers to formal schooling that took place within school buildings, although the informal 'hedge schools' are briefly discussed. The chapter supports the view of the editors developed in the introduction, that many national education systems have maintained their cultural peculiarities, and indeed that 'national and local differences can only be explained historically'. While German and French education history emphasizes the central role of the state (see Cohen in this book), both Irish and American studies have a regional focus, and in Ireland the dominant role of the churches in education is striking. Indeed, the significant contribution of Irish Roman Catholic nuns, priests and brothers to education in the United States has left an imprint that also merits close examination.

Also worthy of attention, in the Irish context, is the way in which culture – particularly fiction, poetry and drama – has mediated the history of schooling, while offering interpretations of education change. Indeed, the poetry of W.B. Yeats provides a useful lens on schooling and change. In February 1926, Yeats paid a visit to a school in Waterford. By that time, he was already a Senator of the Irish Free State, a recent Nobel Prize winner, and – as a man in his early sixties – had witnessed much change in Ireland. In the opening stanza of 'Among School Children', he wrote: 'I walk through the long schoolroom, questioning. A kind old nun in a white hood replies. The children learn to cipher and to sing, to cut and sew, be neat in everything, in the best modern way.'

The school of which Yeats wrote, St Otteran's, had been founded only a few years earlier and it was the first Mercy convent school in Waterford City, situated in the south of Ireland. The presence of the 'kind old nun' is significant in this context, as it indicates the role of the Catholic Church in schooling after centuries of suppression. Moreover, the observation about the children's activities is not accidental, as it refers very directly to the new Free State curriculum. Thus, the question arises: what, by the time Yeats was writing, was the 'best modern way' in Irish education, and how had it been attained?

Without doubt, it was a continuation of the explicitly political function of schooling in Ireland, which dated from the sixteenth century. At that time, schooling had been harnessed in support of the spread of the influences of the Reformation. Tudor policy included the passing of a series of laws to proscribe Catholic education and secure support for Protestantism and loyalty to the crown. The Catholic Church lost its public role in Irish education and a series of penal laws prohibited Catholics from having their children educated by Catholic priests and nuns, either at home or abroad. It also banned Catholic teachers from running schools or teaching children. However, as scholars have noted, many Irish Catholics flouted the law, opting to secretly send their sons abroad to be educated in seminaries in France and Spain. Others availed themselves of the subversive system of 'hedge schools' that spread throughout the country. By the end of the eighteenth century, this illegal system catered for the majority of the Irish school-going population, which attended approximately 9,000 small schools.

Despite repeated 'official' efforts to provide schools for the poor, which would be an alternative to the hedge schools, no legislation was passed to organize a system of mass education. Instead, in the early nineteenth century, government funding for schools was channelled through Protestant voluntary societies. The Kildare Place Society (KPS), founded in 1811 with the aim of affording 'the same facilities for education to every denomination of Christians without interfering with the peculiar religious opinions of any' (Statement of the Committee of the Kildare Place Society, 1820) was particularly successful. However, it was never likely to succeed as the acceptable face of mass education. In KPS schools, the Bible was read 'without note or comment' (Statement of the Committee of the Kildare Place Society, 1820), a practice unacceptable to the Catholic Church. At the forefront of public opposition to the KPS, Daniel O'Connell argued the case in the name of Catholic parents and advocated for allocating a share of the parliamentary education grant to Catholic schools. A campaign for reform, led by Archbishop John McHale of Tuam and Bishop James Warren of Kildare and Leighlin, resulted in a petition to Parliament submitted in 1824 and the subsequent Commission of Irish Education Inquiry (1825), which recommended that public funding should be withdrawn from Protestant education societies. Instead, it was argued, a government board of education should be established for building and maintaining national schools and Catholic and Protestant children should be educated together for secular instruction and separately for religious instruction.

The proposal can now be seen to have anticipated some of the changes that we are presently witnessing in twenty-first-century Ireland, with its vision of non-denominational national schooling and its respect for religious difference. However, in the intense political climate of early nineteenth-century Ireland, and at a time when the Catholic Church was becoming increasingly vocal, lack of tolerance for mixed secular instruction was evident. The Catholic demand was for an explicitly Catholic school system, while the Established Church and the Presbyterian Church required scriptural reading to have a central position in education. By the time the chief secretary of Ireland, Lord E.G. Stanley, formulated an acceptable version of non-denominational national education in 1831, Catholic emancipation had been granted and there was considerable urgency to solve the problem of mass schooling. With over 6.5 million Irish Catholics, out of a total population of some 8 million, it was necessary to accommodate the majority. What Stanley envisaged as a system of 'combined literary and a separate religious education'[2] became, de facto, the system of denominational national schooling that was to survive, remarkably intact, until the current move towards greater pluralism.

State funding was granted to support teacher training, the building of schools, and the production of textbooks, while existing schools, including those managed by Catholic orders, such as the Presentation Sisters and the Christian Brothers, could apply to the new National Board for financial support. By the end of the first decade of its existence, the National Board had 1,978 schools operating under its control. Many of those with religious affiliations, such as convent schools, were single-sex and the overwhelming majority catered to Catholic families. The number of these denominational schools reached over 8,000 by the end the century.

At the same time, the secondary education system was developing. Traditionally the preserve of a small minority of Anglican families, secondary schooling gradually became available to Catholics after Catholic emancipation and the consequent emergence of many teaching religious orders in Ireland. Large diocesan boarding schools were founded by the bishops, to provide the education of Catholic boys as well as to facilitate recruitment of future members of the clergy. St Patrick's College, Carlow (1793), St Jarlath's, Tuam (1800), St Finian's, Navan (1802), St John's, Waterford (1807) and St Peter's, Wexford (1819) all offered a classical education for Catholic boys, while also functioning as minor seminaries that prepared some of them for their future role as secular priests (see Raftery and Relihan, 2012). The religious orders also expanded their network of schools and, by 1867, there were forty-seven Catholic colleges for young men in Ireland, under the direction of the Dominicans, Jesuits, Holy Ghosts, Vincentians and others. For girls and young women, education was supplied in day and boarding schools run by various orders originally established on the continent, including the Loreto, Ursuline and Dominican Sisters, while two Irish congregations, the Presentation Sisters and the Sisters of Mercy, also established a network of girls' schools throughout the country.

In 1878, the Intermediate Education (Ireland) Act was passed, legislating for a system of examinations that offered prizes and scholarships as well as supported exhibitions. Similar to the Cambridge and Oxford 'Local' Examinations, the Intermediate Examinations were to become the route into civil service jobs and to university degrees, giving Catholics access to managerial and professional jobs that had traditionally been denied to them. By the end of the nineteenth century, a particularly Irish – and, it must be said, Catholic – form of schooling had been developed. Thus, the Church retained an almost vice-like grip on what was a largely single-sex system into the early twentieth century.

Although there is not consensus among scholars regarding the legacy of such control, it is generally conceded that the Church made a sustained contribution to the spread of literacy and numeracy and vastly improved the prospects of the ordinary Irish population.

It would be simplistic to suggest that the path of progress in nineteenth- and early twentieth-century schooling was straightforward. In truth, it was beset with obstacles. For example, national schooling was heavily invested with political significance and even a cursory glance at the curricula of that period reminds us that, while the function of the national school was the creation of the citizen, there was a changing conception of 'citizenship' as Catholics became increasingly articulate and the rhetoric of nationalism found its way into the debate pertaining to education. The National Board provided all national schools with a set of 'compulsory' graded lesson books, which formed an official curriculum and encouraged much rote learning and memory work – methods abhorred by a significant number of educationists and political figures at the time, including Padraig Pearse. While the first and second readers taught simple lessons, the advanced readers included lessons on the British monarchy and the geography and history of England. Scholars agree that these books formed part of the British cultural assimilation policy for Ireland and the inclusion of well-known Protestant evangelical writers made them largely unacceptable to Catholics.[3] Indeed, the Christian Brothers made an early withdrawal from their affiliation with the National Board, in part because of their objections to the pervasive influence of British and Protestant culture in national schools.

In 1863, another significant gesture that brought about change in the culture of national schooling was the ban imposed by Paul Cullen, Archbishop of Dublin, forbidding Catholics to participate in the state system of teacher training at the non-denominational college in Marlborough Street, Dublin. The concession by the government, in 1883, of state support for denominational training colleges was a marked victory for Catholics and, by 1903, five of the seven teacher training colleges were Catholic. With the Church jealously guarding its position in education, it is not surprising that Irish schooling retained a political function into the twentieth century. Donald Akenson has argued that the success of the Catholic Church in education was not that it gained such complete control, but rather that it articulated the needs of the population. 'Lest the arrangement of Irish educational institutions to suit the church be misrepresented', he notes, '. . . the overwhelming majority of the laity seem to have been satisfied with the situation' (Akenson, 1975, p. 97). As the Church's distrust of state activities was shared by the people at large, it was not difficult to persuade the public that schooling should be managed by the Church.

Unsurprisingly, when Ireland gained political independence in 1922, it was content to leave education in the hands of priests, brothers and nuns. It has been shown that the new Irish Free State effectively preserved the administrative structures of the national school system (Raftery and Relihan, 2012). John Coolahan has commented on the new Irish administration's unwillingness either to establish a commission on education or introduce legislation in the area (Coolahan, 1981). Instead, the overwhelming concern was to strengthen the national fibre by ensuring that the Irish language, history and culture dominated schooling. From March 1922, the teaching of the Irish language became compulsory in national schools and it was later made compulsory for state examinations (in 1928, for the Intermediate Certificate, and in 1934 for the Leaving Certificate). In 1928, the Department of Education issued a memorandum to the publishers of books for national schools advising them that school books should have an 'Irish outlook and a definite rural bias'.[4] By 1933, with the publication of *Notes for Teachers*, the Department of Education articulated its commitment to restoring the 'characteristically Gaelic turn of mind' (Department of Education, 1933, p. 55), while resisting the effects of 'foreign penetration by newspaper, book and cinema' (p. 55).

With over 90 per cent of national schools under Catholic management by 1930, the conflation of the 'Gaelic ideal' with Catholicism was commonplace. In national schools, books contained lessons that included references to families saying the rosary and children going to Sunday Mass. The rhythms of religious life, such as prayer and devotions, pervaded secondary schooling even more fully and the Church controlled almost all second-level schooling. Ecclesiastical authorities defended their involvement in education on the grounds that their motive in education was the salvation of souls.[5] However, the historian E. Brian Titley argues that the Catholic Church 'insisted on and vigorously defended the type of clerical control which prevailed in both primary and secondary education' because Catholic schools 'were the principal agencies for the recruitment of clergy and for the maintenance of a middle-class laity which was unquestioningly loyal to the church' (Brian Titley, 1983, p. 143). This rather persuasive view has been developed by Tom O'Donoghue, who details the success of the Church in recruiting priests and nuns from schools and juniorates (O'Donoghue, 2004). Still, it is an incomplete account of the function and the undoubted success of the Church's involvement in education at that time.

The fact remains that the Catholic Church was uniquely positioned to provide secondary education to Irish people for three important reasons: (1) it had the sympathy of a population that had been denied the expression of its religion; (2) it could provide labour and resources at little cost to the exchequer; and (3) it had an educated workforce. The 'grammar school' model of education, which had been introduced in 1878 with the passing of the Intermediate Education (Ireland) Act, required teachers who knew classical and modern languages and history, in addition to mathematics, algebra and natural sciences. However, educated priests and nuns were best equipped to teach Catholic secondary school children. Indeed, so effective were their efforts that the Catholic schools regularly 'topped' their leading Protestant counterparts in the annual competition for Intermediate medals and distinctions and for awards from the Royal University of Ireland, established in 1879. The consequences of this discrepancy were noted by, among others, Maurice Hime, who drew up a list of 'successful' Irishmen educated at Clongowes Wood College, Vincentian College Castleknock and Belvedere College (Hime, 1889), while *The Irish Catholic* newspaper reported triumphantly on the success of K. Murphy, Dominican Convent Sion Hill, who took first place in the MA Degree in Modern Languages at the Royal University examinations in 1892:

> We do not wish to make any ungenerous comparisons but . . . it cannot be uncalled for to state the fact that on this, the first occasion when the Alexandra College and a convent school came in to open competition for the great prize in connection with the examination for the highest degree in Arts, the convent school remains the victor.
> (*The Irish Catholic*, 1892, cited in Raftery, 1995, p. 7)

Almost all of these Intermediate schools, however, were 'fee-paying': that is, annual fees for tuition were required. This meant that second-level education remained the preserve of the middle classes, until the middle of the twentieth century, with the move towards free education in 1966. In this respect, Ireland lagged behind France and the United States, where free secondary schooling was introduced in the early 1930s (see Cohen's chapter in this book). Irish education rhetoric and policy paid little attention to the ideals of 'democratic equality, social efficiency, and individual social mobility' before the middle of the twentieth century.

The classroom described in Yeats's 'Among School Children', with the 'kind old nun' and the children learning their lessons 'in the best modern way', will remain as an astonishingly accurate snapshot of Irish schooling in the early decades of the twentieth century, nodding, in the process, to the legacy of O'Connell, Pearse and Paul Cullen. The distinctly 'Gaelic' and Catholic education that the children are shown to be receiving was sufficiently new and remarkable that it merited the attention of Yeats. Many other Irish writers have since reflected on the place of both the Irish language and the Catholic clergy in their experience of education. As we move towards what will now, without a doubt, be a new era in state provision of schooling, accommodating more of E.G. Stanley's nineteenth-century vision of schooling than that of Archbishop Cullen, it remains to be seen what will emerge as the next 'best modern way'. Irrespective of the next developments, the history of Irish education suggests that Irish schools are 'culturally and historically specific', and are not easily compared with schools in other countries (Raftery *et al.*, 2008; and Aubry *et al.* in the Introduction to this volume).

Notes

1   The original draft of this chapter appeared as a shorter article in the centenary issue of *Studies* (Dublin, 2012), and is reproduced with kind permission of the Editor.

2   Letter from the secretary for Ireland to his Grace the Duke of Leinster on the formation of a Board of Education, 1837 (485) ix 585. In: Hyland and Milne (1987, p. 100).
3   See, for example, Goldstrom (1972) and Raftery (2009).
4   National Archive, Dublin, Ed/File No. 22299/Box 495 (cited in Raftery and Relihan, 2012).
5   See, for example, Rev. Michael Maher, cited in E. Brian Titley (1983, p. 143).

References

Akenson, D.H., 1975. *A Mirror to Kathleen's Face: Education in Independent Ireland, 1922–1960.* Montreal and London: McGill-Queen's University Press.

Brian Titley, E. (ed.), 1983. *Church, State and the Control of Schools in Ireland, 1900–1944.* Dublin and Montreal: McGill-Queen's University Press.

Coolahan, J., 1981. *Irish Education: History and Structure.* Dublin: Institute of Public Administration.

Department of Education, 1933. *Notes for Teachers.* Dublin: Department of Education.

Goldstrom, J.M., 1972. *The Social Content of Education, 1808–1870: A Study of the Working Class School Reader in England and Ireland.* Shannon: Irish University Press.

Hime, M.C., 1889. *The Efficiency of Irish Schools and the Superiority to English Schools, as Places of Education for Irish Boys.* London: Simpkin, Marshall.

Hyland, A. and Milne, K. (eds), 1987. Letter from the secretary for Ireland to his Grace the Duke of Leinster on the formation of a Board of Education, 1837 (485) ix 585. In: *Irish Educational Documents,* 1. Dublin: C.I.C.E., p. 100.

O'Donoghue, T., 2004. *Come Follow Me and Forsake Temptation.* Bern: Peter Lang.

Raftery, D., 1995. Ideological differences in the first formal programmes of education for Irish women. *Proceedings of the International Standing Conference for the History of Education.* Montreal, p. 7.

Raftery, D., 2009. Colonizing the mind. The use of English writers in the education of the Irish poor, c.1750–1850. In: M. Hilton and J. Shefrin (eds) *Educating the Child in Enlightenment Britain: Beliefs, Cultures, Practices.* Farnham and Burlington, VT: Ashgate, pp. 147–162.

Raftery, D. and Relihan, M., 2012. Faith and nationhood: church, state and the provision of schooling in Ireland, 1870–1930. In: L. Brockliss and N. Sheldon (eds) *Mass Education and the Limits of State Building, 1870–1930.* Basingstoke: Palgrave Macmillan, pp. 71–88.

Raftery, D., McDermid, J. and Jones, G., 2008. Social change and education in Ireland, Scotland and Wales: historiography on nineteenth-century schooling. In: J. Goodman, G. McCulloch and W. Richardson (eds) *Social Change in the History of British Education.* Abingdon: Routledge, pp. 45–62.

Statement of the Committee of the Kildare Place Society, 1820. *Eighth Report of the Society for Promoting the Education of the Poor of Ireland,* Appendix No. VI. In: A. Hyland and K. Milne (eds) (1987) *Irish Educational Documents,* 1. Dublin: C.I.C.E., pp. 60–64.

Chapter 11

Make the nation safe for mass society

Debates about propaganda and education in the United States in the twentieth century

Norbert Grube

While analysing the relationship between education and the state, this chapter tries to expand the perspective of educational history by considering aspects of communication history. As Timothy Glander stated:

> Education and communication are fundamentally linked, inescapably affiliated in theory and in practice. Educational philosophers from Socrates to Dewey to Freire have recognized this and have sought to make this relationship clear. Education and communication cannot be separated, although our present academic arrangements make believe that they can be so partitioned.
>
> (2000, p. x)

The chapter examines concepts and ideas of intellectuals, philosophers, politicians, and especially mass communication researchers, about the role of schools, education and governmental propaganda and their aims to reach national homogeneity, coherence, or even conformity, in the United States in the twentieth century. Debates about the ideals of social harmony and community were not restricted to the United States as the chapter of Veronika Magyar-Haas shows. They still had great and global attractiveness at the beginning of the twentieth century, especially the communist utopia of classless equality (see the chapter of E. Thomas Ewing). However, this utopia ended in so-called collectivism, which was a stark contrast to equality because a small but powerful circle of communist leaders divided the society into comrades and varmints (Baberowski, 2008, pp. 120, 160). Somehow similar, the fascist promise of national community (*Volksgemeinschaft*) (Frei, 2002, pp. 105–113) resulted in racist selection of members of the German people and their enemies. According to Hannah Arendt (1996, pp. 657, 682), totalitarian formations of social and of national unity were the result of widespread perceptions of increasing social disorder, decomposition of class structures, and unstructured mass society. Despite violent ordering of society in the first half of the twentieth century, European totalitarian governments did not renounce education, but rather focused their attention on school instruction as a tool for stabilizing socialist and national community and forming allegiance prospectively.

The fact that totalitarian tyrannies support school education – perceived as an instrument of a rather liberal nation state of the nineteenth century – can be referred to the competition of nation states and of ideological systems. In contrast to totalitarian movements neo-liberal governmental concepts did not aim to overcome social classes, but they intended to create social balances, homoeostasis and equilibrium (Foucault 2001, pp. 290–291) by state interventions. Similarly, instead of attempting to reach social equality, the neo-liberal version suggested common welfare. For this purpose, the government should start to retreat from regulating society, and the market should be a reflection of the new ordering power of social relationships and interactions. The constitutional state should, rather, guarantee security so that almost everyone of the population can participate in economic progress. State interventions should mainly serve one aim – mobilizing human resources in order to increase economic growth that should guarantee social harmony and balance. According to Foucault, neo-liberal governments did not only have the possibility but the duty to arrange state interventions as a tool of preventative social policy. It comprised educational and health care policy to activate the resources of the *national* population (Foucault, 2004b, pp. 124, 198), in an attempt to increase national welfare.

However, in the light of huge and diverse mass society in the first third of the twentieth century, many public intellectuals, educational reformers and politicians asked if the United States were one powerful and effective nation. This question was intertwined with several other important questions: (1) how to mobilize national human resources not only for welfare but also for warfare, and (2) how to control and direct public opinion or mass communication at the same time. Although public communication of mass society was judged as necessary for the circulation of goods and trade (Foucault, 2004a, pp. 52, 73), it should still be predicated on common shared values, or rather on a broad acceptance of national aims and a broad affirmation of the government. National planning of social, economic, political and educational developments became necessary a tool that should promise security for national welfare, the population and the government. Therefore, sociology, mass communication research, psychology and, foremost, the university as a whole were seen as an important means to reconcile the citizen with his or her state (Loss, 2012; Park and Pooley, 2008; Popkewitz, 2010).

Much is written about different educational debates and reforms in the era of American progressivism in the first third of the twentieth century (Kliebard, 1995; Tyack and Cuban, 2001). I will sum up only the main points, because I will focus on propaganda and on the relationship between education and propaganda, addressing comparisons, definitions and intersections. I will prove the question of how political propaganda would compensate civic education at schools from the 1920s to the 1940s. The focus on the connection between propaganda and education seems to be helpful to stress the interdependency of education and the state. The next two sections deal with widespread notions that, in the process of mass industrialization and complex mass society, schools could not prepare young citizens rapidly and sufficiently for overseeing complex democratic and global decision-making processes. Therefore, political propaganda could have been seen as an efficient tool for occasionally imparting the most important facts and preparing the population for the approval of the national government. In the fourth and fifth sections, I will present activities and engagements of mass communication researchers for governmental propaganda organizations in the First and Second World War, before closing with a summary and an outlook.

Propaganda can be defined as a symbolic and ideological form of communication characterized by appeal, and by reduced and selected information. It is designed to form efficiently popular opinions and attitudes by evasion of the public (Arnold, 2003, pp. 64, 78–79; Bussemer, 2005, pp. 29–30, 36). In contrast, education and schools of the nation state are in a latent conflict, as they try to develop *individual* rationality, emancipation and talent on the one side and to stabilize national values, *community* and welfare by integrating the individual in mass society on the other side (Böhme and Tenorth, 1990, p. 161). The exact understanding and realization of education depends on accepted and dominating cultural norms and national expectations towards education. In this utilitarian sense, individual skills have to serve the needs of society, as Carleton Washburne (1889–1968) proposed in the Winnetka Plan 1912 (Kliebard, 1995, p. 181).[1] Harold Dwight Lasswell (1902–1978), the father of modern propaganda studies and a propaganda expert, attempted to provide a double definition of education and propaganda by comparing, contrasting or, better, relating one to another:

> Propaganda may be defined as a technique of social control, or as a species of social movement. As technique, it is the manipulation of collective attitudes by the use of significant symbols (words, pictures, tunes) rather than violence, bribery, or boycott. Propaganda differs from the technique of pedagogy in that propaganda is concerned with attitudes of love and hate, while pedagogy is devoted to the transmission of skill. . . . When the word propaganda is used to refer to social movement, it is often contrasted with education. The spread of controversial attitudes is propaganda; the spread of accepted attitudes and skills is education. It is proper to speak of communism as propaganda in Chicago and as education in Moscow.
> (Lasswell, 1935, p. 189)

While the main task of propaganda, the control and standardization of the public, has been studied (Gary, 1999, pp. 60, 63), less attention has been paid to the relationship between propaganda and education. Of the studies on this topic, some have occasionally stressed distinctions, others similarities (Gary, 1999, pp. 91, 114). According to Lasswell's definition, propaganda and education are both attempting to contribute to national unity and formation, but they differ in their methods. Whereas propaganda addresses emotions and tries to call upon feelings by visual or audio symbols, slogans and posters, education aims to develop rational skills mainly through teaching reading. In this chapter, it will be shown that propaganda was regarded as organizing social and cultural homogeneity, political integration and loyalty faster than education, all of which reflect important aspects of time and efficiency.

Mass society, world war, economic depression and social crises: the historical context of governmental propaganda and educational policy in the United States in the first half of the twentieth century

In the progressive era, the United States of America tended to be a highly industrialized and urbanized nation with rapid growth of the population due to migration and increasing birth rates. Cities had more than one million inhabitants and many quarters of immigrants were set up in New York, Chicago, Philadelphia or Detroit. The population increased from 37 million in 1865 to more than 100 million inhabitants in 1915 and this trend was increasing (Heideking and Mauch, 2008, pp. 192, 208–209, 233; Jäger, 2001). The vast country – once very difficult to develop and to traverse – was increasingly characterized by vast mobility because of the rapid development of railway, subway and highway networks. President Theodore Roosevelt (1858–1919) established the supremacy of the United States in northern and middle America after the Spanish-American War of 1898, and Woodrow Wilson (1856–1924) subsequently demanded that the United States should be a great power throughout the world, claiming with self-confidence to 'make the world safe for democracy' (Osterhammel, 2009, p. 575). This slogan aimed to legitimize the Americans entering the First World War in 1917 and attempted to establish a global post-war arrangement. However, these early visions of the so-called One World under American leadership soon failed.

At the same time, the rising American mass society challenged the established political system and nation state. Crime, the misuse of alcohol, poverty, child labour, prostitution, corruption in urban administration by dubious bosses and an upcoming gap between the haves and have-nots threatened cultural values, political participation and democracy. Republican ideals of local community – once stated by Thomas Jefferson – had to be modified, renewed, or compensated by alternatives. The so-called progressive movement demanded many reforms to solve social problems. But it was too heterogeneous to fulfil these ambitious intentions. Political leaders such as Woodrow Wilson or even Theodore Roosevelt tried to adapt progressive calls for new social policies. The interests of big industrial companies and banks, for example US Steel, Standard

Oil of New Jersey, General Electric and American Telephone & Telegraph (AT&T), should be intermingled with the interests of workers, especially of great labour unions, to create a strong community in favour of increasing national welfare. But Wilson and others favoured demands for more and broader participation in public affairs rather rhetorically. Instead of the revitalization of republican local communities, the establishment of an enormous nationwide bureaucracy proceeded irresistibly. Standardization, centralization, statistics and scientification were the key words to describe the attempts of administrative progressives at the efficient exploitation of national human resources. However, because of the lack of sufficient social security in cases of disease and unemployment, the world economic crisis (*Weltwirtschaftskrise*) aggravated social problems and this has persisted since 1929. In the process of economic depression and national erosion, the New Deal under President Franklin D. Roosevelt (1882–1945) prevailed as the dominant model and solution. Governmental interventions should serve to stimulate economic boom and social policy should give answers to social crises. For some American intellectuals the 'National Recovery Administration' (NRA) of the New Deal revealed several parallels with European cooperative models and autarkic policy of land use regulation and economic policy, especially in fascist Italy. There were also some similarities between the American and German, Italian and Soviet political solutions and performances in the 1930s concerning their anti-liberal impetus and new forms of intensive governmental propaganda (Otto, 2007, p. 80; Schivelbusch, 2005, pp. 23–33). This propaganda should establish public allegiance to governmental aims and activities. For example, the NRA started the 'Blue Eagle' Campaign to mark businessmen, entrepreneurs and consumers visibly and symbolically for their support for national economy and welfare. The inscription on the medal was 'We do our part' (Schivelbusch, 2005, pp. 82–83) and should signalize self-evident engagement for national welfare.[2]

Efficiency as the new aim of pedagogy and mass communication research

The success of this form of propaganda was not surprising if one considers that, in the 1930s, propaganda was based on social empirical data of content analyses of newspapers or public opinion research in order to address diverse target groups *efficiently* (Lasswell, 1931, 1941, 1957). *Efficiency* and *target group* were not only core concepts for mass communication experts, as they were also the key words to legitimize new educational reforms, as Miriam Cohen shows in her chapter. The child-study movement in particular, being deeply convinced of directing the success of learning, demanded more extensive knowledge and data in the field of teaching and school psychology. The children and pupils became the new target group for psychologists and sociologists, including G. Stanley Hall (1844–1924) (Kliebard, 1995, pp. 38–41). In the struggle for dominance over the American curriculum, many reformers proposed different solutions for the improvement of schools. Nevertheless, there were some important common innovations, such as the belief in scientific curriculum-making, the consideration of the children's abilities, and the deep conviction that schools had to strive towards improving national welfare and standards of living. Therefore, school reformers, one of whom was John Franklin Bobbitt, wanted to make education more applicable. In their opinion, schools had to equip their students with skills that matched the needs of the job markets and industrial factories. This view became intermingled with demands for a child-centred curriculum. Thus, some subjects, including Latin, History and Literature, were regarded as waste that should be abolished from schools (Kliebard, 1995, p. 85). Moreover, the curriculum should be adapted to the children's abilities, and consequently should be tailored to different target groups, for example boys, girls, or children from well-educated families. In this view, pupils were perceived as consumers whose needs were analysed and satisfied by various curricular offers or even products. Still, it would be misguided to think that this child-centred curriculum derived from idealistic goodwill. In fact, scientific curriculum planning should serve to exploit the children's resources more efficiently. Partially, the ideal of some educational reformers in the United States was the promise of Frederick Winslow Taylor (1856–1915) and industrial psychologists to manage labour and factories by means of an efficient system (Kliebard, 1995, pp. 82–84). According to David Tyack and Larry Cuban (2001), Herbert Kliebard (1995) and David Labaree (2011, p. 190), there was a shift in the educational propositions in the United States from traditional local republicanism and participation to efficiency to prepare the youth for the demands of the economic national market. In particular, the so-called administrative progressives – academic experts, educational professors, superintendents or commissioners of education in diverse American states, for example David Snedden (1868–1951) in Massachusetts, Charles A. Prosser (1871–1952) and Clarence Darwin Kingsley – inclined towards this new premise of efficiency. They favoured the centralization, the state administration of schools, expert-driven and scientific curriculum planning, and the grading of pupils based on intelligence tests (Labaree, 2005). To a lesser extent the development of individual talents and skills in schools should serve individual autonomy or emancipation, but rather purposed to increase national welfare, progress and national or social coherence. The struggle for the American curriculum stemmed from different plans and notions of how schools and education could contribute to solving problems of rapid economic and social change. Some preferred the traditional curriculum, some focused on academic subjects, and others preferred vocational education with manual training.[3] New subjects, including modern languages, social studies instead of history, or science instead of biology and physics, should consider economic needs and should help to educate children more successfully. Even if it is true that the child replaced the curriculum, the school still had to serve national aims and the wishes of the children. This applied to all the different approaches of progressive school reformers.

The main protagonist of pedagogical progressives, John Dewey, wanted to strengthen democratic community by considering the experiences of the child as the starting and reference point of education. In contrast to administrative progressives, pedagogical progressives aimed to promote 'discovery and self-directed learning' of any subject, as this helps students learn how to learn and should strengthen self-responsibility and the capability to solve problems. In other words, they aimed to promote 'values of community, cooperation, tolerance, justice and democratic equality' (Labaree, 2005, p. 277). Therefore, for them, subjects such as art, literature, or music were equal to the ones that promised utilitarian application.

Although this approach still emphasized the functional link between school and democracy, in the Cardinal Principles of Secondary Education (1918) democracy was only a subordinate consideration. Civic education, once a value of its own, seemed to be subordinated under the ideology that schools should serve the needs of the economic market. The notion of educational efficiency and of precise scientific planning of schools that seemed to promise success of learning and application of skills became more persuasive.[4] From the 1930s to the 1950s, people believed in the progress of school education and therefore in national and economic progress by means of improving school education. Referring to and trusting in polls of George Gallup (1901–1984), Tyack and Cuban (2001, p. 13) pointed out that most people were convinced of the effectiveness of the advancement of schools, when compared to their quality in early times. Scientific planning of education raised expectations that schools would increase the standard of living, as children would learn more and gain better skills than their parents had done.

The belief in sciences was overwhelming in the first third of the twentieth century (Bussemer, 2005, p. 254) and this fact perhaps explains the successful entry of psychology into the field of pedagogy. However, social sciences and especially pollsters of public opinion research institutes also promised precise planning, prediction and efficient, preventive application of the data in the fields of social policy, political communication, consumption and the use of mass media (Gary, 1999, p. 73).

While, in the era of American progressivism, educational reformers turned to methods of empirical social research, psychology and communication research as tools for planning the curriculum efficiently, the communication experts and sociologists on the other hand legitimized their activities with ambitions and impacts of civic education. For example, researchers of public opinion, including Elmo Roper (1900–1971), George Gallup or Hadley Cantril (1906–1969), idealized polls as a communicative instrument to reorganize and re-establish the traditional New England town-hall meeting under conditions of complex national mass society. Similar to John Dewey, they pointed out the democratic potential of polls to create a new national communication community. Therefore, Gallup's column in 106 newspapers, in which he presented current poll data, was titled 'America Speaks!' (Igo, 2007, p. 117). In fact, the data were not produced to serve active nationwide communication, but rather to observe the passive consumer, voter and user of mass media. Therefore, the origins of professional and scientific mass communication research went along with the needs of business, governments and administration to obtain information pertaining to the unknown mass in order to guide it. In this context, the creation of the average American (Igo, 2007) should help to normalize and standardize wishes, notions and opinions. In doing so, the average was represented only by the white middle class. Polls, legitimated as an instrument of national integration with democratic implications, were in fact an instrument of inclusion and exclusion.

Pollsters were successful in establishing not only private but also new academic institutes of public opinion research in Princeton or Newark. Social scientists and mass communication researchers such as Hadley Cantril and Paul Lazarsfeld (1901–1976) managed to obtain financial support from big foundations after convincing them that their research on the effects of media use was efficiently applicable to political, economic and media leaders' agendas. The Rockefeller Foundation gave 67,000 USD for the Princeton Radio Research Project (Bussemer, 2005, p. 269; Gary, 1999, p. 89; Glander, 2000, p. 115) and invested millions of dollars into research on the effects of propaganda during the Second World War. The effects of the radio, in particular, were in the core of mass communication research because it was judged as a new tool with educational impact – especially after the increasing use of radio sets from 400,000 in 1922 to 51 million in 1940 (Glander, 2000, p. 1). According to social scientist Hadley Cantril, it can serve to increase 'our sense of membership to the national family'. He hoped that the radio 'may produce a nation of attentive listeners' and therefore may create a direct media-based relationship between rulers and ruled, between the President and the people by broadcasting the fireside speeches of Franklin D. Roosevelt (Cantril and Allport, 1935/1986, p. 254). Researchers and pollsters regarded themselves not only as observers of the social but as experts 'for fostering democratic values and improving citizenship' (Igo, 2007, p. 122) and for establishing national coherence.

Propaganda and education – two sides of the same coin?

The establishment and the difficult balance of mobilization and stabilization of national community was the main aim that education and propaganda had in common. However, the more schools shifted towards child-centred curricula and the utilitarian application of education in the fields of technology, business and science, the more civic and republican education could be neglected. The lack of efficient political instruction was increasingly filled by propaganda. For example, the Cardinal Principles of Secondary Education (National Education Association, 1918) aimed, among other things, to exploit time resources by using leisure time efficiently by introducing activities that served towards improving national welfare. The utilitarian orientation of secondary education should help to create a community that depends on division of labour, workmanship, output for the national good and meritocracy. Ideally, it should strive towards formation of employers and employees and thus stabilize and increase national welfare. The importance of civic education as a school subject in its own right decreased – it was only one (the fifth) of seven utilitarian and functional aims of secondary education. According to Labaree (2011, pp. 186–187), the Cardinal Principles were no longer an acknowledgement to republicanism and democracy, but to useful skills that were applicable in the job market and for the management of factories. Indeed, civic education in secondary schools had still to strengthen the democratic nation state, but as one aim among others:

> the comprehension of the ideals of American democracy and loyalty to them should be a prominent aim of civic education. The pupil should feel that he will be responsible, in cooperation with others, for keeping the nation true to the best inherited conceptions of democracy, and he should also realize that democracy itself is an ideal to be wrought out by his own and succeeding generations.
> (National Education Association, 1918, p. 14)

Therefore, 'the class as a whole develops a sense of *collective* responsibility. Both of these devices give training in *collective* thinking' (National Education Association, 1918, p. 14). The training of responsibility no longer referred to individual freedom and to critical political participation, but rather served to create one powerful American formation with allegiance towards values and the main guidelines of current governmental policy. Clearly, the adjective 'collective' does not only remind us of the key word of socialism in the Soviet Union, which was founded only one year before the publication of the Cardinal Principles, but also aligns with Harold Lasswell's definition of propaganda as 'the management of collective attitudes by the manipulation of significant symbols' (Lasswell, 1927, p. 627).

This tendency of rhetoric convergences – at least on a functional level – between educational reformers and propagandists can be easily confirmed. One year after Lasswell's essay on propaganda was published, the main protagonist of pedagogical progressivism, John Dewey, maintained, 'Propaganda is education and education is propaganda' (1928, p. 222, in Boydston, 1984). Dewey's statement might be influenced by his visit to the Bolshevist society in the Soviet Union in 1928. Being very impressed and enthusiastic about the creation of a new socialist society, he judged it as a successful model to establish a valuable community. This fact might be an indication that Dewey's judgement was not only the result of an individual short-term error, but was an opinion that matched with widespread notions of collective community and the pedagogical implications of propaganda. For Dewey, propaganda and education could intersect when related to 'the universal good of universal humanity' (1928, p. 222, in Boydston, 1984).

Dewey was not the only public intellectual and philosopher who stressed the parallels between propaganda and education – many communication researchers and experts did so (Glander, 2000, pp. 5–8, 25–26). Edward Bernays (1891–1995), the nephew of Sigmund Freud and one of the first Public Relations advisers in the United States, lifted propaganda within the ranks of imparting information and knowledge (Bernays, 1928a, p. 114) and maintained, 'Honest education and honest propaganda have much in common. There is this dissimilarity: education attempts to be disinterested, while propaganda is frankly partisan' (Bernays, 1928b, p. 959).[5] But in pointing out these dissimilarities, Bernays imputed that education only suggests all-party and unselfish motivation, whereas propaganda does not hide its intention to persuade and is therefore perhaps more trustworthy than education.

Even if experts such as Lasswell tried to differentiate between propaganda and education (as we have seen in the quotation of Lasswell in the introduction) and stressed that education refers to learning of 'accepted attitudes and skills', norms and values, whereas propaganda serves to change existing norms by the implementation of new ones (Lasswell, 1935, p. 189), they brought propaganda closer to education. The reason for pointing out these parallels might be the attempted transfer of the positive connotation of education to gain legitimation for propaganda (Lasswell, 1928, p. 261). For the same reason, Lasswell might also compare the propagandist with an advocate who 'contributes to social harmony by satisfying various individuals and groups that they had a fair chance to put their views before the community, and that it is no disgrace for them to abide by the result' (1928, p. 262).

What stood behind these notions that propaganda can fulfil similar functions and aims to those of education? The rapid growth and change of American mass society, the consequences of industrial work in huge companies, vast mobility, the introduction of mass media, mass communication and consumption, as well as increasing anonymity at the same time, forced many public intellectuals, philosophers and educational professors to sceptical estimations about the role of schools (Glander, 2000, pp. 74–75). Walter Lippmann, in particular, who was a journalist and a spin-doctor of President Wilson, was doubtful about efficient civic education in schools. In his books, *Public Opinion* (1922/1965) and *The Phantom Public* (1925, pp. 53, 146) he stated that schools could not keep pace with rapid political changes and the development of mass media. Because teachers are educated under outdated assumptions and preconditions, they only disperse fears about the 'swarming confusion of problems' (Lippmann, 1925, p. 24) in politics and economy instead of solving them. 'Because the school teacher cannot anticipate the issues of the future' (Lippmann, 1925, p. 35) he or she cannot teach new skills and knowledge. Armed services, industry and especially mass media became new educational agencies (Bernays, 1928a, p. 125), which competed successfully with schools. The ideal of a rational, participatory, politically engaged citizen had nothing to do with reality, as most people were excluded from political decision-making processes, were not able or willing to participate, or acted destructively and indifferently; in contrast, a small group of elite experts, the insiders, had access to information and the power to decide. This diagnosis, partially shared by John Dewey in *The Public and its Problems* (1927, in Boydston, 1984), went along with notions that the public faded, was eclipsed or is only a phantom. However, while Dewey wanted to strengthen public education, Lippmann estimated the democratic potential of the population sceptically and preferred elitist people's instruction by the propagandist use of selective, simplified information, symbols and persuasion (Gary, 1999, pp. 29–36; Grube, 2010a). But considering the fact that Dewey equated propaganda and education in 1928, the distinction between 'Lippmann's "realist" and Dewey's "idealist" positions' (Gary, 1999, p. 37) is not as clear-cut as it might seem at first glance.

Lippmann's opinion and concepts were partially shared by Edward Bernays, who pointed out, 'Public Opinion is slow and reactionary, and does not easily accept new ideas' (1928b, p. 959). To some extent, Harold Lasswell (1928, pp. 259, 263) shared the notion that public opinion is dull, lethargic, selfish, irrational and influenced not only by stereotypical pictures in our heads (Lippmann), but rather by prejudices and taboos (Bussemer, 2005, p. 297). Only propaganda and manipulation 'entails the removal of a prejudice' (Bernays, 1928b, p. 971) and can thus not only get over traditional habits and attitudes, but also promise efficient progress and social harmony at the same time.[6] Psychological and sociological diagnostic abilities serve the propagandist to observe and to teach the public. Propaganda, as defined by Bernays, becomes a tool of enlightenment and 'has methods adapted to educating the public to new ideas, to articulating minority ideas . . ., to making latent majority ideas active' (Bernays, 1928b, p. 961).[7] According to Lasswell, the civic duty of public participation competed with 'many other forms of social activity: sport, amusement, crime', and propaganda was therefore needed 'to stimulate public attention to political matters' (1928, p. 263). Stating the superiority of mass persuasion in comparison with school propaganda promised to orchestrate public opinion by creating emotional and dramatic circumstances, for example conferences, events and films. These circumstances or scenarios and the use of mass media, especially the radio and mass press as the new agencies of public education (Bernays, 1938, p. 125), managed to draw attention and curiosity to policy and successfully address opinion leaders, who then delivered the messages to others.

Propagandists and mass communication experts as the new national educators

Lippmann, Bernays, Lasswell and other researchers of mass communication, including Paul F. Lazarsfeld, George Gallup and Hadley Cantril, did not remain in the academic ivory tower of critical research of propaganda, for example by the Institute of Propaganda Analysis. In fact, as experts, they advised governments on how to create national support and conformity towards governmental decisions. Bernays drafted campaigns for the US President Calvin Coolidge (1872–1933) and several big companies. In particular, both world wars accelerated the rise of governmental agencies for propaganda, which were funded by enormous sums. National unity and conformity between the government and public opinion, as well as the mobilization of the support of the people for the American entrance into the First World War, were regarded as indispensable for the victory. In 1917, the US Committee on Public Information (CPI), under the leadership of George Creel and with the engagement of Lippmann, orchestrated the acclamation for the war, which was a difficult task after years of neutrality in foreign policy (Gary, 1999, pp. 18–19, 32). The CPI was one of the first modern propaganda organizations. Despite the controversy regarding whether propaganda should replace education as the function of the school, the CPI achieved 'nearly full control of the nation's publishing organs during the war' (Bussemer, 2005, pp. 74–80; Glander, 2000, pp. 3, 7). The so-called Educational Division of the CPI, headed by the historian Guy Stanton Ford, who was president of the University of Minnesota from 1938 until 1941, managed it to influence public opinion in favour of America's entrance into the war by various means. As a result, 75,000 volunteers addressed the people at public places and held speeches no longer than four minutes. These so-called 'Four Minute Men' resulted from the presupposition of the inattentive and uninformed public needing short and simple messages to implement political orientation and allegiance. Furthermore, 75 million brochures and leaflets were produced and often used in schools, and even a newspaper – the *National School Service* – was founded. Ford tried to establish the Educational Division even when the war was over and legitimized his demands in a letter to the National Education Association (NEA) in 1918, with remarks about the main 'task to make an Americanized nationalized American nation' (cited in Glander, 2000, p. 9).

The concept of expert-guided democracy remained attractive for many intellectuals all over the world and especially in the United States.[8] Bernays called for an expert who:

> would be, rather, a trained technician who would be helpful in analysing public thought and public trends, in order to keep the government informed about the public, and the people informed about the government. America's relations with South America and with Europe would be greatly improved under such circumstances. Ours must be a leadership democracy administered by the intelligent minority who know how to regiment and guide the masses. Is this government by propaganda? Call it, if you prefer, government by education. But education, in the academic sense of the word, is not sufficient. It must be enlightened expert propaganda through

the creation of circumstances, through the high-spotting of significant events, and the dramatization of important issues. The statesman of the future will thus be enabled to focus the public mind on crucial points of policy, and regiment a vast, heterogeneous mass of voters to clear understanding and intelligent action.

(Bernays, 1928a, p. 114)

Similar to Bernays, Lippmann demanded the foundation of a ministry of information and Lasswell maintained, 'Democracy has proclaimed the dictatorship of palaver, and the technique of dictating to the dictator is propaganda' (1927, p. 631). All these requests became real during the Second World War, when mass communications experts, such as Lazarsfeld or Lasswell, pollsters such as Cantril, Roper and Gallup, psychologists including Jerome Bruner or Carl Hovland, and other intellectuals such as Margret Mead, Edward A. Shills and Herbert Marcuse (Müller, 2010), as well as immigrants such as the German poet Carl Zuckmayer (Nickel and Schrön, 2002), cooperated with several governmental propaganda organizations funded by the CIA (Bussemer, 2005, pp. 300–303; Glander, 2000, pp. 48–49, 88–89). These organizations were founded in 1941 or 1942 and were named Office of Civilian Defense (OCD), Office of the Coordination of Information (COI), Foreign Information Services (FOS), Office of Facts and Figures (OFF), Office of War Information (OWI) and Office of Strategic Services (OSS), the last two being the most important ones (Gary, 1999, pp. 112–113, 130, 154). They had to observe public opinion, and strengthen morale and civilian defence, as well as achieve compliance with governmental warfare and national consensus. The names of these agencies clearly indicated that the onus was on information instead of propaganda, as this term was hidden. They promised the transfer of reduced, basic, selected *knowledge and facts*. Again, propaganda is presented in a certain context of education. Or, in the terms of Hadley Cantril, they provided information and support, that the 'President can become a more successful educator' of the nation (cited in Glander, 2000, p. 89). A similar ascription of the political leader as the first teacher of the ideological or national collective was used in the propaganda trials in Moscow 1938 to characterize Stalin as a caring father of the people (Baberowski, 2008, p. 150). This parallel might indicate some affinities in the notions of state interventions and governmental people's instruction between the American New Deal and the Bolshevist regime.

This fundamental people's instruction by governmental propaganda seems to contradict Foucault's thesis about the governmental retraction from social ordering in favour of the economic market, which should regulate the society much more efficiently. Still, governmental propaganda can also be seen as an instrument of preventative social policy (Gary, 1999, pp. 33, 68, 72–74) aimed at gaining security, establishing control over conflicts and supporting national welfare.

Summary and outlook: education and propaganda in the Cold War

The entanglement of governmental propaganda and education became apparent in the concept of post-war re-education. However, now America did not address only its own population, but also other nations, especially Germany. Again, this effort was aimed at rapidly achieving allegiance to Western values of democracy, free market and economy. Because the concept of enemy changed at a fast pace, from National Socialist Germany to communist Soviet Union, the efficient attainment of national, ideological or Western consensus was delegated to propaganda and schools. Still, time and efficiency were again the most important criteria. Mass communication researchers, sociologists, pollsters and educational reformers adopted these criteria and promised efficient planning of social unity and welfare (Schumacher, 2000).

These promises were seldom reflected critically in the atmosphere of ideological competition in the Cold War, as Soviet campaigns and agitation were regarded to be much superior to Western propaganda. This perception or even historical construction of political and ideological inferiority of the Western world in relation to the so-called Communist Bloc was a main factor that initiated, for example, the Smith-Mundt Act in 1948 (Glander, 2000, p. 60–62; Schumacher, 2000, pp. 70–72).

Propagandists such as Bernays and Lasswell could present themselves as public educators because cultural and educational policy and social research became part of national security. This is evident in the naming of acts and important governmental reports, for example the National Defense Education Act, after the shock of Sputnik in 1958, as well as the report, *A Nation at Risk* (Tröhler, 2010, pp. 9–10). The intersection of education and national security is akin to the so-called 'mental national defence' (*Geistige Landesverteidigung*) in Switzerland from 1930 to 1960 – a period that is characterized by attempts to form Swiss conformity and national consensus in the light of threatening totalitarian movements in Europe (Mooser, 1997). Efficiency remained the key aim of school education from the 1920s to the bi-polar conflict of the Cold War, characterized by comparison and competition with the Eastern Bloc. Indeed, school subjects, such as mathematics, natural sciences and modern languages, attained new relevance because they were applicable and seen as serving to strengthen technological innovations and economic boom in relation to the Soviet Union. Nevertheless, at the same time, school lost its monopoly on education for two reasons. First, various new locations with educational impacts, for example department stores and television, raised activities in leisure time. Here, children learned other skills faster than they could do so in schools. Second, as the criteria of speed and measurability became the most important indicators and values of educational success, the aforementioned perception of schools as slow, inefficient and less competitive supported the notion of propaganda as the main instrument towards achieving national community. Since the beginning of the Cold War, the House Committee on Un-American Activities (HCUA), a Committee of the House of Representatives, became a powerful agency, dominating the political discourse and manifesting the friend–foe image. Even though the HCUA published a five-part booklet, *100 Things You Should Know About Communism in the U.S.A.* in 1948 (Tröhler, 2011, p. 12–16), the placement of reduced, selective information and facts was only one propagandistic form. Another approach attempted to gain intellectual dominance by opinion leaders and media supremacy – namely that, in the global conflict of the Cold War, the creation of Western coherence and community should be achieved as a counterpart of the Eastern Bloc. Therefore, public intellectuals, such as the European authors Manes Sperber or Arthur Koestler, were seen as responsible for spreading messages of democracy and freedom and were imbedded in the 'Congress of Cultural Freedom' that was funded by the CIA (Hochgeschwender, 1998).

These attempts at propaganda and education resulted from a certain concept of democracy that was not based on deliberative participation, but rather on acceptance and acclamation of governmental leadership. This acceptance was observed and gauged by social sciences – the so-called sciences of democracy. They should serve to create the average as the new point of reference for national community and integration. Furthermore, successful forms of American propaganda, including the 'Four Minute Men', were adapted in West Germany by the founding of organizations such as 'Mobilwerbung' or 'Arbeitsgemeinschaft Demokratischer Kreise' in the early 1950s. They were presenting short lectures and films, with the intent to inform the so-called uninterested rural population about governmental messages (Grube, 2010b). Therefore, in the early stages of the Cold War, in West Germany, democracy was introduced by re-education *and* propaganda.

Notes

1   Thanks to Veronika Magyar-Haas for this hint.
2   As another example of propagandistic ambitions, the Farm Security Administration (FSA) – founded in 1937 – did not document only the everyday activities of workers, but also praised the severity, staying power and action for the national community. The bombardment of public opinion in favour of national coherence was the aim of the activities of the FSA.
3   The president of the University of Chicago, Robert Maynard Hutchins (1899–1977), pleaded for the maintenance of a traditional canon of subjects and books of higher education and refused educational utilitarianism and the notion that schools have to equip students with skills relevant only to jobs, business and technology.
4   The administrative progressives had important offices in school administration and acted as school practitioners, whereas philosophers such as Dewey rather remained in the academic ivory tower (Labaree, 2005, p. 280) – although he gained public relevance.
5   Intersections between propaganda and education can be detected in the text 'Propaganda as a weapon' ('*Propaganda als Waffe*'), by the German communist media mogul Willi Münzenberg (1889–1990) (1937/1977, p. 176). They are also mentioned in the book by the Austrian social psychologist Peter Hofstätter (1954,

pp. 322–329), who served as a military psychologist for the German army during the Second World War. From 1949 until 1956, he taught at American universities.
6 In a similar way, Paul F. Lazarsfeld, Bernard Berelson and Hazel Gaudet (1944) maintained that polls were a useful tool against prejudices and racism.
7 'Every man who teaches the public how to ask for what it wants is at the same time teaching the public how to safeguard itself against his own possible tyrannous aggressiveness' (Bernays, 1928b, p. 960).
8 It was even promoted by many German intellectuals in the first third of the twentieth century, albeit with some modifications, as they supported the concept of mental aristocracy.

References

Arendt, H., 1996. *Elemente und Ursprünge Totaler Herrschaft. Antisemitismus, Imperialismus, Totale Herrschaft.* Munich: Piper.
Arnold, K., 2003. Propaganda als ideologische Kommunikation. *Publizistik*, 48(1), pp. 63–81.
Baberowski, J., 2008. *Der rote Terror. Die Geschichte des Stalinismus*, 2nd edn. Frankfurt: Fischer.
Bernays, E.L., 1928a. *Propaganda.* New York: Horace Liveright.
Bernays, E.L., 1928b. Manipulating public opinion: the why and the how. *American Journal of Sociology*, 33(6), pp. 958–971.
Bernays, E.L., 1938. Public education for democracy. *Annals of the American Academy of Political and Social Science*, 198(July), pp. 124–127.
Böhme, G. and Tenorth, H.-E., 1990. *Einführung in die Historische Pädagogik.* Darmstadt: Wissenschaftliche Buchgesellschaft.
Boydston, J.A., 1984. *The Later Works of John Dewey, Volume 3: Essays, Reviews, Miscellany, and 'Impressions of Soviet Russia'*, Carbondale, IL: Southern Illinois University.
Bussemer, T., 2005. *Propaganda. Konzepte und Theorien.* Wiesbaden: Verlag für Sozialwissenschaften.
Cantril, H. and Allport, G.W., 1935/1986. *The Psychology of Radio.* Reprint. Salem, NH: Ayer.
Foucault, M., 2001. *In Verteidigung der Gesellschaft. Vorlesungen am Collège de France (1975–76).* Frankfurt: Suhrkamp.
Foucault, M., 2004a. *Geschichte der Gouvernementalität, Bd. 1: Sicherheit, Territorium, Bevölkerung.* Frankfurt: Suhrkamp.
Foucault, M., 2004b. *Geschichte der Gouvernementalität, Bd. 2: Die Geburt der Biopolitik.* Frankfurt: Suhrkamp.
Frei, N., 2002. *Der Führerstaat. Nationalsozialistische Herrschaft 1933 bis 1945.* 7th edn. Munich: DTV.
Gary, B., 1999. *The Nervous Liberals. Propaganda Anxieties from World War I to the Cold War.* New York: Columbia University Press.
Glander, T., 2000. *Origins of Mass Communication Research During the American Cold War. Educational Effects and Contemporary Implications.* Mahwah, NJ: Lawrence Erlbaum Associates.
Grube, N., 2010a. Mass democracy and political governance. The Walter Lippmann–John Dewey debate. In: D. Tröhler, T. Schlag and F. Osterwalder (eds) *Pragmatism and Modernities.* Rotterdam: Sense, pp. 145–161.

Grube, N., 2010b. Aushandeln, Gestaltung und Resonanz von Regierungspropaganda seit der Ära Adenauer im Spannungsfeld von Politik, Wirtschaft, Wissenschaft und Medien. In: K. Arnold, C. Classen, S. Kinnebrock, E. Lersch and H.-U. Wagner (eds) *Von der Medialisierung der Politik zur Medialisierung des Politischen? Zum Verhältnis von Medien und Politik im 20. Jahrhundert.* Leipzig: Leipziger Universitätsverlag, pp. 267–285.

Heideking, J. and Mauch, C., 2008. *Geschichte der USA*, 6th edn. Tubingen, Basel: A. Francke Verlag.

Hochgeschwender, M., 1998. *Freiheit in der Offensive? Der Kongress für Kulturelle Freiheit und die Deutschen.* Munich: Oldenbourg.

Hofstätter, P., 1954. *Einführung in die Sozialpsychologie.* Stuttgart, Wien: Humboldt-Verlag.

Igo, S.E., 2007. *The Averaged American. Surveys, Citizens, and the Making of a Mass Public.* Cambridge; MA: Harvard University Press.

Jäger, F., 2001. *Amerikanischer Liberalismus und Zivile Gesellschaft. Perspektiven Sozialer Reform zu Beginn des 20. Jahrhunderts.* Gottingen: Vandenhoeck & Ruprecht.

Kliebard, H.M., 1995. *The Struggle for the American Curriculum 1893–1958*, 2nd edn. New York, London: Routledge.

Labaree, D.F., 2005. Progressivism, schools, and schools of education: an American romance. *Paedagogica Historica*, 41(1–2), pp. 275–288.

Labaree, D.F., 2011. Citizens and consumers. Changing visions of virtue and opportunity in US Education, 1841–1954. In: D. Tröhler, T.S. Popkewitz and D.F. Labaree (eds) *Schooling and the Making of Citizens in the Long Nineteenth Century. Comparative Visions.* New York, London: Routledge, pp. 177–192.

Lasswell, H.D., 1927. The theory of political propaganda. *The American Political Science Review*, 21(3), pp. 627–631.

Lasswell, H.D., 1928. The function of the propagandist. *International Journal of Ethics*, 38(3), pp. 258–268.

Lasswell, H.D., 1931. The measurement of public opinion. *The American Political Science Review*, 25(2), pp. 311–326.

Lasswell, H.D., 1935. Subject and object of propaganda. *Annals of the American Academy of Political and Social Sciences*, 179(May), pp. 187–193.

Lasswell, H.D., 1941. The World Attention Survey. *Public Opinion Quarterly*, 5(4), pp. 456–462.

Lasswell, H.D., 1957. The impact of public opinion research on our society. *The Public Opinion Quarterly*, 21(1), pp. 33–38.

Lazarsfeld, P.F., Berelson B. and Gaudet, H., 1944. *The People's Choice. How the Voter Makes Up His Mind in a Presidential Campaign.* New York, London: Duelle, Sloan and Pearce.

Lippmann, W., 1922/1965. *Public Opinion.* New York: Free Press.

Lippmann, W., 1925. *The Phantom Public. A Sequel to 'Public Opinion'.* New York: Macmillan.

Loss, C.P., 2012. *Between Citizens and the State. The Politics of American Higher Education in the 20th Century.* Princeton, NJ: Princeton University Press.

Mooser, J., 1997. Die 'Geistige Landesverteidigung' in den 1930er Jahren. Profile und Kontexte eines vielschichtigen Phänomens in der schweizerischen politischen Kultur in der Zwischenkriegszeit. *Schweizerische Zeitschrift für Geschichte*, 47(4), pp. 685–708.

Müller, T.B., 2010. *Krieger und Gelehrte. Herbert Marcuse und die Denksysteme im Kalten Krieg*. Hamburg: Hamburger Edition.

Münzenberg, W., 1937/1977. Propaganda als Waffe. In: T. Schulz (ed.) *Willi Münzenberg. Propaganda als Waffe. Ausgewählte Schriften 1919–1940*. Jossa: März-Verlag, pp. 173–315.

National Education Association, 1918. *Cardinal Principles of Secondary Education*. US Bureau of Education Bulletin. Washington, DC: Government Printing Office.

Nickel, G. and Schrön, J. (eds) 2002. *Carl Zuckmayer. Geheimreport*. Gottingen: Wallstein.

Osterhammel, J., 2009. *Die Verwandlung der Welt. Eine Geschichte des 19. Jahrhunderts*, 4th edn. Munich: Beck.

Otto, I., 2007. 'Public opinion and the emergency'. Das Rockefeller Communications seminar. In: I. Schneider and I. Otto (eds) *Formationen der Mediennutzung II. Strategien der Verdatung*. Bielefeld: Transcript, pp. 73–91.

Park, P. and Pooley, J. (eds) 2008. *The History of Media and Communication Research. Contested Memories*. New York: Peter Lang.

Popkewitz, T.S., 2010. The university as a prophet, science as its messenger, and democracy as its revelation. In: D. Tröhler, T. Schlag and F. Osterwalder (eds) *Pragmatism and Modernities*. Rotterdam: Sense, pp. 99–121.

Schivelbusch, W., 2005. *Entfernte Verwandtschaft. Faschismus, Nationalsozialismus, New Deal 1933–1939*. Munich, Wien: Hanser.

Schumacher, F., 2000. *Kalter Krieg und Propaganda. Die USA, der Kampf um die Weltmeinung und die Ideelle Westbindung der Bundesrepublik Deutschland*. Treves: Wissenschaftlicher Verlag.

Tröhler, D., 2010. Harmonizing the educational globe. World polity, cultural features, and the challenges to educational research. *Studies in Philosophy and Education*, 29, pp. 5–17.

Tröhler, D., 2011. Historiographic challenges in history of education. *International Journal for the Historiography of Education*, 1(1), pp. 9–22.

Tyack, D. and Cuban, L., 2001. *Tinkering Toward Utopia. A Century of Public School Reform*, 8th printing. Cambridge: Harvard University Press.

Chapter 12

Conceptualizations of dignity and exposure in critiques of community
Implications for ethics and educational theory in the work of Plessner and Nancy

Veronika Magyar-Haas

Policy documents in Germany, from federal and state ministries, organizations and commissions, have long been shaped by the discourse of 'activating a new communality' (*Gemeinschaftlichkeit*). This 'new communality' has been evident in politically initiated and promoted strategies of communalization, for example in the context of social work, at least since the 1990s (Kessl, 2000; Magyar-Haas, 2009, pp. 79–80). These indicate a displacement of social responsibilities to individuals and small communities, which can be explained (see, for example, Ziegler, 2001, pp. 7–8) with reference to the crisis of the Fordist model, and the associated decline in the importance of quasi-universal (welfare-)state normality.[1] The 'decreasing benefits for the poor and poorest' reflect the crisis of the welfare state, which is also regarded as the 'crisis of the social' (Brumlik, 1995, p. 34). The 'restructuring of the welfare state' in Germany has included the demand that state or communal services that no longer seemed affordable in terms of tax funding should be made 'cost-efficient, effective and flexible' (Brumlik, 1995, p. 34). This has been evident in various political reports referring to 'communality', a concept linked with norms and values such as commitment, reciprocity, and self-efficacy for the community. These norms and values are in turn deployed in an instrumentalizing, moralizing way (see Magyar-Haas, 2009, p. 80). There are complaints about the loss of values, disintegration and anomie, for which the proposed solution is 'calls for a revitalization of subsidiary, primary communities (*Lebensgemeinschaften*)' (Brumlik, 1995, p. 34), both in politics and in certain areas of the social sciences. Philipp Sandermann (2009) argues that the striking renaissance of postulations of 'community' (*Gemeinschaft*) and 'communality' (*Gemeinschaftlichkeit*) in the German debates has to do with the reception of communitarian approaches from the United States. The publications subsumed under the 'communitarian' label are quite heterogeneous, but are linked by their role, since the 1980s, as the expression of a kind of 'intellectual counter-movement' to liberalist concepts in US social philosophy and political theory – such as those propounded by John Rawls (Brumlik, 1995, p. 35; Gutman, 1985). In keeping with this, the arguments used in communitarian approaches can only be understood in light of the criticism of (neo-)liberal concepts (see Sandermann, 2012, pp. 101–103). It is more than ironic that communitarian perspectives – now that they have been 'imported' into Germany – seem highly compatible with a neo-liberal policy of activation on the part of the state.

This may be connected to the fact that, in the arguments of those authors associated with communitarianism,[2] 'society' is 'systematically conceived only on the level of "community", and "community" [is] ultimately [conceived] only on the level of subjective obligation towards the "community"' (Sandermann, 2012, p. 108). This notion that the self has an obligation and a responsibility towards the 'community', its way of life and 'values', means that the aspirations, ideas and wishes of individuals are subordinated to those of the community, and thus lends itself particularly well to political instrumentalization.

This chapter is based on the assumption that this *potential for instrumentalization* offered by 'community' – which is, depending on the configuration of the state, charged with moral significance or treated as morally insignificant, and prized or rejected as a concept – is primarily connected with the mythical, controversial *concept* of community. This concept requires a close analytical and critical examination, which will be undertaken here. The first step will be to outline the constitution of the 'we', then to ask on what levels this allows discussion of 'community'. This involves taking a closer look at two critiques of community, which come from different historical contexts but are very similar in their criticisms: Helmuth Plessner's liberal critique of postulations of community in the Weimar Republic, and Jean-Luc Nancy's deconstructive critique of mythologizing ideas of community, particularly in communitarian approaches, in the 1980s. Of course both critiques have to be defined in terms of their socio-cultural and temporal contexts, yet it would be simplistic to position these approaches solely as part of their respective historical contexts, and to assume that these critiques are strictly a product of history.

The discussion begins with the social theory of Helmuth Plessner, written in the 1920s, which is experiencing a certain renaissance in current German (Eßbach, 1994; Fischer, 2008; Krüger and Lindemann, 2006; Richter, 2005), Dutch (de Mul, 1991; Ernste, 2004) and Italian (Accarino, 2009; Rasini, 2007) philosophy and sociology. Plessner's concept of community, which proves fruitful for analysis for several reasons, is the result of a clear-sighted examination of the situation in Germany at the time, informed by a premonition of the dangers of totalitarian thinking. His critique of community and radicalism, set out in the 1924 work, *Grenzen der Gemeinschaft. Eine Kritik des sozialen Radikalismus*, recently translated into English as 'The Limits of Community. A Critique of Social Radicalism', seems, for his time, both paradigmatic and unique. Plessner's socio-philosophical interpretation in his critique of community is connected with an anthropological and socio-ethical line of argument. The focal point of his social ethics here is a definition of the soul, and the concept of 'ontological ambiguity' (1924/2003, p. 63); Plessner's interpretation of dignity builds on this concept. These interconnections are pivotal for the analyses in the chapter, as it is here that implications and links for pedagogy and educational theory become discernible.

The next section focuses in particular on Jean-Luc Nancy's critique – based on the theory of difference – of communism and of neo-liberal and communitarian perspectives, and his conceptualization of communality. Nancy (1986/1988, p. 68) redefines 'the being of community' as 'the exposure of singularities', according to which definition 'exposure' and 'sharing' (*partage*) constitute the being of community. Even though no social ethics of responsibility is made explicit in Nancy's work, such an ethics does seem to be implied, and does appear to offer possible connections with educational theory.

The last section focuses on the implications that the previously discussed concepts of community have for educational theory; in particular, it explores the scope of Plessner's critique of community for traditional, closeness-based approaches and concepts in educational and school theory. The final section of the chapter offers a conclusion.

The question of the 'we'

> And as we know, community (as an organicistic or mystical construct, i.e. in essence in all its well-known, philosophical or political forms) always and fundamentally excludes.
>
> (Nancy, 1994, p. 194)

The question of the 'we' is always political. Behind this term there are always ideas about subjects, persons or individuals, about I and you, about selves and others, 'plural singularities' (Nancy, 1996/2004), the question of the 'between' or the 'third party'. This 'we' ostensibly simulates similarities, common features, equal status towards the inside, by setting limits to belonging towards the outside, or by classing particular characteristics as relevant and thus producing differences and thereby non-belonging, that is, a 'not we'. What is constructed in the process is a *myth of homogeneity*, concealing the *dimension of power* in communal relations.

Limits are also placed on this 'we' in the political power context, or conceptually, in scholarly analysis. Depending on where the line is drawn, this 'we' merges into community, society, state, nation or into amalgamations thereof, for instance when there is talk of the international community, the community of states, of the state as a community of solidarity etc. These amalgamations, of which community will be examined more closely in the following text, are by no means clearly definable, and have been subject to a variety of conceptual interpretations and historical instrumentalizations.

The concept of community is neither neutral nor purely descriptive (see Gertenbach et al., 2010, pp. 10–13). It may imply the idea of collective care and social bonds and thus be linked with 'welfare' and 'social well-being', but it may equally be exclusionary, if it has the connotation of a strong common identity. In this respect 'community' can limit individual freedom and be intolerant towards difference (Mooney and Neal, 2009, p. 2). 'Community' may also be evoked nostalgically, as if there had once been a coherent community (Clarke, 2008).[3] The concept of community is part of historically specific academic and societal developments and political contexts and has divergent connotations in different national contexts. Here the conceptualization, ideology and practice of community can be subjected to scholarly examination (see Amit and Rapport, 2002). If community is dealt with as a *political-ethical category*, analysis of its forms, representations and normative justifications in their historical contexts and conditions seems crucial. As a further line of discourse, theoretical perspectives can be identified in which community is examined as an *ontological category*. In these it tends to be 'ahistorical questions of human coexistence and sociality' (Gertenbach *et al.*, 2010, p. 20) that are discussed. Following this logic of differentiation, we can state that interpretations of '*community*' that are primarily political-ethical consider community in its various forms (family, collective, political association etc.), while analyses based on ontological arguments hypothesize '*communality*' as a genuine coexistence. While Plessner's analyses, which will be discussed in the following section, can be assigned to the former category, Nancy's analyses fall more into the latter category.

Contexts of Helmuth Plessner's critique of community and his interpretation of dignity

In the first third of the twentieth century, in the German-speaking context, as in the US-American discourse (see Dewey, 1927; Grube, 2011; Lippmann, 1925), the debate about the establishment and collapse of communities developed in connection with in some cases sceptical, pessimistic perceptions of industrialization, urbanization and the emergence of anonymous masses – even if divergent conclusions were drawn in the different discourses (Magyar-Haas, 2009, p. 82). In the German context, community frequently has positive connotations as a refuge from the coldness[4] of society in industrial, capitalist modernity, and – in the spirit of social romanticism – is usually associated with warmth and feelings of security (see Gertenbach *et al.*, 2010, pp. 30–39; Nolte, 2000, pp. 108, 159–169). These debates about communality were conducted not only in the framework of sociological and philosophical analyses (Kracauer, 1927/1977), which will be the main focus here, but also in the context of art, architecture,[5] literature and theatre (Fischer-Lichte, 2004, pp. 82–83; Magyar-Haas, 2009, pp. 82–83).

'The idol of this age is community', Helmuth Plessner observes in 1924, and criticizes the emergence of this phenomenon as the result of an 'excessive cooling of human relations due to mechanical, commercial, political abstractions', which lead to the 'excessive counter-model in the ideal of a glowing ... community' (Plessner 1924/2003, p. 28). By analogy, decades later, Zygmunt Bauman (2009, pp. 43–45) reveals strategies aimed at reviving a 'feeling of community' in the factories, as a way of compensating for the coldness caused by capitalist production methods. Gerd Bauman (1996, p. 15) also stresses: 'Yet the word [community] retains connotations of interpersonal warmth, shared interests, and loyalty.'[6]

In 'The Limits of Community', Plessner engages explicitly with the social formations 'community' and 'society' (*Gemeinschaft* and *Gesellschaft*), a distinction that had a formative influence on the sociological and philosophical debate in Germany, particularly in the first half of the twentieth century. This relationship between community and society had, on the one hand, already been theorized in the work of Ferdinand Tönnies (1887/1926)[7] – an interpretation that experienced a wide reception in the decades that followed; on the other hand, it begins to develop its problematic aspects, politically and socially, in the Weimar Republic. Tönnies differentiates between the two social forms as follows:

> All – both relationships and collectives (*Samtschaften*), and corporations (*Körperschaften*) – are communal, in that they are based on direct mutual affirmation, i.e. 'natural', essential will (*Wesenswille*); are societal, in that this affirmation has been rationalized, i.e. established through 'rational', arbitrary will (*Kürwille*).
>
> (Tönnies, 1887/1926, p. xii)

According to this, community is constituted on the basis of 'vegetative life', through 'parental descent and sex' (Tönnies, 1887/1926, p. 8), while society presupposes a rationalized will to connect (for this, see also Haus, 2003, pp. 95–97). Tönnies thus conceived 'community' in the sense of a collective with a common, connecting 'mentality' and with a unified 'will', in which a shared understanding is more or less inherent, and not the result of discussions or communication (Magyar-Haas, 2009, p. 81).

Tönnies juxtaposed these two forms of sociality, with their different logics of constitution, perhaps not explicitly as 'antitheses'[8] (Plessner, 1924/2003, p. 11), but in a polarizing manner as 'normal types . . ., between which real social life operates' (Tönnies, 1887/1926, p. xii). He thus contributed substantially to an understanding, in subsequent sociological or philosophical discourses, that the relationship between community and society is *dichotomous or dualistic*. In the reception of Tönnies in the German-speaking context, this relationship tends to be construed as exclusive, either in the sense of two different forms of social integration, or in the sense of a historical shift from community towards society, which also implies exclusivity (Haus, 2003, p. 95). This exclusivity does not, however, seem to play a decisive part in the US-American discussions, where community does *not* function as the opposite of society. Instead, John Dewey's (1927) construction of society as the Great Community points to the interconnectedness of the two social forms. Dewey devises his concept of community in a somewhat programmatic respect as a communicative community, which is constituted through exchanges about common actions and experiences and which is nonetheless supposed to 'improve' the communicatively loose, unconnected (mass) society (Magyar-Haas, 2009, p. 82).

Helmuth Plessner, on the other hand, in his 1924 critique in the context of the Weimar Republic, reconstructs 'blood' and 'the ideal' (*die Sache*) as community-building elements. Even if Dewey's understanding of society as a Great Community suggests the relevance of proximity, his conceptualization, unlike Plessner's, is not so much about the form of the social, which limits behaviours and gives expectations of particular modes of action. When proximity is meant, this tends to be in a spatial sense, in terms of neighbourhood, where, however, common experiences are also given concrete form through communication. Dewey's concept of community should therefore *not* be regarded as if the members were, so to speak, only loosely linked, and as if they engaged in communicative exchanges when jointly affected by a topic. In his arguments, mutual support on the basis of common experiences is central. Dewey's concept of community is based on experience, communication, but also action. His ideal is a renaissance of the community of virtue, which was to be reactivated in large communicative spaces through the popularization and publicization of scholarship.[9]

In Plessner's work (1924/2003, pp. 41–45), on the other hand, community is interpreted critically as an association marked by directness, closeness, intimacy, genuineness, unreservedness and immediacy, which therefore restricts the behavioural options of the individual, signifies the 'abolition of the private sphere of the person' (Plessner, 1924/2003, p. 45) and thus *impacts on human dignity*. It is therefore not particularly surprising that it is *not* the characteristics of community that Plessner (1924/2003, p. 41) identifies as 'factors securing human dignity', but the characteristics of society. Plessner understands society, in a liberal interpretation, as the social form which, thanks to its characteristics of impersonal relationships, distance, indirectness, reserve and opportunities for play, is most apt to do justice to the human constitution and is thus able to ensure human dignity.[10] Here dignity 'always [concerns] the whole of the person, the harmony between their inside and outside, and designates that ideal condition which people strive for' (Plessner, 1924/2003, pp. 75–76). Thus this 'harmony' can, according to this logic, only succeed when opportunities for distancing and dissimulation are available and no fixations on a particular suchness (*Sosein*) are undertaken. Thus Plessner observes critically that the form of communality smooths out the individual differences among people, that it demands the surrender of their identity, and rejects interpersonal space, distance and boundaries. It is precisely these, however, that Plessner conceives as constitutive elements of personhood, thereby legitimating the necessity of sociality in anthropological terms, with reference to his *conceptualization of soul*, which he equates with an 'inwardness incomparable in depth and inner abundance of qualities' (Plessner, 1924/2003, p. 62; see also Magyar-Haas, 2009, p. 84).

On the one hand, Plessner (1924/2003, p. 63) argues, the soul (*das Seelische*), which is becoming and being (*Sein*) in one, does not tolerate 'any final judgement, but resists any fixing and formulation of its individual being (*Wesen*)'; on the other hand, it needs to be seen as well, since 'the soul suffers from nothing so much as a lack of attention (*das Nichtbeachtetsein*)'[11] (p. 64). This ambiguity, the simultaneity of visibility and invisibility, of revelation and concealment, recognizability and the propensity to be mistaken for something else, is referred to by Plessner (1924/2003, p. 63) as 'ontological ambiguity'. It is in 'unfixability' or 'indefinability' (*Nichtfestlegbarkeit*) that the playful evasion, the diversity of representational possibilities, is revealed. 'Ontological ambiguity' gives rise to 'the two fundamental forces in the life of the soul: the urge for revelation, the need for recognition, and the urge for restraint, modesty' (Plessner, 1924/2003, p. 63). If this simultaneity is suspended in specific social situations in favour of one of the two poles, Plessner (1924/2003, p. 70) argues, if the psyche (*das Psychische*) dares to emerge 'naked', this entails 'the risk of ridiculousness'. The loss of face resulting from the momentary revelation of the soul requires, according to Plessner (1924/2003, p. 72), a compensation, 'a clothing with form' by means of masks, opportunities for dissimulation, the drawing of artificial boundaries, in order to preserve one's own integrity and dignity, the 'idea of a harmony of the soul, and between soul and expression, soul and body' (p. 75; see also Magyar-Haas, 2009, pp. 84–85). Thus, according to Plessner (1924/2003, p. 82), the 'moment of dignity is given in the endlessness and inviolability of the personal soul'.[12]

Since the risk of ridiculousness impacts on dignity, Plessner (1924/2003, p. 79, emphasis VMH) argues that there is a need for forms of co-existence that 'ensure the greatest possible wealth of spiritual relationships between humans but at the same time the greatest possible *mutual protection* from one another'. As explained above, Plessner (1924/2003, p. 80) describes these forms and situations, 'the virtuoso handling of the forms of play in which humans approach one another without colliding, in which they move away from one another without offending by indifference', as societal. While society, along with its soothing anonymity, explicitly responds to the 'longing for masks, behind which immediacy disappears' (Plessner, 1924/2003, p. 41), community, which is characterized by closeness and intimacy, restricts opportunities for dissimulation and social play. '[I]n the unreservedness of openness towards one another' (Plessner, 1924/2003, p. 58), it prevents play with masks, and thus impacts on dignity: 'All signs of affiliation with a community ultimately mean the suspension of the individual's private sphere, if not affectively as in the bonds of biological kinship, then intellectually, imaginatively and symbolically' (Plessner, 1924/2003, p. 45). In contrast, Plessner argues, society lives 'solely from the spirit of play. It plays the games of implacability and those of joy, since there is nothing man can prove his freedom in more purely than in distance from himself' (Plessner, 1924/2003, p. 94). The ethos of the social order of life is 'grace and lightness', 'in which nothing is aimed at intimacy, everything at distance, and it is not the triumph of the value over the purpose, but the victory of play over seriousness, which is most highly esteemed' (Plessner, 1924/2003, p. 38). Such an 'order of life' 'cultivates everything which leads from intimacy to distance, from unreservedness to restraint'[13] (p. 41).

In his early 'manifesto against the "tyranny of intimacy"' (Lethen, 2002, p. 41), which Helmuth Lethen (2002, p. 39) also interprets as a 'behavioural theory of distance', Plessner the social theorist explicitly shows his awareness of the dangers and uncertainties of the social game, stating that *Öffentlichkeit* (public, publicity, the public sphere)[14] brings with it 'the whole risk of the debasement of human dignity' (Plessner, 1924/2003, p. 82). He defines *Öffentlichkeit* as the 'embodiment of relations of possibility' (Plessner, 1924/2003, p. 55) and as the 'embodiment of people and things which no longer "belong", but which have to be expected' (p. 48).[15] These 'relations of possibility', according to Plessner, not only correspond to the special constitution of the human soul, with all its ambivalences and paradoxes; rather, they explicitly allow the art of dissimulation, the masks, the social (role) play – but at the same time also demand these (Magyar-Haas and Grube, 2009, p. 11). For this 'battleground of the public sphere', Plessner argues (1924/2003, p. 82), the individual must 'give [himself] a form in which he becomes unassailable, a suit of armour, as it were', he must become generalized through masks, 'but without completely disappearing as a person', he must dispense with 'being heeded and being respected as an individuality', in order to 'be respected . . . at least in a representative sense'. Thus, in order to avoid the risk of ridiculousness and to be able to preserve dignity, individuals are constitutively reliant on social masquerades (*Maskenspiele*, literally 'mask plays') in this arena of public space – although here, on the 'battleground', the concept of play hardly seems suitable. Plessner thus argues from two perspectives: on the one hand, masks are relevant to do justice to the ambiguity of the soul, and to preserve dignity in indefinability, and, on the other hand, exposure in public demands the art of dissimulation, and also makes this possible. In terms of Plessner's analytical perspective, form gives security, masks – in the sense of public roles[16] – offer protection; through them, people become visible and concealed at the same time. 'Only the great exhortation to respect individually shaped human dignity . . . compels this protection, and thus establishes the logic of the public sphere' (Plessner, 1924/2003, p. 103). Thus Plessner gives the following thoroughly anthropological summary in his work of social theory:

> If life, the body, the intellect did not already ensure that there must be commerce and public sphere, official and professional duties, and that a thousand allowances must be made on all paths, then the soul, for the sake of its own self-respect and that of other souls, would have to invent this public sphere and these transactions, these distance-commanding offices, professions, activities, this ceremonial of working day and holiday, the power of artificiality, all that saves face; and as has been shown, it would have the strength to do so.
>
> (Plessner, 1924/2003, p. 105)

Helmut Lethen (2002, p. 47) makes the critical objection that 'admittedly those situations in which appearing in armour has an unintentionally comic effect, in which being unarmed would be more appropriate, [escape] Plessner's attention'. For the outlined passages in 'The Limits of Community', Lethen's criticism is certainly apposite. Used in this way by Plessner, the concept of the mask recalls the artificial, the dissimulated, or possible available roles that might hide something 'authentic', that which is 'individual'. It is only decades later, in his 1967 work on the philosophy of expression, *Der Mensch im Spiel*, that Plessner (1967/2003, p. 310) writes: '"Persona" means mask', and refers back to the ancient Roman understanding of persona, in that he defines man as the 'actor of his own self' (p. 311), and explains the importance of masks and roles in human behaviour in anthropological terms, while also perpetuating them in his social theory.

Plessner's social science analysis, that is, his examination of different social relations, which are than referred to generically as communal or societal, is associated with a political-normative definition of the concept of society. In his analysis he distances himself from both individualist and socialist positions, stating: 'The individualist revokes society in favour of the great individual, the socialist in favour of the community' (Plessner, 1924/2003, pp. 33–34). First and foremost, however, he is distancing himself here from radical demands and forms of different radicalisms.[17] His criticism is aimed not at community in itself, but at the elevation of this social form above the social, the propagation of community as the *only form of life* – as is currently also apparent in communitarian debates:

> This is not directed against the right of the 'life-community' (*Lebensgemeinschaft*), its nobility and its beauty. But it is directed against its proclamation as the only form of coexistence worthy of humans; not against communio, but against communio as a principle, against communism as an attitude to life, against the radicalism of community.
>
> (Plessner, 1924/2003, p. 41)

Redefinitions of the concept of community in its political and ethical dimensions: Jean-Luc Nancy

In 1986, roughly sixty years after Plessner's critique of community, the French philosopher Jean-Luc Nancy produced a critique of the instrumentalized, 'set in motion' community in the treatise *La communauté désœuvrée*. Here he argued against apparently totalitarian calls for community, against the idea of 'the originary', and against homogenizing ideas of 'becoming one' in these calls.

In the mid-1980s, in the period shortly before the end of the Cold War, during the gradual collapse of communist systems and the hegemonic rise of neo-liberal political models (see Dallmayr, 2008, p. 109; Gertenbach *et al.*, 2010, p. 158), Nancy distances himself from both communism and individualism, from both communitarian and neo-liberal/individualist positions:

> The most significant and probably the most painful thing to which the modern world bears witness ... is the evidence of the dissolution, the collapse or the shaking up of the community. Communism is "the insurmountable horizon of our time", ... and it is this in more than one respect: viewed in political, ideological or strategic terms; what is actually most important ... however ... is the following: the word "communism" symbolizes the wish to discover or rediscover a place for the community.
>
> (Nancy, 1986/1988, p. 11)

This is how, in 1986, Nancy begins his discussion of community, and this is the point where his critique starts. Here he is not only concerned with the 'betrayal' of the word and the idea of 'communism', or of the ideas of justice, freedom and equality invested in the ideal of communism. What he sees as problematic, instead, is the 'basis of the communist ideal itself', that is, the human being who is defined as a *producer*, or who is *defined* at all, who 'is fundamentally understood as the producer of his own work in the form of his labour or his works' (Nancy, 1986/1988, p. 13). This problem of being defined, being determined as something, can be connected with Plessner's critique of the way people are fixed.

According to Nancy (1986/1988, p. 13), the betrayal of communist ideals by so-called 'real communism' '[weighs] on us on the one hand as unbearable suffering (alongside other no less unbearable sufferings which our liberal societies impose on us), and has, on the other hand, decisive political weight'. At the same time he clearly sees the extremely problematic possibility that a 'whole society' could allow itself to be made *obedient* – though here Nancy himself, homogenizing and disregarding difference, constructs 'whole societies' – and that the community, in the name of production, could be taken to be an operative goal to be implemented and fulfilled (see Dallmayr, 2008, p. 111).

What remains when 'community' is dissolved is the individual,[18] by name: the atom, the indivisible, the 'absolutely detached "for-itself" as origin and certainty' (Nancy, 1986/1988, p. 15). Nancy's critique is aimed at individualistic, atomized perceptions that overlook the fact, on the one hand, that the 'individual' displays totalizing, 'immanentistic' features and, on the other hand, that 'individual atoms do not make a world'. On the contrary, this requires an 'inclination', for which Nancy uses the term *clinamen*. The perspective of the 'inclination', which could be the starting point for the analysis of 'being-in-common', is scarcely to be found in theories of the individual, and also marks – like community – a striking gap in the metaphysics of the subject (whether this is taken to mean the individual or the state) (Nancy, 1986/1988, p. 16). Nancy criticizes the metaphysical idea of being as 'ab-solutum' in the sense of a detached, separated, self-contained, *relationless* being (*Sein*) as an 'inauspicious logic', since something that is absolutely separate must include the separation itself, and would thus have to be without an exterior: 'In order to be absolutely alone, it is not enough that I am alone, instead it is also necessary that I alone am alone. Precisely this, however, is a contradiction. The logic of the absolute does violence to the absolute' (Nancy, 1986/1988, p. 17). Finally, being (*das Sein*) 'itself' reaches a point where it can 'define itself as a relationship,[19] as non-absoluteness, and, if you will . . . *as community*' (Nancy, 1986/1988, p. 20, emphasis in original).

Nancy devises a modified concept of community that relates to being-in-common, being-shared. Such an *understanding of community*, which Nancy develops *in* and *through* his criticism of diverse calls for community – calls propagating unity, 'becoming one' *communion* and the originary, and oriented towards assumptions of homogeneity and immanence – is a specific one. It is as *in*compatible with the concept of community developed by Tönnies, for example – as the counterpart or complement of society – as it is with the idea propagated in the US-American debates on community, especially in the work of John Dewey, on the construction of the 'Great Community' (Dewey, 1927; see also Bittner, 2000, p. 84), which can be understood as the reconcilability of both social forms – society and community. Community is – as we learn from 'The Unrepresentable Community' (*Die undarstellbare Gemeinschaft*)[20] (Nancy, 1986/1988, pp. 26–29) – not an empirically discoverable fact, to which Dewey also likes to refer. It did not exist as a lost 'golden' age, nor in early Christian churches, though this is an idea – suggesting unity, harmony and familiarity – that has consistently been evoked over history, whenever the need arose to abandon diversity and uniqueness in favour of identification with the 'living body of the community' (Nancy, 1986/1988, p. 27). 'Community is thus by no means something which society has broken or lost, but something that *happens to us* – as a question, expectation, event, exhortation –, that is, something *emanating from* society that happens to us. So nothing was lost, and therefore nothing is yet lost' (Nancy, 1986/1988, p. 31) – this is the optimistic and pugnacious message of a deconstructivist thinker. 'That which was "lost" from the community – the immanence and the familiarity of "becoming one" – is only lost insofar as such a "loss" is constitutive for "community" itself' (Nancy, 1986/1988, p. 32). In this sense, Nancy argues, this is not a loss, since this is the *only* way community can mark its own boundaries. Summarizing, Nancy emphasizes, with reference to George Bataille, that community is 'neither a work to be created, nor a lost communication, but space itself, the opening up of a space for the experience of the outside,[21] of being-outside-oneself' (Nancy, 1986/1988, p. 45).

In the course of his critique of both ideologies of community and the individual, and to distance himself from communitarian and neo-liberal positions, Nancy develops the concept of 'singular plural being', borrowing but critically expanding Heidegger's[22] (1927/2001) concept of *Mitsein* ('being-with'). In 'The unrepresentable community' the 'singular being' already functions as a central figure of argument, which is neither to be equated with the concept of 'individual'[23] nor with the 'subject': 'A singular being *appears* . . . in the touching of the skin (or the soul) of another singular being, at the outermost limits of *the same* singularity, which, as such, is always *other*, always shared, always exposed' (Nancy, 1986/1988, p. 62, emphasis in original). Singularity as sharing does not refer to some 'social bond' or an 'intersubjective nature', but rather to existence as communication,[24] to the *between* as such: 'The common being (*das gemeinsame Sein*) is neither tissue nor flesh, neither subject nor substance, and hence there is also no laceration (*déchirure*) of this being, but there *is* sharing out ... The "laceration" consists solely in being exposed to the outside' (Nancy, 1986/1988, p. 67). The following insight could offer a fruitful link for the theory of recognition and (social) pedagogy: 'that *I* am first of all exposed to the other and to the exposure of the other' (Nancy, 1986/1988, p. 68).

Nancy systematically takes up and develops the aspects of *exposure*, of being-with (*Mitsein*), in the short work *La Communauté affrontée*[25] in 2001, and in his volume of essays, *Être singulier pluriel*, in 1996. Clearly distancing himself from Heidegger, Nancy emphasizes: '*The plurality of beings is at the foundation of Being*' (Nancy, 1996/2004, p. 34, emphasis in original, tr. Richardson and O'Byrne, 2000, p. 12) and thereby stresses his desire to formulate a 'plural ontology' (Nancy, 1996/2004, p. 12), after all, being 'cannot be anything but being-with-one-another, circulating in the with and as the with of this singularly-plural coexistence' (p. 21, tr. Richardson and O'Byrne, 2000, p. 3). This 'with' functions here as Nancy's 'minimal ontological premise' (Nancy, 1996/2004, p. 54, tr. Richardson and O'Byrne, 2000, p. 27). Against this background, he engages critically both with atomistic, neo-liberal perspectives and with calls for community that operate with a phantasm of unity: 'Omnipotence and omnipresence are always the things which are demanded from community or sought in it: sovereignty and intimacy, self-presence without rupture and without exterior', Nancy (2001/2007, p. 12) comments critically in the short work 'The confronted community'. Here he also subjects his 1986 work to criticism, formulating:

> I have thus chosen to shift focus and concentrate my work around the "with": almost indistinguishable from the "co" of community, it nonetheless bears a clearer hint of the distance at the heart of closeness and intimacy. The "with" is dry and neutral: neither communion nor atomization, simply the sharing of a place, at most contact: a being-together without merging. (In this spirit one must continue an analysis of *Mitdasein* which remained unfinished in Heidegger's work.)
>
> (Nancy, 2001/2007, p. 31)

Implications for educational theory in the concepts of community

'This intelligent little book belongs more to ethics than to sociology. Indeed, it has an immediate pedagogical purpose', states Tönnies (1926, p. 458) in his review of Plessner's 'Limits of Community', without elaborating on this purpose. The aim of the following section is to investigate and reconstruct to what extent Plessner's and Nancy's critiques of community offer fruitful links for educational theory. This question essentially depends on how one interprets the term 'education'.

As mentioned at the outset, education here is not taken to mean only scholastic education, nor – as in the chapter by Norbert Grube in this book – education that should be captured and extended or directed socio-empirically, or that is understandable as propaganda. Following Rita Casale (2011, p. 322), education is taken to mean a 'cognitive process aimed at the realization of the dignity of humans as a species'. The idea of using this concept of education is to break up the apparently obvious nexus between education and school, in order to explore what else comes into view when education is broadly conceived. Casale creates an explicit link between the concept of dignity and pedagogy, even if she leaves the concept of dignity somewhat underdiscussed. In this sense dignity could be defined as an objective formulated in terms of educational theory, which, however – depending on the interpretation of the term 'dignity' – is not necessarily predetermined in its content, and thus does not have to have explicitly normative connotations. Casale (2011, p. 322) follows on from a humanistic concept of education that is unwilling to play off the *self-determination* of the individual against his *structural dependence* 'on his body, on his psyche, and its fantasies', and on others. This concept of education may also reflect the power and powerlessness of the individual, as also pointed out by Käte Meyer-Drawe in 1990, through her interpretation of the sujet-subject. So how can all this – a conception of society based on distance and the safeguarding of dignity, and this concept of education, aimed at the realization of human dignity – be brought together?

The relevance of Plessner's analysis of community for questions of educational theory arises, generally speaking, from the ethical dimension, with which his definition of the terms community and society is connected. In philosophically and sociologically oriented readings of Plessner, however, it is a core aspect, whether his social theory in 'The Limits of Community' is conceptualized in terms of individual or social ethics. While Helmut Lethen (1994), in his monograph *Verhaltenslehren der Kälte* ('Behavioural Theories of Coldness'), focuses on the 'cold persona' and interprets Plessner's approach as belonging to individual ethics, Joachim Fischer (2002), for instance, emphasizes a socio-ethical interpretation. This, he argues, can be justified not only by the fact that Plessner explicitly had social ethics[26] in mind (Plessner, 1924/2003, p. 13), but is also quite clear from Plessner's line of argument, in that he – primarily in his conception of the shared world (*Mit-Welt*) – focuses on the intersubjective sphere. According to Fischer, the interactions in the 'between', propagated by Plessner and referred to as societal – along with the relevance of the masks – are relevant with regard to self-respect for the sake of not only one's own soul, but also the souls of others (Fischer, 2002, p. 87). Plessner's analyses and his social ethics seem productive for perspectives in educational science for several reasons, which will be outlined in the following section.

The concept of dignity

In the light of the previous discussion of Plessner's social theory, the following aspects in Plessner's work can be emphasized: (1) in his major anthropological work, *Die Stufen des Organischen und der Mensch* ('The Levels of Organic Being and Man') (1928/2003), Plessner defines man as an open being – this is the main point of his approach, as he undertakes a definition of man without defining or fixing particular characteristics; (2) this perspective of openness is also associated with an ethical demand for 'not-fixing', and recognition of the other; (3) the communal, constituted by closeness and constriction, reduces the range of possible behaviours, pre-structures these, and prevents any 'individualistic' behaviour; (4) society is, rather, the social form that does justice to the soul's ethical demand for distance, play, masking; and, finally, (5) to emphasize what sets apart Plessner's relationing of the social: the systematic inclusion of the relevance of human dignity, the possibility of which he connects with social distance.

Alongside the concept of openness, Plessner's *conceptualization of dignity* seems to offer ample scope for connections. As Kai Haucke (2003, p. 17) argues, 'with the talk of human dignity, an appreciation of the indeterminacy of human existence [is] indirectly expressed'. This, he argues, is shown in historical experiences, for example in the 'rejection of political discrimination on the basis of social, cultural, ethnic and sexual characteristics'. It is significant, however, that Haucke argues on a semantic level, based on the fixing of the concept of dignity in legal foundations, and not on empirical insights with regard to massive, diverging experiences of discrimination. According to Haucke, Plessner makes reference to the 'historical experiences' of the rejection of political discrimination when he positions the category of indeterminacy as constitutive of the concept of *dignity*. Alongside the humiliation and degradation of being fixed to certain characteristics and attributes (with regard to race, class, gender) and thereby *reduced* in the diversity of human existence, Haucke (2003, pp. 17–19) outlines a further form of humiliation, which becomes apparent in overlooking, ignoring, or in indifferent tolerance.

Public sphere, tact

Plessner thus uses 'the public sphere' (*Öffentlichkeit*) to designate the 'open system of intercourse between unconnected people' (Plessner 1924/2003, p. 95) and understands this as a form of interaction characterized by distance, dissimulation, masquerade and different roles, and thus suitable for personhood. According to Plessner, it contains – unlike communities based on shared ideas and values – options for diplomacy (in the governmental sphere) and above all for tact (in the private sphere), and therefore the need to keep face amid the relations of possibility (Magyar-Haas, 2009, p. 92). Here diplomacy and tact are characterized as 'social arts'.

Artificiality and distance, according to Plessner, are constitutive of the public sphere, in which a two-fold rupture is inherent: 'the impossibility of balancing out the opposition between situation and norm, and private person and "official" person' (Plessner, 1924/2003, p. 96). In this respect, Dewey's (1927, p. 31) idea that the distinction is not between individual people and an impersonal collective, but between people in their private and in their official capacity, is close to the comments of Plessner, who distinguishes between private and official persons and assigns them the options of tact and diplomacy, which are constitutive of negotiation. Diplomacy and tact are necessary to find a balance 'between norm and life, that is, between what is worthy of humans, logically, morally, religiously, aesthetically necessary, and what the situation demands here and now' (Plessner, 1924/2003, p. 97). While diplomatic relations between 'unrealized persons, functionaries, "officials", business people' (Plessner, 1924/2003, p. 109) play the game of 'threat and intimidation, cunning and persuasion, dealing and negotiation' (p. 99), while respecting the dignity of the other, the 'ambit of tact [reveals itself] between natural persons' (p. 109), 'while carefully maintaining distance' (p. 110). Tact is 'the art of inner social differentiation' (Plessner, 1924/2003, p. 109), 'the ever-alert respect for the soul of others, and thus the first and last virtue of the human heart' (p. 107; see Magyar-Haas, 2009, p. 93). This division between norm and situation may be paradigmatic for pedagogical contexts. Here the humanities tradition in pedagogy seems particularly susceptible to focusing on norms, and disregarding the situation. Plessner's critique of radicalism can apply to this tendency, as well as to positivist positions.

Plessner's 1924 work may imply the 'pedagogical' by systematically asserting the saliency of tact and the public sphere. In doing so he neither turns explicitly to 'pedagogical matters', nor does he deal with the 'how' to any great extent. The following questions are relevant in terms of educational research, and might offer links for further studies; one framework in which they could be examined is that of empirical social research: how can tact arise or develop as a constitutive element of the public sphere? Just as diplomacy remains the preserve of a governmental elite, tact is also not given to everyone, let alone at all times – especially when Plessner defines it as a 'social art'. How can this art be acquired? Does this art arise and develop solely through operating in the public sphere? What conditions and resources must be present in order to be able to master the social masquerade and thus the social 'art' of tact (and of diplomacy in the governmental sphere)? What (socio-political, economic) conditions preventing social play and tact can be – above and beyond the 'communal ethos' – analytically and also empirically discerned and reconstructed?

Plessner's anthropology of openness allows homogenizing ideas in conceptions of society to be subjected to a well-founded critique. 'Homogenizing ideas' that are still potent today are those which, by focusing on similarity, can exclude plurality and otherness, or seek to construct common ground (on a normative horizon, a common system of values) through the construction of foreignness (*Fremd-Sein*). Such concepts of society have a genuinely community-like character in Plessner's terminology. The Plessnerian conception of society and the public sphere, however, enables one to conceive of society as genuinely heterogeneous, and assumes a heterogeneous sociality,[27] which, through distance, allows dignity, integrity and recognition. Here the recognition of otherness could be understood as education – which can hardly do without tact and without negotiation in the social sphere – insofar as every prohibition and prevention of the most diverse self-projections can be considered unworthy of humans in social and religious respects.

Conclusion

Whether community impacts on the dignity of the self, or offers protection in order to safeguard the dignity of the self, does not depend solely on whether one is pursuing an anthropological, socio-ontological or sociological line of argument. Another decisive factor is the extent to which community is conceived as open or closed/excluding, and how dignity and exposure are defined in these conceptions. Plessner's conceptualization of *dignity* is focused, socio-ethically, on compensation and balance, in that he defines it as 'the idea of a harmony of the soul and between soul and expression, soul and body' (Plessner, 1924/2003, p. 75). In this perspective, situations in which there is a danger of losing face or being ridiculous could be understood as situations of potential vulnerability, which affect dignity. From a socio-ontological perspective, bodily being – through its dependence on others and on social, political, economic and ecological conditions – could genuinely be recognized in its helplessness, vulnerability and endangerment (Butler, 2010, pp. 2–3). Here vulnerability, violability or 'precariousness' would be a 'generalized condition', 'not simply . . . a feature of *this* or *that* life' (Butler, 2010, p. 22) and any conceptualization of dignity would have to account for this exposure and constitutive vulnerability, or take these as its starting point. Here questions about, for example, the historically, socially and culturally diverging *ways of dealing with* the constitutive conditionality of bodily being and of the conditions surrounding it would certainly be *pedagogical* questions.

This chapter has explored two theories of community. Plessner and Nancy can be situated as prominent thinkers of the paradoxical. While Plessner devises the 'fundamental anthropological laws' of 'natural artificiality', 'mediated immediacy' and the 'utopian standpoint', using obviously paradoxical expressions and taking a dialectical stance, Nancy's critique (1996/2004, p. 23) counters immanence and 'the originary' with the concepts of the 'originary plurality of the origins' and the 'continuous creation in discontinuity'. Both focus their analyses on the political-ethical dimension, but combine this with an anthropological (Plessner) or ontological (Nancy) perspective – a combination in which implications for educational theory and pedagogy become evident. Here Plessner (1924/2003) bases his argument on the self's need for protection, and Nancy (1996/2004) on the exposure of the 'singular plural being'. A certain *need of the self for protection* and *exposure* of the being is observed in each case, but is dealt with differently – depending on how the self or the being is conceived and how the historical context is regarded.

Plessner occasionally distances himself from a Heideggerian-style ontology in his critique of community, but does so explicitly in the work *Macht und menschliche Natur* ('Power and Human Nature') (1931/2003). Nancy, in turn, further develops and criticizes this in his critique of ideologies of community, connected with a readjustment of the concept of community (1986/1988, 2001/2007). Plessner – as Schürmann (2006, pp. 36–37) also argues – rejects every 'apriorism' and emphasizes that talk of man's 'being' (*Wesen*) is necessary, but that the definitions of being are never necessary, but contingent. Plessner's anthropology (1928/2003), in which he defines 'man' as unfathomable and undetermined, anticipates this positioning. Man exists in a relation of indeterminacy towards himself and the world around him (his *Mitwelt*), as an 'unanswered question' (Plessner, 1931/2003, p. 188) – which, however, contains no arbitrariness, but can instead serve as the basis for a social ethics. Such an interpretation would purport to '*hold off* a content-related or formal theoretical fixing as …, which would wish to subject his history, right into the past and the future, to an extra-historical schema of historicity' (Plessner, 1931/2003, pp. 190–191). Nancy does not formulate such a fundamental critique of ontology (see Norris, 2012, p. 147), but clearly denies the possibility of an ultimate cause, stating: 'We must take up fundamental ontology . . . again – and this time definitely *assume the singularly plural nature of the origins*, that is, assume *being-with*' (Nancy, 1996/2004, pp. 52–53, emphasis in original). In Nancy's 'plural ontology' there is no possibility 'of an ultimate foundation of the social' (Marchart, 2010, p. 87), but this does not exclude the many attempts at fixing that seek to give the social a foundation (Marchart, 2010, p. 16). Both philosophers discern these attempts at fixing in positions on the ideology of community, which they criticize and – Nancy in particular – deconstruct (see Sheppard et al., 1997). Plessner does so by establishing the idea of *keeping face*, for the sake of the self and others – an idea connected with the concept of 'ontological ambiguity' – as the socio-ethical basis of his analysis of community, and also formulating it as his normative horizon. Nancy does so by postulating a plural ontology on the basis of the exposure of the singular, and implies, but does not make explicit, a social ethics of responsibility.

While Plessner's anthropologically based approach of constitutive openness was an impressive analysis in the context of the historical situation in Germany in the 1920s, Nancy's conceptualization of the singular plural or, vice versa, the plural singular, based on the theory of difference, and his propagation of a 'plural ontology', which always points to the 'with', seem to be a productive analytical and political-ethical basis in the context of recurring political and pedagogical radicalisms propagating distanceless closeness and immanence.

Notes

1 The regulating, managerial state can therefore only set the parameters – and 'activate' the individuals and communities (Ziegler, 2001, p. 18). For more on the state's managerial governance, see Ziegler's chapter in this volume.
2 Philipp Sandermann (2012, pp. 103–104) reconstructed four main characteristics that can be found, on a *structural* level, in the arguments of the authors associated with communitarianism, for example Charles Taylor, Robert Bellah or Amitai Etzioni: the 'highlighting of communal cultural values as a crucial factor in private and public education', the 'questioning of the possibility of collective social endeavours without the active involvement of the social collective as such', the 'identification of a community-oriented understanding of individuality and authenticity', and the 'emphasizing of the importance of social embedding for the development of modern individuals'.
3 John Clarke (2009) has demonstrated how the discourse about 'migrant Others' evokes myths about a stable, 'coherent community' 'that has been dis-integrated' or had its coherence endangered by the 'migrant Others'.
4 The concept of 'coldness' could be used to subsume exploitative relations, specifically: exploitation of the worker's body and time. On the Janus-faced nature of the capitalist system and industry, see Bauman (2009, pp. 35–37).
5 Volker M. Welter (2010, p. 63) demonstrates that:

> in historiography of early-twentieth-century modern German architecture and urban planning, the idea of community has been a major analytical category. Whether garden city, garden suburb, workers' housing, factory estate, or social housing estate, the often unified architectural forms seem to suggest community. Any enclosing geometric urban form is often understood to strengthen the introverted character that clearly separates such settlements from the big city. In short, these communities are depicted as shining beacons of a new social order in the otherwise harsh urban surroundings of society.

6 With reference to Gilroy, Gerd Bauman (1996, p. 15) quotes the assertion that community 'signifies . . . a particular set of values and norms in everyday life: mutuality, co-operation, identification and symbiosis'.
7 Tönnies' 1887 monograph *Gemeinschaft und Gesellschaft* recently appeared in English translation (2001) with the title 'Community and Civil Society' (Cambridge).
8 Even if Tönnies tried to overcome the exclusivity of the two social forms, he does in many places invite a reception based on exclusivity:

> The group which is formed through this positive type of relationship is called an association (*Verbindung*) when conceived of as a thing or being which acts as a unit inwardly and outwardly. The relationship itself, and also the resulting association, is conceived of either as real and organic life – this is the essential characteristic of the *Gemeinschaft* (community); or as imaginary and mechanical structure – this is the concept of *Gesellschaft* (society).
> (Tönnies, 1887/1926, p. 3, tr. Loomis, 1957/2002, p. 33)

9 For this see the article by Norbert Grube in the present book.
10 The 'essential characteristics' of society and community outlined above have, according to Plessner (1924/2003, p. 33), 'ethical character'.

11 It would be enlightening to investigate to what extent Plessner's approach of 'ontological ambivalence' can be linked with reflections based on the theory of recognition: to what extent could suffering caused by a lack of attention be connected with suffering due to a lack of recognition? Do both concepts refer to a normative horizon that must be internalized or at least used to experience attention and recognition?

12 Such expressions encourage interpretations that read Plessner's social theory in terms of individual ethics. Plessner does not, at this point, discuss to what extent preserving the dignity of the self simultaneously allows or prevents the preservation of the dignity of others. It would be worth asking, however, to what extent it is possible to speak of a 'balance' between 'inside' and 'outside', if the dignity of the other is not preserved in the process. It would thus be quite possible, in mutual respect and consideration for the dignity of the other, to support a reading in terms of social ethics.

13 For an analysis of the closeness of Plessner's notions of artificiality, masks and dissimulation to the aristocratic element in seventeenth-century French classicism, see Eßbach (2002, pp. 73ff.).

14 Plessner scarcely differentiates systematically between the terms *Gesellschaft* ('society'), *Gesellschaftlichkeit* (socialness, sociality, sociability), and *Öffentlichkeit*. In some places the terms are used virtually synonymously.

15 In this sense, according to Plessner (1924/2003, p. 55), the 'irrevocableness of the public sphere' also marks the 'essential boundary' of the ethos of community.

16 Further studies would enable us to discuss the extent to which Plessner's concept of masks and their relevance for the social is related to the role concepts of George Herbert Mead (1934) and Erving Goffman (1959), or which aspects of role theories are anticipated by Plessner's work.

17 Plessner (1924/2003, p. 15) uses 'being radical' to subsume the 'overemphasis on spirituality', 'moralization of achievement, distrust of joy and pleasure, contempt for appearance, lightness, anything which happens on its own'. Here radicalism is taken to mean the 'emancipation of the spirit from reality, nature, life' (p. 16).

18 'When the *I* cannot say that it is dead, when the *I* actually disappears in *its* death, in that death which is in fact its very own thing, the most inalienable thing, then this is because the *I* is something other than a subject' (Nancy, 1986/1988, p. 36).

19 Being must define itself as a relationship, otherwise it would be meaningless immanence – and, according to Nancy, absolute immanence is impossible.

20 In French: *La Communauté désœuvrée* ('The Inoperative Community').

21 For the concept of the 'outside', see also Nancy (1986/1988, pp. 73–74):

> We are equals, because we, every single one of us, are exposed to the outside which *we are for ourselves*. An equal is not someone identical to me. Neither do I find myself in the other, nor do I recognize myself in him: I experience, in or through him, the otherness and the alteration which, 'in my self', places my singularity outside myself and thus makes it end endlessly.

22 Rita Casale (2010, pp. 10–11) points out that, while the 'complicity of Heidegger's philosophy with the political history of the last century' attracts special attention in Germany, this tends to play little role in American and French research – for example, in the work of Derrida and Foucault. Casale shows the specificity of the political reception of Heidegger and Nietzsche in the Italian context, where they were referenced as critics of capitalist rationality, and 'Heidegger's involvement in National Socialism has hardly any importance even today'. The translation of Heidegger's main work, *Sein und Zeit* ('Being and Time'), into Italian by Pietro

Chiodi in 1953 contributed, according to Casale, to Heidegger's 'denazification', and thereby helped to make him, and also Nietzsche, especially in the 1960s/1970s, into 'theoretical reference points of a whole generation of left-wing intellectuals'.
23 'Whereas the individual knows nothing but another individual, which is identical with him and at the same time stands next to him like a thing – i.e. as the identity of an object –, the singular being does not know *his own kind*, but feels it: "Being is never me alone; it is always *me and my own kind*." [quoted from Bataille] This is its passion. Singularity is the passion of being' (Nancy, 1986/1988, p. 72, emphasis in original).
24 Here it would be worth explicitly comparing Dewey's and Nancy's positions with regard to the 'communicative community', precisely because both accord saliency to communication, but take this to mean different things.
25 The first version of the essay *La Communauté affrontée* served as a preface to the second edition of the Italian translation of Maurice Blanchot's (1983) work *La Communauté inavouable* (the Unavowable Community) (Nancy, 2001/2007, p. 6). In the following analysis, the German translation of 2007 is used.
26 That Plessner's ethics are not to be regarded solely in terms of individual ethics, but also of social ethics, is also evident in his concept of closeness and distance, which aims not at an 'either-or' but at a 'both-and', since '[o]nly indirectness creates directness, only separation brings contact' (Plessner, 1928/2003, p. 332).
27 Perhaps this is at the same time where the potential threat of the public sphere lies, or where the uncertainty comes from, since there can hardly be any 'right' mask or role.

References

Accarino, B. (ed.), 2009. *Espressività e Stile. La Filosofia dei Sensi e dell'Expressione in Helmuth Plessner*. Milan, Udine: Mimesis.
Amit, V. and Rapport, N., 2002. *The Trouble with Community. Anthropological Reflections on Movement, Identity and Collectivity*. London: Pluto Press.
Bauman, G., 1996. *Contesting Culture. Discourses of Identity in Multi-ethnic London*. Cambridge: Cambridge University Press.
Bauman, Z., 2009. *Gemeinschaften. Auf der Suche nach Sicherheit in einer Bedrohlichen Welt*. Frankfurt: Suhrkamp.
Bittner, S., 2000. German readers of Dewey: before 1933 and after 1945. *Studies in Philosophy and Education*, 19, pp. 83–108.
Blanchot, M., 1983. *La Communauté Inavouable* ('The Unavowable Community'). Paris: Les Editions de Minuit.
Brumlik, M., 1995. Der importierte Kommunitarismus: Plädoyer für die verbandliche Wohlfahrtspflege? In: T. Rauschenbach, C. Sachße and T. Olk (eds) *Von der Wertgemeinschaft zum Dienstleistungsunternehmen. Jugend- und Wohlfahrtsverbände im Umbruch*. Frankfurt: Suhrkamp, pp. 34–53.
Butler, J., 2010. *Frames of War. When is Life Grievable?* London: Verso.
Casale, R., 2010. *Heideggers Nietzsche: Geschichte einer Obsession*. Bielefeld: transcript.
Casale, R., 2011. Über die Aktualität der Bildungsphilosophie. *Vierteljahrsschrift für wissenschaftliche Pädagogik*, 87(2), pp. 322–332.
Clarke, J., 2008. What's the problem? Precarious youth: marginalisation, criminalisation and racialisation. *Social Work and Society International Online Journal*, 6(2). Available at: www.socwork.net/sws/article/view/62/364 (accessed 9 January 2013).

Clarke, J., 2009. Community, social change and social order. In: G. Mooney and S. Neal (eds) *Community. Welfare, Crime and Society*. Maidenhead: Open University Press, pp. 65–98.

Dallmayr, F., 2008. Eine 'undarstellbare' globale Gemeinschaft? Reflexionen über Nancy. In: J. Böckelmann and C. Morgenroth (eds) *Politik der Gemeinschaft. Zur Konstitution des Politischen in der Gegenwart*. Bielefeld: transcript, pp. 106–132.

de Mul, J., 1991. History and pluralism. Plessner: a postmodernist avant la lettre? In: J. v. Nispen and D. Tiemersma (eds) *The Quest for Man. The Topicality of Philosophical Anthropology. Die Frage nach dem Menschen. Die Aktualität der Philosophischen Anthropologie*. Assen, Maastricht: van Gorcum, pp. 47–51.

Dewey, J., 1927. *The Public and its Problems*. New York: Holt.

Ernste, H., 2004. The pragmatism of life in poststructuralist times. *Environment and Planning*, 36, pp. 437–450.

Eßbach, W., 1994. Der Mittelpunkt außerhalb. Helmuth Plessners philosophische Anthropologie. In: G. Dux and U. Wenzel (eds) *Der Prozeß der Geistesgeschichte. Studien zur Ontogenetischen und Historischen Entwicklung des Geistes*. Frankfurt: Suhrkamp, pp. 15–44.

Eßbach, W., 2002. Verabschieden oder retten? Helmut Lethens Lektüre von Helmuth Plessners 'Grenzen der Gemeinschaft'. In: W. Eßbach, J. Fischer and H. Lethen (eds) *Plessners 'Grenzen der Gemeinschaft'. Eine Debatte*. Frankfurt: Suhrkamp, pp. 63–79.

Fischer, J., 2002. Panzer oder Maske. 'Verhaltenslehren der Kälte' oder Sozialtheorie der 'Grenze'. In: W. Eßbach, J. Fischer and H. Lethen (eds) *Plessners 'Grenzen der Gemeinschaft'. Eine Debatte*. Frankfurt: Suhrkamp, pp. 80–102.

Fischer, J., 2008. *Philosophische Anthropologie. Eine Denkrichtung des 20. Jahrhunderts*. Freiburg: Karl Alber.

Fischer-Lichte, E., 2004. *Ästhetik des Performativen*. Frankfurt: Suhrkamp.

Gertenbach, L., Laux, H., Rosa, H. and Strecker, D., 2010. *Theorien der Gemeinschaft zur Einführung*. Hamburg: Junius.

Goffman, E., 1959. *The Presentation of Self in Everyday Life*. Harmondsworth: Penguin Books.

Grube, N., 2011. A 'new republic'? The debate between John Dewey and Walter Lippmann and its reception in pre- and postwar Germany. In: R. Bruno-Jofré and J. Schriewer (eds) *The Global Reception of John Dewey's Thought. Multiple Refractions Through Time and Space*. New York, London: Routledge, pp. 196–214.

Gutman, A., 1985. Communitarian critics of liberalism. *Philosophy and Public Affairs*, 14, pp. 308–322.

Haucke, K., 2003. *Das Liberale Ethos der Würde. Eine Systematisch Orientierte Problemgeschichte zu Helmuth Plessners Begriff Menschlicher Würde in den 'Grenzen der Gemeinschaft'*. Wurzburg: Königshausen & Neumann.

Haus, M., 2003. *Kommunitarismus. Einführung und Analyse*. Wiesbaden: VS.

Heidegger, M., 1927/2001. *Sein und Zeit*. Tübingen: Niemeyer.

Kessl, F., 2000. Wiederentdeckung der Gemeinschaft? Zur Verschränkung der Diskurse 'Aktivierung neuer Gemeinschaftlichkeit' und 'Soziale Arbeit'. *Widersprüche: Zeitschrift für Sozialistische Politik im Bildungs-, Gesundheits- und Sozialbereich*, 20(76), pp. 19–35.

Kracauer, S., 1927/1977. Das Ornament der Masse. In: S. Kracauer *Das Ornament der Masse: Essays*. Frankfurt: Suhrkamp, pp. 50–63.

Krüger, H.-P. and Lindemann, G. (eds), 2006. *Philosophische Anthropologie im 21. Jahrhundert*. Berlin: Akademie.
Lethen, H., 1994. *Verhaltenslehren der Kälte. Lebensversuche Zwischen den Kriegen*. Frankfurt: Suhrkamp.
Lethen, H., 2002. Philosophische Anthropologie und Literatur in den zwanziger Jahren. Helmuth Plessners neusachliches Mantel- und Degenstück. In: W. Eßbach, J. Fischer and H. Lethen (eds) *Plessners 'Grenzen der Gemeinschaft'. Eine Debatte*. Frankfurt: Suhrkamp, pp. 29–62.
Lippmann, W., 1925. *The Phantom Public*. New York: Harcourt, Brace.
Magyar-Haas, V., 2009. Gemeinschaftskritik–Maske–Würde. Die Relevanz Plessners Ethik für die Soziale Arbeit. In: B. Grubenmann and J. Oelkers (eds) *Das Soziale in der Pädagogik*. Bad-Heilbrunn: Klinkhardt, pp. 77–96.
Magyar-Haas, V. and Grube, N., 2009. Sicherheit. Anspruch–Versprechen–Utopie. *Soziale Passagen: Journal für Empirie und Theorie Sozialer Arbeit*, 1(1), pp. 35–48.
Marchart, O., 2010. *Die politische Differenz. Zum Denken des Politischen bei Nancy, Lefort, Badiou, Laclau und Agamben*. Frankfurt: Suhrkamp.
Mead, G.H., 1934. *Mind, Self, and Society: From the Standpoint of a Social Behaviorist*. Chicago, IL: University of Chicago Press.
Meyer-Drawe, K., 1990. *Illusionen von Autonomie. Diesseits von Ohnmacht und Allmacht des Ich*. Munich: Kirchheim.
Mooney, G. and Neal, S., 2009. Community: themes and debates. In: G. Mooney and S. Neal (eds) *Community. Welfare, Crime and Society*. Maidenhead: Open University Press, pp. 1–34.
Nancy, J.-L., 1986/1988. *Die Undarstellbare Gemeinschaft*. Stuttgart: Schwarz.
Nancy, J.-L., 1994. Das gemeinsame Erscheinen. Von der Existenz des 'Kommunismus' zur Gemeinschaftlichkeit der 'Existenz'. In: J. Vogl (ed.) *Gemeinschaften. Positionen zu einer Philosophie des Politischen*. Frankfurt: Suhrkamp, pp. 194–196.
Nancy, J.-L., 1996/2004. *Singulär Plural Sein*. Berlin: Diaphanes. (Trans. Richardson, R.D. and O'Byrne, A.E., 2000. *Being Singular Plural*. Stanford, CA: Stanford University Press.)
Nancy, J.-L., 2001/2007. *Die Herausgeforderte Gemeinschaft*. Zurich: Diaphanes.
Nolte, P., 2000. *Die Ordnung der Deutschen Gesellschaft. Selbstentwurf und Selbstbeschreibung im 20. Jahrhundert*. Munich: C.H. Beck.
Norris, A., 2012. Jean-Luc Nancy on the political after Heidegger and Schmitt. In: P. Gratton and M.-È. Morin (eds) *Jean-Luc Nancy and Plural Thinking. Expositions of World, Ontology, Politics, and Sense*. Albany, NY: State University of New York Press, pp. 143–158.
Plessner, H., 1924/2003. Grenzen der Gemeinschaft. Eine Kritik des Sozialen Radikalismus. In: G. Dux, O. Marquard and E. Ströker (eds) *Helmuth Plessner. Gesammelte Schriften V*. Frankfurt: Suhrkamp, pp. 7–133. (Trans. Wallace, A., 1999. *The Limits of Community. A Critique of Social Radicalism*. New York: Humanity Books.)
Plessner, H., 1928/2003. Die Stufen des Organischen und der Mensch. Einleitung in die Philosophische Anthropologie. In: G. Dux, O. Marquard and E. Ströker (eds) *Helmuth Plessner. Gesammelte Schriften IV*. Frankfurt: Suhrkamp.
Plessner, H., 1931/2003. Macht und Menschliche Natur. Ein Versuch zur Anthropologie der Geschichtlichen Weltansicht. In: G. Dux, O. Marquard and E. Ströker (eds) *Helmuth Plessner. Gesammelte Schriften V*. Frankfurt: Suhrkamp, pp. 135–234.

Plessner, H., 1967/2003. Der Mensch im Spiel. In: G. Dux, O. Marquard and E. Ströker (eds) *Helmuth Plessner. Gesammelte Schriften VIII*. Frankfurt: Suhrkamp, pp. 307–313.

Rasini, V., 2007. Natura e artificio. Un confronto tra Scheler, Plessner e Gehlen. *La Società Degli Individui*, 28(1), pp. 67–78.

Richter, N.A., 2005. *Grenzen der Ordnung. Bausteine einer Philosophie des politischen Handelns nach Plessner und Foucault*. Frankfurt: Campus.

Sandermann, P., 2009. *Die neue Diskussion um Gemeinschaft. Ein Erklärungsansatz mit Blick auf die Reform des Wohlfahrtssystems*. Bielefeld: transcript.

Sandermann, P., 2012. Die kommunitaristische Gesellschaft der Sozialen Arbeit. In: B. Dollinger, F. Kessl, S. Neumann and P. Sandermann (eds) *Gesellschaftsbilder Sozialer Arbeit*. Bielefeld: transcript, pp. 101–122.

Schürmann, V., 2006. Vermittelte Unmittelbarkeit. Plessners taktvolles Spiel mit der menschlichen Würde. In: K. Röttgers and M. Schmitz-Emans (eds) *Mitte. Philosophische, Medientheoretische und Ästhetische Konzepte*. Essen: Blaue Eule, pp. 34–46.

Sheppard, D., Sparks, S. and Thomas, C. (eds), 1997. *On Jean-Luc Nancy. The Sense of Philosophy*. London: Routledge.

Tönnies, F., 1887/1926. *Gemeinschaft und Gesellschaft. Grundbegriffe der Reinen Soziologie*. Berlin: Karl Curtius. (Trans. Loomis, C.P., 1957/2002. *Community and Society*. Mineola, NY: Dover; trans. Harris, J. and Hollis, M., 1887/2001. *Community and Civil Society*. Cambridge: Cambridge University Press.)

Tönnies, F., 1926. Rezension von 'Grenzen der Gemeinschaft'. *Kölner Vierteljahrshefte für Soziologie*, 5(4), pp. 456–458.

Welter, V.M., 2010. The limits of community – the possibilities of society: on modern architecture in Weimar Germany. *Oxford Art Journal*, 33(1), pp. 63–80.

Ziegler, H., 2001. Prävention – Vom Formen der Guten zum Lenken der Freien. *Widersprüche: Zeitschrift für sozialistische Politik im Bildungs-, Gesundheits- und Sozialbereich*, 21(79), pp. 7–24.

Chapter 13

'Taking the path of least resistance'

Expulsions from Soviet schools in the Stalinist 1930s[1]

E. Thomas Ewing

Introduction

In Moscow School No. 326, teacher Karpova, unable to maintain order in her sixth-grade class, turned for help to the director of instruction Seleznev, who immediately sent four pupils home. Afraid to tell their parents, the four boys fled Moscow for the city of Tula, where they were apprehended by the police and sent home. The poor discipline in Karpova's class and the poor leadership by Seleznev, cited by inspectors as the two causes of the incident, led to sanctions against both educators in early 1938 (GARF 2306/69/2405/8).

This chapter examines the expulsion of pupils from schools as a pedagogical tactic that defines the boundary between education and the state. Teachers such as Karpova and Seleznev, who expelled students from their schools, were in effect disclaiming responsibility for the education of these particular children and turning them over to the organs of the state. In this case, however, state authorities, initially in the form of police and then the Communist Party officials who investigated the incident, in effect repudiated this decision by educators. These state authorities demanded that the schools, and particularly teachers, reclaim responsibility for educating these students, regardless of their transgressions. Sanctioning Karpova and Seleznev was an assertion by Stalinist authorities that disciplining children was an obligation of schools, separate from the state's claims to maintain order in society. By asking what course was taken by an authoritarian system when teachers responded to disobedience by expelling children from schools, this chapter argues that maintaining order through expulsion illustrated a key, and contested, relationship between education and the state.

The defining characteristics of the authoritarian school in the Soviet Union during the 1930s included explicit proclamations that education must serve the needs of the Communist Party, educational rhetoric proclaiming unquestioned loyalty to Stalin, a centrally imposed curriculum, prohibitions on teachers' autonomous professional organizations, total censorship of non-conformist ideas, school spaces penetrated by the security apparatus, and even the arrest, imprisonment, and execution of individuals (Ewing, 2002; Holmes, 2006; Kelly,

2007). Expulsions would seem to fit this pattern, because teachers and school directors often followed the dominant pattern of Stalinism by responding to perceived threats by isolating, exposing, and eliminating individuals. Yet a careful study of the actual practices related to expulsions from Soviet schools, based on archival documents (such as the report cited above), published articles, and oral histories, reveals the underlying tensions involved in the exercise of this form of power.

Comparative and historical perspectives on expulsions

To explore the question of expulsions in a historical context, this chapter draws on comparative approaches to understanding expulsions in a contemporary context. Recent scholarship on the use of expulsions as a disciplinary tool reaches a general consensus that this approach does not succeed in improving behavior and generally exerts a negative influence on both the individuals and the culture of the school (Bock *et al.*, 1998; Brownstein, 2009; DeRidder, 1991; Noltemeyer and Mcloughlin, 2010). According to educator K. Wayne Yang, in situations where exclusions are used extensively, particularly against certain categories of the school population, students "are collectively impacted by the culture of removal – *even if they themselves are not punished*" (Yang, 2009, pp. 50–51). These scholars argue that the more times students are expelled from schools, the more likely it is that they will become "pushouts" who will never complete schooling. In the contemporary United States, so-called "Zero Tolerance" policies, which require the same punishment for designated offenses regardless of circumstances or context, have led to widespread use of suspensions and expulsions. Educational researchers are generally in agreement that Zero Tolerance policies are ineffective, because they tend to exacerbate the practices they are supposed to control, while stigmatizing individuals and groups of pupils. Arguing that the "primary reason for application of disciplinary procedures should be to aid students; that is, applying discipline should be done in an appropriate manner so as to assist students' functioning and learning," a team of educators has argued that suspension and expulsion might seem "on the surface" to be "a reasonable form of punishment"; in fact, the number and nature of negative consequences are too significant to justify these measures (Bock *et al.*, 1998, pp. 50–52).

The significance of expulsions can also be interpreted using Foucault's analysis of "an economy of power" (1980, p. 119). Expelling students from classrooms or schools is part of a broader pedagogical effort to define certain behaviors as "deviant" and subject to punishment, and other behaviors as "normal" and deserving of rewards. In contrast to other forms of classroom discipline that are most effective as they become more invisible, the expulsion of pupils exposes the operation of power in the school or, more specifically, the powerlessness of teachers to control all the students within their classrooms and under their authority.[2] To a certain extent, expulsions are contrary to the emphasis placed by Foucault and those inspired by his work on ways in which schools become modern institutions that create productive and docile subjects through strategies of power, such as increasing visibility, partitioning space, accumulating knowledge, imposing perpetual scrutiny, and constructing norms (Deacon, 2005; Dwyer, 1995; Gunzenhauser, 2006; Hall and Millard, 1994; Jones, 1990; Marshall, 1996; Mayo, 2000; Ryan, 1991; Simmons, 2010).

This chapter draws on new research on the nature of the state in authoritarian systems, such as the Soviet Union under Stalin. A recent collection, *Beyond Totalitarianism*, takes up the same issues as this chapter, by exploring "the everyday micro-mechanisms of a violent regime" (Geyer and Fitzpatrick, 2009, p. 12). The new approaches characteristic of the "beyond totalitarianism" paradigm are suggestive because they move away from assumptions about monolithic power, obedience enforced by terror, or social passivity and atomization, asking instead: "who controls the act of governing . . . and what, if any, its limits are" (Geyer and Fitzpatrick, 2009, p. 29). By asking similar questions about the exercise of power in the Stalinist school, this chapter contributes to this scholarship, while also suggesting new perspectives on the relationship between education and the state.

This chapter engages with the pedagogical approach associated with the Soviet educator, Anton Makarenko. Although his canonical status in Soviet pedagogy was fixed only after his death in 1939, the powerful symbolism of the collective associated with Makarenko's assertions certainly shaped Soviet education in the 1930s. Makarenko argued that the collective was the most important unit in Soviet society, and thus the most valuable tool for disciplining individuals, including pupils in school. According to Makarenko, the collective is "an organized community of personalities pursuing a clear purpose and governed by its collective bodies" (Baker, 1968, p. 288). Although Makarenko's theories were developed in colonies for orphaned or homeless children, rather than in the system of formal schooling, official Soviet pedagogy endorsed the central role of collective discipline in maintaining order in schools. With regard to expulsion, Makarenko's opposition was clearly illustrated by the numerous examples of youth who were threatened with expulsion from a colony because of their misbehavior, yet were successfully rehabilitated through reintegration into a process of collective discipline. Given the emerging influence of Makarenko on Stalinist education in the 1930s, the practice of expelling pupils was certainly inconsistent with the strong preference to discipline children through a comprehensive system of collective obedience.

This research on expulsions from school also addresses the recent, and influential, historiographical arguments made by Oleg Kharkhordin, who traces the tension between the collective and the individual in Soviet political theory and Communist Party practice. According to Kharkhordin, Communist leaders initially preferred to elicit self-criticism that led to self-correction, rather than demanding the expulsion of Party members who diverged from the prevailing orthodoxy. During the 1930s – the period covered by this research on expulsions from schools – this system of vigilance deteriorated into "an indiscriminate hunt for enemies within Party ranks" (Kharkhordin, 1999, p. 158). Thus, the question this chapter will aim to answer, by drawing on the work of Kharkhordin, is whether a similar cycle took place in Soviet schools in the 1930s, as a regulated system of collective disciplinary mechanisms gave way to an unregulated cycle of accusations and expulsions.[3] On the contrary, as this chapter will argue, Stalinist educational officials and state organs worked out mechanisms that sought to keep children under the control of their school's disciplinary regime, in spite of efforts by teachers to expel specific children.

This chapter thus explores the meaning of "exclusionary discipline" (Noltemeyer and Mcloughlin, 2010, p. 60) in a context where expulsion was an instrument of political repression deployed by the Stalinist regime. During the early 1930s, several million so-called "kulaks" were expelled from their homes and villages for their resistance to collectivization. At the height of the terror, in the late 1930s, more than a million convicted "terrorists" and "anti-Soviet" agents were exiled to the forced labor camps of the Siberia and the Far East. Following these dominant political trends, many teachers and principals apparently saw expulsions as an effective way to get rid of disruptive or insubordinate students, thus allowing them to concentrate their attention on more docile and productive classmates. Statistical data, inspectors' reports, school records, and personal accounts testify to the widespread pattern of expulsions, especially in the middle of the 1930s. Yet these practices were subjected to scrutiny by educational and political officials, for whom the prospect of large numbers of young people at liberty outside the confines of the school raised fears of juvenile delinquency, social disorder, and educational failure. The state accused teachers of pursuing the "path of least resistance" when they decided to expel students, thus violating a principle of emerging Stalinist pedagogy – but not political culture – which asserted that, with proper training, guidance, and leadership, all children could be successful students. The central question for this chapter, therefore, is why the state criticized teachers for engaging in a disciplinary practice that it deployed on such a broad scale and with such devastating consequences for millions of its own citizens.

Expulsions as contested pedagogy

Soviet policy on expulsions was inconsistent and contradictory during this era of political terror and educational expansion. In a 1932 decree, which laid the foundation for increasingly traditional forms of classroom pedagogy, the Communist Party Central Committee called for teachers and school administrators to devote more attention to "strengthening conscious discipline" in schools. Yet this decree also defined the following measure as official policy:

those pupils who act as hooligans, insult school personnel, violate the administrative rules of the school and teachers, destroy or deface school property, will be expelled from the school without right of return to the school for a period of one to three years.
(Ob uchebnykh programmakh, 1932, pp. 161–164)

Three years later, in a subsequent decree that further reinforced these tendencies in Soviet schools, the Central Committee stated that "the right to expel students on the basis of transgressions (*prostupki*)" was within the jurisdiction of regional or city educational departments, upon the recommendation of the school director (Ob organizatsii uchebnoi raboty, 1935, p. 165). According to these decrees, official policy permitted expulsions of students, if appropriate approval was provided by school directors, district educational departments, and regional authorities.

Rather than prescribing clear guidelines for the use of expulsions, these policies prompted debate and even disagreement over the use of expulsions as a legitimate tool for disciplining pupils. At a December 1934 meeting, an educational official called expulsions a "disgrace" to the school, as the expelled students spend their entire days outside the school. Emphasizing instead the need for inclusive discipline, this speaker reminded educators that they were responsible for every expelled child. Revealing the contested natured of this issue, however, a later speaker at the same meeting invoked the Central Committee decree permitting expulsions for a designated period of time, and explained that this tactic was an acceptable way to compel students to improve their behavior when they were readmitted to the school (GARF 2306/70/2018/8–9).[4]

Through their statements and actions, teachers revealed the tension between the preferences of those working in schools and the desires of those who set policies.[5] In the fall of 1937, two years after the Central Committee had established new school policies, an elementary school director, G.N. Shevchenko, wrote to his district educational department asking if it was possible to expel two pupils who had been held back a year and were still failing in their courses. According to a pedagogical expert who received this letter, the expulsion of failing pupils was prohibited, even if they remained for a second or even third year in the same grade. The proper approach, according to this expert, was to "take all necessary measures" to return these children to the school and create the conditions that would enable them to complete the elementary grades. These measures included providing the needed textbooks, organizing additional lessons at the school, ensuring that home conditions did not interfere with homework, and ensuring that all children successfully completed elementary school (NA RAO 10/1/95/9/21).

The confusion regarding the rules can be seen in this question sent by a village soviet official near Orenburg to the Central Scientific Pedagogical Institute in Moscow: "Is it possible to expel from the school undisciplined pupils who insult instructors and break school property? If this is not possible, what should be done with them?" To this, and to similar questions from other school directors and teachers, the representative of the Institute replied with the terms set out in the 1932 Central Committee decree: expulsion of one to three years was permitted, but only in exceptional cases when incorrigible pupils had proven all other methods of instruction and guidance unsuccessful (NA RAO 10/1/95/23–24). Responding to a similar question from teacher Voinov, who asked whether it was possible to expel a student for "lack of discipline" even when that student had good grades, the pedagogical expert stated that, although expulsions were permitted, this measure should be taken only in exceptional cases and only after "all possible educational measures" (*vse mery vospitatel'nogo poriadka*) had been taken to deal with students violating school discipline and order" (NA RAO 10/1/95/202).

According to these pedagogical experts, if teachers who loved their work and loved children, worked effectively in the classroom, and formed a "united front" with public organizations and parents, "the question of expulsions, and even of reprimands, would never even arise" (NA RAO 10/1/95/81–87). According to an official in a Moscow research institute, a teacher who took a proper approach to working with pupils and their parents would never have to contemplate resorting to expulsions or even reprimands.

Yet, examples of cases where expulsions were justified were occasionally cited. A 1934 report cited the example of a pupil expelled from school for "poor behavior," yet he continued to attend lessons. At one point, he attacked another pupil and caused significant injury. This example of an expelled pupil who remained in the school was then associated with other problem behaviors, such as pupils who stole from classmates and threatened teachers (Lerd, 1934, p. 2). In a diary entry from early January 1938, secondary school student Nina Kosterina described how a classmate was "kicked out of school for rowdyism," despite the fact that a favorite teacher "vouched for him twice" (Kosterina, 1968, pp. 57–58).

As indicated by the title of this chapter, the most pointed criticism of teachers who expelled students was the accusation that they were "taking the path of least resistance," as stated in a 1938 editorial in the Uzbek newspaper, *Pravda Vostoka*. Teachers who "simply expelled" students for their undisciplined behavior were failing to engage in proper educational work (*vospitanie*): "It is very easy to expel, but to educate (*vospityvat'*), of course, is difficult" (Khudaikulov, 1938, pp. 2–3). According to this report, teachers who expel children "wholesale" and "without any review" were causing children to become "undisciplined hooligans and forcing them out among the criminals." This editorial included a sweeping condemnation of this approach to discipline: "mass expulsions are not a form of education (*vospitanie*)."

The same language appeared several years earlier, in a 1935 Narkompros report on secondary schools, which charged that teachers who did not use appropriate disciplinary methods were "taking the path of least resistance – that is, expulsion from the school" (GARF 2306/70/2567/99–100). Examples sent from localities to Narkompros indicated that pupils were being expelled not only for hooliganism and insulting the teacher, but also for poor academic performance, alien social origins, or even getting pregnant. Parents were not always notified, which meant that children as young as 12 were left on their own, vulnerable to the influence of delinquents on the street and in the markets.

In some cases, denunciations of teachers included examples of behavior clearly intended to expose the incompetent or malicious nature of teachers' actions. In a Moscow school, a teacher named Svechina expelled a boy from her classroom after he drew a picture of Stalin, which the teacher deemed an "anti-Soviet action" (RGASPI 1/23/1265/34). Similarly, a Moscow teacher named Levshina, a Communist Party member, had aggravated relations with one pupil, Voropaev, to such a point that, in one incident, she brandished a chair at him and declared "I am stronger than you, and I will do with you whatever I want" (RGASPI 1/23/1265/33). Levshina removed Voropaev from the class, forcing him to flee from the school without a coat and causing him to miss two days of school. Reports that expelled students exhibited "hooligan behavior" on the street provoked further concerns, thus reinforcing perceptions that teachers and school directors were failing in their primary duty – to discipline children within the boundaries of the school. In the city of Tula, for example, an expelled pupil returned to the school each day to harass former classmates, apparently without any sanction by educational or police authorities (RGASPI 1/23/1128/68–70).

Criticism of this pedagogical tactic was also directed at expulsions of so-called "incorrigibles" (*neispravimye*), because of the implication that teachers and school directors had decided that certain pupils could not be corrected (Shkolu blizhe k rebenku!, 1929, p. 1). In other cases, the criticism focused on the number of pupils or the length of expulsions, particularly when the actions seemed to have been taken arbitrarily or precipitously. In early 1935, for example, the author of an article on Kursk schools complained that students were expelled for months at a time in response to almost any kind of violation of school rules. Warning that many expelled students never returned to schools, joining youth gangs instead, Party officials called on teachers and school directors to recognize that "the task of the school is to prevent hooliganism by means of constant educational work in every possible way" (Saplin, 1935, pp. 10–11).

In other cases, teachers and school officials were denounced for expelling pupils for insufficient cause. In Smolensk, a school director expelled a 14-year-old girl because she had been held back for a third year in the same grade (Arshinov, 1936). A report to the Komsomol Central Committee identified expulsions, along with corporal punishment and abusive language, as examples of inappropriate discipline by teachers. In one case, a teacher expelled nine pupils and made four pupils stand in the corner in the course of a single lesson (RGASPI 1/23/1128/67). In the Far East, school director Starodub expelled an 8-year-old boy from his first-grade class after the boy engaged in so-called "diabolical intrigue in the trade of feathers!" In this case, the Pioneer leader in the school brought the case to the attention of the district educational department. This example was cited as evidence that many teachers were too quick to apply the label of "hooligan" or "disorganizer" to their pupils, rather than working with each child "like a gardener cultivates a tree" to prepare them to be future workers in a socialist society (Ponomarev, 1937, p. 43). To illustrate this condemnation of teachers who refused to work with children perceived as problematic, this article cited the example of a fourth-grade teacher in Khabarovsk who delivered this "ultimatum" when she demanded the expulsion of a pupil: "It's either me or him in this classroom" (p. 41).[6]

Some educators were condemned for seeing expulsions as a means of compensating for their own deficiencies.[7] In the Smolensk region, teacher Shmiakov made this dramatic announcement in early 1935: "The method of expulsion from the class is the only method which the teacher can use now to increase discipline." This statement was criticized by the educational newspaper as an example of attempts by certain teachers to "revive the spirit of the old school and its rods (*palochka*)" (Buntar' and Shnaider, 1935, p. 3). The director of a Khabarovsk elementary school made a request to the city educational department for the expulsion of several pupils called evil, incorrigible, hooligans, and disorganizers. Yet the regional educational journal declared that these same pupils had been in school with this director for several years, which meant that their disorganizing tendencies must have been developed under his leadership (Ponomarev, 1937).

In November 1937, a mother complained that, in her son's school, pupils were removed from history class every day – as many as ten kids in one day's lesson, a pattern that was cited as evidence that teachers were not serious about improving discipline in the school (Tsemakhman, 1937, p. 3).[8] In a Khar'kov school, during the 1937–1938 academic year, teachers reportedly kicked out pupils from their classes "in bunches," while suspensions of up to one month were so common that teachers did not even have to ask the director of instruction, but imposed these sanctions themselves.[9] While expulsions achieved limited objectives of intimidating students and imposing order, these examples suggest that they were less effective at creating the docility and productivity that were the ultimate objectives of Stalinist education. In the spring of 1936, a leading Communist official criticized teachers for wanting to establish special schools as a way to get "difficult" pupils out of their classes (RGASPI 77/1/583/305). In July 1936, teacher Mirolibova of the Ivanov region was accused of committing an "anti-pedagogical" action by throwing a pupil out of the classroom during a lesson (RGASPI 1/23/1188/113).

In exceptional cases, such acts of expulsion could have unanticipated results. In December 1936, Moscow school director Devina kicked a pupil out of the school, without his coat, and even held the door to prevent him from returning. At this point, a crowd gathered and began to make "anti-Soviet" comments: "So this is how they educate (*vospityvat'*) children in a Soviet school" (RGASPI 1/3/177/93).

Yet expulsions could also provoke a different kind of political intervention into schools. Accounts from emigrés suggest that, by the later 1930s, it was virtually impossible for teachers to have any students expelled or even transferred from their classes (Harvard Project A, No. 387, p. 20; No. 1517, p. 10). A former teacher interviewed in emigration declared that a Soviet teacher "actually has little control over the student. He cannot criticize sharply, hit the child or expel him from class. His job is to persuade and influence the pupil to improve himself" (External Research Staff, 1956, p. 130). Echoing official policy, this teacher recalled that pupils could be expelled only with the "permission" of the district educational department. A former school director interviewed in emigration recalled that he sought to have some students expelled because they "were neglecting their work very seriously" (Harvard Project B4, No. 428, pp. 15–16). At a teachers' meeting, this former director declared that these students lack the "aptitude" needed for successful schoolwork. In his comments, he "unwittingly" used a term for "aptitude" (*sposob*), which had recently been condemned as part of the Central Committee's repudiation of pedology, and particularly any claims that certain categories of students lack the capacity to study successfully. The other teachers at the school refused to support his demand that the students be expelled; in his interview, the teacher blamed this opposition on the fact that the teachers "were friendly with the parents" of these Komsomol youth. The director ignored the majority position of the teachers, and expelled the students, which created further problems, as "apparently" one of the teachers "informed" on his actions, which led to threats to have him arrested "as propagator of the anti-Soviet doctrine of pedology." It was only by using his connections at the regional level that this former school director avoided arrest (Harvard Project, B4, No. 428, pp. 15–16). Although no further information was provided about the fate of students, this incident clearly illustrates how, in the Stalinist political environment, the question of expulsions could implicate teachers and school directors in broader conflicts.

According to one former teacher, Soviet schools had chronically poor discipline because of the "lack of authority of the teacher and lack of punishment of the students for their misconduct and misbehavior" (Harvard Project A, No. 1517, pp. 9–10). This former teacher provided an extended account of an adolescent boy who used insulting and obscene language in talking to a female teacher. However, there was nothing she could do, except "perhaps leave class for a while and weep quietly." To illustrate his point that, in Soviet schools, "the exclusion of a student from the school was allowed in an exceptional case, but, practically, this was never done," this former teacher described how the same boy engaged in various kinds of theft in and out of the schools, and was "finally expelled" based on the unanimous recommendation of teachers (Harvard Project A, No. 1517, pp. 9–10). Yet his father, a prominent Communist official at the local level, intervened in ways that prevented the district educational department from carrying out the decision. The school director had to readmit this pupil, "despite the protests of the teachers' staff," who now had to deal with the negative effects of "a bad example [that] has a great influence upon young people" (Harvard Project A, No 1517, pp. 9–10).[10]

The number and proportion of students expelled from schools is an important interpretive question, because it asks how extensively this disciplinary sanction was being applied.[11] Unfortunately, only partial data for the rates of expulsions pertaining to the Soviet Union in the 1930s are available. A survey of 3,680 schools enrolling some 450,000 pupils in the Moscow region for 1931/1932 recorded 479 expulsions. These students accounted for just 0.1 percent of all pupils, and 1 percent of the approximately 42,000 pupils who had left a particular school during the year. This information suggests that, while leaving schools may have been a real concern (approximately 10 percent of the pupils left a school during the year), expulsions contributed relatively little to this problem (NA RAO 12/1/127/60).[12] Five years later, however, a Komsomol report charged that Moscow city educational departments did not even know how many pupils had been expelled from their schools. This report also noted that many pupils expelled from one school quickly found places in other schools, even when the expulsions had been imposed due to hooliganism and disobeying a teacher (RGASPI 1/3/177/91–92).

Very low numbers of expelled students, by contrast, elicited praise for teachers and school directors who seemed to maintain exemplary discipline through inclusive methods. An inspection of thirty schools in the Voronezh region in 1937 found that no students had been expelled, which was cited as evidence of excellent order and instruction in these schools (GARF 2306/70/2438/47). In a 1941 article, school director Chegasov declared with pride that there had been only two expulsions in three years, and both had been exceptional cases (Chegasov, 1941).

The numbers of expulsions were also contested. In the spring of 1937, for example, a published report indicated that a district educational department had "expelled" 512 pupils. In fact, educational officials from the region declared that this figure referred to the number of pupils who had "dropped out" of schools, and in fact only five students had been expelled by the district educational department. Regional officials protested that the publication of the incorrect figures portrayed the district in a negative manner, and they demanded a retraction of the published report (GARF 2306/69/2328/12).

Maintaining order through inclusive discipline

These tensions surrounding teachers' disciplinary methods were also evident in the question of whether outside authorities were more effective in maintaining or restoring order in a classroom. The higher power of political authorities was clearly evident in an incident described by Abraham Kreusler, who, when he began teaching in Soviet schools in Western Ukraine in 1939, faced such chaos that he appealed to the Komsomol organizer (*komsorg*) to regain control of his classroom:

A dead silence fell over the room when he entered it. There was a brief, ominous pause; he looked around, assuming the manner of an orator at a mass meeting. He opened his speech softly, mildly. Then, in a crescendo voice, he began to deliver his harangue. He played on the children's feelings of loyalty to the Soviet state and school. He reminded them that they owed a debt of gratitude to the government at whose expense they were being educated, that it was a privilege to enjoy the benefits of better schooling. He made them feel that the eyes of the world were turned upon them and that they were disgracing not only themselves, but, more importantly, their fatherland by behaving like a pack of uncivilized brutes. Then some threatening notes crept into the *komsorg's* peroration. He drew their attention to the fact that their conduct smacked of sabotage and "wrecking" as he called it, and that grown-ups suffered heavy penalties for such actions.

Having achieved the desired intimidating effect, the *komsorg* switched tactics and reminded the students that their cooperation, including reporting all cases of "insubordination" to the Komsomol, was necessary to ensure that all pupils observed classroom rules. After this intervention, Kreusler recalled, he did not have any further problems maintaining discipline (Kreusler, 1965, pp. 20–21).

Yet just two years earlier, Komsomol inspectors concluded that summoning political authorities – such as the Komsomol organizer – to restore order, had only limited effectiveness and, more significantly, undermined the authority of teachers who would then have even greater difficulty maintaining discipline. Whereas Kreusler's experience testified to the potential power wielded by political authorities, the Komsomol inspectors were more concerned with techniques that could be employed to sustain discipline without the need for obvious and disruptive acts of political intervention (RGASPI 1/3/177/110–111). In a similar fashion, a local Party official complained in late 1936 about teachers who sent pupils to school directors because they were unable to resolve even "the most trifling questions" (Kuprianov, 1936, p. 4). In one school, twelve pupils were sent to the director as "violators of discipline" during just part of one day. Citing the example of a teacher who sent for the director because she was unable to get a pupil to remove his cap, the Party official condemned this approach to classroom management: "Such weakness, such helplessness, cannot help to establish discipline" (Kuprianov, 1936, p. 4).

Soviet pedagogues also claimed successes of this model of disciplining pupils through strategies of inclusion, rather than exclusion.[13] In the spring of 1935, for example, teachers in a school near Odessa did not know how to handle several students acting like "hooligans." Even threats of expulsion or arrest, according to a later report, did not deter their delinquent behavior or their negative influence on the school. With the appointment of a new director and teachers who took an "individual" approach to each pupil, however, discipline improved and order was restored. Echoing a common element of the transformative narratives later made famous by Makarenko, a girl named Raisa Nikolaevna Pavlenko, the former "ataman of the hooligans," became the leader of a new group that spent time discussing literature, playing games, and producing a newspaper; her transformation became the headline of the article: "How 'disorganizers' became model pupils" (Migolat'ev, 1935, p. 2).[14]

Conclusion

This chapter has engaged contemporary scholarship by examining historical examples where "exclusionary discipline"[15] was the subject of contestation between educators and state officials.[16] Thus, it expands the current understanding of the relationship between education and the state in a context where the "normal" attributes and functions of schooling were conditioned by a dictatorial regime that used terror against individuals as a governing instrument. Most importantly, for the purpose of this volume on education and the state, this chapter asks to what extent schools, and more specifically classroom spaces, were shaped by the same broader processes of state power characteristic of a violent dictatorship, and to what extent the exercise of power in relations among teachers and pupils was shaped by additional factors that complicate understanding of a dictatorial state.

The most praised practices of Stalinist pedagogy are suggestive of contemporary discussions of "inclusive discipline" as an alternative to expulsions. In the words of educator Yang, best practices in school discipline include exercising judgment and personalizing disciplinary action, providing an engaging and challenging academic environment, providing effective counseling, involving families respectfully, intervening early, and ensuring that students are engaged with the school community (Yang, 2009). According to American educator DeRidder, the "best programs" are "nonpunitive," are designed "to help each student by identifying and remedying the factors that contributed to the discipline and academic programs," provide "caring, personalized, individualized assistance to each student at an appropriate level of academic and psychological functioning," and are "oriented toward helping the student to become involved in the learning process positively through successful experiences" (DeRidder, 1991, pp. 44–47).

These approaches to discipline involve a negotiation of the proper relationship between education and the state. Inclusive discipline, as advocated by both Stalinist pedagogues and contemporary educators, is designed to keep children within the boundaries of the school, rather than turning them over to the authority of the state. From this perspective, educators who take the "path of least resistance" by expelling students from the school are relinquishing their proper role as the agents most responsible for the education of children. By claiming authority over children, even those deemed as incorrigible or delinquent, educators who practice inclusive discipline are also protecting the boundaries that separate the school from the state.

Notes

1 Funding to support the research for this chapter came from the Spencer Foundation, the National Council for Eurasian and East European Research, and the Department of History, the College of Liberal Arts and Human Sciences, and the Office of the Vice President for Research at Virginia Tech. None of these organizations is responsible for the views expressed in this article. My thanks to the participants in the 2011 conference, Education and the State, for their suggestions and recommendations regarding analysis of Stalinist power in Soviet schools.
2 For discussion of the exercise of power within schools, see the chapters by Geiss, Kafka, and Grube in this volume.
3 For discussion of the relationship between the political climate and debates on school disciplinary regimes, see Kafka's chapter in this volume.
4 These allegations seem to confirm the argument made by American educators that, when schools reject students by expelling them, the students respond by rejecting the school (DeRidder, 1991, pp. 44–47).
5 For a similar example of teachers seeking clarifications on disciplinary policies, see the chapter by Kafka in this volume.
6 See discussion of similar demands from teachers in the chapter by Kafka in this volume.
7 For a firsthand account of a new teacher resorting to sending children to the office, and a reflection on the meaning of such practices, see Yang (2009, pp. 49–50).
8 In a similar manner, L.M. DeRidder claims that schools with high rates of suspensions tended to have "clear disciplinary policies emphasizing standards or controls rather than instruction, community involvement, and student-centered environments" (DeRidder, 1991, pp. 44–47).
9 See the comparable observation, made in the contemporary American context: "some teachers expel children from their classrooms in huge numbers" (Yang, 2009, pp. 59–60).
10 For an interpretation that argues against the expulsion of so-called "bad influences, vectors of malignant behavior that spread like contagion through the classroom," see Yang (2009, p. 50).
11 See, for example, the numbers used in recent American articles designed to emphasize just how extensively expulsions are used to discipline children (Brownstein, 2009).
12 By contrast, schools in the United States expelled 100,000 students, which was approximately 0.2 percent of the total school population (Noltemeyer and Mcloughlin, 2010, p. 59; see also Brownstein, 2009).
13 A recent article makes the case for "Schoolwide Positive Behavior Support (SWPBS)," which is described as "a comprehensive approach designed to promote the appropriate behaviors of all students and enhance the capacity of systems to design positive environments for students" (Noltemeyer and Mcloughlin, 2010, pp. 68–69).
14 The term "ataman" is a reference to leadership among Cossack brigades.
15 This term is used in Noltemeyer and Mcloughlin (2010, p. 60).
16 For tensions in the educational perspectives of teachers and administrators, see the chapter by Geiss in this volume.

Archives

GARF (Gosudarstvennyi Arkhiv Rossiiskoi Federatsii, State Archive of the Russian Federation).

NA RAO (Nauchnyi Arkhiv Rossiiskoi Akademii Obrazovaniia/Scientific Archive of the Russian Academy of Education).

RGASPI (Rossiiskii Gosudarstvennyi Arkhiv Sotsial'no-Politicheskoi Istorii/Russian State Archive of Social and Political History).

References

Arshinov, P.S., 1936. Vykorchevat' iz soznaniia uchitelei vrednoe pedologicheskoe nasledstvo. *Uchitel' i Shkola*, 10, pp. 5–7.

Baker, B., 1968. Anton Makarenko and the idea of the collective. *Educational Theory*, 18(3), pp. 285–294.

Bock, S.J., Tapscott, K.E., and Savner, J.L., 1998. Suspension and expulsion: effective management for students? *Intervention in School and Clinic*, 34(1), pp. 50–52.

Brownstein, R., 2009. Pushed out. *Teaching Tolerance* (e-journal), 36(Fall). Available at: www.tolerance.org (accessed June 20, 2012).

Buntar', G. and Shnaider., L., 1935. Pokonchit' s nedootsenkoi vospitatel'noi raboty. *Za Kommunisticheskoe Prosveshchenie*, February 26, p. 2.

Chegasov, P.M., 1941. Poriadok v shkole kak faktor vospitaniia soznatel'noi distsipliny. In: G.A. Komissar, E.I. Monoszon, and N.P. Storozhenko (eds) *Vospitanie Soznatel'Noi Distsipliny v Shkole*. Moscow: Pedagogika, pp. 5–11.

Deacon, R., 2005. Moral orthopedics: a Foucauldian account of schooling as discipline. *Telos*, 130, pp. 84–102.

DeRidder, L.M., 1991. How suspension and expulsion contribute to dropping out. *Education Digest*, 56(6), pp. 44–47.

Dwyer, P.J., 1995. Foucault, docile bodies, and post-compulsory education in Australia. *British Journal of Sociology of Education*, 16(4), pp. 467–477.

Ewing, E.T., 2002. *The Teachers of Stalinism: Policy, Practice, and Power in Soviet Schools of the 1930s*. New York: Peter Lang.

External Research Staff, 1956. *The Soviet Union as Reported by Former Citizens*. Washington, DC: US Department of State.

Foucault, M., 1980. *Power/Knowledge: Selected Interviews and Other Writings, 1972–1977*. New York: Pantheon.

Geyer, M. and Fitzpatrick, S. (eds), 2009. *Beyond Totalitarianism. Stalinism and Nazism Compared*. Cambridge: Cambridge University Press.

Gunzenhauser, M.G., 2006. Normalizing the educated subject: a Foucaultian analysis of high-stakes accountability. *Educational Studies*, 39(3), pp. 241–259.

Hall, C. and Millard, E., 1994. The means of correct training? Teachers, Foucault, and disciplining. *Journal of Education for Teaching*, 20(2), pp. 153–160.

Harvard Project on the Soviet Social System, n.d. *Schedule A and Schedule B Interviews*. Available at: http://hcl.harvard.edu/collections/hpsss/index.html (accessed June 20, 2012).

Holmes, L.E., 2006. Ascent into darkness: escalating negativity in the administration of schools in the Kirov region, 1931–1941. *History of Education*, 35, pp. 521–540.

Jones, D., 1990. The genealogy of the urban schoolteacher. In: S. Ball (ed.) *Foucault and Education. Disciplines and Knowledge*. London: Routledge, pp. 57–74.

Kelly, C., 2007. *Children's World. Growing Up in Russia 1890–1991*. New Haven, CT: Yale University Press.

Kharkhordin, O., 1999. *The Collective and the Individual in Russia*. Berkeley, CA: University of California Press.
Khudaikulov, I., 1938. O rabote v shkole. *Pravda Vostoka*, January 6, pp. 2–3.
Kosterina, N., 1968. *The Diary of Nina Kosterina*. New York: Crown.
Kreusler, A., 1965. *A Teacher's Experiences in the Soviet Union*. Leiden: Brill.
Kuprianov, G., 1936. Pedagogi eshche ne ispol'zuiut svoikh prav. *Za Kommunisticheskoe Prosveshchenie*, December 2, p. 4.
Lerd, L., 1934. Vypol'nit' reshenie. *Za Kommunisticheskoe Prosveshchenie*, March 4, p. 2.
Marshall, J.D., 1996. *Michel Foucault: Personal Autonomy and Education*. Dordrecht: Kluwer Academic.
Mayo, C., 2000. The uses of Foucault. *Educational Theory*, 50(1), pp. 103–116.
Migolat'ev, A., 1935. Kak "dezorganizatory" stali primernymi shkol'nikami. *Za Kommunisticheskoe Prosveshchenie*, March 14, p. 2.
Noltemeyer, A.L. and Mcloughlin, C.S., 2010. Changes in exclusionary discipline rates and disciplinary disproportionality over time. *International Journal of Special Education*, 25(1), pp. 59–70.
Ob organizatsii uchebnoi raboty i vnutrennem rasporiadke v nachal'noi, nepolnoi srednei i srednei shkole, 1935. In: *Narodnoe Obrazovanie v SSSR. Obshcheobrazo-vatel'naia Shkola. Sbornik Dokumentov 1917–1973*. Moscow: Pedagogika, 1973, pp. 171–172.
Ob uchebnykh programmakh i rezhime v nachal'noi i srednei shkole, 1932. Postanovlenie TsK VKP (b). In: *Narodnoe Obrazovanie v SSSR. Obshcheobrazo-vatel'naia Shkola. Sbornik Dokumentov 1917–1973*. Moscow: Pedagogika, 1973, pp. 161–164.
Ponomarev, A., 1937. Po shkolam g. Khabarovska. *Dal'nevostochnyi Uchitel'*, 2, pp. 35–43.
Ryan, J., 1991. Observing and normalizing: Foucault, discipline, and inequality in schooling. *The Journal of Educational Thought*, 25(2), pp. 104–119.
Saplin, P., 1935. Za vyderzhannoe kommunisticheskoe vospitanie v shkole. *V Pomoshch' Uchiteliu* (Kursk), 1, pp. 5–15.
Shkolu blizhe k rebenku!, 1929. *Vecherniaia Mosvka*, September 13, p. 1.
Simmons, L., 2010. The docile body in school space. In: T. Monahan and R.D. Torres (eds) *Schools Under Surveillance. Cultures of Control in Public Education*. New Brunswick, NJ: Rutgers University Press, pp. 55–70.
Tsemakhman, S., 1937. Po povodu odnogo pis'ma. *Uchitel'skaia Gazeta*, November 29, p. 3.
Yang, K.W., 2009. Discipline or punish? Some suggestions for school policy and teacher practice. *Language Arts*, 87(1), pp. 49–61.

Chapter 14

Utopia, state and democracy

Jürgen Oelkers

'Staatsromane'

In 1855, Robert von Mohl,[1] a liberal German professor of law at the University of Heidelberg, coined the term '*Staatsromane*' in reference to a series of historical works, 'which endeavour to answer the question of the most just and effective way to organise a state and how to order society in a beneficial way by depicting a fictitious ideal' (Mohl, 1855, p. 167).

Mohl, however, added, 'with the sole exception of Utopia by Thomas More', there is scarcely or never a mention of these books nowadays. One could assume 'total ignorance' of the reading public (Mohl, 1855, p. 167). The subject of *Staatsromane* is 'the depiction of an ideal society and political life' and the aesthetic form can be 'a journey, a statistical account or a life story' (Mohl, 1855, p. 170).

Mohl starts the list of *Staatsromane* with Thomas More and excludes antiquity, considering that Plato's *Politeia* was not a *Staatsroman* because it did not include any 'specific contrived state' and it offered no 'poetic representation' (Mohl, 1855, p. 172). This division has been followed throughout literature. There have been 'utopias' only since the publication of Thomas More's *De optimo reipublicae statu deque nova insula Utopia* in 1516, which was dedicated to Erasmus of Rotterdam (Morus, 1516). The first 'utopia' written in the German language was the translation published eight years later, in 1524, under the title *Von der wunderbarlichen Insel Vtopia genant, das ander Buch* ('Of the Wonderful Island called Vtopia, the Other Book') (Morus, 1524).[2] The translator of this work was the humanist Claudius Cantiuncula[3] from Basel, who, as the title suggests, only covered the second book of the first *Staatsroman*.[4]

Social utopias in the sense of the *Staatsromane* have been around since the early modern period. In his time, Mohl discussed fourteen of these works, which are all structured in a similar way. They portray journeys to faraway islands or continents, create social counterworlds that could be placed even in ideal cities, describe a harmonious society and are organized along predominantly socialist lines; and this applies equally to the education of children. There is almost no private ownership. Thus, these counterworlds are often small and isolated.

The world learns of them from visitors who can observe the society, but are never allowed to fully integrate and ultimately have to leave the paradise.

This vision of a completely different world in a faraway place is a fascination that actually goes back to antiquity. In other words, utopias were around *avant la lettre*. Nonetheless, Mohl's classification of *Staatsromane* still resonates today, at least in the German-speaking world. Texts preceding More do not belong to the genre, and those published after More are limited in number. In France, the *utopie* or *le roman utopique* only became an accepted literary genre towards the end of the eighteenth century (Funke, 1983, p. 96); before that they may have been neutrally referred to as travellers' tales, political or heroic novels or merely chimaeras (Funke, 1983, p. 95). The name of the genre gave rise to the problem of classification, and thus to the question of numbers and completeness. How many utopias are there? Only fourteen?

Mohl (1855, pp. 170ff.) commented that he could not guarantee that the bibliography he cited was 'absolutely complete', not least because he did not have access to all the titles. This was the case, for instance, for the satire *I Mondi celesti, terrestri et infernali*, published in Venice in 1552, in which Anton Francesco Doni[5] used the technique of literary reflection to attack the customs of his country. Doni, who was referred to as 'bizzaro', portrays – in the footsteps of Dante – a journey through the seven worlds that lead to a utopian city, which must be interpreted as being a counterworld to the then infamous Venice. Today, Doni is considered a mannerist. However, he was, first and foremost, a composer and musician, one of many with utopian interests.

Another title that Mohl was also unable to consult was called *La République des Cessarès*, which is thought to have been published in London in the eighteenth century (Mohl, 1855). This was *An Account of the First Settlement, Laws, Form of Government, and Police, of the Cessares* by James Burgh, an epistolary novel about a fictional people in the far south of South America between Chile and Patagonia, which was published in 1764. The author was the teacher and political writer James Burgh,[6] who in the mid-eighteenth century espoused the right to free speech, a democratic society and equal rights for both sexes. Burgh's widow Hannah was a great support for the young Mary Wollstonecraft (Johnson, 2002, p. 125).

Still, these two were not the only titles missing from Mohl's collection of *Staatsromane*. In 1941, the scholar of English and later Editor-in-Chief of *Webster's Third New International Dictionary*, Philip Babcock Gove,[7] counted 215 titles of imaginary journeys published in various languages during the eighteenth century alone (Babcock Gove, 1941, pp. 295–300). Depending on the definition of utopia, current bibliographies count thousands of titles (Heyer, 2009; Schaer and Sargent, 2000), and in the period between antiquity to the early twenty-first century their number has only continued to grow. It appears that this genre is not waning in literary or political significance. Moreover, given current research, 'total ignorance' is certainly not the right description.

Mohl's *Staatsromane* have the common feature that they are static in their conception. They describe a state of society that never changes because the social order in the place is considered perfect. Even if, like Karl Marx in the nineteenth century, who linked utopia with class struggle, you add dynamics and relate it to a historical process, there is still an expectation of a certain final state that neither desires nor allows further development. The teleology of history has been fulfilled, or, in other words, in the end, the Hegelian dialectic gives rise to something supreme that finished dialectic itself.

History and finality

Ralf Dahrendorf, later famous rector of St Anthony's College in Oxford, referred to the problem of finality in his dissertation work on *Der Begriff des Gerechten im Denken von Karl Marx* ('The Concept of Right in the Thought of Karl Marx'), Hamburg, 1952. For Marx, Communist society is simultaneously the objective and the outcome of history (Dahrendorf, 1953, p. 91), which continues – Marx is not a chiliast (p. 95) – or even just starts, but no longer changes the new society. All prior history, as it is famously formulated in the Communist Manifesto of 1848, is 'pre-history', that is, that of class struggle.

In the new society, man is free from exploitation of every kind, the means of production have been socialized, bourgeois ownership has been abolished (Dahrendorf, 1953, pp. 99–100) and the 'all-round development of individuals' has become a reality (p. 105).

History can achieve no more. More precisely, the prior history changes its character and becomes a function of society. Many intellectuals believed in the last and perfect society, but not so Dahrendorf, who was 23 years old when he wondered: 'Marx appears not a moment to have considered the idea that even Communist society could disintegrate into a new, substantially different form, that it too could give rise to inner contrasts that develop to become contradictions' (Dahrendorf, 1953, pp. 95–96).

Darwin's theory of evolution emerged at the same time, offering an entirely different vision – a general theory of life that professes nothing more than continual change by adaptation; this would rule out history having any objective. Every species, and thus every social species or every society, can be overcome by adapting to new circumstances, and will either develop further or die out.

The new Communist society is the last one in history, and the first to be there only for man. The 'universally developed individual' Marx wrote about in *Das Kapital* is ironically the Crown of Creation.[8] Moreover, the non-contradictory Communist society represents the 'true realm of freedom' and sustainably aligns social existence with the freedom and needs of the individual. It resembles Christian creation in which there is no longer any change after the creation; however, in communism, the revolution represents creation and God is no longer needed.

For Marxists, the endless evolution of life is a grim notion, no matter how much Marx may have admired Darwin because of the consequences of his theory for Christian theology. Yet, the theory of evolution is based on assumptions that undermine any concept of a final history. The history of society can similarly lack objective and fail to end at an ideal place; yet, this is exactly what the social utopia served to do since the readings of Thomas More in the seventeenth, eighteenth and nineteenth centuries. Marx differed from this view only in the concept of dialectic. Communist society is not simply given, but rather emerges from the class struggle, whereby the realm of freedom comes about through historical necessity. With the proletariat, history has a final subject that liberates itself through struggle and has no pursuit other than Communist society.

The prize is that, in that case, either a final situation that can be filled with notions of paradise or its demise must be conceived. Utopias have always implied dystopias, without changing the fundamental model of thinking. In terms of political ideology, 'demise' is merely the opposite of 'progress'; in both cases, the social movement ends in its final state; however, in one case it terminates at a pinnacle of history and, in the other, at the lowest point. 'Growth' in economic terms has no end, but only rises and fluctuations, whereas positive and negative utopias must describe a final place in which history can never change society again.

Elizabeth Hansot (1974), American historian of education, commented that there could be two modes of utopian thought – perfection and progress. In one case, the perfect world will already exist and thus only needs to be discovered and, in the other, it will have to be pursued by gradual progress or created through revolution. More precisely, the Marxist revolution only creates the preconditions for the emergence of the new society through the socialization of property. The revolution is then transferred into communist education – education that creates 'new man', conceived in a process that would last generations and have no completion date. It is a new form of endlessness and one of the reasons why 'real socialism' ended in 1989. No promise of the future will pass generations without being tested.

The link between utopia and history is only established in the eighteenth and nineteenth centuries (Manuel and Manuel, 1979), with the concepts of historical progress, on the one hand, and Hegelian philosophy of history on the other. The humanistic utopias that emerged in the two centuries after More portray perfect societies that can be held up in contrast to the real world. This motif of a place of hope to be found somewhere long defined the utopian novel (Gnüg, 1999). The sole goal of which was to see in utopian pedagogy the best education being provided in the best of all worlds.

The idea of eternal order and endless stability fascinated intellectuals at a time when no social order existed. Thomas More's England was not a 'society' in our sense but an order of permanent disorder caused by poverty, hunger, a high death rate, illiteracy and a ruling class that did not know any common good. Hence, in a way, modern utopia is a fantasy about order and righteousness at times when no legal state existed. It was Robert von Mohl who coined the term '*Rechtsstaat*' ('constitutional state') in German history of law.

The term 'dystopia' can be traced back to John Stuart Mill, who, in an address to the British House of Commons on 12 March 1868, described the British government as a bunch of 'dys-topians' in reference to their Ireland policy. 'What is commonly called Utopian is something too good to be practicable; but what they (i.e. the government) appear to favour is too bad to be practicable' (Mill, 1988, p. 88).

In fact, dystopias go back further than this, and Mill's formulation of 'too bad to be practicable' missed the religious core of the problem, which pertains to the concept of the beginning and end.

Expectations of the end of the world at a given point in time are characteristic of antiquity and the Middle Ages, both the Christian and the pre-Christian eras (Carozzi, 1996; Cohn, 1997). The motif of final salvation at the Last Judgement is not exclusively Christian. The Book of Revelations is based on various older sources, all of which agree that there must be an end if there was also a beginning. Creation and demise are thought of as birth and death, except that the Last Judgement neutralizes death itself and offers everlasting life to the Chosen People, which, by definition, will not include all.

Utopia is a counterweight to this concept, as it promises redemption from evil in this world without having to wait for the intermediate state and the resurrection. In the Christian versions of Utopia, the promise is an assurance of being better placed to make it to the afterlife. The demand for a better world is closely related to the consciousness of life and death, and can be answered religiously or secularly. The answer must not be given worldly and spatially, because – as Augustine showed – the best world can also be connected with mercy and, therefore, understood as being unattainable. Yet, the unattainability is not the central motif in utopian literature, which seeks to educate that there are better worlds and one can find them.

Notions of a better world beyond the one that is known have not only been around since More. Thus, the term 'utopia' was coined in 1516. Counterworlds were also recorded in the literature of antiquity – for instance, the Elysian Fields in the Odyssey, the Elysium in Hesiod's Theogony,[9] or journeys to other worlds that Pliny the Elder described.[10] In addition, better societies were created with the aim of revealing the shortcomings of the world in which one lives, and creating the longing for the better. This literature was originally not intended to have a political message in the modern sense.

The historical development of utopia

In around 300 BC, in his work 'Sacred History' (*Hiera anagraphe*), the Greek philosopher and writer, Euhemerus of Messina, described a journey to the island of Panchaea at the eastern end of the known world, where he claimed to have discovered a sacred inscription and a utopian society. Although, inspired by Plato's description of Atlantis, Euhemerus turns his work into a manifesto of materialism. The inscription in the temple exposes the gods as 'deified men' (Braunert, 1980, p. 261) and therefore as mortals; thus, belief in them is nothing more than a form of domination. There was no private ownership in this society, the children were a common commodity and the island has therefore repeatedly been mentioned in connection with communism of antiquity (for example, Pöhlmann, 1901, pp. 55–70).

Another example is the autobiography of the Greek merchant Iambulos, which has survived in fragments in the work of the Greek historian Diodorus Siculus. In this work, a journey to an island is described again, whereby, after being taken captive by thieves in Arabia, Iambulos and a companion ended up in the hands of Ethiopians and were taken to the Ethiopian coast. Because they did not fit in with the strictly measured fabric of the generations, they were sent out into the Indian Ocean by boat. They were told they must sail to the south, where they would come upon a paradise island inhabited by honourable people, who would offer them a blessed existence (Diodorus Siculus II/55).

After months of odyssey, the pair finally reached an unknown island and discovered a completely different type of society. Gradually, it becomes clear that the society has spread to various islands, due to their primary distinguishing characteristic – physical constitution; all islanders had flexible bones, and the exact same height. Their proportions made them beautiful and much stronger than the strangers. Moreover, the island dwellers were giants and had a lifespan of 150 years.[11] They had two tongues and could converse with two people at the same time (Diodorus Siculus II/56). They lived in abundance and had more food than they could eat. No more than 400 relatives formed a social community, living together peacefully with all the others.

The communities were engaged in the sciences, especially astrology. The islanders also developed their own writing system, in which the alphabet was sorted by sound and, although it had only seven letters, they could each be used in a variety of ways. Writing was not performed in horizontal lines, but vertically from top to bottom. The islanders were largely free from illness and ailments, although anyone who became crippled or suffered long-term pain was forced into suicide, as prescribed by an irrefutable law – something of an antique law of eugenics. The length of life was strictly limited, and anyone who grew older would, as the law prescribed, have to lie themselves down under the tree of death to die (Diodorus Siculus II/57).

They inhabited a total of seven islands, in a community of goods; there were no rules on marriage and therefore no compulsion to remain monogamous. Men and women could freely exchange partners, children belonged to the community, rather than the parents, and their education was public. There was no private space. Often, the women did not know whether the children they raised in the community were their own or not. Because everything, even the children, belonged to everyone, the community was free of rivalries. The inhabitants never experienced social disorder and never ceased to stress the meaning of the inner harmony of their community (Diodorus Siculus II/58).

In each group, the eldest male was the leader and, when he died, he was succeeded by the next elder. In spite of the abundance, the islanders led a simple life, in harmony with their needs. They had no enemies, and even the giant snakes on the islands presented no danger (Diodorus Siculus II/59). The inhabitants worked according to their abilities, and served the needs of others in an exact cycle that was in tune with nature. Their religious feasts and festivals worshipped the God of the sun, who also gave his name to the islands (Diodorus Siculus II/59). It was Rousseau who revived the idea of living according to natural needs without being disturbed by civilization.

Christian Paradise does not have a door, but a way out. And this is also true for the story of Iambulos. After seven years, he and his companion were forced to leave the island against their will; they were held to be sinners and stood accused of corrupting morals with their evil influence. They were guilty of promoting a negative education that could only be ascribed to outsiders. Thus, the strangers had to make another dangerous voyage by sea. The story ends with a shipwreck in India, which led to the death of his companion and a happy return of Iambulos to his home in Greece (Diodorus Siculus II/60). The island itself remains as it is, for the strangers left no traces.

Thomas More may have known the *Bibliotheca historica* of Diodorus Siculus, as this work of universal history written in the first century BC was an important and often quoted source in the sixteenth century. The analogies to Utopia are so evident that the genre of utopian literature cannot simply be ascribed to More, as is usually assumed (Claeys, 2010; Vosskamp, 1982). What distinguishes More's Utopia, however, is the explicit criticism of society and hence the political links that had been sought long before Marx. Yet, More did not originate the criticism of private ownership and socialism as a model of society.

Utopian works were also produced in the Middle Ages to justify heretical movements (Seibt, 1969), for instance, or to illustrate the Christian faith, as in 'Le purgatoire de Saint Patrick' in 1186.[12] This work describes the desire for a place to absolve sins and hence attain salvation; the place for that was found at the end of the world, in the northern part of Ireland, where pilgrims could find a purgatory that would not burn but save them. Christian visions of the 'other world' were numerous (Easting, 1997), but worldly experiences could also be transcended into utopian worlds. The much renowned *Roman de la Rose* by Guillaume de Lorris and Jean de Meung, which was finished in 1270, relates the story of a long dream about love, which ends almost misogynously. It led to the first literary debate on a utopian work, as Christine de Pizan challenged the portrayal of women in the second half of the work (Hicks, 1977).[13]

Travellers' tales have also been published since the fourteenth century; for instance, the *Itineraria* or *Livre des merveilles du monde* by John Mandeville,[14] written between 1355 and 1357 in Liège (Mandeville, 2000), gives an account of a fantastical journey spanning decades, across the known world to China. Finally, the salvation of the soul from all worldly dependencies and every form of domination, which was described by Marguerite Porète around 1295 in her 'Le Miroir des simples âmes', does not stem from the modern period. Even the risks of utopia are not modern; following a long trial, Marguerite Porète was publicly burned on 1 June 1310 as a heretic (Porète, 1986).

After the Reformation, the question of church authority was newly raised, as many asked – do we really need churches and hierarchies? The merchant and mystic Henry Niclaes (Hendrik or Heinrich Niclaes, Nicolas de Munster), from the town of Emden, conceived his 'family of love' or the 'land of Pietas' (of the true faith) in his book *L'Evangile de Royaume* (1540);[15] as this land was not a place but just harmonious relationships, he believed that it could be achieved throughout the world. It was the first 'utopia' that described an order of emotions, as follows: Niclaes had numerous followers, particularly in Britain, who referred to their community as the 'family of God'. God was reached purely on a spiritual level, the Bible was read allegorically, and heaven and hell were not considered to be real places, quite different to the Christian eschatology (Marsh, 1993).

The social utopia in its modern sense refers to a better world in the future, which can be seen as a political option of the present. This view was not possible in antiquity simply because the concept of 'future' for the Greeks and Romans did not span very far and their spatial knowledge of the world was also limited. It is only the notion of the future as indefinite and distant, yet potentially subject to influence from today, that allows a move away from static models of the best of all worlds. Neither in antiquity nor in the Middle Ages were there notions of a utopian city (Kruft, 1989) or a utopian society that was linked with the expectation of a distant and better future. This only became possible with the link between utopia and history.

The travellers' tales of antiquity have didactic intentions; their utopian worlds are not conceived as an objective of history, but rather portray an ideal society with the aim of teaching or educating the reader. Plato's *Politeia* on the theory of the state, which was written around 370 BC, does not describe a counterworld; instead, it designs an ideal for the existing society. Still, in many respects, *Politeia* is the benchmark for utopian literature, whose authors read Plato not with the eyes of antiquity, but those of the early modern period. A precondition for this perspective – one that Plato, of course, could not have known – was the Christian faith and its claim of redemption, which was gradually conferred on the future of society. It was only in this way that the 'future' in the current sense could actually come about, as an extended horizon that can constantly regenerate itself, yet nevertheless allowing continuities that point beyond the present.

From a literary point of view, the utopias of the early modern period are the consequence of discoveries, particularly the exploration of the world made possible by new maritime routes that had been mapped out exactly, in contrast to antiquity and the Middle Ages. The expanding knowledge of the world was reflected in countless works, ranging from travellers' tales to the discovery of new societies. Anglo-Saxon literature alone counts more than 400 works published during two centuries that can be described as 'utopian' in the narrower sense. Works of this type appeared in all civilized languages and always described not only social but also educational utopias. Thus, the concept of 'utopia' is closely linked with ideas of better education.

Utopian society and education

One of the earliest German examples is Johann Eberlin von Günzburg's description of the 'land of Wolfaria', which appeared as a pamphlet in the late summer of 1521, immediately after the beginning of the Reformation.[16] A former Franciscan friar, Günzburg was a lecturer and preacher in the city of Ulm and had converted to the teachings of Luther. He was so articulate, eloquent and sharp of tongue that he became known as one of Luther's best propagandists.

'Wolfaria' is the old German word for 'welfare state'. Günzburg describes the well-organized model state of the new faith, where idleness is forbidden, all are compelled to work and begging in any form has to be punished. Catholic feast days should be curtailed, even the misdemeanours of the preachers are punishable, marriage is no longer a divine sacrament, and clandestine marriages without public testimony are annulled by drowning. Monastic benefices were rescinded and handed to the hospitals, preachers could only preach in places where at least 500 followers of the new faith resided, and worship of any deity other than Our Father was punishable by decapitation. Anyone who travelled to Rome was considered bound for Sodom and Gomorrah and, to avoid this demise, all schools were to hold two lessons each day on proper thinking and behaviour according to the new faith. 'Wolfaria', or 'prosperity' (*Wohlfahrt*), as the name implies, would only be possible in this structure (Günzburg, 1521/1896).

Utopias also emerged in the context of the Catholic Renaissance; for instance, the 'new world' of Anton Francesco Doni, mentioned previously, described an egalitarian society in which labour is divided rationally for all, money does not exist and governance is modelled on the family. One year later, in 1553, Francesco Patrizis published *La Città felice* – an example for all utopias that described the perfectly organized city with a limited number of citizens, all of whom are known to each other. Here, education was considered greatly important – prudish on the one hand, but intended for practical benefits on the other. Grammar, music and drawing were thought among the practical arts and served to propagate happiness.

In 1555, Caspar Stiblin (Gaspar Stiblinus) from Würzburg, later a lecturer at a gymnasium there, described a Catholic *Coropaedia*, including a theory of the state. The *Coropaedia* is an early theory of girls' education provided at convents; the state is considered a eudaemonistic republic based on collaboration and therefore autarkic. Stiblin emphasizes female ability to learn, albeit under the conditions imposed by a closed world, as venturing out of the convent was forbidden for these women (*Coropaedia*, 1555). Girl education did not remain 'utopian' for very long though. In 1574, in his role as General-Superintendent of the March of Brandenburg, the Reformist Andreas Musculus[17] (Andreas Meusel) announced a girls' school (*Jungfraw-Schul*) that provided a programme of education – albeit not restricted to convents – that became schools after the Reformation. Of particular importance was the daily singing, something that is scarcely mentioned in social utopias. Musculus did not intend to achieve the best of all worlds, but rather a format similar to the existing girls' education (Musculus, 1574).

The social utopias of the late sixteenth and early seventeenth century were visions not of the religious world, but of the naturally organized one. Arcadia, for instance, in Philip Sidney's widely read novel *The Countess of Pembroke's Arcadia* (1590), has the God of nature on its side, which can only be good. According to Sidney, 'Nature promises nothing but goodness', and this also applied to children's education (Sidney, 1891, p. 15ff.). Rousseau also later adopted this idea. On the other hand, in his Catholic *Repubblica immaginaria* in 1580, musician and composer Ludovico Agostini saw the absolute necessity of a Christian confession of faith. His country of nobles is a Spartan state in which public education is based on religion and morals, which are considered to be more important than schooling (Agostini, 1957; see also Rawson, 1991, p. 172ff.). In a way, Rousseau again adopted this idea.

The completely different concept of a cooperative-based society stems from the Dutch author Peter Cornelius van Zurick-Zee (sometimes cited as Plockhoy or Plockboy). In 1659 in England, he published the work *A Way Propounded to Make the Poor in these and other Nations Happy*, in which he developed the concept of the 'little commonwealth' that would make the people self-sufficient. They would come together voluntarily in cooperatives and work for the common good without any coercion. A special source of income would come from the schools, the quality of which was so high that the rich would send their children there and, in this way, allow them to come into contact with cooperative thought (*Genossenschaften*). Education would therefore have a subversive effect. Although no particular religion was taught, saints were still held up as role models (Plockhoy, 1659).

Classical utopias have always required the best – albeit closed – place, access to which could be controlled so that only a limited number could enter. And there is only one such place, rather than many – certainly not many identical places around the world. This also holds true of the Christian utopias, which no longer have faraway islands as their theme, but the city of God, which should be understood as a bastion in the seventeenth century. Tommaso Campanella's

La Città del sole of 1602 is organized in this way, as is Johann Valentin Andreae's *Christianopolis* of 1619.

They use their social utopias to articulate a widespread religious vision. Redemption on entering the one heavenly Jerusalem in imitation of Christ can be seen in many depictions from the Middle Ages. Yet in the early seventeenth century, there was more to this than merely a pictorial affirmation of faith. The heavenly city was brought to earth and interpreted as a social model colony of Christianity, Catholic for Campanella and Reformed for Andreae. Both are educational states that prescribe a utopian place (Oelkers, 1993).

Tommaso Campanella was a Dominican monk and a close pen friend of Galileo Galilei. His work *La Città del sole* was written while in captivity in Spain in 1602,[18] with a Latin version appearing in 1623 in Frankfurt. However, the German translation became available only in 1789.

La Città del sole depicts a communist state with no private ownership; economic production is not for profit, but is designed solely to meet the needs of the society, which are calculated exactly in the form of plans; the institution of the family is abolished because it protects private ownership; women and children are common property; the state is solely responsible for education; and political power lies in the hands of a clerical oligarchy based on the concept of a universal papal monarchy (Campanella, 1964).

La Città del sole is therefore a Catholic theocracy with a communist society, which, given the subsequent history, could almost be regarded as irony. However, in 1602, the notion of the ideal society was not led by materialistic criticism of religion, as in the nineteenth century. The pope and communism were considered compatible, by Campanella at least.

The frontispiece of the 1619 Strasbourg edition shows Christianopolis as an island city, apparently in heaven, while it is purported to be a real, existing state. It depicts wide moats surrounding the fortress with a bridge on each side of the square city (Andreae, 1975, p. 25) and one positioned exactly at the centre. The bridges lead to the gates controlling entry and exit. The way in and out can be closed or opened at will, so that those inside can be sure that entry to anyone else can be precisely controlled. The opposite is also true, as no one can leave the Christian city unchecked, but, of course, no one would want to leave either.

Exactly at the centre of the heavenly city is a temple to which paths from all entrances lead, taking you directly to the inner sanctum. The temple is the Christian church and the Christian crucifix is visible for everyone within the city. The houses are community quarters; there are no individual houses, only quarters arranged in rows, akin to the block of flats predominating in early twentieth-century socialist architecture. There are towers at each end that serve as outward and inward boundary markers. The rows are tapered inwards and the temple is surrounded by a gigantic square to fully express the power of the temple. Protruding into the water on each corner are Christian hearts that are clearly recognizable as embankments. They are so pointed that they could even be spears, indicating that the might of God should be seen as both love and sword. And they point in all directions.

The tale then repeats the tried and tested utopian formula of a shipwreck and a strange world. Christianopolis is arrived at by a shipwrecked voyager, who is portrayed as a wanderer of the world who, albeit involuntarily, reaches his final destination. The city itself is depicted as 'perfect' for the shipwrecked voyager, who enters by passing various controls: 'The appearance of things is the same everywhere, neither ornate nor wretched, and planned for the enjoyment of the open and fresh air. There are about 400 citizens living here, perfect in religion and perfect in civility' (Andreae, 1975, pp. 25–26).

Their entire life, work, sociability, religion and not least education is precisely ordered. Aside from education and morality, work is always the central factor in utopias. On work, it is noted:

- The citizens of Christianopolis preferred to speak of 'exercise of the hands', as labour was neither pain nor suffering.
- The city was a 'single workshop' where one hand passed to the next.
- Each problem was solved with the 'wealth of ingenuity' of the citizens, who were given to cooperation and applied their 'spirit' for the common good.

A utopia like this still influences popular thinking on education, which favours the 'exercise of the hands', the school as a 'workshop', the joy of working, the cooperation of all children and the 'spirit for the common good'. Although my task here is not to comment on the language of education, it is still worth noting how many popular metaphors of education have survived from history.

In many respects, the limited diversity in these utopias is surprising. The basic expectation is always of a strictly egalitarian republic of virtue where equal distribution is intended to negate any egoism. Egoism (the self-love of Augustine) is the exact opposite of the love of God, which (in a sense that it implies morality and piety) promotes what egoism repudiates. This occurs essentially through working and nurturing with a sense of public spirit, that is, through education. The purpose of working is to do good deeds in and for the community and not in order to achieve profit or personal wealth. All property is common property; everything belongs to everyone, but nobody may make use of their share individually.

In contrast, the early dystopias presented the ideal of the new world as an escape from the old one; the new world existed without any new education. In his satire, *Mundus alter et idem* (1605/1607), the English bishop Joseph Hall[19] describes the '*terra australis*', which is so remote that the inhabitants are able to laugh at their enemies. The new world comprises the lands of Crepulia, Viraginia, Moronia and Lavernia, and their inhabitants are described as gluttons, nags, fools and thieves. Through this the reader learns that, at the end of the world, nothing remains but the familiar old London (Hall, 1607).

Henry Neville's *Isle of Pines* (1668) tells of the re-establishment of society by castaways on faraway islands in East India. After George Pine and four women are shipwrecked, he has sexual relations with all of them, and they bear him children who, over the years, produce distinct tribes that gradually break away from the laws of the patriarch and become increasingly primitive. The people do not have to work as they live from nature but, because of this, they forget the technologies brought with them from England and regress. Neville thus describes a dystopia, a negative utopia; the island is discovered by Dutch explorers who do not see this as a superior world but rather as a primitive race that is on the brink of civil war and has a foretaste of its own demise (Neville, 1668).

Dystopias are never associated with education. When Rousseau wrote in *Emile* about '*éducation négative*', he was referring to the protection of the child's nature against society rather than an educational system leading to demise. In contrast, utopias are linked to education and have continually influenced pedagogic thought since the Reformation. The ideal-typical relationship between utopia and education consists of the following elements:

- The first utopian location is clear and manageable.
- Only a few chosen individuals are allowed to enter it and receive the new education.
- These chosen few spread the spirit of their education throughout the world.
- Many different locations touched by this new education create a common effect and reshape the world.
- The old world disappears as the new one emerges.

The central element in all this is education. Only education guarantees the continuity of the 'New Man'. In the famous utopias of the seventeenth century – from Samuel Hartlib's republic of scholars in *A Description of the Famous Kingdom of Macaria* (1641), to James Harrington's civil republic in *The Commonwealth of Oceana* (1656) and Antoine Legrand's utopian kingdom *Scydromedia* (1669) – 'education' is never considered independent. It is a function of the new society that is meant to reproduce itself perfectly without contributing to its transformation, which must be ruled out. Education simply serves to reproduce society and, because the latter is perfect, education can be nothing but positive.

Even those like Francis Godwin in *The Man in the Moon*, who locate utopia outside the Earth, do not have any other model to follow.[20] In his novel, published posthumously in 1638, the bishop tells of how an astronaut named Domingo Gonsales flies in a chariot pulled by trained geese to the moon, where he discovers a new society with perfect education. Godwin (1985) was working on the assumption that the moon was inhabited by intelligent beings. In his work *Mathematical Magic*, John Wilkins, bishop of Chester and secretary of the Royal Society, toyed with the theoretical possibility that an earthly vehicle could be driven by internal forces and raised from the ground (Wilkins, 1648, ch. xvi). This inspired, among others, Cyrano de Bergerac's *Histoire comique des états et empires de la lune et du soleil* (1655) and Daniel Defoe's satire *The Consolidator* (1705).

Gabriel de Foigny's *La terre australe connue*, which was first published in 1676 in Geneva, presents a communist social utopia. It describes a society of androgynes, called the 'Australians', who are far more advanced than Europeans, because no religion has hindered them in their development. This is reflected in their technological superiority and an egalitarian society, organized as a group of 15,000 identical citizens (*seizans*) with no distinctions based on personal refinement. All forms of governance and institutions are unknown and everyone receives the same amount of education. Conflicts are settled spontaneously as ongoing differences do not exist.

The major social utopias from More to Fourier and nineteenth-century socialism were neither democratic nor did they predict a specific political role for the people. Utopia itself is a socialist vision of order with no democratic legitimation, without any voting or participation. Social Order, rather than the people, creates justice and, for this reason, order is inviolable. Democracy implies necessary change, which is not incorporated in the utopian models that cannot be changed for their own sake. On the other hand, democracy is itself a utopia, or at least a utopian requirement, and this will be the subject of my next and last discussion pertaining to the question – why is there this demand for democracy and where does it come from? And what has it to with education?

The utopian requirement for democracy

It is generally well known that the first theoretical justification of a connection between education and democracy stems from Montesquieu. In his major work, *Esprit des loix* of 1748, he presented a typology in which the form of education was dependent on the form of government. According to this work, the laws of education correspond to those of government and cannot be determined independently. Governments vary, as does education, which cannot be unified; on the contrary, it must be understood from a functional point of view.

The basic premise is summarized as follows at the beginning of book 4:

> Si le peuple en général a un principe, les parties qui le composent, c'est-à-dire les familles, l'auront aussi. Les lois de l'éducation seront donc différentes dans chaque espèce de gouvernement. Dans les monarchies, elles auront pour l'objet l'honneur; dans les républiques, la vertu; dans le despotisme, la crainte.
>
> (Montesquieu, 1950, p. 54)

A monarchistic or despotic government does not require any virtue in order to exist; it simply requires genealogy, power and the symbols of honour, on the one hand, and the authority of terror on the other. The opposite is true of an '*état populaire*'; this can only exist if education provides for virtue, which for Montesquieu is tantamount to abiding by the laws (1950, pp. 26–27). Education is, therefore, fundamental for preserving democracy. The idea of a connection between education and the state was originally put forward by Aristotle; however, it related to Greek policy rather than the people.[21] For Aristotle, democracy, in its pure form, implied the authority of the poor, which needed to be replaced by a mixed government.

What democracy is not is described by Montesquieu with a daunting example from the previous century. Up until the 'glorious revolution' of 1688/1689 and the introduction of the Bill of Rights, the English had tried unsuccessfully to establish a democracy. However, they were lacking in the most important element – virtue. Governments were constantly changing, parties fought against one another and the most courageous were astonished by their successes, which never lasted for long. The consequence was clear – 'Le peuple étonné cherchoit la démocratie, & ne la trouvoit nulle part' (Montesquieu, 1950, p. 27).

Eventually, they had to go back to the form of government that had previously been removed and the king was replaced with the Puritan Oliver Cromwell as a revolutionary interlude (Montesquieu, 1950, p. 27). Cromwell had the English king Charles I executed in 1649 and died from malaria in 1658 as Lord Protector. He was so hated by the royalists that they exhumed him and subsequently hanged him when they returned to power in 1660 and Charles II became king of England.

This was only the French perspective, however. Montesquieu, who, after all, was a member of the Horn's Tavern Masonic Lodge in Westminster, simply focused on the form of government and ignored the political process that in no way restored the status quo. The revolutionary movement was too entrenched for that to happen. An important step was taken with the 'Levellers' manifesto of 1649, the aim of which was to associate political democracy, not simply with virtue but with the approval of the people. The eight-page manifesto on the equality of all citizens was written in the Tower of London. Its authors were John Lilburne, William Walwyn, Thomas Prince and Richard Overton, all four of whom were authors and pamphleteers advocating 'freeborn rights' and thus questioning the privileges of birth and, as such, were controversial.

The name 'Levellers' can be traced back to a calculated defamation, which the English journalist Marchamont Needham had initiated in order to caricature 'freeborn rights'. Needham was the publisher of the royalist *Mercurius pragmaticus*, a newsbook, in which the term 'leveller' was coined in 1648 (Raymond, 2005, p. 169). In their manifesto of 14 April 1649, which was taken as a defence, the four pamphleteers defended themselves against the suspicion that they were striving 'to level men's estates' and stressed that their democratic requirements were obvious. The acceptance by the people of a government's policy can only stem from the people themselves, who have to learn to articulate their opinions accordingly (*A Manifestation*, 1649). It was not yet completely clear as to how this was to come about.

The Levellers stemmed largely from the New Model Army – the parliament's army, which was against the king and was established at Cromwell's behest in 1645. Cromwell commanded the cavalry and thus emphasized his solidarity with the troops. The New Model Army was dissolved in 1660 in the wake of the Restoration. Its officers had previously been on the side of Cromwell's republic. This explains the revolutionary requirements as well as the discovery of the people as the subject and supporters of democracy.

Its list of requirements, the 'Agreement of the People' of 1647, whose final version was adopted in May 1649, is the key document for the development of parliamentary democracy. It was proposed that free, equal voting rights be introduced from the age of 21.[22] The Levellers forbade army officers, chamberlains and lawyers from becoming members of parliament. A central concern was equality before the law, culpability was to be abolished and the death penalty was limited to cases of murder. However, no references to education were made in this document. It was far more concerned with levying taxes in relation to property and thereby doing away with the existing privileges of the rich. Nonetheless, education soon became a topic.

John Lilburne was a Quaker at the end of his life. The term 'Quaker' used with reference to the 'Children of the Light' is again a polemical attribution. The members of the sect were said to shiver or 'quake' in the presence of the divine light and their opponents judged them as ridiculous.[23] Quakers were non-conformists and as such were opponents of the Anglican Church. In 1662, the parliament passed the Act of Uniformity, which stipulated that all rituals and ceremonies should be carried out according to the Book of Common Prayer[24] of the high church and only ordained priests were allowed to lead church services. However, around 2,000 priests did not follow the law and established their own communities. The basic premise was referred to by the Quaker William Penn in 1681 as 'true spiritual liberty', including the freedom to decide on the education of one's own children.

Roger Williams, who founded the first American Baptist Church in 1639 in Rhode Island, called this position 'soul liberty', which was linked to the requirement for a radical separation between the state and the church. The famous manifesto published by Williams in 1644, *The Bloudy Tenent of Persecution*,[25] accused the persecution of heretics by the state, criticized the united church, pleaded for religious diversity and considered that it was possible that 'true civility and Christianity may both flourish in a state or Kingdome, notwithstanding the permission of divers and contrary consciences, either of Iew or Gentil' (Williams, 1644, p. 4).[26]

One of the non-conformist groupings was the Congregationalists, who established the principle of communal autonomy. Their *Savoy Declaration of Faith and Order* of 1658 refuted all religious and political hierarchy outside and beyond the community:

- Each community is an individual church which administers itself and does not require a general priesthood.
- God has granted each of these churches all the power and authority required to maintain order and to distribute the different offices between them.
- Pastors are teachers who are appointed and proclaim their teachings publicly.

Ordination without selection and the prior approval of the community was refused. The acceptance of new members was also dependent on a consensus. No other authority existed apart from the self-governing communities (*A Declaration*, 1658).

The preacher William Bridge (1654, p. 3) said: 'Christ as God, could have been merciful unto us ... but not as our high priest.' Education is thus considered to be of utmost importance: 'Take a civil man, and though he may have moral virtues, what is there in him lies beyond the reach of Nature, with the dye of Gospel-Education' (Bridge, 1654, p. 9). Moreover, John Owen's Theory of Communion of 1657 states that 'Our Communion with God ... cannot be natural. It must be voluntary and by consent. It cannot be in the same actions upon a third party, but in return from one to another' (Owen, 1792, p. 11). Thus, man is bound to God by 'faith, love, trust, joy' (p. 15), rather than organized church. Jesus is the 'mediator' of believers (p. 84) and nobody can proclaim the Holy Spirit except the Spirit himself. Education must therefore also remain within the community.

Because of this proximity with the Quakers, William Penn, the son of Admiral Sir William Penn, fell out with his father, who was one of the richest men in England. William Penn the son had studied theology at Oxford and had been chastised and rejected by his father because of his non-conformist beliefs. Quakers believed uncompromisingly in equality between all people; they refused to pay homage to noblemen and did not pay any tithes in the form of taxes to landlords or the church. It was in this spirit that Penn married the Quaker woman Guilelma Springett in 1673, two years after his father's death. In 1677, he went with her and a group of Quakers to America and founded communities in present-day New Jersey, which strictly followed the principle of equality.

On returning to England in 1682, William Penn wrote the first constitution (frame of government) of the Province of Pennsylvania, according to which the free citizens elected their government, a representative general assembly was established and a provincial council was formed, promoting science and supporting public schools. In the same year, this provincial council was established under the leadership of the governor and remained in existence until 1776. As William Penn had visited Holland and Germany in 1677, his idea of public schools was clearly influenced by Dutch models, a fact which is seldom mentioned. The first public schools were established in Holland in the sixteenth century. The teaching staff received fixed salaries from 1574 onwards. Teachers' examinations were introduced in 1581. In 1583, the first school law in the province of Zealand justified school attendance on the grounds of it being beneficial for the republic.

'Public schools' were established in a similar way in Pennsylvania (Wickersham, 1886, p. 4ff.). As was the case in Holland, these were schools in individual communities that were subsidized by their own funds and were accessible to all the children in the community. When Penn arrived in America, there were no more than two thousand inhabitants in the Quaker province of 'Pennsylvania',[27] which was named after him. A year later, on 26 October 1683, the first public teacher to receive a fixed annual income was appointed in Philadelphia.

Penn had offered his justification in the introduction to the constitution, noting that a government is more than a 'correction'; it must lead the business of the state so that it is far more dependent on the citizens than the opposite. 'Let men be good, and the government cannot be bad; if it be ill, they will cure it.'

Wisdom and virtue do not develop spontaneously or out of nature; rather, they 'must be carefully propagated by a virtuous education of the youth' (Wickersham, 1886, introduction). This is a public task as this is the only way to secure the existence of the community in the long term. Citizens cannot simply consider their private heritage if their government is to be sustained and social continuity is to be secured.

Although I should have closed here, there is an aftermath. The puritan motive, to which the young Michael Walzer (1963) rightly referred as 'revolutionary', was to release different social utopias in England in the seventeenth century, including Samuel Gott's *New Jerusalem* and Gerrard Winstanley's *Restoration of True Magistracy*,[28] neither of which was created as a discovery of the existing perfect world; rather, the powers of social change were to be unleashed (Davis, 1981, pp. 142–203). The existing society was to be radically changed without having to abandon the ancestral world. In other words, utopia was no longer to be sought and found but had to be created.

Samuel Gott's visionary work *Nova Solyma* of 1648 paved the way for his Essay of the *True Happiness of Man* of 1650. The vision of the ideal society (that is, the Holy Land of Jerusalem after victory over the Turks) provided an introduction to the change in society itself. Two Englishmen visiting the newly acclaimed country learned of the conditions for a truly Christian society in which the reorganization of education had to be borne in mind above all. Education is the third greatest force of social control, after law and administration; anyone wishing to change society upon their return will, therefore, have to deal with a pedagogical revolution with stronger puritanical morals and education of the individuals who are beginning to understand how to resist political power. One of the main chapters is entitled 'Honours for schoolteachers' (Gott, 1902).

A similar argument was put forward by Winstanley (1988, p. 247ff.), one of the great English rebels of the seventeenth century.[29] In his first work (1648) he put forward the theory of universal salvation, which substantiated the primacy of individual spiritual experience over all forms of parochial institutions or doctrine. Redemption would be granted not to individual souls, but to the country of England, which was considered a 'tenth of Babylon'. In other words, the religious motif was transformed into a social revolutionary one, which was to remain until the days of Gustav Landauer or Ernst Bloch:

- The true government is one based on belief and freedom.
- Freedom means that every individual is free to make use of the Earth's resources (Winstanley, 1988, p. 176ff.).
- This would create a free republic without any authorities, which would put all official positions to the vote and would subject the legal system to conciliators.
- There would be no bureaucracy.

Based on his theories, Winstanley concluded that only practical experiments with society could provide evidence of how a new social order in the spirit of brotherly community could be possible. The first modern settlement experiment began on 1 April 1649 with the 'Diggers' – a settlement group hoping to secure livelihood by clearing the land. This joint activity was taken as a guarantee that equality and fraternity could be truly experienced and no longer be 'utopias'.

The experiment failed, probably due to the opposition of neighbours, who had no understanding of these foreign masses of ambitious sectarians. The new world did not simply develop alongside the old one. In 1650, Winstanley's experiments were rejected all over England with the greatest possible unforbearance (Davis, 1981, p. 173f.) based on the experience and belief, as what was not meant to be must not be. The resistance had not undermined the attractiveness of 'concrete utopia' – the term used by Ernst Bloch to describe the experiments. Regular failure also offered incentives to try again.

In closing, I would say that the utopian motif aims to overcome the present while fostering an expectation of future improvement and a means of reaching that aim. The classical social utopias are based on the fulfilment of an aim and thus on the completion of a journey. It may be that, in modern literature, dystopias are stronger than utopias because the latter's political significance seems to have been exhausted. However, we can neither develop nor live together in a democratic society if we focus on destruction. A society needs freedom as well as education and a desire for justice. The basic premise, therefore, is that democracy is not a utopia but rather a living reality which can even win over its critics.

Notes

1 Robert von Mohl (1799–1875) was Professor of Political Science at Tübingen University from 1827 to 1846. He was relieved from his post after criticizing the government and subsequently left civil service. In 1847, he accepted an appointment at Heidelberg University. Mohl coined the term *Rechtsstaat* (constitutional state). In 1848, he was a member of the Frankfurt Assembly.
2 Ralph Robinson (1520–1577) provided the first English translation in 1551. A second, revised edition was published in 1556.
3 The Catholic humanist Claudius Cantiuncula taught law in Basel from 1517 and remained there until 1524. He then fulfilled high positions for his native city of Metz as well as the Empire. In 1542, he was appointed Head of the Chancellery of Ensisheim in Upper Alsace, where he oversaw the business of the Austrian government.
4 A complete translation only appeared in 1846.
5 Anton Francesco Doni (1513–1574) was originally to become a priest, but he had to leave the monastery while still a novice and became a renowned writer. In 1548, Doni wrote the foreword to the Italian translation of More's *Utopia*. The translation itself was by Ortensio Lando (Heyer, 2009, p. 187).
6 The Scot James Burgh (1714–1775) was a lecturer at various dissenting academies and a well-known publicist. Along with Joseph Priestley and Benjamin Franklin, he was one of the members of the group of 'Honest Whigs'.
7 From 1924 to 1927, Philip Babcock Gove (1902–1972) was Instructor in English at the Rice Institute and subsequently at New York University until 1942. His work *The Imaginary Voyages in Prose Fiction* explores European studies and was accepted by Columbia University as a dissertation in 1941.
8 The Bible, Psalm 8, 6.
9 The Island of the Blessed was thought to be located at the western edge of the Earth. The darlings of the gods were sent to the island without having to suffer death.
10 *Historia Naturalis*, second book: *Kosmologie* ('Cosmology'). Pliny the Elder (23–79 AD) was a renowned Roman writer, who also held civil and military offices.
11 It refers to Theopompos of Chios and his description of the island of Meropis, where a good society lived alongside a corrupt society.
12 *Tractatus de purgatorio Sancti Patraciii*, by the Cistercian monk Henry of Saltry in Huntingdonshire. In 1624, a print was found in Paris and, presently, 150 copies of the manuscript still exist (Henricus Salteriensis, 1991).
13 This debate resulted in a utopia in *Le Livre de la Cité des Dames*, which Christine de Pizan (1365–after 1430) had completed around 1405.
14 John Mandeville (Jehan or Jean de Mandeville) (d. 1372) was a doctor from Liège.
15 *L'Evangile de Royaume; la terre de paix* (published in the Opuscula of 1540). Henry Nicholis (Henri Nicolas or Heinrich Niclaes), an Anabaptist from Münster, founded the 'Maison d'amour', a sect that wished to found its faith purely on love and compassion. Nicolas also represented the concept of the '*homo novus*'.
16 The description of the social and religious order in the 'land of Wolfaria' was related in a total of fifteen pamphlets written by Johann Eberlin von Günzburg to evaluate the consequences of the Reformation. The pamphlets propose '15 allies' in the struggle for the new order.
17 The militant reformer Andreas Musculus (Andreas Meusel) taught theology in Frankfurt.
18 Tommaso Campanella (1568–1639) was accused of heresy on many occasions. In 1600, the reason given was his participation in a conspiracy in southern Italy with communist objectives. After severe torture, he was condemned to life imprisonment.

Campanella was only released on 26 May 1626, and on 6 April 1629 his name was removed by the Vatican from the index of prohibited books.
19. The English edition appeared in 1609, translated by John Healy. Joseph Hall (1574–1656), who was bishop of Exeter from 1627 and of Norwich in 1641, was the first English satirist to follow the classical standards (*Virgidemarium*, 6 books, 1597/1598). In 1642, he was one of the thirteen bishops to be captured and arrested by parliament and his cathedral was destroyed. Hall was thus forced to become a beggar but still managed to survive until 1656.
20. Francis Godwin (1652–1633) was bishop of Hereford.
21. The role models for Montesquieu (1950, pp. 27, 28) were the '*politiques Grecs*', who followed no other power than that of virtue. 'Ceux d'aujourd'hui ne nous parlent que de manufactures, de commerce, de finances, de richesses et de luxe même.'
22. Including women, but excluding civil servants, beggars and royalists.
23. The founder of the 'Society of Friends', George Fox (1624–1691), was summoned before the court on 30 October 1650 in Derby for blasphemy. He wrote in his journal that the judge called his movement 'Quakers' 'because we bid them tremble at the word of God' (*A Journal*, 1808, Bd. I, p. 130). This relates to different parts of the Old Testament (e.g. the Bible, Ezra 9, 4 and Isaiah 66, 2) and was meant to be patronizing.
24. The *Book of Common Prayer* was written in 1548 by Thomas Cranmer, the Archbishop of Canterbury; the first edition appeared a year later. This was due to the rapid proliferation of the English mass during the Reformation.
25. Written as a dialogue between 'Truth' and 'Peace' based on twelve principles disclosed at the beginning.
26. Religious freedom was generally understood as freedom of opinion that formed the basis of the first amendment to the American constitution, which was adopted in 1791.
27. 'Penn's Woods' – the Latin word '*sylvania*' means 'woods'. King Charles II of England had bequeathed land to William Penn on 4 March 1681 to balance out his debt with Penn's father.
28. Gerrard Winstanley, 1652. *The Law of Freedom in a Platform: or True Magistry Restored*. London (Winstanley, 1988, pp. 152–277). The piece is dedicated to Oliver Cromwell.
29. Gerrard Winstanley (1609–1676) was an apprentice in the clothing trade and became a freeman in the Merchant Taylors' Company in 1637. He married Susan King in 1640 and moved to Walton-on-Thames. The civil war destroyed his business and he became destitute. In 1648, four pamphlets were published against social exploitation and political arbitrariness which brought him instant fame. He founded the Diggers a year later with the aim to create a society without money and wages – one that would be able to organize itself spontaneously without administration and official positions at a local level. Winstanley moved to Cobham in 1660 and later became a Quaker without seeing the expansion of his ideas.

References

Sources

A Declaration of Faith and Order Owned and Practised in the Congregational Churches in England. Agreed Upon and Consented unto by their Elders and Messengers in their Meeting at the Savoy, 12 October 1658. London: Printed for D.L.

Agostini, L., 1957. *La repubblica immaginaria. Testo Critico, con la Biobliografia dell'Autore, a Cura di L. Firpo*. Torino: Ramella.

A Journal or Historical Account of the Life, Travels, Sufferings, Christian Experiences and Labour of Love in the Work of the Ministry, of that Ancient, Eminent and Faithful Servant of Jesus Christ, George Fox. 1808. The Fifth Edition, Corrected. Vol. I/II. Philadelphia: B. and T. Kite.

A Manifestation from Lieutenant Col. John Lilburn, Mr. William Walwyn, Mr. Thomas Prince, and Mr. Richard Overton (Now Prisoners in the Tower of London) and Others, commonly (though unjustly) Styled Levelers. 1649. London: W. Larner.

An Account of the First Settlement, Laws, Form of Government, and Police, of the Cessares. A People of South America. In: *Nine Letters, From Mr. Vander Neck, one of the Senators of that Nation, to his Friend in Holland*. 1764. London: J. Payne.

Andreae, J.V., 1975. *Christianopolis*. Trans. W. Biesterfeld. Stuttgart: Reclam.

Bridge, W., 1654. *Twelve Several Books*. London: Peter Cole.

Campanella, T., 1964. *La Città del Sole*. Milan: Rizzoli Editore.

Coropaedia, Sive de Moribvs et Uita Virginum Sacrarum, Libellus Plane Elegans, ac Saluberrimis Praeceptis Resertus: Gasparo Stiblino Autore. Eivsdem, de Evdaemonensium Republica Commentariolus. 1555. Basilae: Per Ioannem Oporinum.

Cyrano de Bergerac, 1858. *Histoire Comique des États et Empires de la Lune et du Soleil*. Nouvelle édition par P.L. Kajic. Paris: A. Delahays.

Dahrendorf, R., 1953. *Marx in Perspektive. Die Idee des Gerechten im Denken von Karl Marx*. Hanover: Verlagsbuchhandlung J.H.W. Dietz.

Defoe, D., 1705. *The Consolidator or, Memoirs of Sundry Transactions from the World to the Moon*. London: Benjamin Brigg.

de Foigny, G., 1668. *La Terre Australe Connue*. Reproduction du texte originale sur l'unique exemplaire de l'édition de Genève, 1676, avec les variantes de l'édition der Paris (1692). In: F. Lavèche (éd.) 1968. *Les Successeurs de Cyrano de Bergerac*. Genève: Slatkine Reprints, pp. 61–163.

Diodorus Siculus. *The Library of History*. Book II, chapters 35–60. Available at: http://Penelope.uchicago.edu/Thayer/E/Roman/Texts/Diodorus_Siculus/2B*.html (accessed 14 March 2013).

Doni, A.F., 1552. *I Mondi Celesti, Terrestri et Infernali Degli Academici Pellegrini Compositi da Doni, Monondo Piccolo, Grande, Visibile, Immaginato*. Vinegia: appresso Gabriel Giolito de' Ferrari.

Godwin, F., 1995. *The Man in the Moon*. Ed. J.A. Butler. Ottawa: Dovehouse Editions.

Gott, S., 1902. *Nova Solyma. The Ideal City, or: Jerusalem Regained*. London: John Murray.

Günzburg, J.E. v., 1521/1896. New statute die Psicatus gebracht hat uss dem lad wolfaria welche beträffendt reformierung geistlichen stand. Basel 1521. In: *Sämtliche Schriften, vol. 1*. Tubingen: M. Niemeyer.

Hall, J. 1607. *Mundus Alter et Idem Sive Terra Australis Ante Hac semper Incognita Longis Itineri but Peregrine*. Hannovie: per Gulielmum Arconum.

Harrington, J., 1656. *The Commonwealth of Oceana*. London: Printed for J. Streater.

Hartlib, S., 1641. *A Description of the Famous Kingdom of Macaria*. London: Printed for Francis Constable.

Henricus Salteriensis, 1991. *Tractatus de Purgatorio Sancti Patricii*. In: R. Easting (ed.) *Early English Text Society, Original Series, vol. 298*. Oxford: Early English Text Society.

Hicks E., 1977. *Le Débat sur le Roman de la Rose.* Edition critique. Introduction, traduction et notes par E. Hicks. Bibliothèque de XVe siècle, tome 43. Paris: Champion Paris.

Legrand, A., 1991. Scydromedia. In: U. Graff (ed.) *Bibliotheca Neolatina, 5.* Frankfurt: Peter Lang.

Mandeville, J. de, 2000. *Le Livre des Merveilles du Monde.* Edition critique par Chr. Deluz. Paris: CRNS.

Mill, J.S., 1988. *Collected Works. Vol. XXVIII: Public and Parliamentary Speeches Part I: November 1850–November 1868.* J.M. Robson and B.L. Kinzer (eds). London and Toronto: Toronto University Press/Routledge and Kegan Paul.

Mohl, R. v., 1855. *Die Geschichte und Literatur der Staatswissenschaften, vol. 1.* Erlangen: Ferdinand Enke.

Montesquieu, 1950. *Œuvres Complètes.* In: A. Masson (ed.) *Tome I: Esprit des Lois, Lettres Persanes, Considérations.* Paris: Les Editions Nagel.

Morus, T., 1516. *De Optimo Reipublicae Statu Deque Nova Insula Utopia.* Louvain.

Morus, T., 1524. *Von der Wunderbarlichen Insel Vtopia Genant, das Ander Buch.* Basel: Joannem Bebeliu.

Musculus, A., 1574. *Jungfraw Schul: Bestellet und Geordnet Auff die Newlichste Auffgerichten Christlichen Schulen in Gehaltener Visitation der Marck Brandenburgk.* Frankfurt (Oder): Eichhorn.

Neville, H., 1668. *The Isle of Pines. A Late Discovery of a Fourth Island in Terra Australis, Incognita.* London: S.G. for Allen Banks and Charles Harper.

Owen, J., 1792. *Of Communion with God the Father, Son, and Holy Ghost, (Each Person Distinctly) in Love, Grace, and Consolation: Or, The Saints Fellowship with the Father, Son, and Holy Ghost, Unfolded.* Glasgow: W. and E. Miller.

Plockhoy, P.C., 1659. *A Way Propounded to Make the Poor in These and Other Nations Happy, by Bringing Together a Fit, Suitable and Well Qualified People unto One Household-Government of Little Commonwealth.* London: Printed for G.C.

Porète, M., 1986. *Le Miroir des simples âmes.* In: R. Guamieri (ed.) *Corpus Christianorum. Continuatio Mediaevalis, t. 69.* Turnhout: Brepols.

Sidney, P. 1891. *The Countess of Pembroke's Arcadia 1891.* Written by Sir Philip Sidney, Knt. The Original Quarto-Edition, 1590, in Photographic Facsimile, with a Bibliographical Introduction ed. by H.O. Sommer. London: Kegan Paul, Trench and Trünbner.

Wilkins, J., 1648. *Mathematical Magick: Or The Wonders That May be Performed by Mechanical Geometry.* London: M.F.

Williams, R., 1644. *The Bloudy Tenent of Persecution 1644, for Cause of Conscience, Discussed, in a Conference Between Trvth and Peace.* Who, in all tender affection, present to the High Court of Parliament, (as the result of their discourse) these (amongst other passages) of highest consideration. London.

Winstanley, G., 1988. *Gleichheit im Reiche der Freiheit. Socio-philosophical Pamphlets and Tracts.* Frankfurt: Fischer.

Literature

Babcock Gove, P., 1941. *The Imaginary Voyage in Prose Fiction: A History of Its Criticism and a Guide for its Study with an Annotated Check List of 215 Imaginary Voyages from 1700 to 1800.* New York: Columbia University Press.

Braunert, H., 1980. Die Heilige Insel des Euphemeros in der Diodor-Uberlieferung. In: H. Brauert (ed.) *Politik, Recht und Gesellschaft in der Griechisch-Römischen Antike. Collected articles and speeches.* Stuttgart: Klett-Cotta, pp. 255–268.
Carozzi, C., 1996. *Weltuntergang und Seelenheil. Apokalyptische Visionen im Mittelalter.* Frankfurt: Suhrkamp.
Claeys, G. (ed.), 2010. *The Cambridge Companion to Utopian Literature.* Cambridge: Cambridge University Press.
Cohn, N., 1997. *Die Erwartung der Endzeit. Vom Ursprung der Apokalypse. Visions of the Other World in Middle English.* Cambridge: D.S. Brewer.
Davis, J.C., 1981. *Utopia and the Ideal State. A Study of English Utopian Writing 1516–1700.* Cambridge: Cambridge University Press.
Easting, R., 1997. *Visions of the Other World in Middle English. Annotated Bibliographies of Old and Middle English Literature, 3.* Cambridge: D.S. Brewer.
Funke, H.-G., 1983. Die Geschichte der Gattungsbezeichnungen der literarischen Utopie in Frankreich im 17. und 18. Jahrhundert. In: W. Hempel (ed.) *Französische Literatur im Zeitalter der Aufklärung.* Frankfurt: Vittorio Klostermann, pp. 75–107.
Gnüg, H., 1999. *Utopie und Utopischer Roman.* Stuttgart: Reclam.
Hansot, E., 1974. *Perfection and Progress: Two Models of Utopian Thought.* London and Cambridge, MA: Harvard University Press.
Heyer, A., 2009. *Sozialutopien der Neuzeit. Bibliographic Handbook. Volume 2: Bibliography of Sources of Utopian Discourse from Antiquity to the Present Day.* Berlin: LIT.
Johnson, C.L. (ed.), 2002. *The Cambridge Companion to Mary Wollstonecraft.* Cambridge: Cambridge University Press.
Kruft, H.W., 1989. *Städte in Utopia. Die Idealstadt vom 15. Bis zum 18. Jahrhundert Zwischen Staatsutopie und Wirklichkeit.* Munich: C.H. Beck.
Manuel, F.E. and Manuel, F.P., 1979. *Utopian Thought in the Western World.* Oxford: Basil Blackwell.
Marsh, C., 1993. *The Family of Love in English Society.* Cambridge: Cambridge University Press.
Oelkers, J., 1993. Erziehungsstaat und pädagogischer Raum: die Funktion des idealen Ortes in der Theorie der Erziehung, *Zeitschrift für Pädagogik*, 39, pp. 641–648.
Pöhlmann, R., 1901. *Geschichte des Antiken Kommunismus und Sozialismus, 2.* Munich: C.H. Beck.
Rawson, E., 1991. *The Spartan Tradition in European Thought.* Oxford: Clarendon Press.
Raymond, J., 2005. *The Invention of the Newspaper: English Newsbooks, 1641–1649.* Oxford: Clarendon Press.
Schaer, R. and Sargent, L.T. (eds), 2000. *Utopie: La Quête de la Société Idéale en Occident.* Paris: Fayard.
Seibt, F., 1969. Utopie im Mittelalter. *Historische Zeitschrift*, 208(3), pp. 555–594.
Vosskamp, W., 1982. Thomas More's Utopia. Zur Konstituierung eines gattungsgeschichtlichen Prototyps. In: W. Vosskamp (ed.) *Utopieforschung. Interdisziplinäre Studien zur Neuzeitlichen Utopie, 2.* Stuttgart: Metzler, pp. 183–196.
Walzer, M., 1963. Puritanism as a revolutionary ideology. *History and Theory*, 3, pp. 59–90.
Wickersham, J.P., 1886. *A History of Education in Pennsylvania, Private and Public, Elementary and Higher.* Lancaster: Inquirer Publishing Company.

Index

accountability 127, 138, 146–147, 150–155, 163–166
administration: administrative communication 111–12; bureaucratic 114, 163; Bush 32, 148, 150, 155; Clinton 148; legitimation of 109, 115; Obama 32, 152–153, 155; Roosevelt 21
A Nation at Risk 146, 153, 191
Andreae, Johann Valentin 244–245
austerity 78, 79, 81, 82, 84, 89, 91, 93, 95, 97

Bernays, Edward 187–190
'Big Government' 161
Birmingham Education Society (BES) 22
Bloch, Ernst 252
bureaucracy: Grand Duchy of Baden 10, 106, 108, 113–116; Latin America 53; Max Weber 3–4; United States 6, 20, 144, 149, 182; Germany 163; welfare state 163; and utopian ideals 252
bureaucratic hierarchy 163; *see also* administration
bureaucratization of school discipline 10, 121, 124, 133
Bush, George W. 10, 32, 149, 152 *see also* administration

Campanella, Tommaso 11, 243–244
capitalism 40, 86; *see also* overaccumulation of capital; neo-liberalism
Carter, Jimmy 144–145

Catholic: anti-Catholic organizations 31; Church 9, 11, 24, 31, 40, 44, 48–50, 52, 171–172, 174–175; education 172, 176; emancipation 173; faith and religion 49; Irish Catholics 171–173; Latin America 40, 44, 48–52; municipalities107; press 48; republic and state 48, 51; Roman 52, 171; schools 27–28, 172, 175; social teaching 159; teacher training colleges 174; utopia 242–244
Catholicism 49, 51–52
central: anti-centralist tradition 10; Communist Party Central Committee 222–225, 227 government 21–22, 52–53; funding 18; power, control and authority 6, 18, 112; state and administrative structures 6, 19, 107, 159, 162, 165; *see also* centralization; decentralization
centralization: and American progressivism 182; and decentralization 8, 9, 18, 21, 73; and equality 18–19, 21–22, 53; of disciplinary policies and authorities 121, 123, 127, 130, 132–133; of educational policy 25; of education system 18, 33, 53; of government 18, 26, 52, 143; resistance to 154
child labour 20–21, 47, 86, 181
Christianopolis 244–5
citizenship: Ansässen 62–64, 67–73; gender 43; Irish Catholics 174; race 32; Winterthur 62–65, 71–73; *see also* immigrants; suffrage

civic education 179, 184, 186–187
civil society 42–43, 46, 160, 162
class: bourgeois 41;and citizenship rights 63; and collective responsibility 186; distinctions 107; elite, dominant or ruling 39, 43–44, 50, 237; middle 22, 70, 175–176, 185; privileged 23; and race 21,33, 209; social classes 61, 82, 92, 179; struggle 236–237; working and lower 22, 29, 62, 161; utopia of a classless society 178
Clinton, Bill 146, 152; *see also* administration
Cold War 32, 124, 191–192, 204
Common Core Standards Initiative 33, 133, 152–153, 155
communism 34, 180, 192, 198, 204–205, 236, 239, 244; *see also* socialism
communist: Bloc 191; Karl Marx 236–237, 240; officials and leaders 178, 226; Party 219, 221–222, 225; Soviet Union 186, 191, 219, 221, 228; state 244; systems 204; vision, ideal and utopia 11, 178, 205, 236, 239–240, 244, 247
communitarianism 196–197, 204, 206
community: assemblies 67, 72; and citizenship 70–72; and deregulation of public services 162; Dewey's theory of 184, 200–201, 206; education and research 148–149, 153; general concepts of 7,9, 196–198; Great 200–201, 206; and homogeneity 65, 205; Nancy's theory of 11, 197–198, 204–207, 201–212; national 5, 178–179, 180, 182, 185–187, 191–192; as an ontological category 199; Plessner's theory of 11, 197, 199–202, 204, 208, 211–212; as a political-ethical category 199; protests 128–9; school 70–71, 73, 230; and totalitarianism 204; Tönnies' theory of 200, 206–207; utopian ideals of 11, 181, 239–241, 244–245, 249–252; versus society 200, 206

compulsory and obligatory education 4–5, 20, 22–23, 27, 43–48, 50, 52, 64, 67–69, 71–73, 86, 87, 89, 93, 97, 139
conservative: oligarchies 49; party 24, 27; republicans 28, 147; thought and writing 45, 49, 105
Conservatives 24, 26–28, 31, 49, 144, 148, 161
Cromwell, Oliver 248–249
countercyclical policies and investments 78, 79, 82, 84–87, 89–91, 92, 94, 95, 97, 98

decentralization 8–9, 18, 21, 73, 133
deconstructive critique 197
democracy: direct 70; and expertise leadership 189, 192; and propaganda 181, 184, 186, 190–192; representative 70; and self–governing religious communities 248–250
democratic: community and society 184, 235, 252; equality 9, 24, 34, 176, 184; government and state 18; ideals and utopia 11, 122, 247–249, 251–252; legitimation and control 111, 157, 247; movement 70, 73; paradox 66–67; process 112;
democratization 22, 70–73, 112
Democrats and the Democratic Party 144, 147, 151, 154, 167
deregulation 92, 162
Dewey, John 178, 184, 186–188, 199–201, 206, 210
dignity 11, 130, 197, 199, 201–203, 208–211; *see also* Plessner
Diodorus Siculus 239–240
discipline: centralization of school 10, 121–133; and collective obedience 221; exclusionary 222, 230; inclusive 12, 223, 228–230; lack of 125, 219, 223–225, 227
disciplinary responsibility 133
Doni, Anton Francesco 235, 242
dress and grooming codes 128–129
dystopias 237–238, 245–246, 252

economic crisis 82, 84, 89, 93, 98, 182
economic depression *see* Great Depression; Long Depression
economic development 40, 69, 80–81
economic growth 50, 78–79, 82, 86, 87, 92, 95, 97, 179
economic progress 179, 184
education: access to 7, 9, 18, 21–24, 28, 30–32, 61, 64, 67, 92, 146, 251; agencies *see* state education agencies; compulsory *see* compulsory and obligatory education; expenditure on *see* financing; funding; freedom of 27, 44, 50, 116, 249; religious *see* Catholic; Protestant; secular *see* secularization; standardization of *see* standardization
education policy 17, 61, 94, 97–98, 138–139, 141, 146–148
efficiency 23–5, 81, 84, 87, 93–94, 97, 105, 164–165, 176, 181–184, 191
Elementary and Secondary Education Act (ESEA) 138, 141–144, 146–148, 150–151, 154
elementary and primary education 23, 45, 48, 50, 52–53, 86, 87, 88
England 6, 9, 17–19, 21–24, 27–31, 33, 41, 47, 68, 88, 92, 154, 174, 237, 243, 246, 248, 250–252
equality 3, 24, 34, 45, 61, 65, 72–73, 176, 178–179, 184, 205, 248–250, 252
equity 19, 21–22, 53, 62, 65, 72–73, 83, 92, 97, 128, 130, 141, 146, 155
ethnicity 82, 92, 127–128, 147; *see also* race
experts 4, 11, 26, 109, 112, 115, 126, 163, 182–185, 187–190, 224; *see also* mass communication research and experts
expulsion from school: as an economy of power 220–221; in the Soviet Union 219–230; in the United States 122, 130–132

federalism 138–139, 148, 153–155
financing education 9, 61, 87, 139, 160; *see also* funding

First World War *see* World War One
Foucault, Michel 179, 190, 220–1
France 6, 9, 17–19, 21–22, 24, 28–31, 33, 41, 47, 66, 68, 81, 83, 86–87, 89–90, 92–93, 96–97, 154, 172, 176, 235
French Revolution 5, 66
funding: federal 32, 123, 141, 154; private 78, 93–94; public funding and expenditure 17, 51, 78–79, 81–82, 84–87, 89–95, 97, 172

gender 20, 83, 92, 209
Germany 4, 23–24, 34, 41, 46–7, 81, 89, 159–161, 191–2, 196–197, 200, 212, 250
globalization 5, 92, 93–94
government: administration 45; bureaucracy 53; federal 21, 26, 32, 122, 132, 138, 140–142, 144, 147, 154–155; limited 26; local 26, 131, 143; national 21, 27, 40, 42–44, 49, 52, 141, 143, 180; self- 108, 111, 250
Grand Duchy of Baden 10, 106–113, 115–116
Great Depression 19, 21, 27, 30, 89–91; *see also* Long Depression; economic crisis
Günzbürg, Johann Eberlin von 242

'hedge schools' 171–172
Heidegger, Martin 206–7, 212
higher education 44–45, 51, 83, 89–90, 92, 93, 97, 153; *see also* technical education
Hispanic America *see* Latin America
homogeneity: national 11, 178; myth of 198; *see also* social cohesion; unity
hooliganism 225, 228; *see also* misbehavior; school violence
human dignity *see* dignity

immigrants 40, 46–47, 122, 181, 190; *see also* citizenship
implementation 4, 6, 20, 25, 71, 78, 87, 90, 92, 97, 107, 114, 126, 139, 142, 148, 150, 153–154, 187; *see also* state education agencies

Improving America's Schools Act (IASA) 138, 146–147
in loco parentis 122–125, 133; *see also* centralization of disciplinary policies
income 18–20, 25, 62–3, 69, 82, 88, 95, 164, 243, 251
Industrial Revolution 40, 80, 84–86, 89–91
industrialization 42, 86, 89, 180
inequality 9, 25, 72, 79, 94–97, 146, 161
Ireland 28, 171–177, 238, 240

justice 78, 81, 85, 184, 205, 247, 252

Keynesian consensus and policies 92
Knies, Karl 107–10
Kondratiev cycles 9, 79–82, 86–87, 89–91, 94–95, 97
Kondratiev, Nikolai 80
Kulturkampf 107

labor laws 20–1
Labour Party 26
Lasswell, Harold Dwight 180–182, 186–188, 190–191
Latin America: Argentina 40, 44, 46, 47, 50, 53; Brazil 39, 40, 44, 93; Chile 40, 44, 47–8, 50–51, 53, 235; Colombia 40, 44, 48, 52–53; Ecuador 40, 44, 48, 51–52; Mexico 42, 44, 53; Uruguay 40–42, 46–47, 50; Venezuela 44, 53
Levellers 248–249
liberalism 45, 50, 61, 163–164 *see also* neo-liberalism
Liberals 24, 31–32, 48–50, 52, 68, 143
Lippmann, Walter 187–190
literacy 42–3, 53, 174, 237
Long Depression 87, 89; *see also* Great Depression
Los Angeles 10, 121, 124–133

Makarenko, Anton 221, 230
'management by measurement' 10, 165
managerialism 34, 163–167
Marx, Karl 236–237, 240
masks 202–204, 208

mass communication research and experts 178–180, 182, 185, 188, 190–191
mass media 184–185, 187–188
mass society 11, 178–181, 184, 187, 200
misbehavior 123, 126, 129, 221, 227; *see also* hooliganism; school violence
Mohl, Robert von 234–236, 238
Montesquieu 247–248
More, Thomas 11, 234–235, 237–238, 240, 247

Nancy, Jean-Luc: community and being-in-common 198, 206; critique of communism 198, 204; critique of neo-liberal individualism 198, 204–206; plural ontology 207, 212
National Defense Education Act (NDEA) 138, 141, 191
National Education Association (NEA) 144, 186, 189
neo-liberalism 7, 10, 92, 94–95, 105, 161, 164, 179, 197–198, 204, 206–207
New Deal 18–19, 21, 31, 182, 190
No Child Left Behind Act (NCLB) 10, 32–3, 133, 138–9, 147–155

Obama, Barack 151 *see also* administration
overaccumulation of capital 84, 86–87, 91–92, 97

participation 9, 22, 62, 65–67, 69–70, 73–74, 92, 111, 181–183, 186, 188, 192, 247 *see also* suffrage
Penn, William 249–251
Plato and Platonic philosophy 110, 234, 239, 241
Plessner, Helmuth: concept of human dignity 197, 199, 201–203, 208–211; critique of community 11, 197–204, 208, 211–212; theory of masks 202–204, 208; theory of the soul 197, 201–203, 208–211
pollsters 184–185, 190–191
Popular Front 29–30

power: bureaucratic and administrative 115, 140, 144–145, 163; and discipline 124, 220–221; ecclesiastical 49, 244, 250; economy of 220; local or federal 21, 32, 66, 71, 139, 146, 153–154; political, governmental or state 20, 22, 43, 48, 49, 66, 107, 162, 230; and social work 163, 166; suppression of corporate 43; of the United States 181, 186
primary education *see* elementary education
private schools 27, 44, 50–51, 63
private sphere 110, 201–202, 210
procyclical policies and investments 79, 82, 90–92
professionalism *see* social work
progressives 20, 182–184
progressivism, American 179, 184
propaganda: and communism 180, 192; and education 178–192; *see also* mass media; mass communication research and experts; governmental 178, 180–182, 190–191; and social control 180; trials in Moscow 190;
property: church 65; common 63–65, 70–71, 244–5; municipal 63, 67–68, 71; private 63; rights 70, 73; school 223; socialization of 237; taxes 26, 33, 249
Protestant: Church 65; countries and societies 43, 172; culture 65, 122, 174
Protestantism 172
Protestants 49
public education 6, 17–19, 26, 28, 31, 40, 50, 52–53, 78–79, 82, 84, 87, 89–90, 98, 122, 138, 140, 149, 155, 188, 243
public funding *see* funding
public opinion 11, 179, 182, 184–185, 187–190
public sphere 78, 92, 98, 203, 209–11

Quakers 249–50

race 21, 31–33, 126–128, 147, 209, 246
Race to the Top (RTT) 33, 151–55

radicalism 197, 204, 210, 213; *see also* Plessner's critique of community
Reagan, Ronald 145
Rechtsstaat 238
Reformation 172, 241–243, 246
redistribution 33, 91, 94, 142, 144, 162, 164
regulatory state 10, 20, 161–162, 164–165
religion 28, 31, 49–50, 110, 175, 243–245, 247
Republicans and Republican Party 28, 30, 52, 146–147, 154
revolution: of 1848 108; in education policy 148; glorious 248; liberal 51; Marxist 236–237; pedagogical 251; *see also* French Revolution; Industrial Revolution
Roosevelt, Franklin D. 31, 34, 182, 185
Roosevelt, Theodore 181
Rousseau, Jean-Jacques 108, 240, 243, 246

Sallwürk, Ernst von 108–109, 112, 116
Sarmiento, Domingo Faustino 40–41
school blowouts and walkouts 128–9; *see also* student protests
school violence 123–125, 130–131, 133 *see also* hooliganism; misbehavior
school vouchers 34
scientific curriculum planning 183
Second World War *see* World War Two
secondary education 23–30, 44, 50, 53, 61, 90, 92, 138, 141, 143, 154, 173, 175, 184–186
secularization 28, 48–49, 51
separation of church and state 28, 45, 49, 51; *see also* secularization
Sickinger, Anton 110
social coherence, cohesion and unity 9, 11, 78, 89, 93, 105, 183, 185, 191–192; *see also* homogeneity; unity
social disorder 129, 178, 222, 237, 240
social mobility 24, 176
social work: anti-professionalism of 166; autonomy of 165–167; and principle of subsidiarity 159; professionalism of 34, 125, 163, 166

Index

socialists 28–31
socialist society 179, 186, 204, 226, 234, 247; *see also* community
socialism: of Soviet Union 186, 237; as a utopian ideal 234, 240, 247
Soviet Union 186, 191, 219, 221, 228
Sputnik Crisis 32, 191
Staatsromane 234–236
Stalin 190, 219, 221, 225
Stalinism 11, 219–220, 222, 227
Stalinist education and pedagogy 11, 221–222, 226, 230
standardization 4, 8, 10, 31, 33, 66, 105–106, 165–167, 180, 182
state education agencies (SEAs) 139, 141–142, 150, 154
student protests 128–129, 227
suffrage 22–3, 62, 65–66, 70 *see also* participation
suspension from school 122, 131–132, 220, 226; *see also* expulsion form school
Switzerland 4, 18, 46–47, 61, 66, 68, 72, 191
systemic regulation 79, 81–82, 84–85

taxation 78, 85, 89, 91–95, 97–98
taxes 23, 26, 33, 63, 71, 249, 250
technical education 23–24, 90, 108; *see also* higher education; university education; efficiency
technological innovation 84, 98, 191
theology 110, 237, 250
Tönnies, Ferdinand 200, 206–207
totalitarianism 178–179, 191, 197, 204, 221

UNESCO 3, 4, 53
unions: teacher 28, 30, 144; trade and labour 22, 28, 31, 182
United States 6, 9–11, 17–19, 21, 23, 27, 29, 31–34, 41, 43, 46–47, 53, 81, 89, 97, 121–123, 127–128, 133, 138–140, 152, 154–155, 171, 176, 178, 181, 183, 187, 189, 196, 220
unity, national 41, 178, 181, 189
university education *see* higher education
US Department of Education (USED) 31, 139, 144–150, 152–155
US Office of Education (USOE) 10, 139–143
utopia: in antiquity 11, 235, 238–239, 241–242; Christian 238, 240–242, 243, 244, 251 (*see also* Christianopolis); communist 11, 178, 205, 236, 239–240, 244, 247; concrete 252; democratic 247–251; and education 237, 239–240, 242–252; limited diversity of models of 245; in Middle Ages 11, 240–242, 244; during Reformation 241–243, 246; and *Staatsromane* 234–6

Varela, José Pedro 42, 45–47
virtue 201, 210, 245, 247–248, 250–251
Volksgemeinschaft 178
Volksschule 72

War on Poverty 32
welfare state 6, 17–19, 21, 86, 161–163, 196, 242
Wilson, Woodrow 181–182, 187
Winstanley, Gerrard 251–252
Winterthur 9, 18, 61–73
Wohlfahrtsverbände 159–160
World War One 11, 28–29, 31, 181, 189
World War Two 11, 17, 19, 27, 29, 32, 45, 53, 79, 82, 84–86, 90–92, 98, 121, 180–181, 185, 190

Zay, Jean 29–30
"zero tolerance" policies 122–123, 132–133, 220